The Home Office
and Small Business
Answer Book

· SECOND EDITION ·

The Home Office and Small Business Answer Book

· SECOND EDITION ·

Solutions to the

most frequently asked

questions about

starting and running

your business

Janet Attard

An Owl Book

Henry Holt and Company   New York

Henry Holt and Company, LLC
Publishers since 1866
115 West 18th Street
New York, New York 10011

Henry Holt® is a registered trademark of
Henry Holt and Company, LLC.

Published in Canada by Fitzhenry & Whiteside Ltd.,
195 Allstate Parkway, Markham, Ontario L3R 4T8.

Library of Congress Cataloging-in-Publication Data
Attard, Janet.
The home office and small business answer book : solutions to
the most frequently asked questions about starting and running
your business / Janet Attard.—2nd ed.
p. cm.
"First owl edition 2000"—P. preceding t.p.
"An owl book."
Includes index.
ISBN 0-8050-6450-8 (pbk.)
1. Home-based businesses. 2. Small business.   I. Title.
HD2333 A75   2000   00-020819
658′.041—dc21

Henry Holt books are available for special promotions
and premiums. For details contact: Director, Special Markets.

First published in 1993 by Henry Holt

First Owl Books Edition 2000

Printed in the United States of America
2   4   6   8   10   9   7   5   3   1

For Jay, Steve, and Vicki

Contents

Contents

Acknowledgments

Revising and expanding this book and simultaneously keeping our Business Know-How forum and web site and our other business activities running smoothly would have been impossible without the help of a number of very special people. My heartfelt thanks go out to Angelia Hayes, Lisa Freeman, Eldon Beard, Mike Holzschu, John Maihos, Brad Solomon, Sonsie Conroy, Jim Peabody, Robin Ferarro, Michele Popa, Merry Schiff, Jim Smith, Sharon Porpiglia, Paul Mayer, Jeff Chasalow, Kent Seitzinger, Jack Slick, Hal Zoller, and dozens of others who help in the forums and/or provided insights for the book.

I'm deeply indebted, too, to David Sobel and Anne Geiger at Henry Holt for their efforts in making this book happen.

Finally, I would like to acknowledge the role that the Internet and online services have played in making this book possible. Many of the businesspeople and professionals I interviewed were found through my company's Business Know-How forum on America Online, through our web site, and through mailing lists in which I participate. Almost all of the research was done on the Internet, and most of the interviews were done through electronic mail.

The Home Office
and Small Business
Answer Book

· SECOND EDITION ·

Introduction

I was just about to leave for lunch when the switchboard operator told me I had a phone call.

Puzzled, since I was new on the job and was not expecting any calls, I walked back to my desk and picked up the phone. It was my 10-year-old son.

"Hi, Mom, it's me."

"Stephen . . . ? *Stephen?*"

"Yeah, it's me."

"Why did you call? Is anything the matter?"

"I'm at Mike's house."

"You're supposed to be in school. Why are you at Mike's house?"

"The school caught on fire and they sent everyone home."

"What do you mean the school caught on fire . . . ?"

"So I got on Mike's bus and went to his house."

". . . If the school caught on fire and you're at Mike's house, *where's Vicki?*"

"I put her on our bus and told her to go to Nina's."

"Did Nina say it was OK?"

"I don't know, I'm at Mike's house."

As it turned out, 7-year-old Vicki was indeed at Nina's, but that phone call made me start to reconsider whether taking the job as a staff writer on a business trade magazine had been the right thing to do. Although the job was exactly the type of work

I had wanted, and it allowed me to schedule my hours around the children's school schedule, I just didn't feel comfortable about working away from home.

It wasn't long before I started to resent the hour and fifteen minutes I had to spend traveling to and from work each day. I also realized that the costs of going to work (for new clothes, gasoline, tires, lunch from the deli on days I didn't have time to make my lunch or forgot to take it with me) were all eating into the extra income I thought I'd gain by working at a "real" job instead of freelancing from home as I had been doing for the ten years prior.

So a few months later, when my husband took a new job and we had to move to another part of the state, I decided to give self-employment another go-round—at least until the children were a few years older.

That was more than 18 years ago. These days the "children" come to visit on weekends. Stephen is an accountant working for one of the major accounting firms and Vicki is a middle-school teacher in one of the best school districts in the state.

My husband, who once wanted no part of computers (unless they were hooked to laboratory instruments and spat out graphs that looked like EKGs) has, as someone at his office holiday party informed me, become the lab guru for what's on the Internet and how to find it.

Over the years my business has changed and grown just as my children have. I'm no longer a one-person writer and copywriter. Instead, my business, which I've incorporated, is an Internet company that specializes in developing online content, web-enabled databases, and building online communities. (If that description makes your eyes glaze over, strip away the buzzwords and what we are can be likened to a cross between a magazine publisher and a talk show.)

Although you won't find any employees working in my office, I don't work alone. I work with a network of small businesses and freelancers I call on as needed (and as they are available) for various projects. We also have dozens of volunteers who run chats, answer questions on message boards, or contribute articles to our forums and web site. Each are experts in their own fields and participate in our forums as their schedules permit because they enjoy "giving back" and helping others succeed, and also because they derive the same kind of benefits from online volunteer activities as they do from participating in local networking groups. The major difference is that their names and expertise get national—even international—recognition when they participate online.

Each of the freelancers and volunteers work from their own homes on their own computer equipment, and at whatever hours of the day—or night—are most convenient for them. Although some of the freelancers work for me quite often, I've met only a couple of them in person. We communicate primarily via e-mail and instant messages, with occasional phone calls when more detail is needed than can easily be conveyed through the computer.

The arrangement works extremely well for all of us, since it gives each of us the flexibility and independence we want to manage and grow our individual businesses. This virtual business model we've developed is no longer unique, either. Ninety-nine percent of the employers in the United States are small businesses, and many are very small. On Long Island, New York, more than 60 percent of all businesses with payrolls have four or fewer employees according to Department of Labor records. And that doesn't take into consideration all the sole proprietors who have no employees and, for IRS purposes, no payroll.

Not surprisingly the U.S. Department of Labor also reported in their 1999 special report called *Future Work*, that 60 percent of all small businesses start as one-person homebased businesses. They are typically started with existing equipment and without outside capital.

Not everyone finds the going easy, however. For instance:

▸ The highly skilled engineer who wants to kiss his 9-to-5 job good-bye may be at a loss to know how to find customers for the consulting service he wants to start or what kind of health insurance policy to buy when he is no longer covered by the company plan.
▸ The programmer who has developed what could be the hottest new program of the decade may not know how to market her work or how to protect it with copyrights, trademarks, or patents.
▸ The secretary who has started a word processing business so she can stay home with her children may not know how to price her services or whether to believe the salesperson who says if she'll pay a fee of several hundred dollars he may be able to make it possible for her to accept credit cards from her customers.

In the past, finding practical answers to questions like these has not been easy. Although plenty has been written about the benefits of being self-employed and what one *ought* to do to start a business, textbook rules often don't work in real-life home offices and very small businesses.

The *Home Office and Small Business Answer Book* provides those real-life answers. The questions in the book are based on real questions received from business owners and would-be business owners throughout the United States and Canada since 1988 when my company, Attard Communications, began providing home office and small business information first to an online service offered at the time by the General Electric Corporation, and later through our Business Know-How forum on America Online and our web sites, http://www.BusinessKnowHow.com and http://www.BusinessKnowHow.net. The answers are based on information I've gathered during my own twenty years of self-employment and on real-life experiences of business owners and professionals in many different trades and industries.

The book was written with another practical consideration in mind, too: the time crunch every business owner faces. Although it would be useful to learn how to start and run a business one step at a time, few people have the time to do it that way. Instead, they forge ahead, looking for answers and information as they need it at various stages of their business.

This book has therefore been organized to help you find answers as you need them. The first part of the book deals with common questions and concerns about choosing, equipping, and starting small and home businesses. Following that is nuts-and-bolts information about getting customers, running the "business side" of the business, and dealing with problems that may arise along the way. There's also information about growing your business and lists of useful resources. Finally, you'll find references throughout the book to Internet resources as well as tips for using the Internet to *do* business.

In short, the *Home Office and Small Business Answer Book* will help you gather the information you need quickly and easily so you can focus your efforts on running your business and achieving success.

I.

Taking
the Tiger
by the Tail

1.

Can You Really Make
Money at Home?

This week more than 40 million people in the United States are likely to spend some time tapping away at home computer keyboards, tinkering with gadgets in slightly musty basements, loading boxes or barrels or tools into vans or garages, or pursuing any number of other activities, all in pursuit of one common goal—making money at home.*

Who are these people? How successful are they at making money at home? More important, should *you* work at home and will *you* be successful? Here are some insights and information to guide you in your decision.

Q **Who works at home?**

Almost everyone works at home, or so it often seems! There's that guy up the street who has a little wallpapering business on the side, the woman around the corner who translates scientific papers into German, your sister in Chicago who works as a freelance direct mail copywriter, and your brother-in-law in California who leads corporate training seminars.

Then, too, there's the auto mechanic who makes house calls, the homebased word processor your company hires occasionally, the woman who does your taxes every year, the computer consultant who just installed a new inventory system in

---

*This figure is based on a report published in 1999 by International Data Corporation (IDC), a market research firm that provides data, analysis, and advisory services to the information technology industry.

your company's warehouse, the retiree who set up and maintains your web site, and the young man in a suburban New York community who grew his "little" newspaper delivery route into an enterprise so profitable that it let him put aside enough money to pay for his college education *and* make a down payment on a condominium he purchased for rental income—*before he turned 18.* (Because of his age, the young man's parents had to co-sign the contract. Not surprisingly, this individual went on to become an accountant.)

And, let's not forget your old school pal Jim Douglas. Jim is that guy you haven't seen in 15 years who called last week just to say hello—and to share information with you about a wonderful business opportunity he's discovered that could help you save for a financially secure retirement.

Q **How many homebased and small offices are there in the United States?**

U.S. Census Bureau figures available in 1999 show there are 19,286,000 firms in the United States. Three-fourths of those firms (14,325,000 companies) are what the Census Bureau calls "nonemployers"—businesses with no payroll. These businesses are mostly self-employed individuals operating unincorporated businesses in or out of the home. The U.S. Department of Labor estimates that half of the nation's small businesses are homebased.

Q **How much money do people who work at home make?**

Some people run million-dollar businesses from home offices. Others work sporadically from home and make just a few hundred to a few thousand dollars annually. U.S. Department of Labor statistics from 1997 (the latest year available at this writing) show that the majority of people who work in homebased business work less than 23 hours a week and earn less than $25,000.

Individuals who work full-time in successful homebased businesses, however, often make substantially more than people who are not self-employed. Results of a study conducted on our Business Know-How[sm] web site (http://www.businessknowhow.com), suggest that about 51 percent of those who are self-employed full-time or are employees of their own corporation have a gross business income of $50,000 or more. Nineteen percent indicated they had gross incomes of $100,000 or more.*

*The data is from a member survey available on the Business Know-How web site (http://www.businessknowhow.com). Survey data is collected anonymously. About two-thirds of the people who take the survey provide income data.

Research conducted by Cyber Dialogue, Inc.,* an Internet database marketing company, shows that the median household income for adults, in general, in the United States is $36.8 thousand. In comparison, in households in which the primary income is from homebased self-employment, the median income is $49.7 thousand per year.

Q **What kinds of businesses can be started at home?**

Almost any kind! Profitable newsletters, chemical distributorships, electroplating businesses, and mail order companies have all been started at home. So have candy distributorships, used-car sales operations, precision tool-and-die companies, word processing and desktop publishing businesses, catering firms, landscaping services, web hosting, and transcription services.

Q **Is there anything I can't do at home?**

There are certain products that it is illegal to produce in the home. Fireworks and other explosives and medical supplies and drugs are prohibited in most states. The manufacture of food and clothing at home is highly regulated or prohibited in some localities. (If you are allowed to produce food for resale at home, you will have to comply with strict health regulations.) Generally, if what you do can affect the health and safety of others, it will be regulated and could be prohibited as a home business. In addition, some communities have outdated zoning laws forbidding any type of business to be conducted in the home. Often such laws are blatantly ignored; sometimes they are enforced. Check your local laws if you have any doubts. (See chapter 10 for information on zoning and other laws that may affect you.)

Q **Do people ever lose money trying to start a home business?**

Yes, they do. Thousands of people each year throw good money away chasing get-rich schemes and scams. Thousands more see their investments turn sour because what they sell just doesn't attract the demand they expected it would, or because they stumble into some unforeseen pitfall along the way.

---

*Cyber Dialogue provides tools, data, and services to enable senior marketing professionals to identify, segment, and manage online consumers. Cyber Dialogue, Inc., 304 Hudson Street, New York, NY 10013, 212-651-7016. http://www.cyberdialogue.com

In fact, a study published by the Small Business Administration in 1999 found that about 45 percent of businesses that file for bankruptcy had one or no employees. In one-third of the cases, the businesses filing for bankruptcy had under $100,000 in debt.

Nothing can eliminate all of the risks involved with starting a business. But you can minimize those risks. That's why I wrote this book. If you read it closely, it will help you avoid some of the most common start-up pitfalls.

Q   **What are the benefits of working for myself?**

I asked a crusty old industrial plant owner that question years ago, and he wagged his finger at me and said, "Young lady, there is only one reason to be in business: to make money, make more money, and make still more money."

Although this kind of obsession with money is a motivator for some business owners, 41 percent of the people who completed the Business Know-How survey indicated either a desire to be their own boss or a desire to control their destiny as the reason for running their own business. Many others simply want a way to earn a living but also be available to take care of their children, elderly parents, or a disabled spouse.

Even when money is the initial motivator for starting a business, business owners often derive benefits that are equally important to them.

Wendy Enelow, president of Career Masters Institute (http://www.cminstitute.com), has been self-employed since the 1970s. She built and sold two successful businesses before starting Career Masters Institute in 1998. She explains the benefits of self-employment this way:

"Sure, the money is an important factor. However, more important is the self-satisfaction I feel after working with each client, knowing that I have made a real difference. It's immediate feedback which is often a benefit NOT experienced in 'corporate America.' Further, self-employment affords you a tremendous amount of control over your own destiny. What happens in my life is a direct result of what I put into it."

Making money was one reason Randy Cassingham, author of *This Is True* (http://www.thisistrue.com), created his newsletter and books. But it wasn't the only reason. He also wanted a creative outlet to write more, wanted to achieve "a little bit of fame," wanted to be his own boss, and wanted a portable job—one that could go on the road, on vacation, and even on a cruise ship.

Q **Can people who don't have a lot of contacts or a lot of corporate management experience build satisfying and successful businesses from home?**

Yes! They may not be able to build a profitable business overnight, but if they are patient and build the business slowly but steadily, they can build successful and very satisfying businesses.

Jerry Lunsford, a former backcountry ranger, is one good example. Lunsford was seeking a better way of life when he started his business, Camelid Capers, in 1985. At the time, he was searching for something to do that would keep him outdoors. Camelid Capers, which takes tourists on guided picnic hikes in the Point Reyes National Seashore, was born when Lunsford attended a llama auction in Grants Pass, Oregon, and envisioned tourists leading gear-laden llamas. He bought several llamas and built a series of outings around that theme. "The favorite scenario was lunch on the beach with llamas," Lunsford says.

But then the llamas picked up a parasite in the national park area where the tours operated, and all of them died. Lunsford made some changes in the business and now Camelid Capers provides backcountry catering services to outdoor groups "without the use of the llamas." Lunsford also contracts out his seasonal outdoor activities to a local kayaking company, serving the company as a manager, guide, and webmaster.

Q **What are the benefits of starting a business from home?**

The obvious advantage is a reduction in overhead costs. Putting your office in a corner of your home eliminates monthly office rental and utility expenses. In addition, having your business at home may also:

- provide substantial tax deductions
- reduce transportation costs
- eliminate commuting time
- reduce expenditures for work clothes and lunches out
- reduce child-care worries and expense
- reduce interruptions and increase your productivity
- allow you to work when it is most convenient for you to work
- minimize involvement with office politics
- provide better customer service
- let you take control of your own destiny

Q **Are there any drawbacks?**

Yes, there can be some drawbacks. Chief among them is the need to wear all the hats in the business. Instead of being able to delegate marketing, billing, filing, bookkeeping, routine correspondence, and other office functions to a staff, most people who work at home have to handle all of these functions themselves. Other potential problems include:

- finding or attracting customers may be difficult
- getting big fees or contracts may be a problem
- making important business contacts may be harder
- financing and suppliers credit may be hard to come by
- family interruptions may be disruptive
- family members may not be supportive of your business
- family privacy may be disturbed if you have customers come to your home
- start-up expenses may be higher than you expected
- Receivables (payments from your customers) may be slow in arriving—or never arrive at all
- Money for pension, health and life insurance come entirely out of your pocket
- Vacations from work mean vacations from income

Q **What does it take to build a successful home business?**

Business school professors, venture capitalists, and bankers will say it takes a combination of these factors to build a successful business:

- a good product or service at the right price
- a sizable market (a substantial number of customers)
- a clear-cut plan for reaching that market in a reasonable amount of time
- sufficient financing
- an experienced management team
- the technical competence to produce and deliver the product
- the means to market the product or service

- an emphasis on customer satisfaction
- the ability to collect from customers
- an accurate method of keeping records
- an awareness of tax and other laws affecting the business
- a watchful eye on the competition and market trends
- the flexibility to change direction when change is needed
- an owner who is at once optimistic, persistent, realistic, and enthusiastic about the product

Q **Are there any special character traits I'll need?**

People who have bootstrapped their way to success in homebased or other small businesses point over and over again to the importance of the business owner's enthusiasm and dedication.

"Textbook businesses always seem to have investors, be highly capitalized, and have sophisticated business plans," says Duane Long, owner of Long Transportation Services, Inc., a trucking and transportation brokerage in Raleigh, North Carolina. But, while those things are important, says Long, "the textbook scenario is far different than the way the majority of small businesses start."

Long speaks from experience. An entrepreneur himself, he launched his transportation brokerage from his kitchen table in 1984 with only $500. The company, which is no longer homebased, now grosses close to $20 million annually.

As Long sees it, the two traits needed for success in business are knowledge and commitment. "You have to know the product, know what the business is all about, and then put your blood, sweat, and tears into it. You have to become almost obsessed. If you don't, it will fail."

Q **Is it still possible to start a business from the kitchen table?**

Yes, you can. There are still businesses that get started with little more than a manila envelope, a notebook, an index card file box, and the family telephone. Some run that way forever. Others move their businesses into a spare room or out of the house as the business grows and add phone lines and equipment to manage the business.

Q **Besides the willingness to work hard, what other personal character traits do I need?**

Enthusiasm and belief in your product or service are critical to building a successful business. Your ability to convince customers to buy from you, suppliers to sell to you on credit or at a discount, and family and/or friends to loan money to you all depend on your ability to sell others on the value of your offerings. If you dislike the business or what you have to do to make money in the business, your ability to make the needed sales, contacts, and loans will be crippled.

In addition, most successful business owners generally possess the following characteristics:

- They are self-starters. They don't sit around waiting for someone else to tell them what to do or when to do it.
- They get along with most other people.
- They believe in listening to and learning from others.
- They set long-term goals as well as short-term goals.
- They look to the future and live for the future, not the past.
- They are both optimistic and realistic.
- They like to take charge and make decisions.
- They don't complain about life; they make life happen.
- They are flexible but not wishy-washy.
- They are honest and considerate in their dealings with other people.
- They believe in themselves.

Q **I have little children at home. How many hours will I have to work a week to make money?**

There is no minimum number of hours you have to work each week to make money. One of the wonderful things about building your own business is you can build it to suit you and your needs. Your earnings won't be sky-high if you can only work a few hours a week, but you can still make money. Furthermore, if you plan for the long run, the business you start on a small scale now could grow into a substantial source of income as the time you have to devote to it increases in later years.

For example, if you have the skills and equipment, you might want to start a small word processing business from home, doing a limited number of jobs when the children are asleep. As they grow, you might take on more work, take courses in commercial art and layout (if you have the interest), and expand into desktop publishing. Later you might add other services or even move the business out of the house. The same kind of gradual growth and expansion of time and income can be maneuvered in many other fields.

Q   Is there an easy way to make money in my own business?

Working for yourself can be highly enjoyable, highly rewarding, and highly profitable, but there is no easy road to riches.

Q   Is there any good way to make money in a hurry?

Although there are some businesses that can be started faster than others, you can't count on making money in a hurry in any business. Even if you find customers immediately, you may have to wait for payment, or you may need the profits to buy inventory, supplies, equipment, or improve your cash position.

Q   What home and small businesses make the most money?

The businesses that make the most money are almost always those that allow you to hire other people, make commissions on work other people do, or sell products to many people. Income from businesses requiring your individual attention is always going to be limited by the number of hours you can personally devote to client work. If it takes you 50 hours to write a computer program you sell to one company for $1,000, you have made $20 an hour. If you can turn around and sell that same program unchanged to ten other companies, even allowing for marketing time your earnings per hour on that program have multiplied tremendously.

Similarly, if you do word processing and do all the work yourself, the money you make will be limited by the time you devote to marketing the service and performing it. However, if instead of doing the work yourself you become a temporary employment agency and match workers to available jobs, you could greatly increase your income.

Q **Do many home businesses fail?**

There are no accurate statistics on failure rates for home businesses. Although statistics for all small businesses show close to 50 percent disappear within 5 years (either through failure or because they're bought out), such statistics don't really apply to home businesses.

The reason is that many home businesses are run from a corner of the family checkbook as well as a corner of the family den. Having relatively low start-up costs, no business rent to pay each month and no payroll to meet each week, few home businesses ever really fail. Instead, they fade away, as the owner shifts his or her focus to other income-producing activities. If one business idea doesn't work out, the owner of a home business may try some other income-producing activity. Thus, the individual selling decorative wreaths may switch to selling jewelry or collectibles, a seamstress may go into the image-consulting business, or a computer consultant might start a software publishing company. This is particularly true when a business is operated as a moonlight operation, provides a second income for a family, and/or is supplemented with income from part-time or temporary employment.

Finally, when a home business doesn't work out, equipment and supplies purchased for the business can often be used for other purposes. The computer that was bought to run a business may wind up being used by one or more members of a household to prepare homework or to acquire word processing, spreadsheet, or other computer skills needed to get a job. Supplies, samples, or inventory may also get used up by family, given away as gifts, sold in online auctions, or packed up to await sale at the next neighborhood garage sale or a local flea market.

Still, there are many home businesses that do fail because they made expensive purchases they can't use, bought too much inventory, or can't find customers. So look carefully before you leap.

Q **Are there any common traits among unsuccessful home businesses?**

An SBA study on small business bankruptcy found that the top three reasons for business failure were:

▸ Changing outside conditions such as competition, rent increases, or other costs of doing business

- Inadequate financing
- Inside conditions such as mismanagement, bad location, loss of major clients

Some home businesses fall prey to those problems. However, even when cash runs out, the underlying reason for the disintegration of a home business can often be attributed to one or more of these factors:

- lack of owner enthusiasm and dedication
- lack of knowledge of the business or industry
- failure to get to know the customer and/or make contacts
- lack of self-confidence
- no market for the products or services
- the product or service isn't profitable to produce and sell
- the product or service is grossly overpriced compared to comparable products and services
- poor-quality goods or services
- owner's focus is on making money with little or no regard for the customer or what is being sold
- no real product or service is being offered
- lack of professionalism in dealing with and corresponding with customers
- no clear-cut plans
- need for cash
- inability to compete against bigger or more established companies

Q **I have a good idea, but I'm afraid I'll lose money if it doesn't work. Is there any way to avoid the risk?**

No. If you want to be in business for yourself you are going to have to take some risks. But, be sure they are calculated risks. In other words, do all your homework, find out as much as you can about the industry, the customers, the competition, and what it takes to make—or break—the business you want to start. Then decide if you can live with the risk. If you can't, you may have to settle for a different type of business or for working as someone's employee until the time comes when you can afford to take the risk.

Q **Can I work for myself a few hours a week without starting a business?**

There are people who call their businesses a hobby for years. However, there are several problems with doing that:

- If you aren't reporting the income, you are operating illegally and could find yourself sued for tax evasion or fraud sometime down the road by both the federal and state government.
- If you are reporting your income, you may be missing out on important tax deductions and leaving yourself open to penalties (for not paying self-employment tax on business income) if you are ever audited and found to be running a business instead of pursuing a hobby.
- Should you need a business loan to expand your "hobby," you won't have the financial information bankers or other investors are going to want to see before loaning you money.

Q **I'm not sure I want to start my own business. Are there any jobs that would let me work at home?**

More and more companies are experimenting with hiring people to work at home or allowing existing employees to do part or all of their work at home. According to figures from Cyber Dialogue, Inc., there were 16 million telecommuters in the United States in 1999. These people communicate with the main office over the telephone lines, and often deliver work (via computer or fax) over the telephone lines as well.

These jobs aren't easy to find, but if you bang on enough doors, you may be able to turn up something to your liking, particularly if you have computer skills and a computer available to you. If you are employed in an occupation that doesn't require your presence in the office, consider whether your present employer might allow you to work at home part or all of the time. If you can show the employer the advantages of fewer interruptions, increased productivity, and better-quality work—he or she may agree to the arrangement, or at least to test the concept.

2.

The Million Dollar
Question:
What Kind of Business
Can I Start?

You don't have to read many success stories before you start wishing you could work for yourself. The opportunity to be your own boss and the potential for high income are strong enticements. But what can you do? What kind of business would be suitable for you to start? This chapter may help you discover some answers.

Q **I want to start a business, but don't know what to start. How do I decide what would be a good business to pursue?**

The most successful home and small businesses are generally those that:

- are based on the owner's skills, interests, and knowledge
- involve doing something the owner likes to do and does well
- sell products or services that many people need and are willing to buy or must buy
- sell services that other people need and can't do themselves or don't have time to do themselves

One way to close in on the most promising businesses for you, personally, is to get out a sheet of paper and divide it into four vertical columns. In the first column, list everything you like to do, and in the second column, list the things you are expert at doing or about which you have some or a great deal of knowledge. In the third column, list businesses that might make use of the interests and skills you have listed in the first two columns. In the last column, make notations about how many customers there might be for each type of business you have listed (see Table 2. 1 on page 23).

Use the notes you've made as a paper "think tank." They should let you immediately spot which of your interests (things you like to do) match up with businesses that have a potentially large base of customers. If you also have the skills required by the business(es), you now have one or more specific targets to investigate as a possible business.

Here's an example: Suppose you work or have worked as a secretary in a large corporation. Your "Do Well" list might include a variety of job-related tasks such as word processing, scheduling, filing and organizing, taking messages, and answering phones. It is also likely that you've included non-job-related tasks like planning parties, cleaning, organizing school fund-raisers, and cooking.

If your "Like to Do" list includes organizational things like arranging meeting details, running the school fair, or rearranging closets or cabinets for efficiency, businesses that would fit in with what you like to do and know how to do might be a word processing or general secretarial service, a meeting planning service, or a personal organization service—just for starters. For a secretarial service, the "Potential Customer" column might include local businesses, students, and job hunters. You may not know offhand who would buy meeting or planning services, but you can research these if they are of interest and fill them in later.

Have a supportive spouse or friend suggest businesses that match your skills and interests. They may see business possibilities you don't. If your spouse or friends tend not to be supportive, don't discuss your ideas with them. Try to find someone who is, or keep your ideas to yourself.

Q   Where do I get business ideas?

The list of business ideas on page 459, the Yellow Pages of your phone book, and the articles and ads in popular magazines and trade publications are good sources to jog your thinking. However, don't get taken in by the get-rich-quick ads or the "Make thousands of dollars in your own business" ads. Make a list of the types of businesses that pique your interest, then investigate the most promising ones to see if any would make a suitable business for you.

Table 2.1: Business Selection Worksheet

Instructions: Fill in appropriate information under the headings "Like to Do" and "Do Well." Then, under "Business Possibilities," list, in the order they occur to you, any ideas for possible businesses based on your skills and interests. Finally, next to each business idea, put some rough "guestimate" of how many people would buy from the business and who those people might be. Your notations should help you spot potentially good businesses for you to consider.

Like to Do (interests, hobbies, etc.)	Do Well (skills, expertise, experience)	Business Possibilities	Potential Customers and Income

Table 2.2: Sample Worksheet

Like to Do (interests, hobbies, etc.)	Do Well (skills, expertise, experience)	Business Possibilities	Potential Customers and Income
Experiment with new recipes	Word processing	Meeting planner	Large corporations; potentially substantial fee for each meeting organized
Organize school fund-raisers	Scheduling		
	Filing	Word processing service	Students, small businesses, bigger businesses with work overloads; relatively small profit per job but can do many separate jobs
Play the piano	Organizing meetings		
Plan parties	Taking messages		
Travel	Writing letters		
Read	Coordinating multiple tasks		
Rearrange closets		Image consulting and personal organization services	Upper income customers; executive women who don't have time to organize their closets; relatively few customers but fun work
		Wedding or party planning service	Anyone who schedules parties in halls or other major events
		Formal clothing rental service	Party-goers—male and female; likely to be repeat customers
		Complete office and resume service center	Mostly business customers or individuals needing resumes written and typeset; many customers; small profit likely for each sale

Q **What else makes a business successful?**

The businesses with the best track record for success are those for which the owner:

- ▸ knows the business, the industry, and the customer
- ▸ can produce a top-quality product or service for which there is a need
- ▸ can produce the product or service better, less expensively, or more quickly (or sometimes all three) than competitors
- ▸ knows how to reach the customer
- ▸ knows how long it will take to get the business going and plans accordingly
- ▸ starts off with one or more customers, often former employers

Q **Which businesses are the simplest to start?**

A service business in an industry you know well or a service that involves doing tasks others don't like to do or don't have time to do will usually be the easiest to launch. Often such businesses can be started by getting on the phone, calling potential customers, and asking for their business.

Q **Is there anything I should avoid?**

Steer clear of ads or "friends" promising that you can start earning a big income right away, particularly if they ask you to send money for information. For the most part such ads and telemarketing scripts have been carefully written to push your "hot buttons" (greed, desire for status, need to provide for your family) and pry you and your money apart.

Q **How long will it take before the business is successful?**

Don't expect overnight miracles. Like growing flowers, growing a business takes time. If you know who your customers will be before you start your business, you may be fortunate enough to start making sales right away. But it still may take months to build a stream of customers steady enough to make the business successful.

Q **I want to start a business but don't have any skills. Is there anything I can do?**

Everyone has some kind of skill. You probably just haven't discovered yours or may need more training to turn one of your skills into a business. Vocational schools, high schools, and colleges in your area may offer adult education courses that you could take to develop or improve skills. Additionally, you might be able to get a part-time job working for a company where you could gather industry knowledge or on-the-job training.

Q **I'd like to start a business in a totally different field than the one I'm in now. How do I know what kinds of things I'd be best at doing?**

Think about the things you like to do and are good at doing. Do you like to help people? Do you spend a lot of time at a hobby? Do you like to build or make things? Table 2.1 on page 23 should help you explore your interests and skills.

Consider, too, whether there is something you've always wanted to do that makes money but which you were discouraged from doing. For instance, when I was in junior high school I wanted to be a writer. Well-meaning parents, teachers, and guidance counselors all suggested I would be better off pursuing some other career since writers tend not to make much money and because I was "so good in math and science." What they said seemed logical, so I started college as a chemistry major.

No one, including me, ever considered whether I really *liked* math or science. And, despite top grades in the subject, I really didn't like math. In fact, by the end of my first year in college I *loathed* math and changed my major to English. Shortly after graduating college I started working on—and writing for—a daily newspaper.

Is there a writer buried inside you? A photographer? An artist? A dancer? An actor? Or is there some other field you always wanted to pursue but never did? Do you have, or could you acquire, sufficient skills to turn your avocations into a part-time or even a full-time business?

Q **There are a lot of businesses that sound interesting to me. How do I decide which business is the right one?**

Look for the business that comes closest to your interests and capabilities and that fits in with your long- and short-range financial goals. For each business you think you might want to start, ask yourself the questions below. Write your answers down on a piece of paper so you can more easily compare the relative benefits and drawbacks of one business over another.

- Do I really know much about this business?
- Do I have all the skills needed to start and run this business?
- Would I really enjoy doing whatever is necessary to sell this product or service?
- How much money do I need to make each week?
- How much money could this business make each week?
- How long would it take (realistically!) to start generating that much money?
- How much will it cost to start this business and run it until it starts producing income on a steady basis?
- Can I afford to put that much into the business?
- What money will I use to live on until the business starts making money?
- How fast do I need to generate money?
- Are there really enough people who want to buy this product or service? (See chapter 7, "Planning: Your Personal Road Map to Success")
- Do I know how to find them?
- How many hours a week can I work now?
- How many hours a week will it take to do all the work (finding customers, producing or getting the product or service to them, billing them, doing the bookkeeping)?
- How big could the business grow?
- How big do I want it to grow?

Q **Do I need to know about a business before starting it if I'm going to buy a franchise? Won't the franchisor teach me all I need to know?**

People who buy a franchise or a home "business" without knowing anything about the business and without learning about the business in advance are taking a big risk. Without some idea of what the business is all about, you have no way of determining if you will like the business, if there is a market for its products and services in your area, or if you have what it takes to bring in a steady stream of customers. Additionally, while a true franchise provides training, less expensive turnkey businesses and opportunity ventures often provide only a manual and perhaps a little phone support to help you get started.

Q Where do I get the money to start a business?

Most people dig into their own pockets to start their businesses. They pull extra income from weekly paychecks, suck it out of savings accounts, take out personal loans or second mortgages, use charge cards to buy equipment, use inheritances or, occasionally, pension funds, borrow from relatives, barter, make deals, and so on.

Q How much time should I spend investigating an idea?

As much time as you need to get the facts, but no more. Remember, no matter how good your idea is, you can't turn it into a business until you act on the idea. Do take the time to gather all the details you need to determine your chances for success, but don't get so tied up looking into the business that you never get your own business going. If you are procrastinating because you're worrying about failure, try starting the business on a very limited scale to allow you to judge your interest and chances for success if you were to go after the business in a bigger way.

Q How much money will I need to start a business?

People have started profitable businesses with not much more than the sweat of their brow, but realistically you should count on having to spend a minimum of a few hundred dollars, even if the business you want to start can be run without purchasing equipment or inventory. The reason: you will need money for business cards, stationery, phone calls, office supplies, postage, and perhaps for ads or brochures. (See chapter 7 for planning information.)

Q Can I start a newsletter with $200?

Realistically, no. Even if you were to do all the writing, editing, and layouts yourself, you will still have printing, marketing, and mailing and distribution costs. To find out how much money you will need, determine how many pages the newsletter will be, what it will cost to print it, and what it will cost to place ads, create and send out sales literature, and distribute the newsletter to your readers. If the newsletter will be supported by advertising or by subscription fees, they may take time to collect, so allow yourself enough money both to market the newsletter effectively and to get out several issues.

Whether you are creating a newsletter or any other type of business, working out the cost figures is essential. If you see that the costs are higher than you can afford, rethink your idea. Determine if the skills needed for the original idea could be used to start a business that takes less cash. For instance, if you have the skills to write, edit, and produce a newsletter but not the money to print, market, and mail it, consider doing sales and marketing literature for other businesses. You probably *could* get that type of business started with $200 if you had another source of income to pay your bills until the service developed steady customers and income.

Q **But what about Internet newsletters?**

Can't they be started without much money?

If you already have a computer and an Internet connection, you can start a newsletter that is delivered via electronic mail for very little money. But you aren't likely to make much money *directly* from the newsletter. Because there is so much information available for free on the Internet, most people won't pay for subscriptions to an online newsletter unless it is information they can't get in any other way. As a result, most people who publish electronic newsletters do so as a labor of love, or because they use the newsletter as a tool to help sell other products and services.

Some newsletters that are sent electronically contain paid advertising. But publishers need to have many thousands of subscribers before they can expect to make much money from ads in e-mailed newsletters.

Q **I have a lot of expensive computer equipment. What would be the best computer business to start?**

There are only a few true "computer businesses." These are businesses such as selling, programming or repairing computers, selling Internet services, and developing web sites. In almost all other businesses a computer is nothing more—or less!—than a tool to accomplish a specific task. If you used a typewriter instead of a computer to write letters, type spreadsheets, write legal contracts or books, you wouldn't consider yourself in the typewriter business. Using a computer is no different. You start with the skill or business and use the computer to help produce the work of that business faster or more efficiently.

Q **I'm disabled. What kind of business could I start?**

The answer will depend on your abilities and interests. Many people with physical disabilities use computers and the Internet to produce income. Holly Phillips, a Pennsylvania woman who is confined to a wheelchair due to a self-limiting form of muscular dystrophy, has enough strength in her arms and hands to use a computer and has developed a business creating communities on the Internet. Among the communities she has created is the Romance Chat on the Microsoft Network. She also takes digital photographs and acts as an agent for small businesses that want to sell items on Internet auction sites but don't have the computer experience or tools to do so.

James R. Hasse, who was born with cerebral palsy, is another disabled entrepreneur who works on the web. After quitting his job as VP of communications for a Fortune 500 company because he was bored, he spent close to $24,000 trying several ventures including self-publishing. Hasse, who talks with difficulty and requires crutches to walk, says, "Being a business consultant with a disability can be extremely difficult." He eventually founded Hasse Communication Counseling and found his niche developing communities on the web for the disabled. His personal web site (http://www.tell-us-your-story.com) features stories written by people with disabilities.

Other occupations that make heavy use of microcomputers are equally suitable for handicapped workers. Among them are writing, computer programming, computer security, and word processing. If you need information about adaptive devices to help you work at home, contact your state office of rehabilitation or IBM Special Needs Systems, 800-426-4832 (voice) or 800-426-4833 (TDD). Or, visit their web site: http://www.austin.ibm.com/sns.

Q **Should I start several businesses at once to see which makes money?**

I wouldn't recommend doing that. It takes a lot of time and effort to start one business. If you try to start several at the same time, you won't be able to devote sufficient time and attention to any one of them.

If you are seriously interested in two or more different businesses because you like the products and services of each, try this strategy: start one business, get it on its feet and running smoothly, and then start the second venture. If your second venture is in any way related to the first, your start-up will be easier, and you may eventually find that each business can feed customers to the other. If you start a lawn-care service, for instance, and later a pool maintenance service, your lawn-care company should be able to tell the pool service what homes in a neighborhood to target for pool openings, closings, cleaning, and repair. If you are a technical writer and are good at writing manuals, you might start a sideline business doing computer training. Training sessions at corporations may bring you technical or other writing assignments, or your writing may lead to training opportunities.

Be sure, however, to allow yourself time to establish customers and expertise in one business before attempting to start the next.

Q **I'd like to start a little business my spouse could run while I'm at work. What would be good?**

The only good business for your spouse to run while you are at work is one that he or she *wants* to start. Remember, it takes commitment, dedication, and time to start and run a business. If your spouse doesn't have the time or interest to research a business, he or she is unlikely to be very happy or successful running one you start. (The same is true for starting businesses for your children to take over.) If the business is something you'll do as a joint venture, talk it out together. See what he or she likes to do or might like to do and how that matches up with what you could do after work or on weekends. One team-up situation that works well for some couples is for the at-home spouse to be the marketing and customer service end of the business (drumming up business, taking service calls or orders during the day) while the work-away-from-home spouse becomes the one responsible for doing the work or making the product that was ordered.

Q **An acquaintance has asked me to come to her home this weekend to learn how I could make money in my spare time, but she wouldn't tell me any more than that. Should I go?**

That tactic is commonly used to get people to go to meetings to recruit distributors for "network marketing" or multilevel marketing (MLM) organizations. What you will probably hear is that you can make money by being a distributor for the company. As a distributor, one of your main tasks will be to build a "downline," which is to bring more distributors into the organization under you. Your distributors will be encouraged to bring in still more distributors, and so on.

If you attend the meeting be aware that while some people make money in these ventures, many spend far more on sample kits, motivational tapes, and leaflets than they ever make in profits. Furthermore, certain MLM operations are prohibited in some states. Others that pop up from time to time are outright scams. If you decide to get involved, move cautiously and learn as much as you can about the organization. If you have any doubts about a group's legitimacy, check them out with the state or county district attorney's office and/or with the Better Business Bureau. Computer modem users can also get information about MLM organizations they are considering in the Network Marketing Forum at keyword MLM on America Online. (See chapter 4 for further discussion of MLM.)

Q **How can I tell the difference between a real business opportunity and a scam?**

Memorize this phrase: **If it sounds too good to be true, it probably is.** There is no quick and easy way to make money, no way to make megabucks for stuffing or opening envelopes, and no secret method to go from near bankruptcy to Mercedes ownership overnight. Neither is it very likely that you will "start making money right away on the Internet in your spare time" as one infomercial boasts. There are people who make considerable money with a part-time business, but usually they command high fees because they have become experts at something or because they have gradually accumulated a list of repeat customers.

Remember, the only true opportunity is one that will let you make a profit selling a product or service at a reasonable price that people want to buy. If you will have to wheedle, cajole, use high-pressure sales tactics, or stretch or hide the truth to win customers, your business will be short-lived and your profits nonexistent.

Q **What should I do first?**

Once you've chosen a business, there are a number of organizational and legal tasks to perform before you get started. Among them:

- prepare a business plan (explained in chapter 7)
- choose and register a business name
- check zoning laws
- determine what special permits or licenses might be needed and apply for them

- apply for an employer identification number
- apply for a sales tax number (resale number) if needed
- open a business checking account

Some specific steps will vary according to your local laws and the type of business you run. The start-up checklist on pages 39–42 lists some common start-up tasks and includes some suggestions for who to call about various requirements.

Q How long will it take me to get started?

It could take a month or more to complete all the tasks that need to be done. If your local laws require you to place a public notice in a newspaper stating your intent to do business under a fictitious name (or even your own name), you may have to run the notice for several weeks before you can start the business officially. An employer identification number and sales tax number, if you need them, may also take a little time to be assigned. Other tasks usually can be accomplished fairly quickly unless you have to take and pass any tests, as you might need to do in order to get a license or get special insurance.

Q Will I have to collect sales taxes? And if I do, will I have to incorporate?

You will have to find out what products and services have a sales tax in your state and collect taxes if you sell any of those products or services. You don't have to incorporate to collect sales taxes. Your state tax department should be able to give you information about taxable items. Don't be surprised if the regulations seem confusing and arbitrary or if they change from county to county and city to city within your state. You may have several different tax rates if you sell in more than one area of the state. Each sale is subject to the tax rates and regulations that apply to the customer's location.

Q Do I have to collect sales tax on out-of-state sales?

At the time of this writing, mail order and Internet businesses collect sales tax only on purchases made by residents of their own state and any state in which they have nexus. (Nexus means having a physical presence, that is, having a sales agent or other company that services your customers.) This could change, since the impact of the Internet is making some state governments concerned that they may be losing sales tax revenue. To be sure you are operating within the law on this issue check with your tax adviser.

Q Where can I get help if I need it?

The legal requirements for starting a business vary from state to state, and even from county to county or city to city within any one state. They also vary according to the type of business you are starting. Unfortunately there is little consistency in the way the offices responsible for administering the regulations are named. In one locality you might need to contact an office of permits; in another, the county clerk's office. In some cases you will need to comply with regulations issued by several different state or local offices.

The first place you should turn for help, therefore, is the blue government listings in your county or regional telephone directory. For information about registering your business name and getting a business certificate, look for a county or city clerk's office or an office of business permits and licenses. Call and ask if that office is the right place to register your business name, and if there are other local or state regulations that the type of business you are thinking about starting must comply with.

Don't be surprised or get discouraged if the first office you call doesn't have the information you need and doesn't know where to refer you. Clerks in any one government office often know little about what goes on in other government offices. A man in Chicago called and wrote letters to several Illinois state offices; then, when he got no response after two weeks, decided "it was time to trek on down to the State of Illinois Building."

There, he says, he asked four different people if there was "any central office to find out all the licenses and permits that might be required of a business or for a contractor doing a particular job." Three out of the four people he asked were of no help at all. "One of them, upon my saying the word 'job,' said that anyone looking for a job should go see personnel and pointed me in that direction.

"A fourth came through, but not with a one-stop answer. She said that various agencies and departments handled various areas. Incorporation, for instance, would be handled via the secretary of state. Licensing, on the other hand, would be the department of revenue."

If you can't quickly find out what permits and licenses you may need and where to apply for them, a nearby office of the Small Business Administration (SBA) or the Service Corps of Retired Executives (SCORE) should be able to help. Other government-funded agencies that may be able to help you find your way through the maze of red tape are Small Business Development Centers (SBDCs), Economic Development Agencies, and Offices of Women's Business Ownership. (See pages 479–84 for phone numbers of SBA, SCORE, SBDC, and Women's Business Ownership offices throughout the country.) You also can get the phone number of a local SBA by calling the SBA answer desk in Washington, D.C. That phone number is (800) 827-5722. When you dial that number you get a prerecorded message giving you a menu of options from which to choose. One of the options tells you how to contact local branch offices of the SBA.

Local business groups such as the chamber of commerce, regional industrial associations, and Lion's Clubs can be helpful. Colleges and universities that offer business classes may also offer some help.

In addition to securing any necessary licenses and permits, you may also need to apply for a state sales tax number. The place to get that information as well as information about state income taxes is often called the state tax department or state revenue service. (See the list of state tax department addresses and phone numbers in Appendix 5.) If you will be hiring employees, contact your state department of labor to find out about any state labor laws with which you must comply.

Information on federal income taxes for businesses and on payroll deductions you are required to make if you hire employees is available from the U.S. Internal Revenue Service (IRS). Visit a local IRS office, or download the information as well as tax forms from their web site at http://www.irs.gov/. You can reach the part of the web site that focuses specifically on business information and forms from this URL: http://www.irs.gov/bus_info/index.html.

Q   **Should I quit my job to start my business?**

The answer really depends on your financial status. If you need your income to pay for food, clothing, shelter, and bills, try to develop some customers and have at least 6 months' to a year's worth of living expenses put aside in the bank before quitting your job. Here's why:

Suppose you are a graphic artist. You quit your job, start your home business, and, after two weeks, meet someone from a medium-sized ad agency who says he has a job for you but is waiting for the client to give the go-ahead. Two weeks later, the agency contact calls you and sets up a meeting for the following week with you and a copywriter with whom you'll be working.

After the meeting, you do a rough layout but have to wait for the writer to send you the copy before you can continue. That takes another week. You finally finish the job and send it to the agency, they send it to the client, and a few days later the client requests a minor change. You make it, and at long last you can bill for the job.

At this point, a month or more has elapsed since you first heard about the job. *It is likely to be another 30 to 45 days or perhaps longer from the time you submit your bill until you get paid.* That makes the total elapsed time from the day you heard about the assignment until you actually got a check in your hands close to 75 days. If the check is big and drawn on an out-of-town company you may have to wait 5 days more for the check to clear your bank and the money to become available. If the check was drawn on an out-of-state bank, it could take 2 weeks.

While quitting your job may be tempting, a better path to follow, if possible, would be to work at the business part-time until the following factors are in place:

- You have a cash reserve that will last you 6 months to 1 year.
- You have run the business long enough to see there is a lasting demand for the product or service.
- You know how long it takes to collect payment from customers.
- You have a steady stream of customers.
- Profits allow you to pay yourself a salary and replace medical insurance or other benefits you'll lose when you quit your job.
- The business has grown enough that it requires your attention full time.

Q **If I use my own name as the business name do I have to register with anyone?**

That depends on where you live. In some states you are required to register your business even if it operates under your own name. In other states, you don't have to register the business unless it operates under a different name.

Q **Must I have fancy business cards and stationery made up?**

If you are serious about being in business, you should have business cards and business stationery made up. If your business is one where appearances and creativity are important, you will need well-designed business cards, letterhead, and envelopes all printed on a good stock (*stock* is a term used in the printing industry to describe kinds of papers). If your business is something like a car repair service, you can probably get by with a plain white business card and inexpensive stationery. You may also need things like sales slips, shipping labels, and invoice forms.

Q **Do I need a computer?**

Owning and knowing how to use a computer is almost essential in most businesses today. Although there are many businesses that don't require a computer to create or deliver a product or service, most businesses can benefit greatly by using a computer to *run* the business. Doing your accounting, keeping track of sales leads, reminding yourself to make follow-up calls to prospects and customers, and writing letters, sending out mailings and bills, and many other tasks can be done much more quickly and efficiently on a computer than they can be done manually, once you learn how to use the computer and software. Customers may want to send you electronic mail or place orders online, and you may want to look for suppliers on the Internet.

Don't make the mistake of assuming a computer is the magic ingredient that will put you into business, however. If you don't already have a computer available at home, wait to buy one until you know how to use one and know what you will use it for. Most local schools and colleges offer adult education computer courses. (Unless you want to start a new career as a programmer, though, don't bother with programming courses. Look for courses that teach you what you can do with a microcomputer and/or how to use frequently used computer applications such as word processing, databases, and spreadsheets. See chapter 12 for information on buying a computer.)

Q **Do I need any special training to start a business?**

If you have no previous experience running a business, you will need to acquire some basic knowledge of business practices and procedures. Most of that basic knowledge can be acquired inexpensively through reading, networking with other businesspeople, and attending inexpensive business conferences in your area.

Q **I never finished high school. Will I be able to run my own business?**

Yes. One of the nice things about being the boss is there's no one to tell you that you can't be hired because you don't have a high school or college degree.

Q **Do I need an attorney or accountant to start a business?**

It would be wise to consult an attorney or accountant since you will need to know what civil and tax laws affect you and how to keep at least simple financial records. However, many home business owners don't feel they can afford professional help and gather the information they need from books, friends, the library, seminars, or other sources. If you choose to go that route, be aware that there are some situations in which you would be foolish not to consult professional help. Among them:

- if you have to sign or offer contracts
- if you deal in large sums of money or hold money or property for customers
- if you plan to invest a substantial amount of money in your business
- if you plan to buy a business or franchise
- if you have no knowledge of taxes
- if what you sell might potentially cause injury or loss of any kind to someone else
- if you will be working with another person in a formal or informal partnership
- if you are going to incorporate
- when you develop a product, design, or name that you wish to protect from future use by unauthorized parties
- whenever you encounter unfamiliar or puzzling legal or financial matters

Table 2.3. Business Start-up Checklist

The list below is meant to remind you of the tasks you may have to perform to start your business. It includes some contact information and notes that may be of use to many businesses; blank spaces would be filled in on your own list with names and numbers you collect as you proceed with your plans.

Task	Contact	Notes	Date Done
Assess your skills and interests			
Research the business idea		Investigate the business (will it make money? how much? what do you need to start it?)	
Write a business plan and market plan		You may not need an elaborate business plan with high-powered spreadsheets for a small home business. You should at least create an informal plan, however, both to help you decide if the business will make money, and to give your activities focus and direction. If you need financing, you will need a formal business plan.	
Choose a business name and verify right to use the name	Yellow Pages; county clerk's office records	Normally, you can't register a business name if another business is using a similar name. Therefore you should check the Yellow Pages for similar names before going to register yours. It's also advisable to have several alternate choices ready. Some businesses that have registered names may not be in the phone book.	
Register or reserve corporate name		Only if you plan to incorporate.	
Register or reserve state or federal trademark	U.S. Patent and Trademark Office	Advisable if you will be selling nationally and want to protect symbol and names from use by others.	

(continued)

Task	Contact	Notes	Date Done
Register copyrights	U.S. Copyright Office	Registration isn't required to protect your copyright, but registering a copyright gives you more recourse against infringers. It is also inexpensive and relatively easy to do.	
Apply for patent if you will be marketing an invention	U.S. Patent and Trademark Office	Assistance from a patent attorney is advisable.	
Check zoning laws	County, city, or town zoning board		
Choose a location for the business or make space in the house for it			
Register business name and get a business certificate	Usually handled by the county or city clerk's office	A business certificate may be called a DBA (doing business as) or a fictitious name certificate. You may also need a business permit from your town or city to operate your business, as well as other licenses or permits. Determine what you will need by asking local authorities or other local business people.	
File partnership or corporate papers		It is highly advisable to have an attorney help you prepare the papers if you plan to operate as a partnership or corporation. See chapter 11 for additional information.	
Get any required business licenses or permits	City or county licensing or clerk's office		

Task	Contact	Notes	Date Done
Order any required notices of your intent to do business in the community		Some states require you to run a public notice in a newspaper indicating your intent to operate a business. You should be able to find out how to place such notices and how long it must run when you register your business name.	
Have business phone or extra phone lines installed	Local phone company		
Check into business insurance needs		Equipment and auto/vehicle insurance or fire, theft, and liability insurance may be needed. Your personal vehicle and house insurance may not cover your business. (See chapter 22 for additional information.)	
Find out about health insurance if you will not have coverage under a spouse		If leaving full-time employment, make sure your coverage doesn't lapse.	
Apply for sales tax number	State tax department		
Get tax information, such as record-keeping requirements, information on withholding taxes if you will have employees, information on hiring independent contractors, facts about estimating taxes, forms of organization, etc.	Local IRS office		*(continued)*

Task	Contact	Notes	Date Done
Apply for employee identification number if you will have employees	IRS		
Call Department of Labor to determine labor laws if you will have employees			
Find out about workers' compensation if you will have employees			
Open business bank account(s)			
Have business cards and stationery printed			
Place advertising			
Purchase equipment or supplies			
Call everyone you know and let them know you are in business			
Order inventory			
Order signage			
Order fixtures			
Have sales literature prepared			

3.

Cash on the Line:
Connecting to Success
with a Telephone

Until the mid-1990s, most people used telephone lines primarily for live voice conversations and, in business, to transmit fax documents. But now millions of people use standard telephone lines to send and receive written communications, digital photography, and sound and audio clips. Millions more use those same telephone lines to buy and sell products, buy and sell stocks, offer customer support, and process bank and credit transactions without voice contact. As a result, the way we communicate and do business has changed drastically in recent years.

You, too, may be able to make money with your telephone. But to do so you will need to know how to distinguish true income-producing opportunities from the all-too-prevalent get-rich schemes designed to make someone else money at your expense. This chapter will help you gain a better understanding of what it really takes to turn your telephone into a money machine.

Q **How can I use the telephone to make money?**

You can make money either by offering a telephone-based service, by selling telephone services, or by using the telephone (usually in combination with computer or fax) to communicate with customers or an employer and deliver work to them.

Q **Technology helps big businesses, but what about home businesses and people who have lost jobs?**

The advances in telecommunications and computing technology are opening up new opportunities for self-employment and for working at home at salaried jobs. The same technology that makes it possible for you to use your computer, modem, and telephone line to order a new sweater or pair of slacks from the Gap allows employees to do data entry and other jobs for employers without ever setting foot on the employer's premises.

When my own company, Business Know-How (http://www.businessknowhow.com) was building a directory of business associations that we license to corporations for use on their web sites, we recruited a team of freelancers to do the work. The team included a programmer who developed a web-based data entry and display system for us, a project manager, several people who did the research and data entry, and an editor who proofread and released the entries for public viewing. Each of the people involved in that project lived in different states. Each used their own home computer, modem, telephone line, local Internet connection, and web browser to do their part of the project from their own home office. None of the people involved in the project ever met each other in person. I never met most of them, either. With the exception of a couple of telephone calls to the programmer who developed the data entry and display systems for us, all communications among team members were done via e-mail and instant messaging.

Q **What kind of work can be done from a distance?**

Distance workers—sometimes called teleworkers or virtual assistants—can do almost any job involving the creation, recording, or exchange of information, graphics, and increasingly, sound and video. Specific jobs include computer programming, data entry, writing, editing, proofreading, web design, web site hosting, teaching, training, newsletter production, public relations, research, customer service, sales, recruiting, commercial art, mailing services, and more. Using call forwarding, fax, e-mail, instant messaging, and live chat, you could even be (or employ) a secretary who works at home. In fact, about the only type of work that can't be done by distance workers are jobs that must be done on-site such as filing paper, cleaning, landscaping, construction, and other work that requires physically touching something located on a business or consumer's property.

Q Are all teleworkers employees?

No. There are three kinds of teleworkers.

Telecommuters.
Employees who work at home.

Contract workers.
People who work on a project by project basis for many different companies. They are usually hired by and paid by an agency that locates the contract assignments.

Independent contractors.
People who are self-employed. They get no benefits such as sick pay, health insurance, or a pension plan from the businesses for which they work, and are responsible for reporting and paying income tax and self-employment tax directly to the IRS. Most independent contractors work, or attempt to work for more than one company. In fact, making one's services available to the general public is one of the criteria the IRS uses to distinguish independent contractors from employees, since they are treated differently for tax purposes.

Q Do I need any special equipment or skills to be a distance worker?

In most cases you'll need a computer, modem, telephone line, Internet access, and an e-mail account. If you use a computer at home to connect to the Internet, you may already have all of those things, however.

Depending what kind of work you do, you may also need to own one or more specific software programs to do the work. For instance, a company might require you to use a specific word processing, presentation, graphic design, or page layout program. If you are self-employed or are a telecommuter who rarely goes to your employer's office, you may also need additional office equipment. Some companies will pay these costs, but others expect the worker to pay for equipment, phone line, and other costs.

Q **Are telecommuting jobs easy to find?**

No, they aren't. Although there are an estimated 15.7 million telecommuters in the United States and businesses are increasing their use of nontraditional workers, most people who are telecommuters were originally hired to work in an office and spend only some of their time working from home.

Q **Do people telecommute every day of the week?**

It depends on the situation. In some jobs people work from home all of the time, in other jobs the people work from home a few days a week or on a more occasional basis.

Q **What kind of businesses use teleworkers?**

All kinds! Fortune 500 companies and small Internet companies like Business-KnowHow.com use teleworkers. Bigger companies often have formal telecommuting programs for employees allowing them to work at home a set number of days a week. Small companies that are Internet based or that have learned to use the Internet extensively in their business are more likely to hire people to work at home exclusively or to use teleworkers who are independent contractors. Teleworkers are used by service businesses, high-tech industries, banking, advertising, publishing, and insurance companies. Some state and federal government agencies have telecommuting programs in place, too. Many have been started as employee benefits to help attract or retain employees.

Q **Do businesses use teleworkers as a way of keeping costs down?**

Saving overhead costs is usually not the motivation behind telework programs at big corporations. Bigger companies usually put telecommuting programs in place at the request of employees, or as a way to retain valued employees who are moving to another part of the country, want to stay home to raise their children, or for some other reason can't or don't want to travel to the office daily. Some big businesses and government agencies institute telecommuting programs as part of an effort to decrease pollution.

For small companies, the savings on overhead costs often is a factor. NETrageous, Inc. (http://www.netrageousresults.com) is a company that uses teleworkers exclusively. The company, which helps small- and medium-sized companies with their Internet marketing strategies and promotions, has employees located in four different states who work from their homes. "We've saved tens of thousands of dollars by not having to pay rent," says Stephanie Sebeck who is vice president of operations for the company. The company benefits in another way, too: happy employees. "We have extremely happy and loyal employees because they get to work from home. We've had no attrition and we believe this is because our employees are very happy with their setup of working from home," Stephanie adds.

Q **Do businesses advertise for telecommuters? Or, are there lists I can buy of companies that hire telecommuters?**

Most companies don't advertise for telecommuters. There are people who sell lists of companies who hire telecommuters, but usually the only people who make any money from such lists of names are the people selling them. Other types of ads that ask you to send money for information about how to work at home are usually promoting business opportunities, or worse, scams. Do not waste your money sending for information about stuffing envelopes at home, "processing" e-mail, or assembling products at home. You may also see ads in classified ad sections of newspapers and online services that have headlines that say "Work at Home" or something similar. Such ads usually are selling business opportunities that may require an investment of anywhere from $50 to many thousands of dollars. (See chapter 4 for more information on business opportunities.)

Q **Where *can* I find legitimate work-at-home jobs?**

Web sites that list job openings are one good source of information. Search these for the term "freelance" or "independent contractor." Freelance jobs are also sometimes advertised in newspaper help wanted ads. Don't forget about your present employer, either. He or she may be willing to set up a telecommunications program.

Internet companies that publish articles and newsletters or that have large communities (people who come back to the site over and over again) are good prospects, too. Sometimes the people who get hired make themselves known by being volunteers or by participating in the online community as a visitor. Other times they respond to job opening notices found on the web site or distributed in e-mail newsletters from the site.

Q How can I get my current employer to let me work at home?

If the company doesn't have a formal policy, ask if you could work at home on a trial basis. Remind your supervisor that you could be more productive working from home since you will have fewer interruptions and suggest they let you try working from home for one or two days a week. Be sure you get your work done and keep in touch with the office during business hours. If the experiment is successful, consider whether it would be feasible to ask the company to let you work at home more days a week.

Q I have a new baby and two other preschoolers and need money, but no one wants to hire me to work at home. Why not?

The problem could be that you are focusing on your need for money and the time it takes to raise three little children. Employers may sympathize with that, but they don't hire people out of sympathy. They hire people who have needed skills and who have sufficient time available to do work they need done. If you are serious about finding work-at-home jobs, you need to focus on the skills you have and the way your skills will meet an employer's needs. You also need to be honest with employers—and yourself—about the number of hours you can work a week.

Q What are the drawbacks of being a telecommuter?

There are a couple of disadvantages. First, you may lose contact with other staff members and run the risk of being passed over come promotion time. You may also find you miss the camaraderie of office work. Some people discover they dislike the peace and quiet of working at home and would much prefer being with other adults during the day or in a situation where things are "happening." Finally, working at home can be an expense. Depending on your employer, you may have to supply your own computer, fax, modem, or other needed equipment. You might also have to pay your own telephone costs for calling the company or dialing into their network. If you buy these items yourself and are employed by the company (rather than being an independent contractor), you cannot deduct their cost on your tax return.

Q **What online resources are there for teleworkers?**

There are a number of web sites that have sprung up to help put freelancers (or free agents, if you prefer) together with companies that need independent contractors to work for them. Among them are:

http://www.bizbuyer.com/
http://www.elance.com
http://www.mbafreeagent.com
http://www.freeagent.com
http://talentmarket.monster.com
http://www.staffwriters.com/

In addition, there are a variety of information resources on the web covering telecommuting. Among those are:

http://www.gilgordon.com
Resources for telecommuters and managers of telecommuters

http://www.gsa.gov/pbs/owi/telecomm.htm
Government telecommutting programs and information

http://www.telecommute.org
Trade association focusing on telecommuting

Q **Do I need to get my employer to put anything in writing?**

Yes, it's a good idea to get the details of your agreement with your employer in writing. Be sure the agreement specifies how often you'll telecommute, who will pay for the equipment needed, who will pay for phone calls, how many hours a day or a week you'll work as a telecommuter, what those hours will be, and how often you're expected to contact the office or travel to the office.

Q **Is there any way I could deduct the cost of my computer and other equipment?**

If you go into business for yourself you may be able to deduct the cost of your equipment. Many people start off with their last employer as the first customer of their new business. You must be careful to set things up so you are truly independent, however, or you could lose your chance to take business deductions and the employer might get hit with a variety of penalties.

Q **I've seen ads implying that for a few hundred dollars I can buy a 900 number and make several hundred dollars a day. Are these ads for real?**

Many of these ads are misleading at best. While there are legitimate ways to make money with 900-number information services, you are not going to be able to do it on an investment of just a few hundred dollars. Warns Robert Mastin, author of *900 Know-how: How to Succeed With Your Own 900 Number*, "There are a lot of snake-oil hucksters out there."

Q **How can I tell what is legitimate and what isn't?**

Among the companies to be wary of are those that:

▶ Offer you the opportunity to share in the profits if you will advertise and promote their program.
▶ Pressure you to sign up *now*, before all available 900 numbers "run out."
▶ Imply you can get rich by owning a 900 line. A 900 number by itself is worth nothing to you. You must have a product and the money to advertise that product to make money.

Q **Are there any legitimate 900-number services?**

Yes, there are many of them. Among the organizations and government agencies that have 900-number information services now or have used them in the past are: Dow Jones & Company, Microsoft, the New York World Trade Center, the Associated Press, the Michigan Department of Commerce, *Consumer Reports*, and the ABC-TV network.

Among the types of services available through 900 numbers are up-to-the-minute stock quotes, software support, legal advice or faxed copies of legal forms, import/export leads, academic information, medical advice, and counseling for parents. You can also voice your opinion in TV polls or contribute to some fund-raising campaigns by using 900-number services.

Q **How do 900-number businesses work?**

A 900-number business is simply a pay-per-call telephone information service. The 900 number is not in itself a "business." Rather it provides a method for delivering a product and getting paid.

These services generally are offered to consumers as a "team effort" by the following kinds of companies:

- An information provider who creates the information service (or sometimes an entertainment service) and is responsible for its content.
- A service bureau that provides a business message storage system to help the information provider handle the incoming calls. (Some information providers use their own message storage equipment instead of using a service bureau.)
- A long-distance carrier (phone company) that carries the 900 program (AT&T, MCI, or Sprint).
- The local phone company, which is responsible for the billing of the 900 services.

The information provider advertises the service (just as it would advertise any business) through whatever media it chooses. Customers who want to use the service call the advertised 900 telephone number and obtain the information, incurring a fee that has been set by the information provider. At the end of the month, the local telephone company adds the 900-number charges to the customer's regular phone bill. The phone company takes its cut and distributes the balance of the collected fees back to the other players in the chain.

Q **Haven't a lot of people been ripped off by calling 900 numbers?**

There have been some con artists who have used the pay-per-call industry as a new way to work the same old scams that have plagued the mail order and telemarketing industries in the past. Among the advertised 900 numbers that have been most abusive have been services that advertise "guaranteed" credit, ways to get out of debt, and even high-paying overseas jobs. Often the information retrieved from such services is of little true value to the caller. In the past consumers often had no way of knowing in advance exactly how much it would cost to get the advertised information. Only when their phone bills arrived at the end of the month would they discover that the worthless information sometimes cost as much as $50 or more.

The industry also got a bad name in the past because of "adults only" call-in lines. As a result, federal and state regulations were put in place to regulate the industry. These laws have helped clean up the industry, but there are still some hucksters out there.

Q **Can small businesses really make money in the pay-per-call industry?**

It is possible for small and home businesses to make money with their own 900-number information services but not on a shoestring budget. The cost of turning an idea into a 900-number information product and test marketing it normally runs somewhere between $2,500 and $10,000 depending on the media used to advertise the program. If the program is successful and you plan to continue it you should plan on having additional money available since it can take up to two months or more to collect your earnings from the incoming calls.

There is, of course, no guarantee that after spending that much money your information product will be a success.

Q **What regulations affect 900 numbers?**

Under current FCC regulations customers must be told as soon as they connect with a 900-number service what the charges will be and who the information provider is. They also must be given the option to hang up at the beginning of the call without getting billed. (The information provider has to foot the bill for all hang-ups.) Automated collect calls, line seizing, and generation of dual-tone, multi-frequency tones are prohibited.

Consumers also have the option of disputing 900 charges to their phone numbers and cannot have their telephone service disconnected for refusing to pay a bill for a call to a 900 number. Businesses and consumers also have to be given the option by the phone company of having 900 numbers blocked (arranging it so they may not place calls to 900 numbers).

Different states have different regulations regarding the information that may be offered on a 900 number, and at least one state was trying to get legislation passed that would routinely block 900-number access from all phone lines, making it necessary for phone customers to specifically request access to 900 service.

The long-distance carriers and some of the service bureaus have regulations with which you must comply, too. AT&T, for instance, insists on seeing and approving advertising copy that will be used to promote a number as well as the actual information to be delivered once a caller connects with the number.

Q **Can I make money by selling products, services or information over the Internet?**

Yes, there are many ways to connect with customers and profits on the Internet. You'll find examples of companies throughout this book. You must start off with a good product or service and knowledge of how the Internet works, however.

Q **What about selling long distance and other telecommunications services? Is that profitable?**

There are a variety of ways that people make money selling telecommunications services. Perhaps the most common is by being a distributor for multilevel marketing (MLM) companies that sell long distance, paging, or Internet services. The majority of people involved in such opportunities work at them in their spare time, making an average of just a few hundred dollars a month. About 10 percent of the people in this field work full-time and bring in a full-time income. About 1 percent make $100,000 or more per year. A few people make significantly more than that. Jacqueline Freeman, a national training director with Excel Communications, Inc., estimates that it takes the average person five years working full-time or ten years working part-time to reach the point where he or she can quit a full-time job and live on income as a network marketer selling telecommunications services. For those getting into the field for the first time she suggests that long-term income is dependent on the company's stability and on customer loyalty.

MLM businesses aren't the only ones that sell various telecommunications services. But because of the competition in the market and the trend toward consolidation, small independent businesses are unlikely to succeed in the telecommunications industry.

Q **Could I make money purchasing my own coin-operated telephones and placing them in business establishments?**

Unless you get lucky enough to get an unusually good location, your average take per month will be about $20 per phone. Areas that do best for pay phones are bars and other busy locations where people might normally be expected to make many phone calls. Any money that is in the coin box gets split with the owner of the establishment in which you have placed the phone.

In addition to the low income from pay phones, some would-be business owners who have invested in pay phone "opportunities" have had difficulty getting the number of phones they purchased, getting the pay phones placed at business locations, and getting the promised training.

4.

Low-Cost Home Franchises, Business Packages, and Multilevel Marketing: Are They Any Good?

Sometimes it seems like the hottest business of the decade is the business of selling business opportunities.

Open any magazine aimed at small business owners and people who want to start businesses, and you will see page after page of ads promising to help you get started in allegedly lucrative businesses. You'll find ads for franchises that will put you into the "exploding" service industry, ads promising to send you "confidential reports" about some questionable new home business opportunity, and ads for franchises with familiar names like Merry Maids or Meineke Discount Mufflers.

Reading these ads is one way to answer the universal question, "What kind of business can I start?" But will purchasing the franchise or business plans or equipment advertised in such ads really lead to easy money?

Here are some tips and real-life experiences to help you decide.

Q **Is buying a franchise a good way to go into business?**

It can be. The International Franchise Association estimates that about $1 trillion in sales (about 40 percent of all retail sales) were made through franchised establishments. While not every franchise or every franchise owner is successful, franchising does reduce some of the risk of launching a new business by letting you copy a business concept someone else has already made successful.

Q **What specific benefits does a franchise offer?**

Depending on the franchise, among the benefits you might gain are:

- a business concept with a track record for success
- name recognition for the business
- management training
- access to proprietary methods and/or processes used in the business
- a ready-made business or marketing plan to follow
- ready-made ads, brochures, and other sales and marketing aids
- help with financing

Q **What are the disadvantages?**

The security you acquire by licensing someone else's business methods and practices has its price. Among the drawbacks of being a franchise are:

- Your start-up costs can be high.
- You will have to follow the franchisor's rules. That means you might have limitations placed on everything from what products and services you sell to what goes into ads, where you are allowed to sell, and even how your business is furnished.
- You will have to pay a percentage of your sales and/or a flat fee to the franchisor (company from which you purchase the franchise) each year.
- Your success is dependent in many respects on the talents, foresight, and stability of the franchisor.
- You will be locked into the terms of the contract with the franchisor whether your operation is successful or not.

Q **What should I look for in a franchise?**

First and foremost you want to took for a franchise that sells a product or service you would enjoy producing and selling. Your best bet is to find a franchise in an industry you know at least a little bit about. All too typical is the case of the Chicago car salesman who decided to change careers and go into business for himself. He bought a basement waterproofing franchise but then found the business boring. He wanted to sell it, but sales weren't as high as he had expected they would be and he had trouble finding a buyer. He was stuck paying off the franchise fee and working at a business he didn't enjoy.

Once you've pinned down some possibilities, you should get and carefully scrutinize a disclosure document called the Uniform Franchise Offering Circular (UFOC) for the franchise or franchises you are interested in. This disclosure document will give you the information you need to help you determine the answer to these and other important questions:

- How stable is the franchise and what is the background of its officers? (Any history of litigation or bankruptcy of the franchise or its officers is supposed to be included in the UFOC.)
- What will *all* your costs of purchase be? Advertising, training, inventory, insurance, and all other costs in addition to the franchise fee and royalties should be spelled out.
- How well established is the franchise? Have they been in business for many years or are they brand-new? How many other franchises have they opened and where are they located?
- What kind of track record do they have? Have most of their franchisees been successful? Names and addresses of franchisees in your state should be provided before you sign any contract. Call the people on the list and ask about their experiences.
- What kind of training and support will they provide as part of your franchise fee?
- How close to your store can the franchisor let another franchisee set up shop?
- Will you be required to purchase supplies or products from the parent company? If so, compare your cost to the local retail prices of the same goods. There have been instances where the price from the franchise company for goods was *higher* than the price of the same goods in local retail stores. Selling anything under such conditions would be quite difficult.
- What do the contract terms say about ownership? Can you sell out to someone else if you wish? If you want to continue when the contract expires, will it be automatically renewed? Will you be able to convert your store into an independent operation if you should want to?

- Determine how disputes will be handled should they arise. Watch for clauses requiring arbitration in the franchisor's home state if it is different than yours. Should a dispute arise, you'd have to travel to that state for arbitration hearings.
- What criteria does the franchise use in selecting franchisees? Do they do any screening? Or, do they seem more interested in getting your franchise fee?
- Does the franchise use high-pressure sales techniques to get you to sign on the dotted line?
- Do you like the people you are dealing with?
- How big is the market for the franchise's products or services in your area and how much competition is there now?

Q **Will the franchise limit competition?**

The franchise will generally give you a territory in which you may operate and agree not to allow anyone else to open one of their franchises in your territory. However, they have no control on competing franchisors opening up a franchise in your territory (for example, if you own a PIP quick print franchise, a McPrint outlet may very well open across the street), and they have no power to keep independents with the same type of business from opening in your area.

Two other things you need to watch out for are the size of your territory and that any verbal territorial claims or promises actually get included in your final contract. No matter how helpful and friendly the company may be, when push comes to shove, the only thing that matters is what it says in the contract.

A franchisee for a company that sells products to a very specific niche market learned that lesson the hard way. He signed a contract with the franchise to open a store in a suburban East Coast community. His contract with the franchise stated that competing stores had to be located at least 7 miles away from one another. When he questioned whether this allowed proximity might hinder business, he was shown figures indicating that stores in a nearby city were profitable even though they were that close together and was also told the franchise company wasn't planning to open any other stores in his state for 3 years. Thus, they said, he would have plenty of opportunity to build his business and become established.

Less than a year later a second store from the same franchise company was opened in the area. The store was more than 7 miles away from the first one but close enough to seriously cut into the business. Warns the owner, "Buyer beware. A seven-mile territory in a densely populated city may be fine, but seven miles is nothing for some kinds of businesses in the suburbs. You wind up doing the advertising for the other store."

Q **Can I get copies of franchises' Uniform Franchise Offering Circulars (UFOCs) before I talk to any franchise management so I can compare several before calling a company?**

There is a company called Frandata that can send most franchises' UFOCs to you for a fee. You can reach that company for information by calling or writing:

Frandata
1130 Connecticut Avenue, NW
Washington, DC 20036
(202) 659-8640
http://www.frandata.com

Q **What will it cost to buy a franchise?**

Depending on which franchise you are interested in, your initial franchise fee could be as little as $1,000 or as much as $100,000 or more. On top of any initial fees will be other start-up costs, which could run from a few thousand dollars to $500,000 or more.

Q **What's involved in running a franchise?**

Even if you will be able to hire other people, you yourself will need to know how to operate all phases of the business since you may need to train employees or fill in for them when they are absent or if they leave. You will also need to be a good manager and salesperson and keep good records.

Q **Can I avoid market research by buying a franchise?**

No. While the franchise company may help with site selection and other details, there is no substitute for doing your own research. Remember, a franchise isn't something you can walk away from easily if it doesn't work out. Therefore *before* you sign the franchise agreement, make sure you determine how many sales you will have to make to be profitable and whether your territory has the population and the demand to make it likely you can reach that sales figure even if a competitor opens.

Q **Can I sell the franchise?**

Some franchises allow you to sell if you can find a buyer, and some don't. The UFOC will tell you what the franchise's regulations are regarding sale or transfer of your contract to anyone else.

Q **Is there any place where I can get more information about franchising?**

The International Franchise Association has a catalog that includes various publications about franchising. For information about the association or to get a catalog, call or write:

International Franchise Association
1350 New York Avenue, NW
Washington, DC 20005
(202) 628-8000
fax 202-628-0812
http://www.franchise.org

In addition you can find information about franchising quite regularly in *Entrepreneur* magazine (http://www.entrepreneurmag.com), *Inc.* magazine (http://www.inc.com) and in *Small Business Opportunities* magazine. *Enterpreneur* and *Inc.* both have searchable franchise databases on their web sites.

Q **Are there any inexpensive home franchises?**

Some franchises can be run from home and, therefore, may have lower start-up costs since you won't be required to build or rent space. But, most of the low-cost home "business opportunities" are not franchises. They are either multilevel marketing or direct selling opportunities, or package deals that promise to give you everything you need to start a business.

Q **What's the difference between a business opportunity and a franchise?**

When you buy a franchise, the relationship is ongoing. The franchisor is likely to have some say about the quality of the goods or services you sell and the methods you use to acquire the products or provide the service. They will also collect a royalty or other fee from you on an ongoing basis. In return they will give you guidance and training as well as name recognition.

A business opportunity does not usually come with the control or the support that a franchise does. However, sometimes the company selling the opportunity may act as a service bureau. And sometimes the opportunities are structured in such a way that they appear to be franchises even though they aren't. Some states now require business opportunities to register in the state and to provide disclosure documents to consumers intending to purchase the opportunity. See Appendix 5 for a list of states that have franchise and business opportunity laws.

Q **How much does it cost to buy a business opportunity?**

Prices vary widely from under $100 to $10,000 or more. And that's just the price to purchase the opportunity. You will have to allow additional money for marketing, office expenses, and other routine costs of doing business.

Q **Is there much risk involved with buying a business opportunity?**

Yes, there can be, particularly when the purchase price is significant and you need a storefront as you would for most franchises.

One would-be business owner—we'll call him "Joe"—sold a rental property he owned to raise the money to purchase an automotive parts business opportunity. The business looked like a franchise because it was to be operated from a storefront location and would sell the opportunity company's brand of merchandise. But as Joe discovered after the fact, the company was not a franchise but a seller-assisted marketing plan.

Before Joe had all the up-front money in place to get the business going, the opportunity company found an existing auto parts store and negotiated a price for him to purchase the store. This was a separate transaction from the purchase of the opportunity. Once the store was turned over to Joe, the opportunity company removed all of the inventory in the store and replaced it with their own branded merchandise. "The business failed after about a year of sucking me dry, and I filed legal action to recoup my losses," Joe explains.

To help prove his case, Joe ran an ad in a state-wide automotive periodical asking for information from people with similar experiences. He was inundated with responses and won his case against the company, but not until after the business had forced him into bankruptcy.

Looking back, Joe says he believes the company put unsuspecting consumers in business to fail so the opportunity company could profit by "repossessing more than they supplied." In the agreement, he says, "they lien everything on the premises of the store, not just what they finance you for. That would include thousands of dollars of shelving, displays, cash registers, computers, signage, and many other peripherals of doing business."

Joe advises others who are looking for business opportunities to treat the purchase the way you'd treat the purchase of an automobile. "If it's not what you want exactly, at the right price and the right conditions, be ready to walk away. I didn't do that. I let my mind overlook some obvious shortcomings for what I thought would be a positive result no matter what." He also advises to learn the laws covering franchises and opportunities in your state and to read all disclosure documents carefully. "No one will do it for you. You must do your homework."

Q **I want to work at home on my computer. Are the computer business opportunities that are advertised worth buying?**

It depends on the specific opportunity purchased, the purchase price, and who you ask. Some opportunities provide you with information, software, supplier lists, and instructions that would be quite time-consuming to gather any other way. Others provide little of value. Generally the bigger the income claims made in the ads and the less the "opportunity" costs to purchase, the more likely you'll get ripped off. But paying a high price to buy a computer business opportunity (or any other kind) is no guarantee you'll be satisfied, or that you'll be able to get a refund if you purchase the opportunity and aren't happy with what you get.

Before you make any purchase investigate the company and get details of the return policy (if any) in writing. If at all possible, use a credit card to make your purchase. That way if you aren't satisfied with the purchase and if the vendor won't refund your money you may be able to dispute the charge through the credit card company. If you send a check, your only recourse would be to sue, and that would probably cost more than the money you'd recover if you won.

Q Do many people lose a lot of money buying opportunities?

Unfortunately, yes. Although the Federal Trade Commission, state attorney general offices, and the government in Canada and other countries are constantly working to stop opportunity frauds, the legal process involved takes time. Furthermore some less-than-opportune opportunities manage to skate along at the edge of the law.

Q Why is it so difficult to spot these con artists?

The companies usually go to great lengths to make themselves look respectable. As a result, even people who have the skills and experience to do well in a particular industry can easily be fooled.

Lori Collins, an Ohio resident, bought a medical billing business opportunity after attending a seminar her husband heard advertised on a local radio station. She had done medical billing before interrupting her career to have children, so the opportunity seemed a natural.

"The seminar lasted an hour," Lori recalls. "They made the field sound like a piece of cake. They didn't promise they would obtain doctors for me; however they did make it seem like there was a high demand and that you would be tripping over them." They also touted their professionally created marketing materials, and that seemed like an advantage to Lori, too. "The only part at this point that made me swallow hard was the $8,000 initial fee. We had checked into franchises, so we talked ourselves into the fact that even though there was a high fee, it was minimal compared to the franchise costs," she adds.

The information package and videotape the company supplied were slick. "It all came very professionally packaged, which helped add to the thought that this was a top-notch company." The company's history stated they had been in business for 13 years, and the salesperson Lori had been dealing with "went out of his way to act like he was my new best friend."

Lori checked with the Better Business Bureau in the state in which the company was based. The BBB showed only three complaints had been filed and that each had been resolved. Lori and her husband refinanced their house to get the cash to buy the opportunity. Not long after they did, the opportunity company was sued by the FTC and went bankrupt. Looking back, Lori says the one thing she should have researched but didn't was the reputation of the people selling the opportunity. "If I had checked out the head people associated with this company, I would never have gone with them."

Q **Does anyone really make money from these turnkey businesses?**

A few people do. However, like any business, it takes time, hard work, and some trial and error to build the business and make it profitable.

Q **Is it mostly uneducated people and opportunists who lose money on business opportunities advertised in magazines?**

The amount of education you have seems to have little to do with who loses money or makes it. People who lose money in turnkey businesses or other business opportunities generally do so for one of these reasons:

- They have unrealistic expectations about how much time and effort they will have to put into selling the product or service to make it profitable.
- They have unrealistic expectations about how much money they can make from the business.
- They salivate on cue (much to copywriters' glee) to words like "easy," "confidential," "lucrative," and "profit," particularly if the ads also include five- or six-digit numbers preceded by dollar signs.
- They don't determine in advance if the product or service will sell, in what quantity it will sell, or what it will cost them to sell the product.
- They don't really like the product themselves or wouldn't buy it themselves at the price they have to charge.
- They discover after buying the business plans or package that the business will require selling and they hate selling.

Q **Is it possible to make thousands of dollars with little effort in my spare time like some of the business opportunity ads promise?**

It depends how much spare time you have. The two most important things to remember about opportunity advertising are:

1. There's no such thing as a free lunch.
2. If it sounds too good to be true, it is.

Remember, even though you may be able to process and fill orders in your spare time, you will have to start out with desirable products or services and will still have to spend time finding customers and doing other routine business chores if you expect the business to be successful. If you can't regularly set aside time to work in the business, you won't succeed.

Q **What can I expect if I send for one of those blind ads that promise to tell me the secrets of getting rich?**

Most of them are reports filled with hype about how the author of the report made his or her fortune (and how you could, too) in real estate or financial deals or repairing credit. Often people send away for the materials out of curiosity or because the ad has a money-back guarantee and therefore somehow seems "legitimate." It is probably the curiosity seekers who keep these advertisers in business.

Q **Don't the advertisers lose money if they offer a money-back guarantee and their program doesn't work?**

Not in practice. The guarantee is an advertising ploy that builds confidence and gets the reader to send in money. Most people never bother to send for their refund if they don't like the materials they get.

Q **How do I avoid frauds?**

There's no foolproof way to avoid scams; however, you can avoid many scams by steering clear of any business opportunity that

- promises unrealistic profits
- promises you can become wealthy working a few hours a day in your spare time
- has agents or distributors that seem more interested in soliciting you than in selling products or services
- discourages or forbids you from contacting other investors, distributors, or licensees of the business

- requires an up-front payment before giving you any details of what the business entails
- claims no experience or skills are needed
- requires you to pay someone money to get at-home work
- makes you an agent for a company that you haven't thoroughly investigated

IMPORTANT WARNING Be wary of travel agent opportunities. Entrepreneurs selling travel services as intermediaries have been sued by their customers when trips have fallen through. If you are considering becoming a sales rep for a travel company, check the company out thoroughly. If you have a computer and modem visit the U.S. Federal Trade Commission's web site (http://www.ftc.gov) and read the publications that are available online there for additional information.

Q **Are sales of franchises and business opportunities regulated in any way?**

A number of states have instituted franchise and business opportunity laws. Fifteen states have laws that require franchisors to provide presale disclosures, known as "offering circulars," to potential purchasers. Thirteen of these state laws treat the sale of a franchise like the sale of a security. Twenty-three states have business opportunity laws. These laws usually require that companies give potential purchasers a presale disclosure document that has been filed with a designated state agency.

Q **What is multilevel marketing?**

Multilevel marketing (MLM—also called network marketing) is a way of distributing and selling products and services through a chain of independent distributors rather than through traditional retail outlets.

Q **How does multilevel marketing work?**

Each distributor has two basic jobs: (1) to sell the company's products or services and (2) to recruit more distributors to sell the company's products or services.

Each new recruit a distributor brings into the organization is, in turn, encouraged to bring in his or her own recruits. The result is that an active distributor eventually develops a hierarchical substructure known as a downline that looks somewhat like an organization chart in a company with a lot of employees.

Each distributor gets sales commissions on his or her own direct product sales. He or she also makes a commission on the sales of the distributors in their downline. There are also likely to be performance bonuses available for reaching certain sales levels.

Since each distributor profits not only from his or her own sales but from sales of the downline, it is to the advantage of the distributor to guide and help those below to succeed.

Q **How do people get paid in MLM companies?**

Compensation plans vary from one MLM company to another, but typically distributors' commissions or margins (a discount off the list price) depend on a company's sales volume and where it is in the distributor chain.

In some companies distributors earn a commission on their own sales (say, 20 percent) and a lesser commission on any sales made by people below them. They might make 7 percent on sales made by people they have recruited directly (level 1),

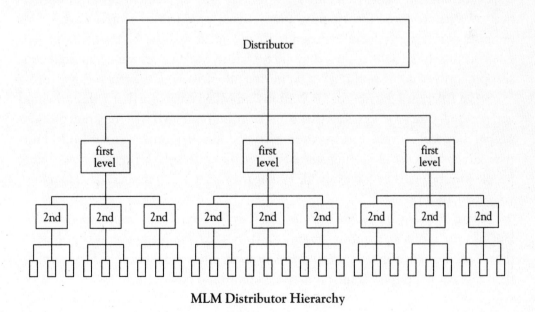

MLM Distributor Hierarchy

5 percent on sales made by the recruit's recruits (level 2), and so on. Thus if a level 3 recruit sold $50 worth of goods, she would make a $10.00 commission on the sale, the person immediately above her (the level 2 distributor in the chain and the one who directly recruited her) would make $3.50 commission on that sale, and the person at the top of the chain (the level 1 distributor) would make a $2.50 commission.

Q **Is there a limit to how big a downline can get?**

Yes. Different MLM companies set different rules about how many levels deep distributors will be paid. Some key the number of levels to the sales volume; others set the number of levels some other way. In addition the MLMs develop some kind of procedures (usually based on sales volume) that lets them break away or go direct—in other words, split off from the parent distributor chain and operate as the head of their own chain.

Q **Getting paid for not working sounds too good to be true. Is it?**

Ideally, that top-level distributor is also selling products as well as getting commissions from his or her downline. They are also responsible for providing training and support services for the downline.

Unfortunately, things don't always work that way. In some MLM organizations new recruits are lured into joining (and buying products or sample cases) with promises of gaining financial independence and great wealth. All they will have to do to become financially secure, they are told, is to work a marketing plan that consists primarily of doing nothing but recruiting others to work the marketing plan.

Steve Bretzke, a distributor for Watkins, an MLM company that sells household and personal care products, says that some distributors for MLM companies promise people they will soon be earning thousands of dollars a month in their MLM business. Since the cost of getting started is usually under $100, Bretzke says, "many people join before they have any idea what they have to do to succeed. Therefore, you see many dropouts."

Before dropping out, some recruits find they drop hundreds or thousands of dollars into the business, spending money on things like sample products they buy for their own use, meeting fees, transportation costs, promotional literature or catalogs they give out to prospects, and promotional tapes and books.

Q **Does anyone ever make money in MLM?**

Yes. Like almost any other industry or business the amount of money that can be made is usually proportional to the effort, time, commitment, and planning that goes into building the business.

Richard Suter, a CPA who specializes in taking start-up ventures public and who has done some work with MLM operations, says, "The ideal distributor is somebody who has the long view and the capital to back it up. They should have sales experience. Dealing with and overcoming rejection problems is the number one problem in all selling."

Bretzke, who says he just broke even the first year he was involved in MLM, agrees that the long view is important. He says it takes distributors about a year of working 10 to 15 hours a week to be able to make an income of about $1,000 a month. Where the real money is, he says, is in residual income, which can take 3 to 5 years of concentrated effort to build.

Q **What is network marketing?**

Network marketing is another name for multilevel marketing.

Q **What should I look for in an MLM company?**

The most important thing to look at is whether or not you like the products the company sells and would buy them yourself if you didn't join the MLM company. People who don't believe in a product or service or think it is too high-priced will have a difficult time convincing anyone else to buy it.

Since your income will be dependent on residuals from future sales, you also need to look very carefully at the overall financial stability and the management ability of the company and its founders. Obtain Dun & Bradstreet or TRW credit reports about the company and try to determine if the founders have been involved in any litigation (perhaps in other MLM organizations) in the past. In addition, request the names of other distributors and ask about payment of commissions and what they think about the organization as a whole. Says Bretzke, "Since it will take three to five years or more to truly make any serious money in this business, you have got to be sure that the company will be there with you."

Be cautious about newly formed MLM organizations. Don't get taken in by overzealous invitations to "get in on the ground floor." Many new MLMs, like many other types of new businesses, fail as a result of undercapitalization, poor accounting practices, inexperienced management, and other problems. Thus if you join a new MLM, don't risk more than you can afford to lose.

Q **What is a compensation plan?**

The compensation plan is the mechanism by which you get paid. It tells you what volume of sales you need to do before you get paid, how many levels deep you get paid, and under what circumstances you will qualify for bonuses. The plans typically have names like stair-step breakaway plan, unilevel, and matrix. There are also "hybrid" plans that combine one or more elements of the basic plan structures. The various types of plans are discussed at length in *Learning By Doing,* by Gary Molatore (888-444-1700). There are also a number of articles on the subject by Molatore located in the Multilevel Marketing Forum on America Online (keyword *MLM*).

Q **Which type compensation plan is better?**

"A lot of people in network marketing feel that whatever plan their company uses is the best, and that is understandable," says Eldon Beard who is a Watkins distributor and assistant forum manager of the MLM Forum produced by Business Know-How on America Online. "Some plans are designed to pay a higher percentage of the available bonus money up front for personal sales and on commissions for group sales in the first 1-to-3 levels. Others are constructed to pay more in the deeper levels, and some spread the bonus payout fairly evenly across all levels of the plan. Regardless of the type of plan, the key to remember is that you can make money with all of the legitimate plans. The product, and your effort, is the key. Good products, at a fair market value, are what drives any compensation plan," he adds.

Q **How are MLMs different from illegal pyramid schemes?**

The primary difference between a legitimate MLM company and a pyramid scheme is that an MLM company makes its money by selling products or services. In pyramid schemes that masquerade as MLMs, people coming into the organization pay money for the right to sell a product and the right to benefit by recruiting others into the organization. Selling the actual product or service, if it even exists, is incidental to recruiting.

Because of their emphasis on recruiting and other practices, some MLM companies that do sell products have been accused of illegal practices in various states. A few have been banned in some states. If you have any doubts about the legitimacy of an organization, check it out by calling your state attorney general's office or city consumer affairs office.

Q **How can I avoid pyramid schemes?**

There are a number of things you should do to steer clear of pyramid schemes and other scams:

- Watch out for claims of being able to make thousands of dollars a month within a very short time.
- Steer clear of any company that pressures you into buying substantial quantities of inventory either to join the organization or move up its ladder. If it doesn't buy back the inventory you can't sell (or if the company goes bankrupt), you will be out the amount you paid for the stock.
- Avoid any organization that requires any kind of significant investment to give you the "right" to bring other people into the organization.
- Watch out for investment or real estate management clubs where the money from the new investors winds up in the pockets of the earliest investors rather than being put into any actual real estate deals.
- Consider how much emphasis is placed on selling the product or service. If the emphasis is entirely on recruiting, the operation may be a pyramid scheme disguising itself as an MLM opportunity.
- Beware of plans that claim to sell miracle products or promise enormous earnings. Ask the promoter of the plan to substantiate claims with hard evidence.
- Beware of shills. When you ask a plan promoter for a list of individuals who have bought their plan, you might be given a list of people who are being paid to give false testimonials about their success in the business.

▸ Don't pay or sign any contracts in an "opportunity meeting" or any other high-pressure situation. Insist on taking your time to think over a decision to join. Talk it over with your spouse, a knowledgeable friend, an accountant, or a lawyer.

▸ Do your homework! Check with your local Better Business Bureau and state attorney general about any plan you're considering—especially those that seem too good to be true.

Q **Where can I find other people to ask about the company or the opportunity?**

Excellent sources of information are the home office and small business areas of any of the online computer information services. AOL, for example, has an entire forum devoted to multilevel marketing opportunities (keyword *MLM*). If you don't have a computer and modem, try asking people in networking or professional associations to which you belong if they know anyone who has heard of or has bought into the plan or business you are interested in. Try to get names and numbers and call the people and ask their opinions. Also check the public library for information, the attorney general's office, and the Better Business Bureau in the area the company is located.

Q **There seem to be more scams than real business opportunities out there. How can I find a business to start without getting ripped off?**

Thoroughly investigate any business opportunity, turnkey business, or franchise you are considering before getting involved. Make sure you can answer each of these questions affirmatively:

▸ Do I personally like the product or service?
▸ Would I buy this product or service at the price I will have to charge?
▸ Would I be satisfied with the quality of this product or service?
▸ Do I trust the people selling the opportunity, the turnkey business, or franchise?
▸ Have I had an attorney review the terms of the contract if I have to lay out much money?
▸ Do I know exactly what I will be getting for my money and what I won't get?

> Have I called or contacted others who bought this business or plan and asked if they were satisfied?
> Will I enjoy doing whatever is necessary to sell the product or service?
> Will I enjoy this line of work?

In addition, make sure you gather the *facts* to answer all of these questions:

> Who will buy this product? (Be specific.)
> Where will I find these people?
> What, specifically, are they looking for when they buy this type of product or service? (Don't guess. Call prospects and ask!)
> How many potential customers are there in the area in which I will be marketing the product or service?
> How many sales will I have to make to be profitable?
> What will it cost me to make those sales?
> Does the product or service lend itself to repeat customers?

5.

Internet and Mail
Order Riches:
Are They for Real?

For years, mail order has been touted as the easy road to riches—the ideal way for anyone with little money and little time to start a business that will stuff their mailboxes with dollars and build incredible wealth. More recently, Internet e-commerce businesses have been promoted in the same way. Put up a web page, place a few free classified ads, and watch the orders—and the money—roll in. Or, so some people would like you to believe.

Industry research makes it appear there is big money to be made by marketing directly to the consumer, too. According to a study conducted in 1999 on behalf of the Direct Marketing Association, traditional direct marketing and e-commerce sales will total more than $2 trillion by 2004. That amount will be split almost equally between business-to-business and consumer sales. And then there are all those stories about young entrepreneurs who turn their ideas and technical skills into multimillion-dollar Internet businesses before they reach their thirtieth birthday.

But are mail order and Internet businesses really as easy to start as some advertisements, articles, and books imply? Can the average person really make much money with a shoestring operation? Or do you need a rich uncle and a lot of luck to make your fortune in mail order or off the Internet?

Read on to discover the "amazing truth."

Q **What is mail order?**

Mail order, as the term is being used in this book, is selling or delivering merchandise through the mail. For very small businesses on tight budgets, that usually means selling through small advertisements in print publications, selling over the Internet, or selling through a catalog mailed to people who have previously bought from a company. Mail order may be your only way of selling products, or it could be an additional sales outlet for products you sell some other way.

Q **What kind of products are suitable for mail order?**

Almost anything can be sold by mail. Consumers and businesses buy everything from pens and pencils to furniture, computers, expensive collectibles, and stereo systems through the mail.

What you need to consider isn't so much the *kind* of things that could be sold by mail but rather the products that would be *practical for you* to sell as a small business. The cost of ads, catalogs, a web site, business stationery, postage, and packaging material can add up quickly. Thus, it is often best for small businesses to focus on products that:

- are targeted at a well-defined market
- do not break easily
- can be sold for a markup that will cover all costs and allow for some profit
- have a big enough market to make the effort worthwhile
- have a market you can afford to reach
- can be adequately described or depicted without using full-color photographs

Q **Where do I find products to sell?**

You can find the products anywhere. In some cases, you may actually manufacture the products yourself. Everything from gingerbread cookies to ink have been literally cooked up in entrepreneurs' kitchens and then marketed by mail.

Products you don't manufacture yourself can often be found in nearby warehouse outlets, manufacturing companies, from distributors, and advertised in trade magazines and in classified ads in newspapers like the *Wall Street Journal* or the *New York Times*. Industry trade shows are another excellent source of ideas for new products to sell. If you know what you want to sell and can't locate a manufacturer or distributor, look up the product in *The Thomas Register of North American Manufacturers* (available at libraries or on the web at http://www.Thomasregister.com). Call the manufacturer and ask for names of distributors. Look in the public library for other directories of manufacturers as well.

Q   How do you know what products will sell well?

The "secret" is to identify a market (group of people who share a common trait) and study that market closely on an ongoing basis to see what needs are unfulfilled or what trends are emerging.

Wendy Lew is the buyer for The Golden Bear, a fine jewelry manufacturer and retailer that sells better ladies' clothing, home gifts, and jewelry from other fine jewelers as well as its own signature line of golden bear pendants. In addition to sales in its two retail stores, the company sells through a catalog, which it mails twice a year to 500,000 people, and through its web site at http://www.thegoldenbear.net.

The Golden Bear's typical customer is 40 years old or older. Wendy, who has been the buyer for both the retail and catalog operations for 10 years, keeps on top of trends by reading trade publications, other company's catalogs, and by attending trade shows. "I read *Women's Wear Daily* [WWD] for ideas on new trends, colors, and fabrics as well as for hints about what's going to be happening next season," she says. "I attend shows such as the Coterie, Style Industry, FAE, Boutique Show, and the New York Gift Show, and pay attention to fashion magazines such as *Elle*, *Vogue*, and *In Style*. I also shop the big guys like Bergdorf's, Saks, Neiman's, Bloomingdale's, and Barney's to see what they have going on."

Q   How do I determine what to charge?

This is where your research comes in. You should have a pretty good fix on how much your customers are willing to pay for the convenience of getting the goods you want to sell through the mail. You should also know what all your expenses will be to advertise, purchase, and deliver that product. While many people in mail order say you should sell merchandise for at least four times what it costs you to buy or produce it, the actual amount depends more on what the market will bear. In some instances, you may only be able to mark up a product 50 percent, but if you can sell it in quantity to customers who will make many repeat purchases, that markup may be sufficient for profit. With other types of products you may be able to mark up your prices tenfold because your costs are extremely low and/or people can't get what you sell any other way.

Q **What kind of catalog do I need? Does it have to be in color?**

The type of catalog you need will depend on your product. If the products are items people are familiar with or that can be described adequately in a few words or sentences, a neat list of items, perhaps with a few simple drawings included to break up the gray look of the type, may be all that's needed. If you are selling clothing or anything that people normally want to see up close before ordering, you will need photographs in your catalog. If people are going to want to see the color of your product, you will need color photos in your catalog, which will add considerably to your printing costs.

Q **Can I print a catalog on my home computer?**

If you have a printer that produces good clear type with no jagged edges, you could print out master pages (called camera-ready copy). The quality of the type would be better if you output your finished work on an imagesetter at a service bureau, but if you can't find a service bureau or don't want the added expense, you can get away with using output from a good computer printer. If you need more than just a handful of catalogs, it will be cheaper and faster to bring the master pages to a copy center or a quick printer. Photocopies can cost as little as 3 to 4 cents a page, depending on where you live.

Q **Are there any alternatives to printed catalogs?**

Yes. You can put a catalog on a web site for a fraction of what it would cost you to print a color catalog and mail it. You can save the most money by doing some of the work yourself or by using ready-made Internet "storefront" software or services that will suit your needs. Some Internet services that offer off-the-shelf solutions for setting up a web site and catalog are iCat (http://www.icat.com/), Netscape (http://www.netscape.com), Yahoo (http://www.yahoo.com), and eCongo (http://www.econgo.com). There are many others as well. Or, you can get shopping cart software—search the Internet for the term *shopping cart software*—and put a catalog and online shopping on your own web site. Companies that offer merchant services (so you can accept credit card payments) should be able to provide you with a list of providers whose software works with their system as well. Be sure to shop around and compare prices before making any decision.

Q **How many items do I need to sell?**

It depends on what your customers want to buy and what you can provide for them. Often companies start out with just a handful of products and describe them on a single flier. Gradually, however, they add to their list of offerings.

Q **Can you sell just one or two products profitably by mail?**

Usually, no. Because of the marketing costs to acquire each customer, mail order companies traditionally make most of their profits by making multiple sales to each customer, usually over a period of time.

That said, if you have a unique product, a very targeted market, and sufficient markup, you might be able to make a small profit by selling a single product.

Depending on your industry, you might be able to get a catalog company to include your item in its catalog. In some industries such as software, however, catalog companies charge for placement in their catalogs.

Another option: find other small businesses who sell to the same market and share the cost of a mailing, inserting several fliers in a single mailing.

Q **What about those mail order opportunities that are advertised in magazines? Does anyone ever make any money from them?**

Very few people make much money this way. Here's why:

When you purchase a mail order opportunity, what you get is the right to buy and sell a variety of gift merchandise that is similar in quality to what you would find in gift shops on boardwalks and other tourist areas. The wholesale price of the merchandise is often too high to make it profitable selling the items by mail, especially when you calculate in the cost of catalogs (which you have to buy from the opportunity company), postage, and other costs of doing business. Complicating matters is the fact that these opportunities are sold to anyone who wants to buy them. So there are many, many people all trying to sell the same merchandise, from identical catalogs or pictures on web sites.

In fact, about the only people who make significant money on such opportunities are the opportunity companies themselves. They make their profits by selling catalogs, selling web page set-ups, maintenance and hosting services, and from commissions they get for selling merchant account services and equipment. The web services and merchant account services can cost would-be business owners $80 to $100 or more per month, and may be tied into noncancelable contracts that keep them paying fees long after it becomes apparent they'll never make any money from the "opportunity."

Q   Can I really make money with little classified ads?

Yes, you can use little classified ads to bring in business and make money. There are people right now making anywhere from a few hundred dollars to $40,000 or more a year in their spare time from mail order businesses they have started with classified ads.

Q   A lot of people say they've placed classified ads and never made a cent. What's the secret to making them work?

The secret to making money with classified ads is to plan on creating a *line of products* and to use classified advertisements as one relatively inexpensive way to find customers for that line. In effect, the advertising buys the customer and you make your money through multiple sales to that customer.

Don't plan on selling anything expensive directly through classified ads. Generally the best things to offer in classified ads are free literature or a very low-cost product. Products that are most likely to sell directly from a classified ad are those priced under $3. When you fill the order or request for information, you send the customer a catalog or sales literature describing other merchandise you have for sale.

Don't expect to be swamped with orders or inquiries from a single ad. Depending on the publication in which you advertise, you will be lucky to get one-tenth of 1 percent of the advertised circulation to respond. A good response from a classified ad in a carefully chosen publication may be as few as 40 to 50 inquiries. You should plan on using the income from your initial sales to pay for additional advertising, thus allowing you to build a customer list little by little.

Plan on advertising repeatedly and in multiple publications. Initially, you will want to test your ad and product in only one or two publications to see if you get any response. If you get enough inquiries to indicate an interest in what you are selling, then you will need to advertise regularly in several publications.

Expect to spend several years building the business. Even if you happen to have the money to take out big ads in a lot of publications all at once, it generally is not advisable to do so. Being new to mail order and new to business you could easily make any number of mistakes. Typical mail order mistakes involve the choice of products to sell, the price at which to sell them, the publications in which to advertise, the time of year to advertise, or even the wording in the ad. (One budding entrepreneur was selling an inexpensive item and forgot to include the price of the item in the classified ad!) Starting small means mistakes will be small.

Plan on increasing the size of your ads as you begin to know what sells and what doesn't. Once you start to get some customers and income as a result of your classified ads, you will want to try using small display ads to attract more attention and bring in more customers. If budget is a consideration, test a small display ad for a short time before agreeing to run it for several months. You will want to be sure the increase in customers will be worth the extra expense.

Plan an doing direct mailings in addition to classified advertising. In addition to responding to advertisements, profitable mail order companies also send out mailings several times a year to people who have purchased from them or responded to ads in the past. These mailings remind customers about the company's products and announce new items that are available.

TIP   Remember that profits depend on satisfied customers and repeat sales. The best source of new business in mail order is always sales to old customers. It is therefore essential to treat the customer as though he or she were your best friend. That means shipping merchandise promptly and offering no-questions-asked refunds or replacement if a customer is dissatisfied or claims an item was damaged or lost in the mail.

Q   **Should I wait until checks clear to ship merchandise?**

Since most customers want their purchases to arrive as quickly as possible, many vendors do not wait until checks clear unless the amounts involved are very large or they have some reason to be suspicious. That is taking a risk, of course, but it is a risk some vendors feel is warranted if the average dollar amount of orders is small, or if they provide goods people can easily purchase elsewhere.

Q **What about accepting credit cards? How do I go about accepting them?**

You will need to apply for a merchant account through a bank or an independent sales organization authorized to grant merchant status to vendors. It is relatively easy to obtain a merchant account if you've never declared bankruptcy, but be on your guard! Watch out for hidden fees, noncancelable equipment or software leases, and other expensive pitfalls. These are discussed in detail in another chapter in this book.

Q **Can I make money selling booklets by mail?**

People do make money selling small booklets and reports by mail. In fact, booklets and special reports can be ideal mail order products because they are lightweight, don't break, and can often be sold for many times your production and mailing costs. However, to make money, your booklets will need to contain in-demand information that appears unique and that can be targeted to specialized audiences. Chances are you won't be able to support yourself on the income; however, you may be able to make a satisfactory part-time income selling information by mail.

Q **Why is targeting so important? Isn't it better to have a big market?**

People today are bombarded with print and broadcast advertising. As a result, they tend to tune out noise advertising—which is anything they are not interested in hearing about or reading about at the moment. The way to avoid being noise advertising is to put your ads in places your customers are likely to search when they want a specific kind of product. Thus, while your potential market for herbs or recipes for making wine might be any adult, the people most likely to buy those items are more likely to look for them in a publication like *Mother Earth News* than in the classified section of the *New York Times*.

Q **What about chain letters that sell recipes or booklets—do they work?**

People who try these chain letters invariably report little or no response to their mailings. Thus they wind up throwing away all the money they spent on paper, envelopes, labels, mailing-list rental, and postage.

The only people who might possibly make money on any of these chain letters are the mailing-list companies that are often named in the letters. These companies often specialize in renting names of opportunity seekers. They may be referred to in letters as a source for fresh, hot, or quality mailing lists that will increase the response to your mailing or make it easier (by supplying you with preprinted labels) to mail out hundreds of copies of the chain letters.

Q **Are such chain letters legal?**

Some chain letters claim to be legal because they sell a product or service. Nevertheless, the United States Postal Service, in a booklet called *A Consumer's Guide to Postal Crime Prevention*, has the following to say about chain letters:

> *Don't waste your money . . . chain letters are a form of lottery and may violate federal mail fraud laws. The same three elements that apply to lotteries (payment, prize, and chance) also make these schemes illegal.*

Q **Should I rent a mailing list and send everyone on the mailing list a catalog or brochure describing my products?**

You have to work out the mathematics to decide whether the cost of the mailing-list rental, the postage, and the preparation of a direct mail package would bring you enough new customers and potential repeat customers to be worthwhile. If you have a clear picture of your target market (for example, all chemical engineers with IBM computers or 25-year-old males who like water sports) and can find an appropriate mailing list to rent, you may get a 1 to 2 percent response rate to your mailing. The 1 to 2 percent figure is about average for a targeted mailing that is not to already-existing customers of a company. Your actual response rate, depending on the product, what actually goes into the mailing, and many other factors, could be much higher or lower.

If you think you can make a profit on a 1 to 2 percent response rate and won't go broke if you try and don't make a profit, do the mailing. (You may have to order a minimum of 5,000 names. Ask ahead of time if you want to rent fewer than that.)

TIP

If you are on a tight budget and can't afford to take a chance sending out 5,000 brochures in the mail, try building your own small mailing list if you sell to businesses. Often buying guides in trade magazines will list contact information for companies. You could also call businesses you think might be potential customers and ask who is responsible for purchasing what you sell. You may also be able to swap customer lists with other small, noncompeting businesses. If your small list draws enough responses, then consider renting a larger mailing list.

Response rates on residential mailing lists will be much, much lower. One-tenth of 1 percent or less is a typical response to mailings sent to all people in a neighborhood.

Q **What laws do I need to know about?**

Most of the laws that affect mail order businesses are the same as those affecting any business selling any product. Your advertising can't be deceptive or purposely misleading, and you may need to be concerned about product liability, warranties, and the legality of selling your products.

You should also be aware that you can't ship unordered merchandise and bill customers for it. You must be able to deliver what you have advertised within the time you state in your ads or within 30 days of the time you receive orders if no time is stated in the ad. If there is a delay due to some unforeseen circumstance, you have to notify the customer and offer to refund his or her money.

Q **Do I have to collect tax on out-of-state mail order sales?**

At the time this book was written you were not required to collect sales tax on out-of-state purchases unless your business had a physical presence (office) in the state in which a sale was made.

Q How do I ship orders?

You can ship orders using either the United States Postal Service or any private shipping service. It is important to find out ahead of time how the merchandise should be packaged for safe shipment. There are any number of packaging companies that can supply boxes, tapes, cardboard envelopes, or other packaging supplies for shipping. When you are just starting out, you may want to buy the supplies you need in small quantities from the large office supply stores such as Office Max, Staples, or Office Depot. But once you need to buy more than a few boxes, envelopes, or other packaging at one time, you'll do better purchasing your supplies in bigger quantities elsewhere. If you can't find a local distributor for packaging in the Yellow Pages, search the Internet for paper and box suppliers.

TIP Not all products can be shipped to all locations by mail. Be sure to check with the U.S. Postal Service or any other shippers you plan to use. You should also call the Department of Commerce to determine whether there are any regulations restricting the sale or shipping of your merchandise to any foreign countries.

Q What is drop shipping?

Drop shipping is an arrangement in which you take orders for a company that manufactures or supplies one or more products your customers want. You send the orders to the suppliers along with shipping labels (usually), and then the manufacturer or supplier sends the product to the customer. You don't need to retain inventory or do any actual shipping, but you also don't have much control over when the product is shipped or how it is shipped, which can be a problem if a customer claims never to have gotten a product or that it arrived damaged.

Q Will I have to spend a lot of time running a mail order business?

In the beginning you can run a small mail order business in your spare time from home, but as it starts to become profitable and generate a lot of customers you will find that your spare-time business is taking up 30 or 40 hours each week.

6.

Creating Your Own
Business Opportunities

Some people spend months or years dreaming about being self-employed and waiting for the right opportunity to arise. Others think they see the opportunity bandwagon passing by and jump on it without considering where it is going, what it will cost, or whether or not they'll really enjoy the ride.

As you can imagine, neither approach to starting a business is particularly successful. To build a profitable business you have to learn the business and then put yourself in the driver's seat and forge ahead. Here is a brief look at what it takes to create a variety of businesses.

Q **What kind of businesses are easiest to start?**

Service businesses have traditionally been the easiest to start, since they require the least amount of start-up capital. Some require nothing more to get started than the purchase of business cards and stationery.

Businesses that provide services that are in demand are easier to start as well. Database programming, computer graphics, web design, human resource consultancies, and other businesses involving highly specialized knowledge tend to be easy to start for individuals who are outgoing and go-getters. Child care and elder care services, handyman, cleaning, and other services for families with two wage earners that can't do it themselves or prefer not to do it themselves are also relatively easy to start.

Q **What do I need to start a word processing, secretarial, or office support service?**

These services are among the easiest to start, but due to competition, it may take time and effort to get the business going.

You'll need a recent model computer, current or near-current versions of widely used office software (Microsoft Word and other products in the Microsoft Office suite are the most popular products), and the ability to make quality printouts, send and receive faxes, and make photocopies. Due to the competition from others who work at home—or would like to—you will also need a good dose of persistence and determination to get your business started and make it profitable.

A multifunction device that gives you printing, fax, scanning, and photocopying capabilities in one unit is a good choice if you are choosing equipment for the first time. As your business grows, however, you may find you need to add on a stand-alone photocopier (to provide added capabilities and speed), a better scanner, or other peripheral equipment. Such add-ons should be purchased only when you have the business to support them.

If you will be including desktop publishing or web site design in your services you will also need page layout software, a web page editor, computer clip art, and graphic editing software—plus experience using all the software. (Owning the software to do desktop publishing or web site design does not give you the ability to do those things. Both require significant training in addition to learning how to use the software.)

Once you buy and learn to use equipment and software, your toughest job is going to be attracting a steady stream of customers. You may be able to get started by making a lot of phone calls and using personal contacts, but sooner or later most secretarial services find they need to use some form of print advertising. Many office services companies find they do well with a small display ad in the Yellow Pages (an ad that's an inch or so big on the page, for instance). Others find they do well by targeting a niche market and advertising in publications bought by that special market. Someone who likes to type academic papers might advertise in college or university newspapers, for instance, while someone who wants to do typing or transcription for medical or legal professionals would want to advertise in local journals or newsletters that lawyers or doctors in the area read. Sometimes, in fact, your business won't get any calls unless you have an ad in a particular niche publication. A court reporter in South Carolina, for instance, saw her business dry up one year because she had forgotten to renew her ad for the year in an industry directory. Advertising won't work miracles, however, and it also has to be frequent to pay off.

Pricing of the actual services you perform will need to be competitive. Depending upon where you live, the price may run from $12 to $25 an hour for word processing. Typesetting, resume typing, and related work, if you have the software and experience to do a good job, can usually be billed at a higher rate. You do have to check the going rates in your area and keep an eye on costs to stay competitive.

If much of the work you do involves transcription, you'll also need to keep a close eye on voice recognition programs. The technology gets better each year, and at some point could have a major impact on the transcription businesses.

Once you find customers, it is important to provide quality work. Joan Kumpitsch, who ran the Johnstown, New York, company J.V.K. & Associates for 16 years, advises, "Start small enough and do what you do well. You can always add services, but if you start with your sights set too high and end up doing a shoddy or mediocre job, you'll soon be out of business. One bad job or one that is done poorly can cost you several new ones."

Q **What does it take to start a money-making newsletter?**

To publish a successful newsletter you need to start out with a very clear focus of who your potential customers are and what kind of information you can provide for them that is different from what they are now getting from other sources. Once you know the focus you will need to decide:

▸ *What is your income model for the newsletter?* How will it produce income? Will you make money by selling subscriptions, by selling display or classified advertisements, or by giving the newsletter away free in order to build a mailing list of individuals who will buy some other product or service you sell?

▸ *Who will write the articles for each issue?* Will you do the writing yourself? Pay freelancers to write? Hire a writer? Will you have enough information to publish regularly and keep readers interested?

▸ *How will you publish the newsletter?* Will it be published in print and mailed conventionally, or will it be published electronically?

▸ *Will you typeset it and print it yourself?* Or will you need to outsource one or both of those functions?

▸ *Will it need to be formatted for use on a web page or in electronic mail?* If so, can you do the electronic formatting on your own? Or will you need to outsource one or both of those functions?

▸ *How long will the newsletter be?* Subscription newsletters will need to be long enough to make readers feel they are getting their money's worth, but not so long you have difficulty filling them with useful content each month. You'll want to consider postage costs in your planning if you'll be mailing a printed newsletter to subscribers. For electronic newsletters, you'll want to consider the amount of text that's comfortable to read on a computer screen. In most cases, articles are easier to read on a computer screen if they are under 1,000 words in length. If the articles are longer, they should be broken up into a series of shorter pages for the computer reading.

▸ *Will you take advertising?* Your answer to this question will affect the subscription price and may have an effect on the length, design, and shipping weight of your newsletter. One good way to accept advertising without changing your page design in printed newsletters is to include inserts from advertisers in your newsletter. The cost of the insert could be set to cover your mailing costs.

▸ *How will you market the newsletter?* How do you plan to get subscribers? Will you advertise? Will you do direct mailings? Will you post samples of the newsletter on a web site? What will marketing cost? Could you publish and continue marketing if you got less than 1 percent response to your initial marketing efforts? Even though your newsletter may be the best around in your field and you target your market carefully, your response could be as low as 1 percent or even lower.

▸ *What will you charge for subscriptions?* If you will be selling subscriptions to the newsletter, the price you charge should be set based on your costs, the exclusivity of the information, and your target customers' ability and willingness to pay for that information. If you provide industry information that businesses can't get easily elsewhere you will be able to command much higher fees than you would if you were selling a newsletter on cost-cutting for consumers.

▸ *How many subscriptions will you need to break even?* How many to make a profit on all your costs? Don't forget to figure in the costs of marketing, postage, phone calls, Internet access, and web development, along with your other costs. You need realistic figures to determine pricing—and whether or not to proceed with the publication.

- *How much time are you willing to devote to the newsletter?* Unless you have money to hire people to write, edit, typeset, and design the publication, the newsletter is likely to consume every spare minute of your time. Are you willing to devote that kind of energy to it?
- *How much turnaround time do you need to allow?* If you will be mailing your newsletter, remember to determine how much time it will take from when you write and do layouts for a newsletter until you can get it printed, folded, mailed, and actually delivered to the reader.
- *Can you afford to market and publish the newsletter for months without a profit?* Be realistic. Work out all the figures before deciding whether to go ahead with the project. Remember, marketing will have to be an ongoing effort, not a one-time event.
- *Do you have the skills to do any writing, editing, layout, design, or web pages you plan?* Computer equipment greatly simplifies some of these chores but only if you have the basic writing, editing, and production skills plus experience using a computer, page-layout (desktop publishing) and/or web design software. If you don't have this background, the going will be rough.
- *Do you have a method for tracking subscribers and expiration dates, printing labels, and mailing renewals?* You should have all those details worked out in advance. Don't wait to figure out how to use your database until subscriptions start coming in. Get it all set up in advance or have someone who is experienced do it for you.

Q **What is an e-zine?**

An e-zine is a magazine or newsletter that is published electronically. It is often delivered in e-mail and is often free.

Q **How can you make money if you don't charge for your magazine or newsletter?**

The "secret" is to use the free newsletter as a lure to attract customers for some related product or service you sell. Consultants, attorneys, accountants, and other professionals often give away free newsletters to establish themselves as experts in their field or to keep their name in front of prospective customers. Web site owners use free newsletters to get visitors to return to their web site, where they sell advertising space and/or products and services. Similarly, some businesses give away newsletters to qualified subscribers and then sell advertising in the publication.

Randy Cassingham, publisher of *This Is True*, a humorous news commentary e-zine (http://www.thisistrue.com), devised yet another twist on the free newsletter concept. He offers readers a short, free version of his e-zine and uses that as a way both to get fans to subscribe to a longer version of the publication and to build sales for self-published books, which are compilations of the newsletter articles. He sells advertising in the electronic publication as well. Advertising revenue is based on the number of subscribers, so the more subscribers he has, the more advertising revenue he stands to collect. As if all those sources of income from the e-zine weren't enough, Randy also syndicates a version of the publication to conventional print media outlets around the world.

If you plan to give away a publication you have to be prepared for initial losses. It takes time and patience to achieve your ultimate income-producing goal. Even though Randy was publishing his newsletter in e-mail (thus saving printing and mailing costs), he lost $3,000 in sales in the first 6 months he was in business. But he hung in there and 2 years later he was able to quit a $50,000 full-time job and live off the earnings of *This Is True*.

Q **How can I make money as a freelance writer?**

There are many different ways to make money as a freelance writer. Freelance writers have traditionally made money writing for magazines and newspapers, writing non-fiction, fiction, or children's books, and writing product literature, newsletters, press releases, annual reports, product manuals, and other types of business communications.

The Internet is yet another source of freelance writing jobs for some writers. Business web sites need promotional copy and Internet-based newsletters and magazines need columns and feature articles just as print publications do. Some magazines actually publish two separate editions (one in print and one on the Web) and sometimes use two separate staffs.

Freelancers often start out writing for publications in their spare time. Some have full-time jobs as writers in industry; others are independent contractors who write advertising copy, do publicity for business, write technical documentation, or do other writing chores to keep up a steady income. Those who just write books and magazine articles or short stories usually have years of experience as writers and frequently have several books in print.

If you are just starting out, it helps to have a specialty and to realize that you may have to do some writing for very little pay just to get published. Once you get published you will, ideally, be able to use copies of published clips plus good ideas and writing skills to get better-paying assignments.

You will also have to consider the market when you write. You may be the world's greatest writer., but if few people besides you are interested in the subject matter of your article, story, or book, you won't get any traditional publishing companies or magazines to publish it.

Q **What about self-publishing books? Can I make money doing that?**

Yes, you can make money self-publishing books. The Internet is making it easier than ever to do so. But you must be able to write good, interesting copy, have a clear target market, and be able to put a lot of effort into marketing and promoting your book.

Careful planning is essential if you want to make a profit. You need to choose a subject carefully, based on who you can sell the book to. The better you can determine who will buy the book and what specific channels you can use to reach potential customers, the more likely you will be successful at self-publishing.

Contact major book distributors and chain stores to find out what you'd have to do to get them to carry your book. Don't forget the online booksellers such as Amazon.com and Barnes and Noble (BN.com). You may find it easier to get your book distributed through the online stores than through retail stores. As an added benefit, being carried by an online store lends credibility to your book and helps assure customers their order will be fulfilled. That will increase your sales. In a test I ran on my own web site, I got three times more orders for one of my books when I linked an "order now" option to Amazon.com than I did when I had the "order now" button linked to a shopping cart on my own web site.

To keep costs down, find a printer who can work from your disk or from laser printouts. You can find ads from these "short run" (small order) printers in the advertising section in the back of *Writer's Digest* magazine. Expect to pay about $4 to $6 each to print 200 copies of a $5\frac{1}{2} \times 8\frac{1}{2}$-inch book. The actual total will depend on the number of colors you use on the cover of the book and whether there are photos inside. Order only a small quantity of books at first. Use sales figures from the first run to determine how many more copies of the book to order. Be sure to keep track of all your expenses as well as how many you give away to friends, family, or as promotional copies so your estimates of what you can *sell* and what your profit is will be realistic.

In addition to contacting major book distributors, look for niche markets that your book would appeal to. Talk to owners of those stores—or those web sites and see if you can work out some kind of deal to have them sell your book on their web site. Often you can encourage them to sell your book by paying them 10 to 15 percent of the price of each book they sell.

If you don't have the money to have your book printed or want to test the response to it before you do have it printed, consider publishing it electronically. Fatbrain.com (http://www.fatbrain.com/) is one of the companies that facilitates electronic self-publishing by preparing authors' works for electronic publication, cataloging the books on their web site, selling them for you, and doing all the bookkeeping.

Another option is to prepare your book yourself for electronic distribution. Adobe Systems has a version of its Acrobat software that includes encryption routines that will allow you to distribute your book electronically without the recipient of the electronic version being able to copy it and give it away to anyone else.

Q **Can I do my own printing and production with a laser printer and binding equipment?**

Yes, there are some books, primarily manuals, workbooks, and other training materials, that can be produced with your own computer and printer—in the beginning, at least. If volume picks up it may become more economical and more convenient to outsource the printing and binding.

Q **I've got a computer. Would desktop publishing be a good business to start?**

People who create successful desktop publishing businesses often work in advertising or graphic arts for many years before launching their own business. That's because desktop publishing really isn't a business. Instead, the term means using a computer and computer software as a tool to simplify some production chores in the creation of print publications, slides, and multimedia works. If you have experience doing typesetting or commercial art and want to start your own service, it is almost imperative to have desktop publishing tools available to you.

If you have no experience in typesetting, commercial art, or related fields, buying a computer and desktop publishing software is not going to put you into business overnight as a desktop publisher. Typesetting, layout, and design all require special skills and training. While these skills can be learned, it takes time to acquire the basic manual skills and hands-on experience needed to know how to create professional-looking documents. In addition, you will also need to spend time learning to use page-layout and art programs. These programs are quite sophisticated, and as a result have quite a steep learning curve.

If you think you would enjoy using a computer to do typesetting and commercial design work, you should get the training before investing in the equipment. Training is offered in night courses at two-year colleges and technical schools and, sometimes, in adult education classes at high schools.

Q **Can I make money screen-printing T-shirts?**

Screen-printing T-shirts and other garments has proven to be a lucrative business for some entrepreneurs. There are companies that started out as home businesses and within a half-dozen years were taking orders for thousands of shirts at a time and were grossing several million dollars a year. There are also businesses that start in basements or small storefronts and never do much more than break even, if they even make it that far.

Q **Can you still get started in screen-printing at home without spending a lot of money?**

Yes, you can. The cost of a start-up depends on the capabilities you want and whether you can locate used equipment to buy. You can operate out of your basement or garage (if zoning laws don't prohibit it), but what you can produce will be limited compared to larger shops doing screen printing.

Nancy Clayton, owner of Computer Design Concepts in Rowland Heights, California, bought used equipment to start her business for less than $1,000. For the money she got a four-color press, a flash dry, and an exposure lamp. "If you look around," she says, "there are some really good deals out there. You can get by with a homemade one-color press to begin with, but you definitely need a flash cure or your prints will come off the first time you wash them. In fact, you can build your own basic press for even less money with plans in the book, *How to Print T-shirts for Fun and Profit* by Scott and Pat Fresener." The book is available on their web site at http://www.usscreen.com or by phone at (800) 624-6532.

Clayton is an assistant forum leader in the screen-printing forum on America Online. It is one of 75 profession-specific forums in the WorkPlace channel on AOL. She started her business in her garage, but later built a free-standing barn-type building on their property to house the business. In addition to screen-printing T-shirts, she uses heat-transfer to imprint some designs and to put names and numbers on team jerseys.

Q **How long does it take to screen-print a T-shirt?**

The amount of time depends on the design of the shirt and the kind of equipment you have. "If it is a one color design on a white T-shirt, and you use a dryer to cure your ink, you can probably whip out about 10 dozen an hour on a manual press. If you only use a flash cure as I do, then you can print about 60 shirts an hour if you don't waste any time and the phone doesn't ring," says Clayton.

Q **Who buys printed T-shirts?**

Printed T-shirts are purchased by a wide variety of businesses and individuals. Businesses often purchase screen-printed T-shirts for their employees to wear on the job. Churches, schools, civic groups, sports teams, restaurants, and even radio stations or banks are all potential customers, too. The screen printers who make it big, however, are those who go after and get orders from large businesses, universities, and national catalog companies, and those who become licensed to print major sport team logos.

T-shirts aren't the only items you can screen print. Most owners see themselves as being in the screen-printing business rather than the T-shirt business. T-shirts, because of stiff competition, may make up only 20 to 40 percent of their business. The bulk of the business often comes from screen printing other types of items, such as baseball caps, sweatshirts, jackets, and other apparel, as well as mouse pads, bumper stickers, and other advertising specialties. In fact, one screen printer shifted his emphasis from screen-printing T-shirts to screen printing with inks that contain silver—and conduct electricity—onto electronic membranes used in the touch panels of photocopiers and other electronic goods.

Q Can I make money just selling T-shirts or other screen printing without doing the printing myself?

Yes, many people who sell promotional products do that. They work with customers to find the right promotional products to achieve their goals and make a commission on each sale. This is another field in which there is considerable competition, however, so to succeed you have to be a good salesperson and be willing to put in many hours searching out new products for your customers.

Q What's the difference between companies that make a lot of money and those that don't?

"The main difference is quality of the printing and the ability to meet deadlines," Nancy Clayton says. "You might get a lot of first orders, but to really build your business you need to develop repeat business. I have customers who have been giving me work for five years or more. A customer needs to know that if the job is needed on a specific day, it will be there. What good does it do to print T-shirts for a company picnic and have them delivered the day after the event? It can be tricky at certain times of the year, but in nine years I have only missed one crucial deadline and that was due to a major storm and power failure. You also need to stand behind your work and replace anything that is defective."

Q Where can I find information on the Internet about screen printing?

Here are several good places to start gathering information:

http://www.usscreen.com
Screen Printing Professional Forum on America Online (keyword, *screen printers*)
http://www.t-shirtshopper.com/websites/wholesale (an extensive list of T-shirt wholesalers)
http://www.hanes2u.com (general information from Hanes Corp., as well as a source of supplies)
http://www.proworldinc.com (information about transfer paper and printing transfers from your computer)
http://www.geoknight.com/intro.html (general information and supplies for heat transfer)

Magazines
http://www.screenweb.com
http://www.impressionsmag.com
http://www.promomart.com/pmindex htm

Q **What does it take to make it as a consultant?**

The keys to success as a consultant are knowing your industry inside and out, taking the time to know what your client wants, and delivering what your client wants in a professional way. James A. Smith, a Chicago resident who has worked as an independent consultant to radio stations for more than 18 years, says that in his field, a consultant needs "an understanding of how radio stations operate, particularly within a given format and a given market size." The needs of a country music station in Wisconsin are obviously going to be different from those of a rock music station in Detroit.

To make money as a consultant, Smith says, you need to do the following: "(1) keep the customer satisfied; (2) remember you are just advising others how to do things, you are not in control; (3) agree in advance on the goals, expectations, and methods of measuring the success of your work; (4) don't try to change too much or too little [in the client's operation]; (5) don't bite off more than you can chew or let yourself stagnate in a changing field."

Q **How do you put those precepts into practice?**

Whether you are in radio consulting, management consulting, computer consulting, or any other kind of consulting, the way to put theory into practice is to first be an expert in what you do and then to bend over backward to satisfy the client.

José Kirchner, a corporate consultant and human resources trainer in Carmichael, California, describes this scenario as being typical of the kind of effort needed to create a workshop series for one of his clients:

I get a request for a workshop such as a series of five two-hour briefings/workshops on sexual harassment. The target audience is supervisors and managers of all departments. They hired me because word of mouth in a neighboring city said I'd do it right, and their Employee Assistance Program uses me as a trainer—a lot!

I contact the program manager for their Employee Assistance Program (EAP). He tells me the supervisors do not utilize the EAP or its management consultants for corrective actions to the extent other city governments do. He wants me to clarify the role of management consultants and how they can be of help in a case of possible sexual harassment—early on, before it actually becomes sexual harassment, if possible.

Contact with the personnel director will tell me a bit more about what is going on: Is there a policy? Have there been incidents? What are the attitudes? Is there a particular work area where this has been a problem? Is there anything he wants me to cover specifically? Does he agree with my proposed approach?

I will also contact the Health, Safety, and Training Officer to get more specific information on each department and possible contacts in each.

Then I will fine-tune my Power Point presentation, adding and deleting slides, which are the main focus points for the audience. I then prepare some handouts and send them for preparation and distribution.

After the first workshop, I will consult a bit more, especially with the HST Officer, and make any necessary revisions. At the end of the series, I will meet with her, and with the personnel director, then give feedback to the training director and program manager at the EAP. All of my contacts are annotated in my client database. I may also prepare written recommendations and a summary. And all participants fill out a one-page program evaluation, which I review and turn over to the personnel director.

Obviously, the specific tasks a consultant will need to perform will differ depending on the type of consulting job. Overall, it is this kind of client contact and client focus that is required to establish a consulting practice and develop it into a profitable business.

Q How long does it take to build up a good business as a consultant?

Once you have established a track record for solving problems, it will take a year or more to establish a business. Things may be lean at first, but if you continually promote yourself, are good at what you do, and are professional in the way you work, your reputation and business will grow.

Q Can you make money as a homebased travel agent?

Although there have been many changes in the travel industry in recent years, it is still possible to make good money as an outside travel agent for a travel agency (the agencies that hire outside agents are called host agencies). You will, however, need to understand how the industry works and have some experience in it, as well as an outgoing nature, to make this business pay off.

To gather experience and background, consider taking a course on how to become a travel agent. Be wary of opportunities that require you to pay to work, particularly if these are accompanied by income claims or hype about free travel. Travel agent training courses are sometimes available through community colleges. The Institute of Certified Travel Agents, located in Wellesley, Massachusetts (http://www. icta.com) also offers home study courses, professional development courses, and certification.

To gain hands-on experience, try to work for a travel agency as an employee or, if necessary, as an unpaid intern. Consider whether there is a particular type of travel you'd like to specialize in, such as cruises or corporate travel. "Travel companies are no longer relying on leisure travel or business travel," explains Joyce M. Fitzgerald, owner of WorldWide Journeys, located in Richland, Washington. "Now, smart travel agencies are developing specialties and niches. A successful agent becomes a consultant, in the true sense of the word—rather than an 'order taker.' Once you have experience, check with several agencies to see what kind of deal each will make, and whether they specialize in the areas you'd like to focus on."

To keep current with the industry, familiarize yourself with the National Association of Commissioned Travel Agents. There are a variety of resources available for homebased agents on their web site (http://www.nacta.com).

Q Can I make money selling at flea markets?

If you go about it in the right way you can. John Hunter, who runs Tools-N-Stuff, a company that sells tools and other items for automobiles, makes his entire income by selling his wares at flea markets. One of the tricks of the trade, he says, is knowing your products and learning where and how to buy your goods. Your prices should be a little lower than those in retail stores—10 percent or lower works, Hunter says. But the real secret, he says, is selling items that are hard to find at any price in retail stores.

Another key to running a profitable flea market business is to have a wide variety of items in low to medium price ranges so you have something available for everyone. Hunter usually sets out about 500 different items, many of which are priced at $5 or less. These will help attract traffic to the booth. The small sales add up and "keep you from just sitting there all day watching people walk by."

Items you choose should not be prone to fading in the sun and should be attractively displayed. You also need to be equipped to quickly cover everything with plastic and secure the plastic with clips in case of rain. At flea markets that have open-air booths as well as indoor booths, the outdoor vendors often do better than the indoor vendors. In fact, Hunter says, some who have indoor booths rent space outdoors as well.

To locate merchandise to sell, look in *Thomas's Register of Manufacturers* for names of manufacturers, go to trade shows, and look for items to sell in publications such as *Cover Magazine* (24 Grassy Plain Street, Bethel, CT 06801-1725, http://www.sumcomm.com).

The biggest mistake people make in working flea markets, Hunter says, is not being businesslike. You have to get necessary licenses and comply with the tax laws, and you also have to plan. "You can't do things halfheartedly. You have to run it like a business." If you are businesslike, he says, you should be able to gross at least $400 to $500 every day you sell.

Q **What about online auctions? Are they just for hobbyists?**

The majority of people who sell on the auction sites are hobbyists, but there are some who make the equivalent of full-time salaries by selling collectibles or other items through popular sites such as eBay (http://www.ebay.com). Some businesses use auction sites to test the market for new products, and a few people have profited by starting their own auction sites for specialized products as well.

To make a profit with auctions you need to specialize in a particular type of merchandise, know your prices, and the market. To make money on an ongoing basis, you'd also need to have a steady supply of items to sell. One big advantage of selling this way is that you can start off in your spare time without any initial cash outlay to rent flea market, craft show, or retail space.

Q **What about crafts? Is there any money selling them?**

There are a variety of ways you can make money in crafts, but for many businesses that sell handicrafts, the profit is low compared to the number of hours it takes to create the craft items. But as in any field, those who treat their activity as a business and keep a close eye on the market for their goods, their raw material, and marketing costs and the labor costs (including their own time), can make crafting a profitable business.

Terrie and Richard Floyd, owners of Laughing Moon, began designing and crafting collector-quality toys and decorative accessories in 1967. They produced expensive, one-of-a-kind pieces until 1994, and also licensed some of Terrie's designs. "The licensing helped us get more of my art out to the general public," says Terrie, "and also let us see that my artwork was very popular at affordable prices." As a result, they decided to "mass produce" Terrie's jumping jack creations in special limited editions. They now have 15,000 customers, including the Metropolitan Museum of Art, Art Institute of Chicago, Gumps, Flax Art & Design, and hundreds of small, quality art galleries.

To increase profitability, treat crafting as a business and keep a close eye on costs and time. Selling other people's crafts on consignment, selling craft supplies, and selling your own original patterns are other ways to add to craft income.

If you develop unique products or designs as Terrie does, you may want to consider licensing them. Look in department stores and discount stores and attend wholesale shows to see if there might be mass-market applications for your work, and contact any appropriate manufacturers. If you can interest manufacturers in your work, be sure to have a contract drawn up that spells out the specific rights you are granting to the manufacturer. Have an intellectual property attorney go over the contract carefully so you know exactly what you'd be giving away (for instance, can the manufacturer use your design on one type of product, or on any product they manufacture?) and what you'd be getting under the contract terms.

Whether or not you plan to license your designs, be sure to register a copyright on original designs. That way if someone copies your work, you could sue and collect damages and attorney fees (if you win).

Q **Can you run an industrial business from home?**

Yes you can, if zoning laws don't prevent you from working at home and if you can comply with any EPA regulations that might apply to your business. Chemical distributorships, gold-plating operations, and even machine shops have been run or started in garages and basements of people all over the country. You could also start an industrial consulting practice if you have experience. You would need to be a registered professional engineer and be fairly well known in industrial circles. "Advertising for this business just doesn't work," says industrial engineer Lew Merrick, owner of Tangent Engineering in Lynnwood, Washington. "People don't look in the Yellow Pages for an engineer—they call up a couple of friends and ask for recommendations."

Q **I speak Spanish and French fluently. Could I get work as a translator?**

Possibly, but you should know it takes more than the ability to speak a foreign language fluently to make money as a translator.

Q **What kind of qualifications would I need?**

Gabe Bokor, owner of Accurapid Translation Services, Inc., in Poughkeepsie, New York, says, "Some technical background and experience in specific technical fields is as important as perfect writing skills. A very good understanding of both the source and the target language is necessary, too, so that idioms and ideas are translated without losing their original meanings." You will also need some computer skills and access to a computer, modem, fax, and appropriate dictionaries.

Q **Where would I find translating work?**

Translators get work either directly from client companies or through agencies or bureaus.

Q **Where can I find names of trade publications and trade associations?**

Ulrich International Periodicals Directory (available in print and on the web at http://www.publist.com) publishes lists of periodicals. You can find a database of industry trade and professional associations on the Business Know-How web site (at http://www.businessknowhow.com/associations/search_associations.asp) or in the professional forum on America Online.

The reference librarian at your public library will also be able to point out directories of newsletters or other directories of trade associations or publications that can give you the information you want.

While at the public library, you may want to dig up your field's industry statistics by reading back magazine or newspaper articles. The newspaper and magazine indices (available at most libraries) will help you locate these articles. Many libraries now have the newspaper and magazine indices on computer, making it fast and easy to search out articles, and some now have articles on CD-ROM disks rather than on microfilm. The library staff can help you learn how to use these tools if you are unfamiliar with them.

Q **How do I find my niche?**

The secret is to start with what you know or with what you like. Learn everything you can about whatever that "thing" is. You can learn on the job or in your spare time, but learn all there is to know about the product, the service, the market, and the business end. Then, before you start your business, plan it all out in advance. Realize you will have to work hard and be committed to making the business successful and that in almost all cases it will take anywhere from 1 to 5 years or even more to build a successful business. Take a close look at any overnight success and you will discover that many years of training and hard work went into positioning the business or the individual to be in the right place with the right product or service at the right time.

II.

Pulling
the Pieces
Together

7.

Planning: Your
Personal Road Map
to Success

If you are like many people who start and run very small businesses, writing a business plan sounds like a task you really don't have to do, or at least one you don't have to do this week, or this month . . . after all, you know what you want to do with your business, right? You are going to sell your product or service and make money. The way you are going to do that is all in your head. Why take the time to write it down when there are so many other things to do? The answer has to do with focus, realism, and achieving your dreams.

Q What is a business plan and what is it used for?

A business plan is an operational guide to your business. It should be used to define the scope of your business, the goals you establish for the business, the methods you will use to reach those goals, and the potential profitability of your business.

It can also be used as a yardstick to measure your progress toward your goals, as a reference to keep you from veering away from your goals, and as a communications tool to give bankers and investors the information they need if you are looking for a business loan or private funding.

Q Who needs a business plan?

Anyone who wants to start or run a business successfully needs some type of plan. After all, building a business isn't much different than building anything else: there are a lot of pieces to put together and a lot of details that need to be coordinated. If you were trying to erect a building you would need to follow some kind of plan, whether the building was a toolshed in your backyard or a skyscraper in a big city.

Q How can a business plan help me if I'm already running a successful homebased business?

Once you've got the business up and running, a business plan serves as your road map to success. By periodically comparing where you are with where you want to go in the business, you can keep yourself on course, and if you spot problems developing, make necessary changes in either methods or your ultimate goals before little problems turn into big ones.

Q How elaborate does the plan need to be?

The amount of detail that goes into your business plan should depend on what you stand to gain or lose in your business.

If you are going to turn your favorite hobby into a part-time business and won't have to spend more than a couple hundred dollars to do so, your business plan could be just a page or two of notes. You'd want to sketch out what you will sell, how you will sell it, how you will price it, and what start-up steps (getting permits and licenses, business stationery, insurance, and so on) you will need to take.

Considerably more thought and research should go into your plans, however, if any of the following circumstances apply:

> • you will be spending a significant amount of money to launch the business
> • you will be quitting a full-time job to start a business
> • you will be starting the business because you *need* an income and hope it will replace the job you can't find or don't want to get*

---

*The reason for creating a detailed business plan in this case is because it will help you evaluate business opportunities from a rational point of view rather than an emotional one. When money is tight and jobs are scarce, fear of the future and worry make you want to grasp at anything that sounds as if it could help. Unfortunately, however, many of the opportunities advertised in publications or passed along by well-meaning friends either are not worth pursuing or take considerably more money to pursue profitably than originally thought. Careful planning can help you steer around the pitfalls.

- you will be devoting a significant amount of time to the business, which you might be able to use in more profitable ways
- you will be expanding an already profitable homebased or other small business

Q **What goes into a formal business plan?**

If you are doing a formal plan to present to a bank or to investors, you will want to include all of these elements:

- A *brief title page* or cover sheet containing a date and the business name, address, and phone number.
- A *table of contents* for the plan.
- An *introduction*, often called an executive summary. This is a brief overview of the pages that follow. It describes the purpose of the plan and summarizes the key elements in the body of the plan so investors, bankers, and others who read the plan can tell at a glance what the business does and how it is or will become profitable.
- A *history of the company*, including details of when it was founded, who founded it, where it is located, what kind of business the company is in, and what the objectives of the company are.
- A *description of the products or services* the company sells and why they appeal to customers.
- A *description of the market* for what you sell. This section should show who your customers are, how many of them there are, and why they will want to buy your products or services. It should discuss who your competitors are and how what you sell is superior or different from what the competitors sell. It should also analyze industry or market trends and how they might affect the size of the market.
- A *description of how you will sell the product or service*. You can have the world's biggest market, but if you don't have an affordable way of selling to that market you won't make a cent.
- An *operational plan*. How will you produce or acquire what you sell? How will you protect your ideas or processes? How will you deliver the product or service?

▸ *A description of the management and organization of the business.* Who is involved? What talents do they have? What strengths and weaknesses do they bring to the company? Can they handle finance, sales, marketing, technical aspects? Do you have the right "mix" for success? Resumes should be included for the key executives involved in the business. What business structure (regular corporation, S corporation, partnership, etc.) is being used to run the business? How will investors (if the plan is to attract investors) make their profits?

▸ *The financial plan.* This section should include sales projections (how much do you expect to sell over what time period?), cost estimates, and details about how you expect to finance operations and what assumptions you have made to arrive at sales and other projections. (In other words, what basis do you have for thinking you'll sell 50,000 widgets a month? Is the figure based on results of test marketing? feedback from focus groups? demographic information?) You'll also need past and projected cash flow statements, income statements, and balance sheets. Financial ratios showing assets-to-liabilities, debt-to-equity, and rate of turnover of inventory and receivables may also be required depending on the scope of your business and who will be reviewing your plan.

Q **What should go into a business plan if I'm not looking for a loan or investors?**

If you will be investing a significant amount of money or time in your venture, you should create a business plan that at minimum puts the following information down on paper:

▸ *What business am I in?* The answer to this question should dictate the focus for all your operations. For instance, are you in the business of selling dried floral arrangements or decorative home accessories? Do you have a word processing business, a resume service, or a secretarial service? If you offer several different products or services, how do they fit together? What do they have in common? You should be able to summarize the nature of your business in a sentence or two. If you can't do that, your business isn't likely to have the focus it needs for growth and success.

- *Who are my customers and what do they want to buy?* Even though you aren't looking for a loan or investors, you still need to gather facts about your market so you can make realistic sales forecasts.

- *How will I sell my products or services?* Many homebased entrepreneurs get so engrossed in developing their ideas that they forget to determine how they are going to *sell* their products or services and what it will cost them to make those sales. Typical is the person who pulls thousands of dollars out of savings to buy the equipment necessary to run a business, then discovers that newspaper ads cost more than he thought and that he doesn't have enough money left to run ads long enough to have them do any good. The time to make such discoveries is *before* you sink thousands of dollars into setting up your operation, not afterward.

- *What will all of my expenses be?* One of the biggest mistakes made by people who start homebased and other very small businesses is not calculating all of their costs. Production and advertising expenses are only part of the costs you will incur. Even if you work from home you will still have to buy supplies (for instance, just printing out or photocopying a single page of text can cost you anywhere from about 2 to 5 cents, depending on the cost of ink and the type of paper you are using). You will also pay for business cards, letterhead and envelopes, equipment, repairs, gas (if you travel to your customers), professional fees, taxes, insurance, and so on.

- *At what point will I make a profit?* The point of being in business is to make a profit. You must determine how many sales you need to make at what price to make the kind of profit you want or need from the business. You also need to ascertain how long it might take you to reach that level of profit so you can determine if you have enough money to live on and support the business until it does become profitable.

Q **Why do I need to put the business plan in writing if I don't want a loan?**

Putting your plans on paper will help you succeed by forcing you to give direction to your business activities. Writing down your plans will make you set specific goals and make realistic and informed decisions about what methods you will use to reach your business goals and what your costs and profits are likely to be.

Q **What is a marketing plan?**

A marketing plan shows how your product relates to the market. It considers what you will sell, the number of potential customers, the strategies you will use to reach those customers, the percentage of customers you will be able to sell to, and how you will get them to buy your products or services instead of those of your competitors.

Q **When do I need a marketing plan?**

You should develop a marketing plan when you start a business and revise it periodically to adapt to changing market conditions. By doing this, you can keep your business in tune with the needs of your customers.

Q **What factors should I look at when preparing a marketing plan?**

The specifics will vary somewhat according to the nature of your business, but in general, you should attempt to get answers to as many of the following questions as possible:

- What products and services are you selling (planning to sell)?
- Who (specifically) will buy these products and services?

  - How old are your typical customers?
  - Are they male or female?
  - Do they belong to any specific ethnic group?
  - Do they share any occupational characteristics?
  - What is their income level?
  - What is their education level?
  - What other common characteristics do they share?

- Will businesses buy what you sell?
- Which types of businesses can use your products or services?

  - Businesses that provide services?
  - Businesses in a particular industry?
  - Manufacturers?
  - Government agencies?
  - Educational institutions?

- Nonprofit organizations?
- Warehouse operations?
- Contractors?
- Retailers?
- Others?

- Where are your customers located? (in your city? county? state? nationwide or worldwide?)
- How many potential customers are there in your market area (how big is your market)?
- What are the annual sales in this industry?
- Are sales in this industry (or for this product) on the rise, stable, or on the way down?
- What percentage of the market or how many sales will you have to make to be profitable? (Will you need to sell 50,000 bagels a week? If so, are there enough potential customers who will buy from you to reach that goal?)
- How will your customers use your products or services?
- What do the customers expect or prefer when they buy your type of product or service?
- How are they getting this product or service now?
- How will your product or service benefit them?
- How frequently will they buy what you sell?
- How can you reach them to tell them what you sell?

  - Will you advertise?
  - Where will you advertise? (newspapers, on the Internet, trade publications, Yellow Pages, direct mail, TV, or radio?)
  - Will you have a sales force or use independent sales agents, a sales representative, wholesalers, distributors?
  - How might you generate publicity?
  - How can you get word-of-mouth publicity or advertising?

- How will you get the actual products or services to customers?
- What commissions or fees will you have to pay distributors, wholesalers, sales agents, or others who sell for you?

- Who is your competition? (Consider the answer to this question carefully since there can be some surprising answers. The competition for your web design service, for instance, won't only be the web designer five blocks away from you. It will also be the Internet access companies and the latest books and computer programs written to help businesses create their own web pages.)
- How does your product or service measure up against what the competition offers? Is the quality the same, better, or not as good?
- What are your competitive advantages and disadvantages? Some factors to consider:

accuracy	customized service
attention to detail	durability
availability of the product	ingredients
availability of consumables	method of delivery
availability of replacement parts	name brand
better guarantee	portability
price of consumable supplies	speed of delivery
price of the product or service	styling
recyclable (or made of recyclable materials)	versatility
	weight
safety	years in business
size	

- Who are your key suppliers?
- What will you do if they go out of business, raise their prices, or stop selling what you buy from them?
- What new products or services could you reasonably expect to add on and sell to the same customers in the future?
- Where will your business be located?
- If you need retail space, will you be in an area that your customers frequent? If not, how will you convince them to come to you?
- If you are going to work alone, how will you market the product or service and produce it, too? How will you split up your time effectively?
- How could you cope if a strong competitor entered your market?

- Can you meet potential demand for the product or service?
- What problems or obstacles could you run into?

Q **How do I make realistic sales forecasts?**

You start out by getting industry statistics if possible. Trade associations, trade magazines, and newspapers all may have information on the total volume of sales in an industry and how this year's sales compare with last year's sales.

You may be able to get some information about the size and location of your market through the same sources. Demographic information available from the U.S. Department of Labor, the Bureau of Census, the U.S. Department of Commerce, and local or regional economic development agencies can also be extremely valuable.

Other ways you can get the facts you need to predict sales include:

- Using industry averagers to calculate response rates to different advertising and sales methods
- Reading trade magazines
- Asking employees or former employees of competitors
- Asking competitors' customers about typical order sizes
- Asking distributors, wholesalers, or sales representatives or agents what their experience has been with similar products or services
- Getting circulation figures (or audience size) for the media you plan to use for advertising
- Calling other advertisers who use or have used that media in the past and asking what their response rates have been
- Surveying your potential customers (in person, by mail, or on the phone) to find out what they buy, how much of it they buy, what they like or don't like about what they buy now, and what it will take to get them to switch to your product(s) or services

Q **How do I estimate advertising and publicity costs?**

To estimate advertising costs, you will need to get rate cards and quotes from the various media you want to use. You will need to determine how frequently you can afford to advertise, what size ad you want (or how much airtime if you will be advertising in radio or TV), and how frequently you will need to advertise. Find out what

Table 7.1: Income Statement

Date: _____

	Jan	Feb	Mar	Apr	May	June	July	Aug	Sept	Oct	Nov	Dec	Total
REVENUE													
Gross sales													
returns, or discounts													
NET SALES													
(gross sales minus returns)													
COST OF GOODS SOLD													
Materials													
Labor													
Overhead													
GROSS PROFIT													
(net sales minus cost of sales)													
OPERATING EXPENSES													
Selling expenses													
Advertising													
Commissions													

Date: _____

	Jan	Feb	Mar	Apr	May	June	July	Aug	Sept	Oct	Nov	Dec	Total
ADMINISTRATIVE EXPENSES													
Salaries													
Payroll taxes													
Insurance													
Rent													
Utilities													
Telephone													
Professional svcs.													
Real estate taxes													
Repairs													
Maintenance													
Postage													
Supplies													
Licenses													
Interest													
TOTAL EXPENSES													
NET OPERATING PROFIT (gross income minus expenses)													
ESTIMATED INCOME TAX													
ESTIMATED AFTER-TAX PROFIT													

it will cost to produce the ad. (Will you pay someone to do the graphics for you? Will a small newspaper or weekly shopper do the ad for you? Will an ad agency work for you only on the commission it gets for placing an ad, or will it also charge a fee? Will you have to pay photographers or anyone else?) If you are going to use direct mail for advertising, you will also need to determine printing and postage costs.

The cost of publicity will depend on what lengths you plan to go to publicize your business. If you are only going to send out a couple of press releases and make a few phone calls the costs will be negligible. If you are going to send out press kits and photos to a multitude of editors and make a lot of follow-up calls, calculate the costs of preparing and printing the press kits, postage costs, and the phone call charges.

Q **What are income statements?**

An income statement is sometimes called a profit and loss statement or an operating statement. It shows your total sales minus your cost of goods sold and your operating expenses over some specific time frame, usually a year or a period of years. (See Table 7.1.)

Q **What are cash flow projections?**

Cash flow projections are predictions about where the cash will come from and how it will be spent in a given time period or business cycle. It differs from an income statement in that it shows the movement of cash through a company instead of focusing on sales or profits. (See Table 7.2.)

Q **What is a balance sheet?**

A balance sheet is a summary showing what you own, what you owe, and what your net worth is. (See Table 7.3.)

Q **Where can I get an example of a finished business plan?**

You can find instructions for writing a business plan, including a generic sample, on the Small Business Administration web site at http://www.sba.gov/starting/indexbusplans.html. Palo Alto Software, which publishes BusinessPlanPro software, has a number of business planning tools including sample business plans for specific types of businesses, available on their web site at http://www.bplans.com.

Table 7.2: Cash Flow Statement/Projection

Projected Annual Cash Flow

First Year

CASH ON HAND
  (beginning cash balance)   _____

CASH RECEIPTS
  Cash sales   _____
  Receivables collected   _____
  Earned interest   _____
  Loan proceeds   _____
  Investor equity

TOTAL CASH RECEIPTS

TOTAL CASH
  (cash on hand plus
    total receipts)   _____

CASH PAID OUT
  Purchases   _____
  Operating expenses   _____
  Administrative expenses   _____
  Loan principal payments   _____
  Capital purchases   _____
  Income taxes paid   _____
  Other   _____

TOTAL CASH PAID OUT   _____
ENDING CASH BALANCE   _____

Table 7.3: Balance Sheet

Assets

CURRENT ASSETS
   Cash _____
   Accounts receivable _____
   Inventory _____
   Other _____
                    TOTAL CURRENT ASSETS _____

FIXED ASSETS
   Equipment, machinery _____
   Land, buildings _____
   Other fixed assets _____
   Less depreciation _____
                    TOTAL VALUE FIXED ASSETS _____

OTHER ASSETS _____
                    TOTAL ASSETS _____

Liabilities and Equity

CURRENT LIABILITIES
   Accounts payable _____
   Bank loans and other
      short-term loans _____
   Taxes payable _____
                    TOTAL CURRENT LIABILITIES _____
                    LONG-TERM DEBTS _____
                    OWNER'S EQUITY _____
        TOTAL LIABILITIES PLUS OWNER'S EQUITY
             (should equal total assets) _____

Q **Are the computer templates for business plans good enough to use if I'm looking for funding or investors?**

They are a starting point. You will need to add detail and knowledge about your business and should have your accountant look over your plan—and poke holes in it so you can rework it—before you present the plan to bankers and investors.

Q **Are there other sources of help for writing a business plan?**

Small Business Development Centers (see page 455), Service Corps of Retired Executives (SCORE) offices (see page 456), the Small Business Administration Office (see page 455 and local government offices for small businesses often offer free or low-cost help for entrepreneurs trying to write business plans. They will *not* write the plan for you or gather the information you need to put into the plan (and you shouldn't expect them to!), but provided they have the staff, they will help you figure out how to put it all together.

8.

Pricing What You Sell

Major corporations spend millions of dollars each year to determine what to charge for their goods and services. Typically, they'll do extensive market research, plug collected data into spreadsheets only an M.B.A. could love, and then test-market the product at different prices in different geographic locations to determine what selling price will produce the most profits.

Small businesses don't have the time, money, or patience to conduct such extensive studies. So how do successful small businesses determine what to charge? More important, how can *you* come up with the right price for what you sell? Here is a collection of questions and answers to help you set prices that are both competitive and profitable.

Q **What's so difficult about setting prices? Can't I just charge more than it costs me to buy or make what I sell, or a little less than what everyone else charges?**

It doesn't take much seat-of-the-pants logic to realize the best selling price for a product or service should be a price that falls above costs and at or slightly below competitors' prices. But here's the rub: business owners who try to slide by on this logic often overlook some important variables. Among them:

- The amount it costs you to buy or make a product or service is often only a small part of what it costs to sell that product or service. If your prices don't allow for all the other costs of doing business, you could lose money on every sale.
- Neither production costs nor competitors' prices predict whether anyone will buy the product or service from you.
- Buying decisions are rarely made on the basis of logic alone. In fact, customers sometimes equate quality with price. If your prices are too low, they may suspect your goods or services are inferior in quality and not buy.
- Internet-based businesses have been forgoing profits in the name of building a large following. If you sell products or services that compete with such companies, you are going to have to develop a business model and pricing strategy that allows you to be competitive or that focuses on a niche market the money-burners aren't addressing.

Q **What should be considered in pricing a product or service?**

No matter what you sell, your pricing strategy should be based on these fundamental principles:

- In addition to what it costs to make or buy what you sell, your minimum price must take into consideration marketing expenses, operating expenses, labor costs, the amount of profit you want to make, and income and self-employment taxes.
- The price you can get for any product or service depends on the amount of money customers are willing to pay or expect to pay.
- There must be a large enough market to allow you to sell profitably over a long period of time. If there isn't a market for your product or service, it won't sell at any price.

Q **Other than a few supplies, what expenses do small service businesses have?**

Service businesses normally don't have to spend large sums to purchase production materials or inventory, but they can have fairly significant daily operating expenses. Even a one-person service business is likely to have many of the following expenses:

- purchase price and maintenance cost of a computer, photocopier, printers, cameras, tools, answering machine, fax, or other equipment
- telephone line and usage charges
- upgrades to equipment and additional computer software needed to meet customer requirements
- business stationery (business cards, letterhead, envelopes)
- supplies such as notepads, computer diskettes, file folders, printer ribbons, toner cartridges, mailing labels, photocopy supplies, film, art supplies, etc.
- file cabinets, desks, chairs, bookcases, and other office furniture
- cost of trade magazine subscriptions
- cost of membership in professional associations
- client entertainment costs
- sales and marketing literature preparation and printing
- postage and/or express mail and delivery services
- appropriate business insurance (fire & theft, personal liability, errors & omissions and, if you have employees, state compensation insurance)
- your salary (as the owner)
- cost of benefits you'd get as an employee (health and disability insurance, pension plan, etc.)
- federal, state, and city income taxes
- self-employment taxes
- cost of legal, accounting, and other professional services
- nonbillable time

If you have or take on employees, in addition to the cost of their salaries and any benefits you offer, you will have to allow for workers' compensation, employers' share of Social Security benefits, extra office overhead expenses, and benefits.

Q **What is nonbillable time?**

Nonbillable time is the time you spend doing work you can't charge your customers for. Typically such work includes writing proposals; making business contacts; answering customer questions; doing your own filing, typing, and book-keeping; and learning to use new computer programs.

Q **Why is nonbillable time considered an expense?**

In a service business, earnings are tied to the number of hours devoted to income-producing work. In some small service businesses one-third or more of the total working hours each week may be spent doing work that can't be billed to any client. In fact, it's not unusual for the owner of a one-person business to work from early in the morning until late at night without directly producing a cent of income.

Under such circumstances, time is a commodity with a significant value. For instance, assume you work a total of 40 hours a week in your service business and on average you make about $25 an hour on time spent on client work. If you spend 10 hours a week doing nonbillable jobs, you have only 30 hours a week left for paid client work. Thus you are losing $250 a week in sales (the 10 nonbillable hours times $25 an hour). If you normally charge $50 an hour for your time, those 10 hours of nonbillable time will cost you a whopping $500 each week.

Q **How can I factor the cost of nonbillable time into my fees?**

Calculate what your expenses will be for a month. This figure should include a salary for yourself, plus all other expenses including loan payments, if any, allowances for equipment upgrades and repairs, and so on (see list on page 122). Add in an amount for profit. (Your own salary is not profit. Profit is what the business makes over and above your salary and all other expenses.)

Multiply this figure by 12 to determine what the gross yearly income of the business should be. Then divide the gross yearly income by 48 to determine the amount of money the business will need to make per week. (The reason for using 48 instead of 52 is to allow 4 weeks for vacation time, holidays, and sick days.)

Once you determine the amount of money you need to earn per week, divide that amount by your billable hours. If you plan to work 40 hours a week but will spend 10 of them on your own accounting chores or other nonbillable work, divide the weekly gross income needs by 30 to get the hourly fee you should charge.

For example, if you determine you need to bring in $5,000 per month to cover your salary and other business expenses, here's how you would calculate hourly fees:

$5,000 (monthly income) × 12 (months) = $60,000 (gross yearly income)
$60,000 (gross yearly income) ÷ 48 (weeks) = $1,250 (per week)
$1,250 (per week) ÷ 30 (hours) = $41.66 (per hour)

Q **What are typical overhead costs for small offices?**

Overhead is typically 1.5 to 2 times annual salary. If a worker works 1,864 hours during the year, at an average efficiency of 75 percent, the worker's billable hours for the year are 1,398 (30 hours a week). If you are paying the worker $25,000 a year, and your overhead costs are twice salary, the total cost for that worker is $75,000 a year. That makes your cost per billable hour $53.65 for that employee. You have to mark up that hourly cost a sufficient amount to make a profit.

Q **What about independent sales representatives, distributors, agents, and others who work on commission only? How do they make sure they'll make enough to cover expenses and make a profit?**

If your business will be some type of agency, brokerage, or distributorship, the commission you can charge will have to conform closely to industry standards. The way to make this type of business profitable is to know your industry inside and out, maintain close contacts with buyers or purchasing agents, and have top-notch sales skills. Whether you plan to be a print broker, distributor for industrial filters, or a literary agent, you need a good handle on:

▶ which companies are buying what type of products
▶ how much they are paying for them
▶ who makes the buying decisions
▶ how many sales you can realistically expect to make
▶ how long it will take you to make the sale
▶ what it will cost you to make the sale
▶ how long it will be from the time the sale is made until the time you collect your fee
▶ what the likelihood of repeat sales is

Since the amount of money you make will be limited to the commissions you make on each sale, add your estimated expenses and the after-expense income you want to achieve, then choose clients whose goods or services will sell at high enough prices and/or in sufficient quantity to produce the income you want to achieve.

Q How can I make accurate sales or cost estimates if I've never run my own business or been involved in marketing products or services?

Here are several ways to get the information you need to predict sales and costs:

▶ Talk to other business owners. Find out what they charge, and ask how much they spend per year on marketing, advertising, office overhead, etc. At the end of this chapter you will find a list of typical fees charged by different types of businesses. The fees will offer you some guidance, but you should try to get information about prices in your part of the country as well.

▶ Contact industry or trade associations and ask if the association has literature that will help you determine what business expenses you may incur and what the going rates are for the general type of product or service you plan to sell.

▶ If you own a modem, check out online forums (special interest groups) such as those that are part of Business KnowHow or the professional forums area on America Online. Look for active newsgroups for your industry and look at message boards on other services such as Yahoo, Lycos, Talk City, or other online business centers. Owners of small and homebased businesses use these areas to exchange information and network with one another. You'll find many of these people will readily share information about pricing and business expenses.

▶ Read employment ads and call several employment agencies to determine what hourly salary you might expect providing your service as an employee in someone else's business. Check salary surveys available on the Internet as well. Locations that have salary surveys include:

- **The Riley Guide** (links to state and local job and salary information) http://www.rileyguide.com
- **Jobstar** http://jobsmart.org/tools/salary/sal-prof.htm
- **Information Week** (annual information technology salary survey) http://www.informationweek.com/7

▶ Remember to add in the cost of employee benefits, office overhead, and an allowance for a profit for the company.

- Gauge your fees according to what other service providers charge you. For instance, if local services in your area charge an average of $70 an hour for labor (car repair, computer repair, etc.) consider setting your prices in the same range.

- If possible, run the business part-time on a small scale, keeping accurate records of all expenses and income. Also keep track of how much time it takes you to complete work or make sales and how long it takes you to collect from your customers. Review this information once a quarter and make any necessary adjustments in your fees.

- If you sell a product, comparison shop. Check prices of similar products in retail stores, discount stores, shopping clubs, warehouses, and mail order catalogs.

- Test market: your product or service. Advertise it in one publication or do a small mailing to test your response rate.

Q **Is it better to charge for a service by the hour or the job?**

There is no "better way" to charge. In fact, there will be some instances when you charge by the hour, others where you charge by the job, and perhaps still other times where you work on a retainer basis, or get a "per head" fee (for teaching seminars, for instance), a contingency fee, commission (on sales or placement), or royalties.

- *Charge by the hour* if the job is one where the customer is likely to make changes in the job specifications while you are working on the project. Here's the type of situation you need to be wary of: A copywriter, after spending half a day at a client's office getting all the information he needed to write the copy for a brochure and sales letter for one of the company's new products, spent the better part of a second day writing the material. Then, before he had a chance to deliver the assignment, he got a call from the company's marketing manager who informed him the company had decided the mailing should include a limited-time offer, for a large discount on the product. The entire mailing had to be redesigned and rewritten. Had the writer quoted a flat rate on that job he would have lost at least one full day's earnings.

- *Charge by the job* if the client won't agree to an hourly rate. Or, if you know how long it will take you to do a certain type of job (such as write a publicity release), it is often more profitable to charge by the job. For instance, if the going rate for writing a short publicity release is $200, and you can write the release in an hour, it's obviously better to state a flat fee of $200 for writing the release than it would be to charge $200 an hour for your work.

TIP On corporate or other projects where many changes are likely, due to either a difficult client or the need for approvals from multiple department heads in a company, at each phase of a project have someone at the company "sign off" on the work (sign a piece of paper approving the work and authorizing the next step or acceptance). This will allow you to bill for changes made at a later stage that should have been made in early stages of the project (and perhaps help keep you from being held responsible for errors). Be sure to plan your initial estimates to allow for frequent changes, or set a cap on the number of customer changes or the number of hours you'll put into the project for the stated fee. Take the time to educate your client in advance about the amount of time and cost that could be involved if the client changes their requirements partway into the project.

Q **What problems are associated with charging by the job?**

The main problem with a per-job or per-page rate is that a job can look deceptively easy (a directory with relatively few words per page, for instance) but can turn out to be extremely time-consuming, particularly if the client is difficult to work with. The way to solve the problem is to spell out very clearly (in writing) what you will do for the project rate and what services or changes in the project will carry an additional fee.

Q **How do you know how long it will take to do a job?**

You learn that from experience. If you don't have experience, you may be able to get the information one of these ways:

- *Ask other people in the same line of work.* Be sure to give enough detail about the job so people can give accurate advice. Don't just say you have a directory to typeset for a university, for instance; give details, such as "There are ten entries on a page, the name is in bold type, with all related information for the entry indented. The number of lines varies from three to five."
- *Do one small part of the job and time yourself.* Then estimate the total job time.
- *Consider not taking the job* or doing the job for free if you are just starting out in a business and have little experience in the industry. In other words, don't bill customers for the time it takes you to learn your trade.

Q **What about retainer agreements? How do they work?**

A retainer can be a lump sum used as a type of secured credit you draw against as you do work for the client, or it can be a regular monthly fee paid to you to guarantee the availability of your services when the client needs them. Generally the amount of money paid on retainer is based on your normal hourly rate.

Q **How do contingency fees work?**

When you work on a contingency arrangement, you get paid only if the outcome of your endeavors is successful. The actual payment is usually a percentage, such as the percentage of a settlement an attorney wins for his or her client, but it can be a flat fee, too.

Q **How high can I set my fees without pricing myself right out of business?**

To answer that question, you'll have to find out what the going rates are for the type of service you perform. In addition to the nature of the service, your experience, geographic location, competitors, and the clients you target all will have an effect on the maximum rate you can charge without losing worthwhile customers.

Q **How do I find out what the going rates are?**

The best advice on that score comes from Roy Bernstein, president of Demand Research Corporation, a Chicago-based company that conducts market research studies for major corporations. Advises Bernstein: "Instead of diddling around with formal market research, the small business owner should get out in the marketplace and go nose to nose with a few air-breathing clients." In other words, get out and talk to the people you want as customers. Find out what they want to buy, how much they are willing to pay for it, and where they are buying similar services now.

Q **What if no one is selling a product or service like mine?**

Bernstein's advice for introducing new concepts is to "be innovative and non-traditional." Instead of trying to explain how a new product or service will benefit your prospects, show them. That's what Lewis Lehr, chairman of 3M, did when Post-it Notes were developed. To test the acceptability of the notes in real-life corporate settings, Lehr had his secretary send samples of the product to the secretaries of a few dozen CEOs at other Fortune 500 companies. As a result of that test, you now pay premium prices for tiny squares of notepaper.

Q **How do I get up the nerve to ask for high fees?**

Knowing what you ought to charge is one thing; actually asking for your fee and holding out for it is quite another. Here are a few tricks you can use to bolster your self-confidence and determination.

- Pretend you are selling the product or service for someone other than yourself. You are less likely to take it personally if a client rejects you because of high fees (or any other reason).
- Calculate how much it costs you and your family to live for a year. Add in an amount to allow for your business expenses. Now divide that figure by 1,920 (average number of working hours in a year). This will be the bare minimum you have to charge just to keep your head above water.
- Make a list of your personal goals (for example, the new house, expensive sports car, vacation condo, etc.). Imagine yourself enjoying them, then put a dollar amount next to each goal, and set a reasonable date for reaching the goals. Each time you are asked to quote a fee, think of your quote as moving you one step closer to your goals.
- Consider how much money the client saves by buying your services instead of hiring a staff member to do the work. By hiring you on an as-needed basis, the client avoids overstaffing, reduces the need for addi-

129

tional office equipment and space, and saves on expenses such as unemployment insurance, compensation, Social Security, health care plans, and other benefits.

Q Should I ever donate my services or charge very low fees to get my foot in the door?

If you are just starting a new business and have no experience in the field, donating your services or charging low fees can be beneficial. It can help you gain the experience you need and can be a good way to build a portfolio and references to attract higher paying clients.

Additionally, if you are new in a community or want to build goodwill for your business, it may be beneficial to donate products or services to key community organizations or projects. Before accepting charity work, however, consider carefully whether it is something you really want to do, whether you will benefit from the work, and whether you will actually have the time or financial capacity to see the project through to its conclusion. If you already have all the work you can do or have no particular interest in the charity, learn to say no. Otherwise you will find yourself spending a great deal of time doing work that doesn't benefit you in any way.

Q Should I charge friends and family?

That's always a touchy question. When you are just starting out, you may want to do work for friends and family for free to build up credentials, but once you have been in business long enough to have steady customers, you may not have time to do work for free.

If you can't afford the time, you should make clear to friends and family that you are in business and must make money to be profitable. If they don't understand, consider it their problem and not yours. Don't get involved in lengthy disputes. Just say you'd like to help them out but have commitments to paying customers that prevent you from doing so.

Q Should I charge all customers the same fee?

In fairness you should charge everyone the same rate. In reality, however, many small service businesses alter their fees somewhat according to who the customer is, how much the customer can afford to spend, and how badly they want the customer's future business.

> **TIP**
>
> If you charge different clients different fees for similar work, get them to agree in writing not to disclose your fees to other individuals or companies. You might also tell a client that the low fee you are charging is a special rate because you value their business, enjoy working with their staff, etc.

Q **Should I charge for travel time?**

Some businesses charge for travel time, and others don't. Those that do charge reason that the time they spend traveling is time they can't spend on other income-producing activities. You will need to decide what's right for you based on what others in your field do, how badly you want any individual customer, and how much time you will spend traveling for that customer. If you do opt to bill for travel time, be sure your customers are aware of that fact before you start work on any project for them. A written explanation of all your fees presented to the client before you start a project will go a long way toward avoiding billing misunderstandings after you've completed the work.

Q **How much should I charge for travel time?**

Travel time is usually billed at either the full hourly rate or one-half the hourly rate.

Q **Should I undercut the competition?**

If you have many competitors and you are not known, you may have to charge a little less than your competitors to make a name for yourself. Some people who run service businesses say being faster and better is an attractive benefit to their prospects. Others say underpricing can backfire. One disc jockey, for instance, lost a sale when he quoted a price $600 lower than one of his competitors. The client felt the lower price reflected a lower level of professionalism. Others have found that increasing their prices considerably increased their number of clients.

TIP   One strategy that works well for many one- or two-person businesses is to start at a price a little below what the competition charges (if that price is profitable) and then gradually raise prices, eliminating marginally profitable customers as the business grows.

Q   **What costs are associated with selling products?**

Following is a list of some of the expenses you may expect when you sell products. The list is not all-inclusive, since no two businesses are likely to incur all the same costs. It will, however, help you determine what costs should be factored into your selling price.

- wholesale price of products you will resell
- price you pay for materials and supplies used to manufacture the product
- outside manufacturing costs you may incur (for instance, to have dies or molds made or have a product produced to your specifications)
- machinery and tools needed to produce the product
- preparation and production of instruction manuals (writing, design, typesetting, printing, and binding costs)
- preparation and production of other items shipped with the product
- packaging (box, Styrofoam filler, shrink wrapping)
- package design cost
- licensing fees or royalties
- cost of warranty cards and registration cards (including business reply postage) included with the product
- cost of sales brochures, press kits, and other marketing materials
- advertising, copywriting, printing, duplication, or other services you may need to purchase
- labor costs (*your own* plus that of any employees)
- employee benefits, such as vacation time, sick leave, pension plans, insurance (again, don't forget to calculate in an amount for benefits for yourself)
- employer share of FICA (and your own self-employment tax if the business is not incorporated)
- state unemployment and compensation insurance costs for employees

- trade show expenses
- sales literature preparation and printing
- web site development and maintenance
- publicity expense
- mailing costs
- mailing list rental costs
- office overhead (rent, maintenance, phones, and other utilities, equipment, equipment repairs/service contracts, office supplies, etc.)
- business insurance and product liability insurance
- legal and accounting fees

Q **How do I determine the best selling price for products?**

Here are several methods to help you decide what to charge for your products.

*Base the selling price on cost per unit:**

1. Estimate how many sales of the individual product (number of units) you will make within 3 to 6 months or some other given time frame.
2. Add up all the business costs you will incur to produce and sell the product and run the business during that time frame.
3. Divide the total expected costs by the expected number of sales. This will tell you what your costs are per sale (unit cost).
4. Determine the profit you want to make on each sale (per unit) and add the profit (plus an allowance for income and self-employment taxes) to the unit cost. This will give you the minimum price you will need to get for each product to cover your costs and provide a profit. If you sell directly to your customers this would also be the minimum selling price.
5. Determine what discounts you will need to offer distributors or others and any commissions you will need to pay to independent sales representatives. (Distributor discounts are figured as a percentage of a

---

*The cost per unit method works well for many small software companies, such as Survivor Software, a company that sells Macintosh accounting software. Mike Farmer, Survivor Software's CEO, says, "As a rough estimate you can figure the final product will have to have a retail price of twice your per-unit cost."

product's retail list price. Thus if the list price of a widget is $2, and the distributors in your industry expected a 50 percent discount off the list price, the actual amount of the discount would be 50 percent of $2, or $1. Sales representatives' commissions are generally calculated on the selling price, not the retail list price.)

6. Add the discount and/or commission amount to the total cost per unit to arrive at a retail price.

7. Compare the price you determine with the list prices of similar products or products aimed at a similar market. If your price seems much higher, go back and look for ways to reduce your costs.

Decide on a retail price and work backward from the expected retail price, subtracting distributor or other discounts, sales commissions, and your profit. This will give you a cost per unit. If you can't manufacture the product at this cost per unit, change the retail price and work out the figures again.

Calculate your break-even point. You don't need to be a mathematician to calculate break-even points. The break-even point is simply the number of sales you need to make at a given price to cover your costs. To determine break-even points, you divide your total costs by the selling price of the item. Your answer represents the number of products you have to sell at the stated price to pay back your costs (break even). If the number of sales you will need is larger than what you might realistically expect to achieve in a reasonable time, look for ways to lower your costs, or consider raising your price per unit.

If you can't easily produce your product in volume, if there is only a very limited market for what you sell, or if you have only a shoestring budget and can market to only a small fraction of your potential market, you will want to shoot for higher selling prices to achieve a lower break-even point.

For example, suppose you make decorative wooden wall plaques and sell them once a month at craft shows. This is a sideline business, and you can make only about thirty plaques a month at a total cost to you of $360. To calculate your break-even point (the number of plaques you would have to sell just to pay your costs), you would take one or more possible selling prices and divide the selling price into the total cost figure. Your results might look like this:

Break-Even Point Calculation

Your Total Cost	Selling Price	Number of Sales to Break Even
$360	$12	30
$360	$15	25
$360	$18	20
$360	$20	18
$360	$24	15
$360	$30	12

Looking at the figures, you would immediately see that at $12 per plaque you would have to sell every single one just to pay back your costs, and that to make a decent profit, you would have to price the plaques at the upper dollar amounts. If you frequent craft shows (and you should if you expect to sell at them), you will have some idea about whether or not items similar to yours sell in the higher price ranges. If they typically don't sell for much more than $15, you will have to decide whether it's worth your while to make and sell the plaques.

Q **How do I find out what my competitors are charging?**

If you aren't sure what your competitors are charging, either call and ask for prices and product literature; go to retail stores or other sales outlets and price similar products; look through catalogs, magazines, and newspaper ads (don't forget the classified section); or call or contact potential customers and do a survey to find out where they now buy what you plan to sell and how much they pay for it. See if your competitor has a web site, too. If they do, look through the site to see if they have a price list posted. Sign up for any free newsletters. They may send out announcements about pricing changes.

Q **What should I do if my price estimates indicate that I will need to charge more than my competitors?**

Basically you have several options:

- *Look for ways to cut costs*. Consider using less expensive materials, different manufacturing methods, cheaper labor, cutting overhead expenses, or automating jobs to eliminate them.

- *Target the cream of the crop (skimming method)*. Look for ways you can add value to your product or imply added value (better grade of materials used in manufacture, more capabilities than competitor's products, etc.), and target your product at the top end of the market. You will need to know the market for your product well enough to make a good estimate about how many sales you could make at premium prices. Multiply the selling price by the expected number of sales, and compare to the cost of sales.

- *Consider different distribution methods*. Calculate the cost and possible effects of different distribution methods. Would the additional volume a distributor could achieve offset the discounts or the commissions you'd have to give and allow you to sell the product at a lower price? Might independent sales representatives have more industry contacts and thus be able to sell your product or service to more customers who are willing to pay a premium price for what you sell? Could you reduce costs and retail price by selling the product through direct mailings?

- *Don't manufacture or sell the product*. While a particular product may catch your fancy, it's pointless to make or sell a product if your figures suggest you can't manufacture or sell it at a competitive price or in sufficient quantity to be profitable.

Q **What's the going rate?**

Following is a list of typical fees charged for a variety of jobs. The figures are based on the stated fees from businesses in various parts of the country and are only presented as a rough guide. In general, even if you quote a flat fee for a job, the fee should be based on what your hourly rate is and should take into consideration overhead costs, benefits, and profit.

Most of the price figures are given in ranges. If you live in an area where salaries and cost of living are relatively low, where there is a lot of competition for your product or service, and where people can't afford to pay small businesses high fees, the fees you can charge are likely to fall in the low end of the range. The same is true if you have limited experience in a field. Some people find it worth their while to charge slightly less than the going rates if they find a client who will give them work on a fairly regular basis and who pays their bills quickly.

If you are highly experienced and work for companies located in a major metropolitan area with a relatively high cost of living, you should be able to command fees in the higher ranges. In fact, the way pricing works in the "real world" is that many businesses start out working at low fees for small businesses, and as their skill in business and their reputation grows, they work their way up the ladder both in terms of the size of companies for which they do work and the fees they charge for that work.

GOING RATES

Accountants (CPA): $75 to $125 an hour and up. An accounting firm will generally bill for its staff at different rates depending on their experience.

Advertising/marketing copywriting: $35 to $75 per hour and up, with a markup of 17.65 percent on other services purchased for the client.

Advertising sales commission, newspaper: 15 to 20 percent of the dollar amount of the ad.

Artist's representatives or agents: 25 percent commission.

Authors' agents: 15 percent commission.

Attorney fees: $75 to $300 an hour plus expenses, depending on experience, reputation, and specialty.

Bookkeeping, and payroll services: $20 to $60 an hour. At the low end of the range would be fees charged by bookkeepers to accountants. At the top end would be fees accountants bill their clients.

Brochure writing: $40 to $60 an hour. Generally, the bigger the company, the bigger the fee.

Catalog copywriting: $15 to $25 per item in the catalog and up, or $25 to $50 per hour for writing only. If desktop publishing or web page design is needed those charges would be in addition to the writing fees.

Commercial art design fees: $30 to $100 per hour or more. The more experience and skill, the higher the fee.

Computer consulting without programming: $30 to $75 per hour for setting up small microcomputer systems with off-the-shelf software, setting up batch files, backing up, and troubleshooting. In some parts of the country, however, consultants get only $15 to $25 per hour for such tasks.

Computer programming, systems analysis: $40 to $125 an hour.

Computer training: $25 to $75 per hour for private tutoring, or for training services supplied to small businesses; $55 to $90 per head for corporate group training classes with all course handouts included. (Note: due to busy staff schedules some personnel directors are choosing computer-based training programs.)

Consulting, marketing/advertising: up to $100 per hour or higher for experienced consultants in major metropolitan areas, but sometimes done free as a special offer to bring in new clients.

Data entry: by individuals working at home, $8 to $15 an hour; billing rate for data entry from a secretarial service can be up to $30.

Desktop publishing production: $25 to $40 per hour for typesetting only; $40 to $75 an hour for designing page layouts.

Desktop publishing consulting: $350 to $1,000 per day, depending on qualifications and experience.

Direct mail package writing: $35 to $100 per hour; $2,000 and up for a 4-page letter, brochure, reply card.

Graphic design: $50 to $125 per hour.

Letters: to type a generic letter and print multiple copies, no merge, cost of typing the letter plus $.50 to $1 per page depending on the type of paper the letter is printed on and who supplies it.

Letters: to type a generic letter and customize by merging with customer addresses, $.50 and up per letter depending on paper plus setup charges and data entry for addresses. Collating, stapling, stuffing letters in envelopes, printing for envelopes or labels would all be extra. A setup fee is sometimes charged for small jobs.

Mailing list data entry: $.25 per record for records that are 3 to 4 lines in length.

Mail order products: at least 4 times your costs for any item. Some people set $19.99 to $29.99 as a minimum price they find profitable to sell products via mail.

Manufacturer's representative: 5 to 25 percent commission, or more depending on industry and the point in the distribution chain. Sales reps who are also dealers selling to the end-user, and reps who assume all marketing costs, might get considerably more than 25 percent, while someone who reps the product to distributors might only get as little as 2 to 3 percent commission, depending on the industry practices.

Medical claims processing: 5 to 13 percent of collections. In states that prohibit a percent of collections fee, a flat fee is charged.

Newsletters: for a single newsletter written and sold to multiple companies (such as health and wellness newsletters distributed by chiropractors), $800 to $1,000 per thousand, imprinted with logo of the company ordering the newsletter.

Newsletter writing for large corporations (such as an internal or external company newsletter): up to $1,000 or more for a four-page newsletter, research material provided. The exact fee will depend on the company, the nature of the publication, the geographic location, and the writer's negotiating skills.

Newsletter production: *see* desktop publishing prices.

Product fact sheets, writing: $120 to $300 and up.

Photography, brochures, catalogs: $150 to $500 per shot.

Photography, presentation slides: 3.5 to 5 times production costs.

Public relations: $35 to $60 per hour; press releases $150 and up per page.

Research for corporate newsletters: $25 to $40 an hour.

Resumes, writing: $35 to $75 per page.

Resumes, typesetting: $30 to $45 per page.

Resume, storage: $5 per resume.

Resumes, extra printouts: $1 per page or $20 per 25 pages. Blank sheets $.10 a page; blank envelopes $.25 each.

Retainer agreements: Retainer agreements are usually figured by multiplying the normal hourly billing rate times the number of hours the client company wants set aside for its work. Some retainers paid in the Northeast:

▸ $1,700 per month plus expenses for 20 hours of work as a retainer to handle advertising for a company with $20 million in annual sales. Any hours over 20 in any given month are billed at an additional fee whether all hours have been used in preceding months or not.
▸ $1,000 per month plus expenses for computer consulting and troubleshooting for a graphic arts firm with a network of three computers, a laser printer, and an imagesetter.

▶ Retainer for legal research: full expected cost of the research (held in escrow, with charges deducted from escrow account as incurred).

Sales letters, writing: $100 to $500 per page, with highest figures going to seasoned professionals in direct mail.

Tax preparation: tax preparers who are not CPAs often charge by the form, charging about $25 to fill out Form 1040, using the client's figures, and $5 to $15 for each additional form. Bookkeeping or other services and electronic filing are extra. Tax preparation at accounting firms is billed by the hourly billing rate of the person assigned to do the return.

Training seminars: $50 to $90 "per head" or a flat fee, which can run from $500 to $2,000 or more a day, depending on the instructor's reputation. Minimum fee of $300 for short sessions is not unusual.

Trademark search: by an attorney, with an opinion about the availability of the trademark, $200 to $500, with higher fees for searches for unregistered marks. (Preparation of trademark application is extra.)

Translation: agencies charge their customers approximately $.085 to $.13 per word, depending on the client, the language being translated from and to, and the technical difficulty of the work.

Typesetting: $25 to $50 an hour; $30 to $45 per page; one-page flier is $30 to $45; standard letterhead (typeface and logo chosen from sample book) is $15.

Writing, books: depending on the publisher, the experience of the writer, the number of previously published works, etc., $2,500 to $15,000 and up, as an advance against royalties.

Writing, articles: $.02 per word to $1 per word and up. Most established writers try to get a minimum of $.50 to $.60 a word, unless the article can be written very quickly. Pay of $35 a word for a 1,000-word article can work out to over $100 an hour if it only takes three hours to write and research the piece.

Writing, technical: $35 to $60 per hour and up.*

TIP

When estimating the time to write a manual or other kind of technical book for a corporation, multiply the time you think it ought to take by 150 percent. Then multiply that figure by your hourly rate. This allows for jobs that take much longer than expected.

*For additional information on writers' fees, see *Writer's Market,* by Writer's Digest Books. This reference is published annually and should be available in your public library.

9.

Money: What You'll Need and Where to Get It

What does it take to turn your business plans and ideas into a viable business? The answer, in most cases, is money. The amount of money and the time at which that money needs to be invested will vary from one small business to another.

For instance, some businesses start out with only a small investment on the part of the owner and are either kept small or are expanded slowly using the profits of the business to finance growth. Other businesses start out small and then turn to outside lenders or investors for money to expand. Still others need hundreds of thousands or even millions of dollars to launch their businesses and require sophisticated management skills as well as investors with deep pockets.

The bigger the investment required to launch or run a business, the bigger the risk to the owner. Thus, your own willingness and financial ability to accept risk will be a determining factor in the kind of business you start and its eventual size. This chapter presents some of the financing options you may want to consider at various stages in your business.

Q **How much do I need to start a business?**

You need enough money to acquire or produce what you sell, market and deliver the product or service to the customer, keep the business running, and keep your personal bills paid until the business is profitable. If you are starting a service business and will run it in your spare time or if you have a spouse who has a full-time job

143

that will cover all your living expenses and health insurance costs, you might be able to start your business with as little as $200 to $300—or possibly even less. If the business you are starting will require you to purchase expensive equipment, machinery, inventory, raw materials or rent space, hire employees, make significant outlays for advertising or promotion, and/or quit a job that you now rely on to pay your bills, you will need significantly more money to start the venture.

The best way to determine exactly how much money you will need to start your business is to use a worksheet similar to Table 9.1 below to estimate your one-time start-up expenses and the regularly monthly costs of doing business. Because it can take time to get your first customers (and collect from them if you have to bill them), you should plan on having at least enough money to cover start-up expenses and three months of operational expenses.

Table 9.1: Start-up Expenses Estimate

Use the list of start-up expenses below as a guideline to estimate how much money you will need to start your business.

One-Time Expenses	Cost
Permits	$_____
Licenses	$_____
Copyright registrations	$_____
Patent(s) (initial costs)	$_____
Trademark(s), (initial costs)	$_____
One-time legal & professional fees	$_____
Deposits (telephone, utilities, rent)	$_____
Grand opening advertising & publicity cost	$_____
Starting inventory	$_____
Other one-time expenses	$_____
TOTAL A: ONE-TIME EXPENSES	$_____

Monthly Expenses	Monthly Cost
Raw materials & parts	$_____
Supplies	$_____
Inventory	$_____
Shipping costs	$_____

144

Telephone	$_____
Equipment	$_____
Office furniture	$_____
Rent	$_____
Utilities (other than phone)............................	$_____
Fixtures	$_____
Display cases	$_____
Interior or exterior redecoration....................	$_____
Signs (inside or outside)	$_____
Property & general liability insurance.............	$_____
Errors & omissions insurance...........................	$_____
Product liability insurance...............................	$_____
Business auto/truck insurance.........................	$_____
Letterhead, envelopes, business cards.............	$_____
Sales literature (brochures, fliers, etc.)	$_____
Advertisements (production costs)	$_____
Advertisements (media charges)	$_____
Web site hosting & maintenance fees	$_____
Mailing list rental	$_____
Publicity expense	$_____
Postage for direct mail or publicity	$_____
Employee salaries..	$_____
Employee FICA, worker's compensation, etc. ...	$_____
Owner's draw (what you need to live on)	$_____
Health insurance	$_____
Other expenses	$_____

TOTAL MONTHLY EXPENSES	
MULTIPLY BY 3 TO GET:	×_____ 3
TOTAL B: MONTHLY EXPENSES FOR THREE MONTHS	$_____
ADD TOTAL A AND TOTAL B TO GET	
MINIMUM REQUIRED FOR START-UP	$_____

Q **Where do I get the money to start a business?**

Most people get the money to start a business from their personal savings, by taking out personal loans or second mortgages on their homes, and/or by using charge cards to pay for equipment or supplies. Equipment leases and vendor credit may be possible, too. Family and friends or other private investors are also common sources of start-up funds. Sometimes the amount of cash actually needed to start a business can be reduced by bartering or by working out some type of business deal with other individuals or businesses.

On rare occasions a manufacturer, supplier, or even a successful entrepreneur provides some start-up funds, equipment, building, or space. This type of opportunity is one you can't really search out, however. What usually happens is that someone with money or equipment spots a bright, industrious, inquisitive employee and figures that the employee has what it takes to build a new business or take over an existing one.

Q **What kind of deals could be used in place of money to help start a business?**

One type of deal is a sweat equity arrangement, which is basically an exchange of work for ownership in the start-up company. In other words, one person agrees to work for free or at a lower salary than normal and, in exchange, gets partial ownership of the business. A different type of arrangement, also beneficial, is one in which an existing business provides certain services for free for a start-up in exchange for a guarantee of future work if the start-up is successful.

Ben Mandell, an entrepreneur who has built several successful businesses, used this technique to produce the pilots he needed for a TV game show he was producing. He got a lower rate for the pilots with an express written understanding that he would shoot 130 shows at their studio, and pay their daily studio fee, if and when the show is sold. "I have a producer I have worked with before. He will produce a pilot at no cost to me. If the show is sold, he will produce all of the shows the first season." Mandel worked out similar deals with other suppliers as well.

Q **Will the bank give me a loan to start a business?**

Getting a local branch of a bank to give you a loan to start a business can be difficult. Banks are very conservative and are often reluctant to deal with start-up businesses, particularly if the owner has little or no experience running a business. If you have a good business plan and a good credit history, you may be able to find a bank willing to work with you, though you may have to shop around for the right bank. If you can't get a business loan you may be able to get a personal loan or a home equity loan or line of credit. (A line of credit is an agreed-upon amount of money you can borrow when needed.)

Q **How does a bank decide whether or not to approve a business loan?**

The bank will want to know how much money you are requesting, how you will use the money, and how you will be able to repay it. They need assurance that you and any other owners have the management experience and commitment necessary to run the business. They'll expect you and any other principal owners to have invested a significant amount of your own money in the business. Generally banks will expect the owner(s) to have an investment in the business equal to between one-third and one-half the amount of the loan requested.

The way to present all this information to banks is by preparing a loan proposal that includes these elements:

- business name and address
- name, address, and Social Security number of each owner of the business
- exact amount of the loan
- purpose of the loan
- financial statements for the last three years or, if the business is just starting, projections of financial data for three years
- business tax returns for the last three years if available
- tax returns and financial statements for each of the business owners for the last three years
- information about the company's market (how large it is, if the market is growing, who the typical customer is, how your business meets customers' needs)
- business profiles of the owners of the company, indicating management experience, special industry knowledge, skills, education, accomplishments
- an indication of what collateral the owner(s) is willing to pledge as security for the loan (collateral is any asset the bank could take over to get its money back if you can't pay off the loan, such as cash, stocks, real estate, and inventory)

Q **What kinds of bank loans are available to businesses?**

The two general types of loans are short-term loans and long-term loans. A short-term loan is one that has a term (the time from when you get the loan until it has to be paid back) that is usually 1 to 6 months but can be up to one year. Usually short-term loans are made to cover temporary or seasonal financial needs.

Long-term loans are usually made for terms longer than one year. Generally these loans are for major purchases, business expansion, or purchase of equipment or real estate. You will usually have to pledge some kind of collateral to get a long-term loan.

Q **What is a secured loan?**

A secured loan is a loan for which you have pledged assets as collateral (or security). If you can't pay, the bank takes over whatever assets you have pledged to pay off the loan.

Q **What is a revolving line of credit?**

A revolving line of credit works something like bank credit cards. You are granted a certain amount of credit, you may use it up to that amount, pay it off, use it up again, etc.

Q **What is a personal guarantee?**

A personal guarantee is a legal document that makes you liable for the debts of your business. You may be asked to sign a personal guarantee for small loans for which you don't pledge collateral, for business leases, and in some other circumstances. If the business defaults on the loan and you have signed a personal guarantee for the loan, the tender can force you to sell personal assets to make good on the loan if you don't have the cash to repay it.

Q **Can I get a loan without going through my local bank?**

Yes, you can apply for loans on the Internet. One service that makes that possible is LiveCapital.com. To use the service you go to the LiveCapital.com web site (http:// www.livecapital.com) and fill out a short application form. If you are applying for a loan of $50,000 or less, LoanWise can tell you immediately if you will qualify for a loan. (The service uses credit history data.) If you do qualify, you are referred to one of their participating banks. (The site doesn't make the loans itself. The service is an intermediary between the business owner and several banks that offer loans to small businesses.) Many businesses get the loan proceeds much more quickly this way than they would by applying to their local bank.

If you are looking for more than $50,000, you may be referred to a lender that participates in the SBA 7(a) Loan Guaranty Program. For additional information on SBA loan programs, see page 150 or visit the SBA web site http://www.sba.gov/financing.

Q **What about credit cards? How can I use them? Do I have to take out a cash advance?**

Some credit cards offer small businesses a line of credit with their cards. (Mastercard and American Express both offered this option in 2000.) If your credit rating is good, you can get $25,000 to $30,000 or more this way, without the hassle of applying for a bank loan. You may have to pay an application fee, but the application fee may be less than a commercial bank charges you if you apply for a line of credit. And the interest rate may be comparable. There is no restriction on how the money is used. You can either use your credit card for purchases or request that the money be put in your bank account and use it for working capital. As with any loan or credit card purchases you need to use the credit wisely since you will be personally responsible for paying it back even if the business doesn't do as well as you had hoped.

Q **What is receivables financing?**

Receivables financing (also called accounts receivable financing) is short-term financing used to provide companies with a source of cash between the time they sell a product and when they get paid for it. The business pledges the accounts receivable (outstanding bills) as collateral for the loan. If the business doesn't pay back the loan, the lender makes arrangements to have customers of the business pay their bills to the bank instead of to the business.

Q **What is factoring?**

Factoring is the outright purchase of accounts receivable (as opposed to lending against them). The business sells the receivables at a discount, getting, say $70 for every $100 in receivables it is owed. The factor may take over the collection function. The factor used to bear all the risk. Nowadays, however, the factor may have recourse back to the company that originated the sale.

Q   **What is inventory financing?**

Inventory financing is a loan used to bridge the gap between the time a company has to make an outlay for raw materials or inventory and the time the raw materials can be turned into products and sold. Although inventory financing may be used in conjunction with receivables financing (to gear up for seasonal sales, for instance) it is more individualized than receivables financing.

"Some lenders will advance only on raw materials and finished product but not on work in process," explains Larry J. Bister, chief financial officer of Crest Converters, Inc., in Milwaukee, Wisconsin. "Some lend only on raw materials. Most lenders want to make sure that any advances against finished product are only against newly created inventory—they don't want to be stuck with merchandise that is old and has no commercial value."

Q   **How do I get vendors to extend credit to me?**

Often all you have to do is ask or say, "Bill me." Other times, you may have to promise future business in return for the extension of immediate credit.

Q   **What are financials?**

Financials are the income statements, balance sheets, and other financial data you prepare for your business plan.

Q   **Can I get a loan from the Small Business Administration?**

The Small Business Administration (SBA) has a number of loan programs available to help small businesses obtain financing. Most of the programs involve loan guarantees made by the SBA to approved lenders, rather than outright loans. If you don't qualify for a regular bank loan but have a good business plan and are creditworthy, you might qualify for a guaranteed loan since the programs guarantee that the SBA will pay a percentage of the loan if the business defaults on it.

Among the SBA loan programs are:

- The 7a Loan Guaranty program guarantees loans of up to $1 million for 75 percent of the loan proceeds. (Thus the lending bank would have $750,000 of a $1 million loan guaranteed.)
- The LowDoc loan program guarantees loans of up to $100,000 for 80 percent of the loan proceeds. As the name implies, these loans feature a simplified application process. The borrower need only complete a one-page application.
- The MicroLoan program offers very small loans to prospective small business borrowers. Under the program, the SBA makes funds available to nonprofit intermediaries, who in turn make loans to eligible borrowers in amounts that range from under $100 to a maximum of $25,000. The average loan size is $ 10,000. The SBA program is not available in all states and the intermediary agencies change periodically.

The SBA guarantees a variety of other loans for specialized needs such as the purchase of fixed assets, defense diversification, and foreign trade. The best source of information about such loan programs are your local SBA, SCORE, or Small Business Development Center offices. Regional economic development agencies can also provide information and help you find the right funding for your needs. You can find more information about SBA loan programs on the SBA web site at http://www.sba.gov.

Q **Does the SBA offer any other kinds of loans or financial assistance to small businesses?**

Several other types of financial assistance are available through the SBA that can be of value to growing small businesses. Among them:

- *The surety bond guarantee program.* Under this program, the SBA guarantees a bid or performance bond, which may be required to get construction contracts, allowing the small business to qualify for the bond it might not otherwise get. (A bond is a guarantee that work will be performed or completed. If the company being bonded can't complete the project, the bonding company has to step in and complete the contract work or pay any losses caused by default on the contract.)

- *Disaster loans.* Loans to help small businesses recover from disasters such as earthquakes or hurricanes.
- *Export Revolving Line of Credit program (ERLC).* This program offers revolving lines of credit for small businesses that export their products overseas.

The SBA also licenses and provides some of the funding for certain venture capital firms. These firms are known as Small Business Investment Companies (SBICs) and ACE-Net, the Angel Capital Electronic Network. Apple Computer, Federal Express, and Nike are examples of the types and sizes of businesses that have received SBIC funding in the past.

Q **Where can I get more information about financial assistance from the SBA?**

To find out more about these and other SBA financial assistance programs, call the nearest SBA office. You will find the number in the blue pages of your phone book under the federal government listings. You can also call the SBA answer desk at (800) 827-5722 and use the automated answering system to get a prerecorded message giving the phone number of your nearest SBA office or visit their web site at http://www.sba.gov.

Q **Are there other government organizations that will help my business get a loan?**

Depending on the nature of your business and its ownership, you may also be able to get help from numerous other federal or state agencies. Among them: the Export-Import Bank, the Department of Housing and Urban Development, and the Department of Agriculture (see Appendix 4). Generally, none of the agencies will toss money your way just because you think you've got a hot idea for a new business. But they may have loan programs available that will help your business expand and grow or secure certain types of contracts.

You should also investigate state sources of funding. Look in the state government office listings in the phone book for phone numbers of departments with names like economic development or industrial development. Call and ask if your state has any funding programs available that would help your type of business. You may also be able to get this information from a local Small Business Development Center, a Service Corps of Retired Executives office, or an SBA office. Women and minority business offices (state, city, or federal) are still another source of information. You can find links to these resources on the SBA web site or on Business-KnowHow.com.

Finally, don't ignore management help available from regional, state, or federal government sources. The training sessions and one-on-one counseling often provided by government-sponsored organizations can provide needed consulting and other help at low or no cost.

Q **Will the government give me a grant to start a business?**

Chances are you've seen classified ads in newspapers that claim you can get "Free Government Money for Your Business," or something similar. What you need to realize is that while there *is* grant money available from government and other sources, no one is going to give you a grant just because you want to start a business. In fact, rarely does anyone get a grant to *start* a new venture. Grant money that is available is generally awarded for the development of some service that benefits the public or is given to companies that have developed or have the facilities to develop a product or service needed by the government.

Q **Where can I find out what government grants are available?**

The *Federal Register* is one source of information about grants. It is published on weekdays by the federal government and contains a variety of announcements, including announcements of grants. You can find the *Federal Register* at large public or college libraries or access it on the Internet at http://www.nara.gov/fedreg.

Another source of information about federal grants is the Catalog of Federal Domestic Assistance (CFDA), which is published yearly by the government. This publication is available in some large public libraries and college libraries and is also on the web. For information about the CFDA, contact:

Federal Domestic Assistance Catalog
General Services Administration
300 7th Street SW
Washington, DC 20407
(202) 708-5082
http://www.gsa.gov.regions/wk/wku

Finally, your state or city might have grant money available either directly from their own coffers or, more likely, through federal grant programs that are administered locally. The federal government gives grant money to the state or local government; the local government is responsible for handing out that grant money to deserving local businesses that apply for it.

Your state may have one office designated as a clearing house for information about grants. In New York State, for instance, the Assembly Speaker's Office publishes a newsletter called the *Grants Action Newsletter*, which lists available state grants and includes brief summaries of some federal grants that are open. A state (or city) office of small businesses, department of economic development, or department of industrial development should be able to point you toward sources of grant information in your state or region.

Q **Are there any other sources of government money for small business?**

A program called the Small Business Innovation Research program offers small businesses funding to do research for various federal agencies. These research projects are announced quarterly in the *SBIR Pre-Solicitation Announcement*. In fiscal year 1996, federal agencies participating in the SBIR program made awards totaling $916 million.

Q **How does the Innovation Research program work?**

Congress created the Small Business Innovation Research (SBIR) program in 1982 to encourage small businesses to do technological research for the government and to encourage the commercialization of research done for the government.

Federal agencies that participate in the SBIR program select certain research topics for funding and then publish a list of those topics in the *SBIR Pre-Solicitation Announcement* which is published quarterly. Businesses interested in doing research on any of the announced topics contact the appropriate agency for the complete solicitation, which gives more specific information about the type of research desired. If the business still wants to apply for funding after reading the solicitation, they submit a formal proposal showing how their company would handle the research project.

Q **How do the agencies choose which proposal will receive the award?**

Your proposal will be considered along with any others received. If several companies submit suitable proposals for the same project, the best will be selected for the award. If none of the proposals for a particular project are acceptable no award is made. Among the criteria the Department of Defense uses to judge proposals are these:

- scientific and technical quality of the proposal
- relevance to the topic description (with emphasis on the innovation and originality of the proposal)
- qualifications of the principal investigator and other key personnel
- adequacy of equipment or facilities
- anticipated benefits of the research

Among the reasons proposals get rejected are:

- they don't conform to the instructions listed in the Proposal Preparation Instructions and Requirements section (which is included in each SBIR solicitation)
- they don't match the needs specified in the solicitation
- the company doesn't appear to have the stability or experience to complete the project

Q **How much money would I get if I receive an SBIR award?**

There are two levels of awards, Phase I and Phase II. Phase I awards are made in amounts of up to $100,000, with work on the project being started and completed within a six-month period. Phase II awards are for up to $750,000. You cannot apply for a Phase II award unless you received Phase I funding for the same project.

Q **How can I get the *SBIR Pre-Solicitation Announcement?***

Contact the SBA Office of Innovation, Research, and Technology and ask to be put on the mailing list for the *SBA/SBIR Pre-Solicitation Announcement.* The address is:

U.S. Small Business Administration
Office of Technology
409 3rd Street SW
Washington, DC 20416
(202) 205-6450
http://www.sba.gov/SBIR/sbir.html

Q **Once I get a business going and see I need more cash, how can I get it?**

The traditional ways include getting bank loans, inventory or receivables financing, a contract loan (if available), funding from family or friends, or a second or even a third mortgage on your house. You could also take a partner or limited partner (a general partner usually works in the business with you while a limited partner usually just puts up money) or incorporate and seek investors who will give you money in exchange for equity (ownership) in your company.

Q **What is venture capital?**

Venture capital is money invested in a business in return for partial ownership. Generally, venture capital is used to fund high-risk businesses that show the potential for high profit (for example, $50 million in sales within 5 to 8 years). Venture capital firms make their profits by selling shares of stock of the successful ventures to the general public.

Q **What do venture capitalists look for?**

In addition to a product or service that has the potential for rapid growth, venture capitalists want to see a management team that has the ability to take the business concept and make it work. If you want to start a business in an industry you know nothing about, if you have no experience running businesses, or if you want to run the business on your own, don't waste postage sending business plans to venture capitalists.

Q **How much money do venture capitalists usually invest?**

There's no set amount; however, most are looking to invest at least half a million dollars since companies requiring less than that amount are likely not to have the potential to become large enough and profitable enough to make the investment pay off.

Q **Will venture capitalists give me cash to start a business?**

Although some venture capital firms do provide seed money (start-up funds) for some businesses, most of the time venture capital isn't invested until there is an available track record indicating the business is successful and has potential for growth. However, you might find start-up funds from one or more local "angels" (small investors, also known as informal venture capitalists). It is usually through these private investors that new businesses raise enough money to get a business going or to do initial development work.

Q **Where do I find these "angels"?**

The angels often come from your personal contacts—friends, family, professional references. Some people also advertise for investors in the business opportunity section of newspapers. If you plan to advertise for investors, it would be advisable to consult your attorney first to avoid running afoul of laws governing the advertising of investment opportunities in your state. (These laws are often called blue-sky laws.) One way some entrepreneurs try to avoid hassle over investment advertising laws is to advertise for a partner and include phrases in the ad such as "substantial equity position for the right partner."

Q **Where do I find venture capitalists?**

You can locate investors through industry trade associations, attorneys, accountants, colleges and universities that teach business, Service Corps of Retired Executives (SCORE) offices, Small Business Development Centers (SBDCs), or SBA offices. In addition, there are directories of venture capital firms that describe the specialty of each firm, the size of the investments the firm usually makes, and other pertinent information.

Such directories are available at large public libraries. You can also find investors on the web through ACE-Net and other web sites.

Q **Does it matter which venture capital firm I contact?**

Yes. Venture capital firms usually specialize in particular industries. If you are looking for money for a bio-tech company, it is a waste of time and postage to send your business plan to venture capitalists that specialize in entertainment.

Q **What should I do to contact these firms? Do I call? Go to their offices?**

The best way to contact venture capital firms is to get a reference to the firm or investor through your banker, a venture capital club, or some other source. If you can't find anyone to make a reference and don't meet anyone through your own networkings, call firms listed in directories and ask to speak to whoever handles your type of business. If interest is expressed, find out whether the contact prefers to see the plan first or would be open to having you present the plan in a personal interview.

Q **How else can I find investors?**

There are also people who "rep" a plan (find investors for you through contacts they have). Expect to pay a fee to such representatives (as much as 5 percent of the money raised), but this fee should come out of the money raised; you shouldn't have to pay any up-front fees except perhaps for travel, mailings, and similar out-of-pocket expenses your representative may incur. These people are often called financial consultants. You may be able to find them through business brokers or through private networking.

Q **What will investors expect in return for money they invest?**

Investors will expect some degree of ownership and a way to get their money out of the business after a set period of time. The amount of ownership you would have to give up will vary with what you are bringing into the business in the way of experience, money, value of the business at the time of financing, and so on. If you have a great idea but no management team, the venture firm might want to hand-pick people to run the company. The investors will generally plan on getting their money back by selling their shares of the business to others through public or private stock offerings.

10.

Making It Legal

You're honest, hardworking, and you report all the income from your home business. So you don't have to worry about lawsuits, right?

Wrong!

No matter how small your business is, it is likely to be governed by a complex web of local, state, and federal laws. Some of these laws are designed to protect your customers, suppliers, creditors, and employees from being harmed by your business or its activities. Others protect you from competitors, suppliers, and even your clients. Still others exist (as municipal servants will invariably tell you) because "that's the way it's done" or because "that's what the law says."

Typical of this type of law is a statute in a New York State township requiring individuals who want to start a home business to get a building permit, have the home office inspected by a town building inspector, and get a certificate of occupancy for the "office" even if they will be working at the dining room table, won't be making physical changes to the home, and won't be having customers come to the house.

Q **What do I have to do to make my business legal?**

The regulations with which you'll need to comply in order to be legal vary according to what you do and where your business is located, but typically, with a business owned and operated by one individual who has no employees (sole proprietorship), you will need to follow some or all of these steps:

- Register your business name and get a certificate of doing business under an assumed name (commonly called a DBA). In some states you are required to register your business name whether you are operating under an assumed name or not.
- Publish your intention to do business in an official notice (required in some but not all states).
- Get required permits and licenses (these will be in addition to the DBA certificate).
- Comply with zoning regulations, regulations regarding signs on your business property, environmental protection laws (if any apply to your business), licensing laws, etc.
- Make arrangements to collect state sales tax if you sell taxable products or services.
- Keep accurate income and expense records and report your income to the IRS and state tax authorities.
- Pay owed income taxes and self-employment tax quarterly.
- Meet any specific bonding or insurance regulations your locality or state has instituted for your type of business.

Depending on the nature of your business you might also have to comply with noise codes, sanitation regulations, laws governing placement and size of signs, or other laws. If you add employees you will also have to comply with all applicable state and federal labor laws.

Q Are there any laws that could prevent me from starting a home business?

Unfortunately there could be. Despite the millions of people who work at home, many communities have zoning or other regulations prohibiting home businesses. Although the intent of such laws may be to maintain property values and prevent a residential neighborhood from turning into a little Main Street, most home businesses generate less neighborhood traffic and far less noise than the average car- or truck-driving suburban teenager.

Other laws or regulations might also interfere with your work-at-home plans, including labor laws, health codes, and licensing requirements. The only way you will know for sure what rules affect you is to ask appropriate local agencies and officials.

Q Why don't communities change the outdated laws?

Many communities are attempting to change the laws, but often change does not come easily. Municipalities may be caught in an intractable situation involving residents who want the change, residents who fear the change, and residents who howl "not fair" because their type of business will not be included among those deemed acceptable for home pursuit.

The resulting battle can be time-consuming and costly. The town of Southold in New York was sued after it implemented a zoning law change that allowed certain types of home businesses. The citizen who filed the suit (and won) claimed the new law was illegal because the town had not first done an environmental impact study. As a result, the town had to do the environmental study, schedule and hold new hearings, and then vote on the law a second time—a process that took many months.

Q Are the laws the same throughout a state?

No, zoning laws are established locally, often at the township, city, or village level. Furthermore, each town or village decides for itself what types of home businesses it will allow. Thus in one community you might be able to run a home business that has up to two employees while in another community the same business might be restricted from having any employees. In still another community you might be able to have a homebased business if you are a fisherman or carpenter but not if you are a real estate agent or insurance broker.

Q Don't a lot of home businesses just ignore zoning laws?

Many people do operate businesses in violation of zoning regulations. In some communities, there is no attempt to enforce the regulations unless a resident complains and forces officials to close down the illegal home business. In fact, there was one community in Illinois where two trustees of an Illinois town had to excuse themselves from discussions of a proposed zoning law that would legalize home businesses. The reason? Each of the trustees had a homebased business.

You cannot assume, however, that it is OK to disregard local law because *some* town boards don't enforce regulations and *some* people get away with operating on the sly. If there are laws prohibiting your type of home business, it will only take one complaint to plunge you into a pot of legal hot water.

Q **Who would complain?**

Neighbors are generally the source of such complaints. A neighbor may not like seeing your truck parked in the street, may think your equipment interferes with TV reception, or may not like it that you wear a single earring or your son has shoulder-length hair. The motivation for the complaint doesn't matter; if you are in violation of the law and a complaint is filed, town officials have to follow established procedures to deal with the complaint.

Even if your neighbors wouldn't complain, someone outside the immediate neighborhood might. Under the heading of "life isn't fair" comes an incident where zoning officials were alerted to an illegal home business after a postal carrier made a comment to his supervisor about the volume of mail going to one home on his route.

Q **What would happen if someone did file a complaint?**

Usually you would be forced to stop running the business from your home and could be fined, and even possibly put in jail, if you continue to violate the ordinance. Fines can be as high as $75 to $100 a day or more.

Q **Is there anything I can do if town officials say I can't run a business from my home or apartment?**

If your business creates no traffic, noise, odor, or other neighborhood disturbances you might consider trying to get the laws changed. Many communities are beginning to realize their laws are antiquated and need to be updated.

If you don't want to try to change the law, you might want to try to get a variance. A variance is a license allowing you to do something that is contrary to the general law.

Enterprising individuals sometimes tackle the problem in other ways. A woman in Florida who raised plants as a hobby decided to turn her hobby into a business by selling plants at a flea market. She applied for and got a state nursery license, but when she applied for a business certificate from the town, she was told by town officials she couldn't run a business from her home and would be prosecuted if she accepted any money for her plants.

Infuriated, the woman wrote a letter to the town licensing agency and sent copies to county officials. In the letter she compared her business to that of an Avon representative who stores and sorts inventory at home but actually sells the product and delivers it to clients away from the home. She added that if she were denied the right to run her business from home, she would make every possible effort to see that Avon representatives and other people who did similar work would also be denied the right to work at home. The woman got her business license.

Still another tactic was used by the owners of a typesetting company when town officials told them they would have to stop operating their business from a garage on their property. The owners knew it was only a matter of time until the company would outgrow the converted garage, but they weren't quite ready to move. So they challenged the zoning law in court because the town couldn't force them to stop operating the business while they were contesting the law. Although it cost them thousands of dollars in legal fees and they eventually lost, it bought them the time they needed to get ready for the move.

Q **How do I find out about zoning laws?**

To find out what the zoning laws are in your community, look in the blue pages of your phone book (the government listings), and find the number of your town or city zoning board or building department. If you can't find a phone number for either of these departments, call the main administration number for the town and ask where to get the information.

Describe the type of business you want to start and the nature of the location from which you'd like to operate (home, main street, building in an area that appears to be a mixture of residences and offices, etc.). Ask what laws might apply to that type of business and if any special permits or licenses will be needed. If you don't want to give away your identity, call anonymously. If you want to be sure to maintain your anonymity and worry about caller identification services, make your call from a pay phone. (Caller identification systems allow people who are receiving a call to see the phone number of the person making the call.)

Q **If a business was operated on the property before I bought it, will I be able to run a business there, too?**

Not necessarily. If the property is in a residential area, the people before you might have been operating illegally or might have had a special use permit that won't apply to your business. Other factors can also come into play. In Southern California, a horse breeder ran afoul of zoning laws after buying a ranch because he had twenty-nine horses on the ranch, and the zoning laws only permitted twenty-one. The only way you will know for sure is to check the zoning laws or have an attorney do it for you.

Q **Where do I find out about state and federal laws affecting my business.**

Local offices of the Small Business Administration (SBA), the Service Corps of Retired Executives (SCORE), or Small Business Development Centers (SBDC) in your area may be able to provide the information you need or tell you where to get it (see Appendix 1). Look in the blue pages of your phone book under federal government for SBA and SCORE locations near you, or call the SBA automated information system at (800) 827-5722 for the location of the nearest office. If there are any SBDCs in your area they will be under the state listings rather than the federal government listings. Still another possible source of information will be colleges or universities in your region that have small business or entrepreneurial courses or majors.

Q **Should I use my own name or a business name?**

Many people operate under their own name at least during the start-up phase of their business. Doing so lets them avoid having to open a separate bank account for the business. While this works for some businesses, others find that asking people to make checks out to them personally makes the business look small and unprofessional.

Q **Can I add "and Associates" or "and Company" to my real name without having to register it as a business name?**

Adding words to or changing your legal name in any way makes it a fictitious name and will most likely subject you to registration requirements.

Q **What happens if I don't register my business name?**

Most banks will not cash checks made out to your business name unless you have given them a copy of your DBA. Thus, if you don't register your business name and a customer gives you a check made out to that name, you either have to return the check and ask for a new one or register the name and get the DBA before cashing the check. If you try to register the business name and someone is already using a confusingly similar name, you may not be allowed to register your chosen name.

Q **What will it cost to register my business name and get the licenses I need?**

Usually the cost of a DBA is relatively insignificant. Fees quoted from different parts of the country range from $30 to $60. Fees you may have to pay for other permits, licenses, or bonds can be steep, however, running to hundreds or maybe even thousands of dollars, depending on the nature of your business.

Q **What do I have to do to register the business name?**

You should go to the county or city clerk's office and search the records to see if there is any other business in your area using the name you want to use. If no other business is using that name, you will fill out a form, sign it, get it notarized, and pay a fee. In a few states, sole proprietorships and partnerships are registered at the state level rather than local. (Corporations are always registered at the state level, often through the Department of State.)

Q **What can I do if someone else *is* using the name?**

Often, the only thing you can do is choose another name. To avoid wasting time, it would be a good idea to check local phone books to see if anyone is using the business name you want before you register the name and to have several alternatives in mind if the name you prefer turns out to be already in use.

Q **Can I use any name that isn't registered in the local area?**

There may be companies that have registered national trademarks or have prior use rights to a name, which would bar you from using that name even though it is not registered locally. You couldn't call your local computer company Apple Computer, for instance, even if Apple Computer has not registered its name in your locality. You might be able to register Apple Stationery, Apple Chair Company, or other names that combined the word *apple* with something unrelated to computers.

Q **What happens if I do accidentally use another business's name?**

If the business sells in your area and has prior use rights to the name, they could force you to stop using the business name. You would then have to alert your customers, change your stationery, change your phone listings and business cards, and so on.

Q **How can I find out if businesses outside my immediate area are using the name I want to use?**

If you have access to the Internet, you can do free searches for nationally registered trademarks from the U.S. Patent and Trademark office web site at http://www. uspto.gov. Trademarks don't have to be registered nationally to be valid, so it's a good idea to search other sources as well. You can quickly find web sites that may have similar names by searching for the name of the company on popular Internet portals such as Yahoo, America Online, Lycos, Alta Vista, or Dogpile, and by searching Network Solutions (http://www.networksolutions.com) to see if anyone has registered a web site with the name you want. Finally, ask your public library if they have reference books or CD-ROMs that contain trademarks that have been registered in individual states.

Q **Do I really have to go to all that trouble?**

Like so many other things in business, it's a judgment call. If you will be operating only in a small local area, and could, if you had to, change your name without a tremendous loss of money or customers, you may want to skip the national name search and just search for similar names in use in your area. If you proceed this way, you must realize that if some company based in another region is using the name as a trademark or trade name and moves into your area, they might be able to force you to stop using the name.

Q **When do I register a business name?**

The time to register your business name is as soon as you are sure you are going to go into business and decide on a business name. You wouldn't want to go to the trouble and expense of getting business stationery, opening a bank account in the business name, and advertising the name if you won't be allowed to register it.

Q **Do I have to register in every county, state, and city I plan to do business in?**

If you only maintain an office in one location and do not physically travel from place to place selling merchandise, you probably will not be required to register your name in any place other than your own county, city, or state. For instance, if you live in Kansas and have a mail order business that advertises in a national publication, you would not be required to register your business name in every state in which you have customers. (Even though you may not be required to register your business name in other states or localities, you might find it beneficial to register your business name as a trademark either in one or more states or nationally to prevent other companies from using a business name like yours to sell similar goods. See chapter 20 for additional information on trademarks.)

Things work differently, however, if you are a flea market vendor or craftsperson who travels from place to place selling goods. In such cases, you may be considered to have a physical presence (which is called *nexus*) in each locality in which you set up a booth or rent a table to sell your goods. You may therefore be required to register your business, get a license, and to collect and remit local sales taxes. If you are unsure of the requirements, show promoters and other vendors should be able to tell you what to do and whom to contact.*

If you have offices in several counties or states you may be required to register in those areas. If you operate as a corporation you have to register as a foreign corporation in any state you have offices in other than the state in which the corporation secures its charter.

Q How do I sign up to collect sales tax?

If your state collects a sales tax, call the state tax department and ask for information about getting a sales tax number, also called sales tax permit, resale number, or resale permit.

Q Do I have to pay sales tax on items I buy for the business?

What is taxable and what isn't taxable varies from state to state, but generally, if you buy taxable items that will be consumed in operating your business (say, paper or toner cartridges) you either have to pay the sales tax on them when you purchase them or, if you use your reseller's number to avoid paying tax at the time of purchase, you will have to pay a use tax for using the items. The use tax will be equal to

---

*Some flea market vendors and craftspeople ignore the local laws and do not register with the appropriate officials or collect sales tax. Although some get away with it, breaking the law is never advisable. Furthermore, state and local officials often roam through many of the larger flea markets and crafts shows spot-checking for licenses and collection of sales taxes.

the sales tax you would have paid. The difference is that you will send it in at the same time you send in sales taxes collected on items you have sold to your customers.

On the other hand, if you are purchasing something that will be used to make a product you will sell (a hard drive that you will be installing in a computer system you build from scratch for a client, for example), you do not have to pay sales or use tax on the purchase if you have a sales tax number. The reason is that sales taxes in the United States are paid by the consumer, not the manufacturer.*

Q   **Do I have to have an attorney to start a business?**

You aren't required to have an attorney to start a business, and many businesses do not have legal help getting started. If your business is regulated by local, state, or federal authorities, if you will be writing or accepting contracts involving significant sums of money, or if you will be operating as a partnership or corporation, it is highly advisable to consult with an attorney. The money you spend up front to make sure things are set up properly and in your best interests can save you hundreds of thousands of dollars and much aggravation in the future.

---

*In certain countries manufacturers may encounter a value-added tax. With a value-added tax the manufacturer does pay a tax on the goods and supplies used in manufacturing the product. The cost of that tax is added on to the other costs in determining the final price of the product to the consumer. (If the item would cost $100 and the company had to pay taxes equal to $5 for goods used in the manufacture of the item, the purchase price would be $105.)

11.
Who Owns the
Business?

Many people think about starting a business the same way they would think about starting to paint the house, starting a new career, or starting any other big project: they think about *doing something* rather than *owning* something. Yet, when you start a business, in the eyes of the law you become a business owner and have to choose a form of business ownership. The form of ownership you choose has important legal, financial, tax, and marketing implications.

Q **What forms of ownership are there?**

There are three primary forms of business ownership:

- sole proprietorship (you are the only owner)
- partnership (two or more parties join together in the business, splitting up the work load, profits, and financing of the business however they wish)
- corporation (a legal entity, which under law has a "life" of its own separate from any individual who owns the corporation)
- Limited Liability Company, or LLC (a hybrid form of business combining the tax structure of partnerships with the liability protection of corporations)

Q **What are the advantages of a sole proprietorship?**

A sole proprietorship is the easiest form of business to set up and run. Here are a few of the reasons why:

- *You make all the decisions.* You alone can decide what to sell and how to sell it, when to expand the business and when to pull back, when to look for financing, when to buy new equipment, when and how long to work, and when to take the day off—without having to justify your decision to anyone.
- *You can take money out of the business easily.* Although it is not advisable, you don't even have to maintain a separate bank account for a sole proprietorship. As long as you keep accurate records of income and expenses, you could run it out of your personal checkbook.
- *You can use losses to offset other income* on your personal tax return.
- *Start-up costs are relatively low.* You generally have less paperwork and fewer regulations to comply with as a sole proprietor than you do with other forms of business.

Q **Are there any disadvantages of operating as a sole proprietor?**

Virtually every book and magazine article discussing what form of business a business owner should choose will tell you the biggest disadvantage of a sole proprietorship is that you have unlimited liability for the actions of your business. In other words, *you are personally responsible for all business debts and actions and could lose your personal assets if the business goes bankrupt or gets sued.*

But also remember that *as the owner of any small business, you are likely to take the same risk no matter what form of business you start.* Contrary to what you may read in books and how-to articles, incorporating a very small business does not automatically protect you from liability for the company's debts or actions.*

---

*Unfortunately, you will still find many books and articles and even an occasional individual with a degree in law or accounting stating that incorporating shields personal assets from liability. What they don't bother to explain, or perhaps never really investigate, is how that protection comes about or how it changes with the size of the business. See page 176 for additional information.

Other disadvantages of a sole proprietorship include:

▶ *There is no continuity of ownership.* Usually when the owner of a sole proprietorship dies, the business comes to an end. While you could train someone to take over the business and make arrangements to pass on the business to a family member should you die, there may be no one in your family who has the interest or ability to carry on without you.
▶ *Financing your business may be more difficult.* Banks and other lenders may be reluctant to loan you unincorporated business money.
▶ *Fringe benefits you can give yourself are quite limited.* The amount you can put tax-free into pension plans and the deductibility of health insurance premiums are both limited, for instance.
▶ *Getting and keeping good employees* may be difficult as the company grows.

Q How does a partnership work?

A partnership lets two or more people (or in some cases businesses) work together to achieve a common goal. There are different kinds of partnerships, but each partnership must have at least one general partner. (In most very small business partnerships, each partner is a general partner.) The partners share in the profits and the work according to an agreed arrangement. Each general partner can act on behalf of the partnership, doing anything necessary to run the business (hire employees, sign contracts, make purchases, etc.).

Q What are the advantages of a partnership?

The chief advantages of a partnership are:

▶ *It lets you pool resources* with others to build a larger, more profitable business.
▶ *It is easy for the partners to take money out of the business.* This is one of the reasons many professional practices use a partnership format.
▶ *The life of a partnership can be easily limited* to suit your needs. Thus a partnership can be formed for a specific project or to achieve a specific objective and can then be dissolved.
▶ *It may allow you to bring needed capital into the business* to finance long-term projects or growth.

- *You may have lower costs and fewer legal regulations* than you would running the business as a corporation.
- *The partnership itself does not pay income tax.* All profits and losses get passed along to the individual partners.

Q **What are the disadvantages of operating a partnership?**

Disadvantages of running your business as a partnership include:

- *Partners don't always get along.* Frequent causes of disagreements are disputes over workloads (who is doing how much); spending (one partner thinks the other is a penny-pincher and the other thinks the first is a spendthrift); and methods of operation.
- *Each general partner is liable for the actions of all the other general partners.* Thus, if your partner leases a new Mercedes in the partnership name and then skips town with the car, the partnership—and you personally as a partner—would be responsible for paying for the car. The same holds true if your partner commits the partnership to any contract or does anything illegal in the partnership's name.
- *You may incur more legal fees* with a partnership than with a sole proprietorship. Although it isn't always done, it is in your best interest to have a formal partnership agreement with your partners and to have the agreement drawn up by an attorney, or at least reviewed by one. If you don't have a formal partnership agreement and the partnership ends, you are likely to end up with even more legal fees to untangle disputes over partnership debts and assets.
- *Changes in ownership* mean the partnership technically comes to an end (dissolves); if a partner is bought out or a new partner is added, however, the business can continue.
- *Fringe benefits,* as with sole proprietorships, are limited compared to those available with regular corporations.

Q **Does my spouse automatically own part of my business?**

Depending on the state laws where you live, your spouse may automatically have a legal interest in your business and be entitled to a share of the business if you divorce. This holds true even for partnerships. (The partner's spouse may have a legal interest in the partnership even if he or she has never been involved in the operation of the partnership.)

Q **What happens if my spouse and I get divorced?**

Depending on where you live and what precautions you have taken, you might have to "buy out" your spouse's interest in the business as part of a divorce settlement, even if the spouse has never worked in the business.

Q **I'm thinking about going into business with a friend. Are we both sole proprietors?**

According to the Uniform Partnership Act (UPA), which is a body of law that establishes basic guidelines for partnerships,* a partnership is "an association of two or more persons to carry on as co-owners of a business." If you and your friend work together in the business you would be considered partners, whether you formally agree to be partners or not. That means you would each be bound by all the rights and responsibilities and liabilities of a formal partnership arrangement. Thus it would be advisable to have a formal partnership agreement with your friend.

Q **Why do we need a partnership agreement?**

While you and your partner may be the best of friends now, it is very easy for misunderstandings to develop in a partnership, just like it is easy for misunderstandings to develop in any agreement that isn't written down. Several psychologists who were also good friends learned this lesson the hard way. They agreed to open a jointly run practice. They were advised to have a formal partnership agreement, but since they were all "experts" in dealing with human relationships, they decided it wouldn't be necessary. Less than a year later their joint effort ended, leaving them engaged in bitter and expensive legal disputes over ownership of partnership property and responsibility for various debts.

*The Uniform Partnership Act (UPA) has been adopted with some variations by all states except Louisiana.

Q **What should a partnership agreement cover?**

Among the basic points that should be explained in the agreement are:

- the name of the partnership
- the function or purpose of the partnership
- the duration of the partnership
- the duties and extent of authority of each partner
- the number and kinds of partners (limited, general, silent, etc.)
- the method for admitting new partners
- the method for dissolving the partnership should the partners be unable to work together
- the contributions (money, labor, equipment, etc.) of each partner to the partnership
- the method for dividing profits and losses
- how the books will be kept
- how property used in the partnership will be owned
- the method to be used to resolve disputes
- how absences from the business or disability will be handled
- what buy-out procedures should be followed in the event that a partner should leave the partnership or die

Q **What happens if we don't have a partnership agreement?**

If you don't have a partnership agreement and your partnership breaks up, you have no way of proving any verbal agreements about who contributed what to the partnership or whether anything contributed to the partnership became partnership property or remained the property of the original owner. Thus any business equipment you brought into the partnership (your computer system, scanner, and laser printer, for example) could be considered partnership property that has to be sold to pay the partnership's debts or split up between the partners.

Q **Do we need an attorney to write the partnership agreement?**

It is advisable to have an attorney to draw up the partnership agreement.

Q **Are there partners who just contribute money and don't get involved with the business at all?**

Yes. Usually that kind of arrangement is set up as a limited partnership and specifically spells out when and how and under what terms the investor(s) will get back their money. It is frequently used for financing small businesses. Limited partners are not liable for debts or actions of the partnership; the most they can lose is the amount they invest.

Q **How does a corporation differ from a partnership?**

A corporation is a legal "person." In other words, it has an identity that is distinct and separate from the individuals who own the corporation. Like a real person, the corporation is legally entitled to enter into contracts, conduct business, own property, lend or borrow money, and so on.

Q **What are the advantages of incorporating?**

The primary benefits of operating under a corporate form generally revolve around tax and marketing considerations and ease of attracting investors. In real life, while the benefits of incorporation may technically be available to a business of any size, in practice very small businesses may gain little or no benefit by incorporating until they have employees or can reap tax benefits by incorporating.

That said, these are the potential benefits of the corporate form of business:

▶ You may be able to raise capital more easily as a corporation than as a sole proprietor; however, there are no guarantees.*
▶ It may be easier to transfer ownership in a corporation than it is in a sole proprietorship or a partnership.
▶ Under some circumstances your tax rate might be lower.
▶ If you have employees, incorporation may protect your personal assets if an employee does something that causes the company to be sued.
▶ You may be able to give yourself more company-paid fringe benefits as an employee of your corporation.

*Banks are going to look for the same thing whether you are incorporated or not: your ability to repay a loan. Being incorporated may make it appear you are more serious about running your business, but incorporation in no way assures that you will be able to find people to buy shares of the business.

▶ You may be able to get and keep good employees by offering them stock in the company.
▶ You may gain estate-planning benefits.
▶ You might find incorporation preferable to a partnership if you will be going into business with one or more other people.

Q **What are the disadvantages of incorporating?**

Among the disadvantages of incorporating are:

▶ *Your cost of doing business usually increases* due to added fees you have to pay.
▶ *The amount of paperwork you have to do increases* because of legal record-keeping requirements.
▶ *You may be subject to "double" taxation,* having your profits taxed once at the corporate level and once again as an individual.
▶ *The IRS could limit your salary as an employee of your own corporation* to an amount it considers reasonable and treat amounts above the "reasonable" salary to be dividends.
▶ *Your personal finances must be kept completely separate from the corporation's finances.* Thus, you can't dip into the corporate bank account if you come up a little short on personal cash for the week.
▶ *Closing the corporation's doors* permanently can be somewhat complicated and costly.

Q **Doesn't the corporate form of business protect your personal assets?**

No, it won't necessarily protect your personal assets. Here's why:

Even though you, as a shareholder of your own corporation, may not be responsible for the debts of the corporation (since the corporation is a separate "person"), there is nothing to prevent someone from suing you personally for actions you performed. For instance, suppose you personally created an ad campaign for your corporation criticizing a competitor. The competitor views the campaign as malicious and untrue and decides to sue. They might sue your corporation and you, personally, as the creator of the ad. While you would not be liable for any settlement the corporation has to pay as a result of the suit, your personal assets could be attached to pay off any judgment the competitor won in its case against you the individual.

In addition, even though you might not technically be liable for the corporation's debts, if you owned a very small corporation, chances are you would have to dig into your own personal bankroll to come up with the money to fight the lawsuit.

Thus incorporation does not necessarily prevent liability problems. One important step you can take to help protect your assets against loss is to obtain adequate liability insurance (business property, professional errors and omissions, and product liability).

The other fallacy about incorporation is that somehow it protects you from paying off any bad debts the corporation incurs. But things rarely work that way. While you are not automatically responsible for the corporation's debts the way you would be responsible for your sole proprietorship or partnership debts, *rarely will you be able to get a loan for a new small corporation unless you sign a personal guarantee, which means that you, personally, will have to pay back the loan if the corporation defaults.* You may also have to sign personal guarantees on building or equipment lease agreements.

Q **How old do you have to be to incorporate?**

The minimum age ranges from 18 to 21 depending on the state.

Q **Can I start a corporation with only one person?**

Most states allow you to start a corporation with only one shareholder.

Q **When is it a good idea to incorporate?**

A good accountant who is used to dealing with small business tax matters can advise you whether or not to incorporate. In general, he or she should help you evaluate whether business growth or other individual business circumstances indicate that incorporating is likely to benefit you by doing any of these things:

- cut your tax bill
- give you better fringe benefits
- increase the amount of money you can put tax-free into your pension plan

- protect your personal assets if your employees cause your company to be sued
- make your company appear bigger than it is
- allow you to retain money in the corporation to meet some specific need
- allow for smooth transfer of ownership
- make it possible to expand the business by bringing in investors

Q **I've heard it's a good idea to incorporate in Delaware, because of tax breaks and other benefits. Is this true?**

As a small business with just a few shareholder-employees, the easiest and best place to incorporate is usually within your own state. Although Delaware may offer some tax breaks and potentially more statutory protection from liability for corporate directors than your own state, for a small corporation the advantages are likely to be outweighed by the disadvantages. For instance, you will have to appoint someone in Delaware to be an agent for your corporation (there are companies in Delaware that do this); you will have to pay an annual franchise (corporate) tax to the state of Delaware; and if you incorporate in Delaware but do business in another state (the state where you live, for instance), you will have to file an application in your home state to do business as a foreign corporation and will then have to pay a franchise fee as well as income taxes in your home state.

Q **What will it cost to incorporate in my own state?**

The actual fees charged to incorporate may be anywhere from under $50 to a few hundred dollars, depending on what state you live in. Attorney's fees, if you use an attorney to incorporate your business, can run from $400 or $500 to close to $1,000 or more depending on where you are located and how much work the attorney has to do for you.

Q **Should I incorporate to get investors?**

If you have people who want to invest, incorporation is one way to set things up so they might be able to get their money out later. (A limited partnership might also accomplish your goal.) But incorporating won't automatically bring you investors.

Q **What kinds of corporations are there?**

There are two basic forms of corporations: regular corporations (called C corporations) and S corporations (formerly called subchapter S corporations). Small corporations often organize under the S format. Another term associated with corporations is "close" or "closed" (or sometimes, "closely held"). This refers to a corporation that is owned by a few private individuals rather than having its shares available to the general public.

Q **What's the difference between C corporations and S corporations?**

The main difference that is of concern to small businesses is the way profits and losses are handled. In a regular corporation the profits are taxed to the corporation and losses absorbed by it. In an S corporation, profits and losses are passed through to the shareholder and taxed at the shareholder's tax rate.

Q **Which type is best?**

The answer depends on the individual circumstances of your business. If the shareholder's personal tax rate is lower than the corporate tax rate, an S corporation may be preferable. Businesses subject to the alternative minimum tax may find the regular corporate status preferable since the alternate minimum rate is lower for corporations than for individuals.

Q **What types of businesses does the IRS consider personal service corporations?**

Corporations offering services primarily in the fields of accounting, actuarial science, architecture, engineering, health, law, the performing arts, and consulting are considered personal service corporations. Writers, artists, and sales agents do not fall into this classification.

Q **Do I need an attorney or accountant to incorporate?**

Technically you could incorporate without outside help, but it is not advisable. Because of the complexity of corporate law, you should get help and advice from an accountant and/or attorney. But not just *any* accountant or attorney. Look for one who has experience dealing with small corporations. Nadine Keilholz, a newsletter publisher, learned that lesson the hard way. Explains Nadine:

> Before we incorporated, all we had to worry about was a quarterly state sales tax form and payment and a Schedule C along with our personal federal filing. As soon as we incorporated, I started getting forms I'd never heard of, from taxing authorities I didn't even know existed. I was buried up to my ears in 940s, 941s, state unemployment taxes, state intangibles taxes (on the value of stock), and about twenty other things. It seemed that every week I got two or three new forms to fill out. And that doesn't even count the environmental impact statements and other nontax-related things.
>
> Unfortunately, the accountant we had been using was fine for personal taxes and a small personal business—but after about two years, when I started getting notices from the IRS, FICA, the state of Florida, et cetera, that we had unfiled returns and unpaid taxes, I found out that he didn't know how to handle a corporation.

The problem, Keilholz eventually discovered, was that although the accountant had actually mailed in their tax forms and checks for payment, he hadn't submitted the proper transmittal forms with the returns. "All that money was sitting there with the IRS instead of having been forwarded to FICA, or with one state agency instead of having been sent on to another."

Keilhoz has since found another accountant and says, "The peace of mind of just being able to throw all of our receipts, our check register, and the myriad forms that we receive each month into an envelope and send them to him and know that it'll be done—and done right—are well worth his fee."

Q **How do I keep corporate minutes?**

There are companies that sell incorporation kits with fill-in-the-blank forms you can use to record corporate minutes (which are a record of shareholders' meetings). These kits generally have sample articles of incorporation, bylaws, notices of meetings, stock ledgers and transfer ledgers (for recording names and addresses of stockholders), and bank stock certificates. A kit put out by a company called E-Z Legal Forms is available for under $15 at discount office supply stores.

Q **When is it advantageous to form a nonprofit corporation?**

Nonprofit corporations may offer certain tax advantages to corporations formed for charitable or other kinds of work. They may be eligible for certain grants, research money, reduced postage costs, and other benefits. Directors and executives of the corporation can be paid decent salaries and get reimbursed for expenses. The rules covering nonprofits are even more complex than those covering C or S corporations and should be discussed with an attorney or accountant familiar with nonprofit management concerns.

Q **How do I choose a board of directors?**

Your board of directors will generally be responsible for determining corporate policy and deciding how to conduct the business. The directors are elected by your stockholders; the corporate officers are chosen by the directors. Thus, if you are the only stockholder, you might appoint yourself director, then, as director, appoint yourself, or whoever else you choose, to each of the corporate officer positions required by law in your state (generally, president, vice president, and treasurer), unless your state requires that different people hold those positions or requires corporations to have more than one director.

The bigger you grow your business, the more important your choice of directors. If you are looking for outside capital, investors are likely to want to see that your directors and officers are qualified to run the business. If you should have the type of business capable of attracting venture capital, the investors may also become directors.

Q **Can I start the business as a sole proprietor and incorporate later?**

Yes. In fact, it is often advisable to do that since a sole proprietorship is the easiest form of business to start. You simply run the business as a sole proprietorship until it grows big enough to warrant the time and expense of incorporating.

Q **Can I switch back and forth between a regular corporation and an S corporation?**

You must incorporate first as a regular (C) corporation. Then, if the shareholders agree to do so, you may elect S corporation status. If you choose to terminate S status for tax or other reasons, you can do so at any time. However, once you have terminated your S status you may not elect it again for 5 years. There may be other tax consequences as well, so be sure to consult your accountant.

Q **What is a Limited Liability Company?**

A limited liability company (LLC) is a form of organization that has some advantages of a corporation, and some of a partnership. A relatively new form of business, LLCs have only been available as a form of business since 1977. What they offer is the same type of liability protection corporations offer, but with income passing through to shareholders as it does in a partnership. Thus, they are similar in many ways to S corporations. The primary differences between S corporations and LLCs is that S corporations are limited to 75 shareholders, while there is no limit on the number of shareholders an LLC can have. Furthermore, S corporations, like any corporation, are perpetual. They are considered a legal entity of their own. LLCs are not, and technically dissolve when a partner leaves or dies.

LLCs can be more complicated than S corporations to set up, and in some localities cost more than corporations to form. The tax status can vary from state to state, as well, a factor that could cause problems if you plan to operate in more than one state. If you form an LLC, be sure to seek the advice of an attorney and an accountant to be sure everything is set up properly.

Q **Is there any other way of working with someone else?**

If you don't want to form a partnership or corporation, the other way to work with other people is to hire them as employees or retain them under an independent contractor or subcontractor agreement. In either case, the individuals are just working in return for money.

12.

What Equipment, Supplies, and Services Do I Need to Get Started?

Whenever I meet someone who says they have an office in their basement I conjure up images of the first home office I ever saw. It was my father's workshop—a tiny area off to one side of the basement steps that was furnished with an old, scarred workbench and a beat-up metal stool. There, under the glare of a single, bare light-bulb, my father would spend his evenings changing vacuum tubes in TV chassis and trying to coax the broken-down sets back into working order for the people who had asked him to do the repairs.

Television sets and technology have changed a lot since then. And so have the equipment and supply needs of many home offices and away-from-home small businesses. Most businesses today couldn't exist without one or more microcomputers; others feel the world will crash in around them if their facsimile machine breaks down or their Internet connection is unavailable. Some still function quite well with nothing more high-tech than a telephone and a file box.

The variety of equipment available today can make it quite confusing at times to know just what to buy. Generally, if you remember to let the business dictate what equipment you need rather than your emotions, you'll make the right choices. Here, though, are some guidelines to help you determine what you may need when you are starting out.

Q ## Can I work at the kitchen table?

One of the great things about working for yourself is you can work anywhere you find convenient. That means you could work at the kitchen table, the dining room table, the coffee table, or the backyard picnic table. In fact, if the work that needs to be done requires nothing more than a paper, pencil, and your imagination you could plop your body into an oversized tire tube and work while you cool your heels in the backyard swimming pool. What you should consider in choosing a permanent spot to work is how you will keep your work materials organized so they are always together. If you don't want to make space for a formal office in your home at first, buy an inexpensive file box that will let you keep all your papers and notes together in an orderly fashion.

Q ## Do I need to get business cards?

Business cards are one of the least costly and most helpful promotional tools. The card tells people what you do and puts that information in a format they can easily store in a wallet, copy into a phone directory, or file in a card directory so they can have your name and number the next time they need what you sell. Thus, you should get business cards and get in the habit of handing them out to everyone you possibly can.

Q ## Do I need to give myself a title on my business card?

If you are trying to give people the impression your company is bigger than a one- or two-person business, or if you like titles, you can give yourself a title, such as president. If you don't like titles and don't have to impress anyone, you don't have to use a title. The name of your business and your name, address, and phone number should be all you need to include.

Q ## Do I need business stationery?

Business stationery is another essential. Even if you don't often write business letters, there may be times when you need to write to suppliers or customers. If you want your letters to look professional and important, you need letterhead stationery and envelopes printed with your business name.

If you don't think you will need business stationery often, use your computer and printer to print your own, or order just a small quantity from a quick-print shop. After seeing how long it takes to use it up, you can reorder a larger quantity if appropriate. Don't wait until the day before you need the stationery, however. It can take a week to two weeks for a printer to print a job.

Q ## Do I need expensive business stationery?

The type of business you run will dictate how impressive your business stationery needs to be. If you run a simple service business and get customers because of your efficiency and your reasonable prices, very expensive-looking stationery would be a poor choice. Customers would be likely to equate expensive-looking stationery with an expensive service.

If you are in a business where you are expected to be dignified and highly professional, however, you will need to use the best quality paper you can afford.

Your printer should have samples of different papers, stationery designs, and type styles available. He or she may also have books of pictures or symbols you could use if you want artwork on the letterhead, business card, and envelope. You can also purchase stationery by mail from several different companies. These companies all have catalogs showing available designs.

IMPORTANT NOTE

Be sure whatever paper supplies or forms you buy work with your printer before ordering in large quantities. Certain papers are too thick to feed through your printer or photocopier, some make the ink from an inkjet printer look blurry or smudge easily; some won't accept the ink from a laser printer properly (the ink will crack when the paper is folded or will smudge). If you use a laser printer, watch out for raised ink letterhead and envelopes. Many raised inks melt from the heat of laser printers.

Many printers and mail order houses are reasonably knowledgeable about what paper works with what printers and are more than happy to help you make the right choice. Be sure to tell them what kind of equipment you will be using, and if there is any question about what will work, ask them to give or send you a couple of sheets of paper to test.

Q **What about order forms? Where do I get them?**

Order forms, sales call forms, invoice forms, purchase order forms, estimate forms, and even specialty labels can all be ordered with your name printed on them from a local print shop or by mail. They can be purchased as loose sheets or as continuous forms for computer printers that have a tractor feed mechanism (a gear with teeth that catches the holes in computer paper and pulls the paper through the machine).

If you just need forms occasionally and don't want to buy printed forms, you can get packages of forms that have a space to type in your name and address at most office supply stores. Or, if you have a computer, you can use either a word processor, page layout program, or a database program to print out forms as you need them.

If you use a popular accounting program such as Quicken, QuickBooks, or PeachTree, look for invoice forms and laser or inkjet checks that are specifically designed to work with your software. That way all of your data will line up in the right place on the forms and checks.

A few of the mail order companies that print forms and stationery are:

New England Business Service, Inc. (Nebs)
500 Main Street
Groton, MA 01471
(800) 225-6380
http://www.nebs.com

Paper Direct
P.O. Box 2970
Colorado Springs, CO 80901-2970
(800) 272-7377
http://www.paperdirect.com

Quill Corp.
100 Schelter Road
Lincolnshire, IL 60069-3621
(800) 789-1331
http://www.quillcorp.com

Q How much business stationery and how many forms should I buy?

If you have no way of estimating how many letters you will write or how many orders you will get, order the minimum quantities of stationery at the start. For a home business, five hundred letterheads and envelopes will be sufficient unless you are planning to do a large personalized mailing. (In that case order enough stationery to do the mailing as well as a few hundred pieces for routine mail.) Although you can get quantity discounts, there's no point buying and having to find a suitable storage place for a few thousand letterheads and envelopes if it will take you 2 or 3 years to use up that many. If you need order forms and invoices, you might want to use the packaged ones from an office supply store and fill in your business name until you determine how many forms you will need each month.

Q Can I make my own stationery on a laser printer?

Yes, you can if you are using a printer that makes clear printouts and the print doesn't crack or rub off on the pages. Unless you have a good sense of design, look for and use templates that come with your word processing software. The templates will help you choose appropriate size and style type for your letterhead. Paper Direct, which manufactures a variety of colorful preprinted papers suitable for business stationery sells templates as well. Their templates help you position your company name and contact information on their papers as well as help you choose the right size and typeface.

Printing your own stationery is a good idea if you only need a small quantity of paper. If you use a lot of stationery, you'll find it preferable to have it printed professionally. Printing envelopes is still difficult on many inkjet and laser printers, so you may find it preferable to have envelopes printed professionally. If you find you don't need them all, so they won't go to waste cover the company name with a home address label and use them for personal correspondence.

Q **Do I need a separate phone line if I work at home?**

Unless you live alone it is advisable to have a separate telephone line for your business. Having the separate line will let you always answer the phone with a business greeting and will prevent ten-year-old Johnny from picking up an extension and trying to dial a friend's home while you are trying to land a new customer. Equally important, having the separate line makes it much simpler to track business phone expenses for your tax records.

If you are concerned about the price of a separate telephone line for the business, consider less expensive distinctive ring service. It will make incoming business calls sound different (so you will know to answer the phone with your business name). A separate line is preferable, however, so callers can get through if your teenager, your spouse, or your computer ties up the telephone for lengthy periods of time. In fact, many homebased business owners find they need at least three telephone lines: one for the family, one for incoming business calls, and one to use for Internet access.

Q **If I run my business from home will I have to get a business phone line?**

Whether you will need a commercial phone line instead of a residential line will depend on your local telephone company rules. In some localities, you only are required to get a business (commercial) line if you want a listing in the yellow pages. In other parts of the country, other rules apply. Call the business office of your local telephone company or the utilities commission of your state to find out what the rules are.

Q **Should I get an 800 number?**

Some small businesses find that having an 800 number for orders boosts sales, though others find they get few extra calls on their 800 line. Since it is possible to get 800 service for less than $7 a month with calls charged at 10 cents a minute or less, it may be worthwhile. One software developer says his monthly 800 costs are under $70, a price that is more than made up, he feels, by the extra orders he gets.

Q **Should I get an answering machine?**

You need some way for customers to leave you messages when there is no one in your office to take calls. The options available are:

- an answering machine
- an answering service
- your own in-house voice mail system
- voice mail purchased from a private vendor or from the phone company

A *conventional answering machine* is the least expensive option. You can get a reliable answering machine in discount stores for under $70 if you watch for sales. While you can get machines with all sorts of bells and whistles, the useful features are a voice-activated message recording system (this makes the machine keep recording as long as the caller keeps talking) and beeperless remote call-in (which lets you call the machine from any touch-tone phone to retrieve messages or even change the message). Other features you may find useful are the ability to turn off the answering machine from an extension phone (handy when the answering machine is downstairs and someone picks up the upstairs extension), the ability to answer two lines, automatic time and date stamping, and the ability to choose your own call-retrieval code (the three-digit number you punch in to retrieve messages from a phone when you are away from the office).

Answering services that use live operators to take calls are preferred by some businesses—particularly those who must be notified of emergency situations. Some people who have used answering services complain, however, about messages being incomplete or that the operators don't get the right phone numbers or forget to give them the messages. Thus, if you plan to use an answering service with live operators it would be a good idea to ask other businesspeople in your community which service is the best to use.

Your own microcomputer-based voice mail system can be handy if you have an IBM or compatible microcomputer system and enough storage space and power to handle the voice messaging system. These computer-based voice mail systems work—as far as the caller is concerned—just like the voice mail systems they hear when they call large corporations. In other words, they get a menu of choices such as "Press one to leave a message; press two to place an order; press three for customer support . . ." You can even program the systems to call-forward incoming calls to another number if you want. The main disadvantage of these systems is they take up a lot of disk space. Computer programmers and others who have to keep up with the latest computer technology sometimes dedicate their outdated PCs to voice mail functions.

Commercial voice mail systems are offered by some local telephone companies. Paging services often offer a voice mail option that will call your beeper when messages have been left for you in voice mail.

Q **Is call waiting a good service to get?**

Call waiting—which signals you that there is another call coming in and lets you put the first caller on hold while you see who the second caller is—may be convenient for you, but it can be annoying or even insulting to your customers. If you don't want to miss messages while you are on the telephone, consider using the telephone company's voice mail service, if available, instead of call waiting. The phone company's voice mail would pick up if your line is busy and allow callers to leave a message without disturbing the call in progress.

In addition, if you use a computer to receive or send data over telephone lines, the call-waiting signal interferes with and disconnects the computer call. If you do decide to get call waiting, find out if there are ways to temporarily disable it if you use your computer on your phone line. This feature is not available in all communities.

Q **What about Caller ID?**

Caller identification service is useful for screening calls. Depending on the telephone you purchase, you may also be able to use Caller ID to tell who called and hung up without leaving a message on your answering machine. Whether those features are worth the money or not depends on your viewpoint and way of doing business.

Q **How do I choose a photocopier?**

The best way to choose a copier is to make a list of all the ways you expect to use it. Consider not only your present needs but how you expect to use the copier in the next year or two. Here are some needs to consider:

- How many copies will you make at once?
- How many copies do you expect to make every month?
- How frequently will you need to copy multipage documents?

- How often will you need to collate multipage documents?
- What size are the originals, and will you often need to enlarge or reduce them?
- Will you want to photocopy both sides of a page on the front and back of a single sheet of paper?
- Are you going to be photocopying photographs?
- Will you need to photocopy on both legal- and letter-sized paper frequently?
- How much space do you have available for the photocopier?
- Will you need to photocopy on card stock? Overhead transparencies?

Compare this list of needs to the photocopier equipment available at local discount stores, superstores or shopping clubs, and office equipment dealers, comparing features and prices of various units. Be sure to ask about the price of consumable supplies such as toner. The inexpensive personal photocopiers may cost significantly more per page to run than the more expensive office copiers. To get the best buy you will need to compare all your costs.

In addition to the price of the copier, consider how much paper you can put in paper trays at one time, how many paper trays the unit will work with (if any), whether you can add collating equipment later on if you will need it. Be sure to find out about power requirements, too. The photocopier may draw so much power that it will require its own separate electrical line.

If you have any special uses intended for the copier (for instance, copying onto card stock, onto papers with rough or textured surfaces, or copying photographs), test the copier with the actual work you want to do. Look at the quality and speed of the output. If space is at a premium in your office, note whether the top of the copier unit (called the platen) slides back and forth during copying or is stationery, and if it slides back and forth, how much room it needs to operate.

Finally, ask about guarantees, maintenance, and service agreements. If you will be using the machine daily or if it is very heavy, you are likely to want someone to come to your office to service the unit, so ask if a service contract is available and what it costs.

Q **Do I need a facsimile (fax) machine?**

Facsimile (fax) machines are used to send or receive all sorts of printed documents, orders, letters, etc. So there's a good chance you will need fax capabilities.

However, depending on what other equipment you own, you may not need to purchase a stand-alone fax machine.

If you are using a fairly recent model computer, for instance, it probably is equipped with a fax modem. The fax modem will allow you to receive incoming faxes and to send out faxes of any computerized document. If you have to fax something that isn't on your computer, however, a fax modem will be of little use unless you also have a scanner and scan the document into your computer.

If you are purchasing a new printer and only get or have to send a few faxes a day, you can save space and money by purchasing a printer that will send and receive faxes as well as print out documents (see multifunction devices below).

If you must buy a stand-alone fax, the good news is that prices have fallen considerably in recent years. You can get a plain paper fax for under $300 in many parts of the country. (Plain paper faxes print out onto standard papers using inkjet or laser ink. They stay readable much longer than thermal printouts do and are preferable to thermal faxes as long as you don't need to receive faxes that are longer than standard-size sheets of paper.)

Q **What kind of fax should I get?**

There are two broad categories of fax equipment: stand-alone fax machines and fax modems that work with microcomputers. With a stand-alone machine, you feed printed or handwritten pages into the machine, which scans the documents and converts what it scans to a format that can be sent out over the telephone lines to another fax machine. When you use a fax modem, you use a combination of computer software and hardware to send documents that are stored in your computer to a fax. Incoming faxes are received into your computer and can be printed out, or, with the proper software, converted to a format you can put in a word processor and edit.

Which type of fax to get will depend on how you will use the fax and on your preferences. Here are various questions and options you should consider in making your decision:

▶ Where will you get the documents you need to send out? Are they already printed documents such as contract forms or letters printed on your letterhead? Are they formatted documents or drawings that reside in your computer?

- Will you need to send photos or drawings via fax?
- Will you need to send copies of handwritten documents or printed documents that have handwritten notations on them?
- What size are the documents you will want to send or receive? Standard letter size or bigger?
- What will you have to do with a document after you get it via fax? Will you need to just look at it and discard it? File it and store it for any length of time? Will you need to get the document into your computer to work on it?
- How often will you need to send or receive fax documents?
- How often will you need to fax documents that aren't stored in your computer? Is there a quick print shop or other business nearby that you can send such documents from if necessary?
- If you are using a fax modem can you launch the software from within any application?

Q **Is it a good idea to buy one machine that functions as a printer, fax, scanner, answering machine, and photocopier instead of purchasing separate devices?**

If you are just buying equipment for the first time, a multifunction device is usually a good choice. It will let you accomplish most of the tasks you need done, at less cost than you'd have to spend to buy separate machines. Furthermore, the multifunction device takes up less space than multiple machines would. Once your business grows, however, you may discover you need a better scanner, or a separate fax or photocopier in addition to the multifunction device. When that happens, your multifunction device can still serve as your printer and as a backup fax, copier, or scanner.

Q **Do I really need a computer?**

Although some businesses can still function without a computer, sooner or later you are going to need one. Your customers want to communicate with you by e-mail, or your suppliers may expect you to order through their web site. Accounting, taxes, general correspondence, sales call notes, tickler files, and many other chores will be easier and faster in the long run to accomplish by computer than they would be manually.

Your customers or attorney may want to send rough drafts of contracts and other documents via computer to eliminate wasted paper, time and overnight mail costs. Parts lists, and price lists, financial planning and estimating, will all be easier by computer. With the right software you may even be able to design your own simple signs, posters, fliers, and ads.

Q **How do I choose a computer?**

To choose a computer you need to start by considering two things:

- What functions you want the computer to perform (word processing, accounting, financial forecasting, graphics, etc.).
- What computer capabilities the majority of your potential customers expect you to have.

Economy and the availability of a friend who has the same type of computer are worth considering, too, but are unimportant if your potential customers all use IBM-compatible computers and you buy a Macintosh. Although there are many programs that have both Macintosh and PC versions available, there can still be some file incompatibility problems. If you don't know what your customers will use and your business isn't graphic arts, your best bet is likely to be an IBM-compatible computer.

If this is your first computer, look for package deals that include the monitor, software, and a printer. (Even if you later decide you need a better printer, it's always useful to have a spare printer.) If at all possible, try to choose a computer that comes "bundled" with Microsoft Office Professional or Microsoft Office Small Business edition. The Microsoft Office products are in widespread use in business and are more powerful and versatile than Microsoft Works, which is often bundled with new computers.

Keep additional software purchases to the minimum at first, focusing on the key application you expect to be using. Each software package takes considerable time to learn to use properly. If you buy several at once, some of them may have new versions out before you get to learn how to use them.

Q **Where can I get detailed information to help choose computer equipment and software?**

Computer hardware, software, and peripherals (printers, scanners, modem, disk drives, etc.) are constantly changing. Read reviews in recent computer magazines and trade magazines to see what programs are most highly praised. Among the computer magazines you might want to look at are *Computer Shopper, PC/Computing, PC World, MacWorld, Small Office Computing*. Your public library should have back issues of at least several of these publications.

If you have access to the web at work or through a friend, read reviews posted on the Internet as well. CNET (http://home.cnet.com) and ZDNET (http://www. zdnet.com) both carry reviews as does CMP's TechWeb (http://www.techweb. com/shopper) and *PC World*'s Internet edition of their magazine (http://www. pcworld.com). Due to the time it takes to get a magazine into print, new product reviews will usually appear on magazines' web sites before they appear in the printed publications.

Q **How often will I need to replace or upgrade my computer?**

It's not unusual to have to upgrade or replace a computer every two to three years, particularly if you want to use the latest software and hardware add-ons. It's not unusual for one-person businesses to spend $2,000 or more per year on computer hardware and software upgrades, replacements, and new purchases. Businesses that require the latest multimedia capabilities usually need to spend more to stay current.

Businesses that just use their computers for word processing, routine spreadsheets, mailing lists, or other business tasks that don't change much from year to year, may be able to upgrade less frequently.

Q **Should I upgrade a computer or replace it when it's outdated?**

The answer to that question will depend on the going price for new computers, whether you just need more memory or need more hard drive space and ports (connections for new devices) and your satisfaction with your current monitor or laptop display. Yet another consideration is whether you have a backup computer system available to you. If you only have one computer and it is two or more years old, it will probably be a wiser decision to purchase a new computer than to upgrade the old one. Among the reasons is that the price for the new system may be equal to or lower than the cost of upgrading, and you may be able to use the old system as a backup for the new one or network it to the new one for added storage space.

Q **How much memory do I need to get with the computer?**

When it comes to memory, the more the better. I would not recommend buying a computer with less than 64 megabytes of memory. Better would be 128 megs of RAM. If you will make extensive use of graphics, page layout, or multimedia software, you may want even more RAM.

Q **How big should the hard drive be?**

Like memory, the bigger the better. If your budget allows try to get a computer with at least a 9-gigabyte hard drive.

Q **I don't have a lot of room in my apartment. Is it a good idea to get one of those flat screen monitors?**

Flat screen monitors take up much less space than conventional monitors. Thus they are desirable if space is tight. Their pricing is still a big drawback, though. You can expect to pay several hundred dollars more for a flat screen monitor than you would for a conventional monitor of the same size. Furthermore, some people find them hard to look at for long periods of time. If you are considering purchasing one, try them out at stores, and try to make your purchase from a retail or mail order source that will let you return it for a full refund if you are unhappy with it.

Q **Could I use a notebook computer instead of a regular desktop computer?**

If you are comfortable looking at the screen and working at the keyboard you could. Today's notebook computers are extremely powerful and many models are available that have almost as much hard disk space as desktop computers. Some have display screens that are quite big, too. The biggest drawback may be the cost if you don't need the notebook to travel. Notebooks can cost $500 to $1,000 more than comparable desktop computers.

Q **What should I look for in a notebook computer?**

Like all desktop computers, the features and prices of notebook computers change every few months, so the smartest thing to do is to check the sources listed above for reviews and comparisons of the latest laptop computers. Among the essentials, however are:

> **Price.** Compare several models that are available in stores and magazines, and also check the prices on models such as those for Dell Computers, which are sold only over the Internet or by mail order.

> **Weight:** under 6 pounds with the AC adaptor is desirable. Lighter models are available but some have smaller keyboards and may be difficult to type on.

> **Processor and speed:** at least a Pentium II or equivalent with a speed of 366mHz or better

> **Display:** is the display comfortable to look at and easy to read? Display screens that are 13 inches or bigger are easier to view than smaller screens, but can be difficult to open on airplanes if you travel frequently and expect to work on the plane. Check the sharpness of the display as well. Active matrix displays are the sharpest and easiest to read.

> **Memory:** Get at least 64 megs of memory. More would be better if you can afford the extra price

> **Hard disk size and speed:** Four gigabytes is the minimum you should consider, and even that can be restrictive if you use the notebook often or if you use a number of big programs such as Microsoft Office, a graphics program, and a web design program.

> **Modem speed, cost, and convenience.** Is the modem included in the purchase price? If so, is it as fast as modems in most desktop computers? If the modem is priced separately, how much extra will it cost? Can you use the modem while the computer is attached to a network?

> **Drives:** can you use a floppy drive, CD-ROM (or DVD), or ZIP drive with the notebook? Can you use them at one time? Can you use the drives while you are operating on battery?

> **Keyboard:** comfortable and convenient to type on. Test the keyboard, if at all possible. Some have tiny keys or don't have a place to rest your wrists while typing.

- **Battery:** How long will the battery last without recharging? Three hours or more without recharging is best, unless you plan to carry a spare battery. Find out what the cost of replacement batteries is, too.

Q What kind of printer should I get to go with the computer?

Before you decide what type of printer to get, you will need to know what kinds of documents you plan to print out. If you have to print out any multiple part forms, you will need an impact printer. An impact printer is one that has a mechanism that produces an image by hitting an inked ribbon, which then hits the page. Impact printers you can buy today are usually dot matrix printers. They are the printers that use conventional-looking computer paper (the kind with the holes along the edges).

Laser printers and inkjet printers (which are the printers you see most often in magazines and in stores) are not impact printers and therefore won't produce an impression on the second or third sheets of multipart forms.

In addition to whether or not you have to print multipart forms, you need to consider:

- The speed of the printer. Find out how long the printer takes to accept and print a single page of text, how long it takes to accept and print a single page of graphics, and how long it takes to print out multiple copies of a single page. Be skeptical about the time stated in the manufacturer's specifications for the printer. Their "typical" page may have much less text or graphics on it than what you would normally print.

- The quality of the image the printer produces. The quality of the image depends partly on something called resolution, or dots per inch (dpi), and partly on the way the characters (fonts) are generated. Laser printers usually print faster than inkjet printers. The printouts are usually more suitable for camera-ready copy and for delivering black and white work to clients. Color inkjet printers are more versatile, however. At some point you may find you need both a color inkjet and a laser printer.

- The cost and availability of ink cartridges. Find out the cost of the cartridge and the number of pages you can expect to print with each cartridge or ribbon. An ink cartridge that costs $17.98 but only prints 300 pages will cost you about $.06 per page for ink. A cartridge for a different type of printer that costs $100 but prints out 3,000 pages would be about half that amount per page.

▸ The way pages are processed queued up for printing. Some printers will let you queue up a number of files at one time to print, and then let you go back to using the computer for something else while the printer churns out pages. Other printers make you wait until the printer is finished printing to move on to other tasks.

▸ The availability of service. Where can you get the printer serviced and how long will it take if it breaks down? Printers tend to break down much more frequently than any other device.

▸ Portability. Will you be traveling? Will you need to print documents while you are traveling? If so, you might want to look at the printers designed to fit in a briefcase, at least as a backup printer. This type of printer probably isn't going to be suitable for your primary printer, however.

▸ How many sheets of paper can be stacked in the printer at once? Less important, perhaps, than all the other considerations, but it is annoying to send a document to the printer and then find a message on your screen saying the printer is out of paper.

▸ The printer's ability to handle heavy paper and/or envelopes. Printers vary in their ability to print on thick paper and envelopes. Envelopes are of particular importance to test. Some printers, even though they claim to be able to handle envelopes, just don't do a good job of it. Either the method of feeding the envelopes is slow and laborious, or the printer twists the envelope so printing is skewed, or it just kind of munches the corners or leaves black ink smudges on the envelopes. If at all possible, test the printer you want to buy with the type of envelopes you want to use.

Q **What will all of this cost?**

You can buy IBM-compatible computers that are powerful enough for small business needs for as little as $1,000—and sometimes less. If you need speed and a lot of memory and software, you will probably pay closer to $2,000 to $3,000. Inkjet printers can be purchased for as little as $100, and are sometimes free with the purchase of a new computer. Good laser printers and multifunction devices are several hundred dollars. Monitors (the computer screen) aren't always part of the price, so be sure you know exactly what you are going to get for your money. Watch out for very-low cost computers. They may not be powerful enough for your needs long term, or to get a computer at the advertised price you may be required to subscribe to an online service for several years, adding hundreds of dollars to your actual cost.

Q **What will I need to connect to the Internet?**

Most new computers come with a modem that will let you access the Internet over standard phone lines. In addition to the built-in modem you'll need to subscribe to a service that gives you access to the Internet. You can do that by subscribing to a large national or international network like America Online or Microsoft Network or by purchasing Internet services from a local Internet Service Provider (ISP). If you travel for business and want to be able to access the Internet from any place you travel without making long-distance phone calls, your best bet would be to choose a nationally available service.

Q **Are there any other gadgets I'd need?**

If you get a computer system you should be sure to get a surge protector or an uninterruptible power supply. The surge protector is the least expensive and offers some protection to your equipment against power spikes (too much power) that sometimes come through lines. A power spike can destroy computer circuitry, so a surge protector is well worth getting. If you have a lot of very important data on your system or have very expensive computer equipment, you will probably want to price the uninterruptible power supplies.

If you get either, however, it is a good idea to unplug the computer in a thunderstorm. Nothing can survive a lightning hit. You should also unhook the modem from the computer during a storm, since telephone lines can carry damaging power surges if hit by lightning.

You will need a practical way of backing up your computer data, too. Although many computers today have a read/write CD-ROM drive or a ZIP drive that can be used for backups, once you get more data than will fit on the CD-ROM or the ZIP cartridge, backups become a chore. Thus you may also find you want to purchase a tape backup system.

The nature of your business and your personal preferences for how you work will determine whether you need to purchase other equipment. Palm computing devices, digital cameras, and scanners are useful equipment for some businesses, and fun toys or tax deductions for others. Your best bet in choosing equipment for the first time is to buy just the basics, then once your business is running, make additional purchase decisions based on what equipment you need to work efficiently and meet customer demands.

Q **What other office equipment will I need?**

Wrist rests that are designed to help avoid carpal tunnel syndrome, a good ergo-dynamically designed chair, and a work surface that is the right height for you are essential if you will be spending more than an hour or two a day at the computer. The cost of such items is small when you consider the back and wrist injuries they will help you avoid. An adjustable copy holder is useful if you do a lot of typing, too. You will also need at least one file cabinet to hold essential business papers, correspondence, etc. Bookshelves are also useful to have in the office, as is a storage cabinet. Cellular phones, beepers, and other telecommunications devices may be useful, but unless your business is a service business where you travel daily from one customer to another, you probably won't need a cell phone or a beeper to start out.

GETTING TO KNOW THE WEB

Little in recent history has changed the way we work and interact with the world as much as online services and the Internet. Although the Internet was virtually unheard of in the early 1990s, today it is routinely used by consumers and business people to do everything from exchange mail, send contracts, check train or movie schedules, order clothing, purchase parts, find jobs and locate service providers. In short, it has fast become as essential to many people as the telephone and fax.

Yet there are still many small business owners who aren't sure how to take full advantage of it as a business tool.

If you are one of these people, if you just haven't had the time to learn as much about the Internet as you'd like, or if you know a little but aren't sure about the best way to put your business on the web, this section should help answer your questions.

Q **What is the Internet, anyway?**

The Internet is a global network of computers that are linked for information exchange. To understand the concept, picture a map of the country with its network of highway systems linking towns and cities together. The Internet is much like that, but instead of physical cities, there are electronic communities and data centers, and instead of roadways there are telephone, cable, and high-speed telecommunications lines that connect them. Now, picture yourself as a huge giant, with one foot in one city, and your other foot in a city thousands of miles away. You reach out and pick up a new car from a third city, then reach out and drop a letter on your uncle's desk in a fourth city. And you do it all without changing position. That, essentially, is the essence—and the power of the Internet.

Q **What's the difference between the Internet and the Web?**

Technically, the Web (short for the World Wide Web) is one of the networks on the Internet. However, most people use the words interchangeably as I have done throughout this book.

Q **How are small businesses and professionals using the Internet?**

Small businesses and self-employed professionals are using the Internet as a productivity tool, a marketing tool, and a way to conduct transactions. They are also using it to gain name recognition, provide customer support, and to tap into networks of other professionals to exchange ideas, tips, and hints.

By establishing an Internet presence they can communicate any time of the day or night with customers, suppliers, and other business owners. They are selling to businesses and consumers who would never find them without the Internet, and they are gathering research to plan their business or make informed decisions all without leaving their office.

In my own business, I use the web as a means of delivering my product (home office and small business information) to two sets of customers. One set of customers is the Small Office/Home Office (SOHO) businesses who will use the information we provide as a free service through our BusinessKnowHow.com, Business-KnowHow.net, and America Online sites. The other set of customers are the online services, the government agencies, and our advertisers, all of whom pay us to create the content so they can get their messages out through us to that same audience.

So, for my business, the web is an economical delivery system. Instead of mailing a printed publication to our audience daily, we distribute our information on the Internet. And, we reach far more people than we'd reach by mail, at a much lower cost.

At the same time our web site and online forums serve a marketing function as well. When we have specific products such as books to sell, we promote them to our mailing list and in our forums, again reaching far more people at much lower cost than would be possible any other way.

And we use online services to facilitate communications with staff and customers and to provide support and networking opportunities to our forum members.

Other businesses are using their web sites to sell directly to customers far beyond their geographic area, to advertise their products and services, to conduct sales presentations without traveling long distances, and for almost every other imaginable business task.

Q   How do I get on the Internet?

You need a computer, a phone line, a modem, a local or national Internet Service Provider (ISP), and software to use the Internet. You also need a way to dial out to the Internet provider. If you have a recent model computer you probably have all of that paraphernalia built into it. Software for several commercial online services (Microsoft Network, America Online, Compuserve, and possibly others) is likely to be in a folder called Online Services. If you want to use one of those services for access to the Internet all you have to do is load the software and follow the instructions to log on. You'll need to have a credit card ready to give for billing purposes. If you don't want to use any of those services, you can also find local ISPs that will sell you Internet access. You would then need a web browser such as Netscape Navigator or Internet Explorer and a dial-up connection (which is part of the Windows operating system on PCs).

Q   What costs will I incur?

Depending on the which Internet service provider you use, you'll be charged a fee for Internet access that may range from $10 to $25 a month. You'll also be charged a fee by your local phone company for your telephone usage.

TIP

Check to see which Internet service provider phone numbers are located in your calling area. If you have to make toll calls to reach an Internet service provider you may wind up with a big phone bill. You may be able to save money by paying for a year Internet access at one time. Try the service on a monthly basis for a month or two at the beginning to be sure you will use it and are satisfied with it.

If you want a web site with your own domain name, you will also have to pay a fee to register the domain and to have your site hosted (made available to users on the web). The fee for domain name registration for the most common domains (.com, .net, and .org) is $70 for the first two years and $35 thereafter through Network Solutions (http://www. networksolutions.com). You could also register through Register.com.

Web site hosting ranges in price from about $15 to $50 and up per month, depending on the services you need and who does the hosting. If you don't need your own domain name yet, you can create a free web site on America Online, Netscape, or MSN, and at many other locations on the web.

Q **Is there any reason to use an online service like America Online instead of a less expensive local ISP?**

If you travel for business and use the Internet often, you'll want to use an ISP that has phone access lines in many parts of the country. If you don't and you need to connect to the Internet while you're gone, you'll incur long-distance charges for the call to reach the connection that gives you access to the Internet.

Another reason to use a large national online service is that they tend to help organize the Internet and provide a lot of content of their own.

Q **How do I get and send e-mail?**

When you sign up for an online service you'll get a chance to choose an e-mail address. This address will consist of three parts: the name you choose, the symbol @, and the domain name of the site from which you got your e-mail address. For instance, my e-mail address on America Online is JanetAC1@aol.com. (Janet AC1 is the name I chose; aol.com is the domain name for America Online.) My e-mail address on my BusinessKnowHow.com web site is attard@businessknowhow.com. Give your complete e-mail address to friends and business associates if you want them to send you mail. You can test the e-mail address to see if it's working by sending yourself e-mail.

To send someone else e-mail you have to know their e-mail address. You put their e-mail address in the "TO:" line of your e-mail program. Fill in a subject line and write your message. Then press the SEND button in your e-mail program to send it on its way.

Q **What's a screen name?**

A screen name is the term AOL uses to designate the first part of your e-mail address (the part that comes before the @ symbol). When you are sending mail to another person who has an AOL address and you are using an AOL account, you don't need to include the @aol.com part of the e-mail address.

Q **Is e-mail the same as a web site?**

No. E-mail stands for electronic mail. It's a personal message sent from one individual to another, much like regular mail is sent from one individual to another. If you have a web site, you may have your electronic mail delivered to the web site, but you don't have to have your own web site to have an e-mail address or get electronic mail. Internet Service Providers will set up a private electronic mail box for you as part of your Internet access.

Q **How do you know if you have e-mail?**

If you have mail, your e-mail program will usually notify you when you dial up your Internet access connection.

Q **What is an attachment?**

An e-mail attachment is a document, graphic, or other element (such as a mini program) that gets sent along with your e-mail; in effect, it's like a little package pinned onto the e-mail letter. Never open attachments that are sent to you by someone you don't know well. They sometimes contain viruses or trojans that can wipe out your computer system.

Q **What's a web site?**

A web site is a specific location on the web. Think of it as a house or building on a street. It could have one thing in it, or it could have many different nooks and crannies. The actual features depend on what the owner of the site wants to add.

Like a house or building, a web site has a unique address. The address is called a URL, which is short for Uniform Resource Locator. Most (but not all) web sites start with http://www and are followed by a period and the actual name of the site. Thus the URL for BusinessKnowHow.com is http://www.businessknowhow.com. Web site addresses are traditionally written in all lowercase letters.

Q **Some web site names end in .com, others in .net, .org, .gov, or .mil. What do the different endings on web site names mean?**

The endings are supposed to indicate the type of web site they are. The .com designation is supposed to indicate commercial services (and usually does); the .net was originally supposed to be used by networks; and the .org designation was originally to be used for nonprofit organizations. The .gov designation indicates a government web site in most cases, and a .mil ending indicates a military site. However, there seems to be no real restriction on the use of any of these. You do not have to be a nonprofit to use the .org extension to the domain name, and .net names are increasingly being used by businesses because all the good .com names have been used up.

TIP Some companies buy up all versions of their domain name to prevent any other company from using it. Doing so is much cheaper than suing if someone tries to use your trademark as their web site name.

Q **How can I find things on the Internet or on online services?**

There are a number of "portals" such as America Online, Netscape, CompuServe, Yahoo, Lycos, AltaVista, Excite, and HotBot that create vast indices of web sites and serve as electronic entry points to the Internet. Most of the portals organize their indices into categories and subcategories creating menu-type listings that help you find web sites of interest. All of them let you search for web sites by keywords as well.

Q **What do you need to set up a web site?**

A web site, technically, is nothing more than some files on a computer that serve (makes available) the files to web users. Although you could set up a personal computer to serve files to the Internet, doing so is impractical because personal computers aren't likely to be as powerful as computers used to serve up Internet pages. Nor are they likely to be hooked to a high-speed connection 24 hours a day. Thus, most people use Internet hosting services to host their web site and make it available to web users.

In addition to a hosting service, you will need a means to create web pages, a way to digitize (convert to computer format) images if you plan to use any on the site, a way to optimize those digitized images for web use, and a way to transfer your web pages to the host site.

If you have the patience to learn how to write the HTML code used in web pages, you could create them with a text editor like notepad. Another option is to use the HTML conversion features in Microsoft Word or Publisher to create web pages. But if you are going to create your own web pages, you will probably get better results if you purchase a web page layout program such as Microsoft FrontPage, Macromedia's Dreamweaver, or some other program specifically created to make web sites.

You could bring images to a store like Kinko's or to one of the big office supply stores to have them digitized. Or you might want to use purchased computer clip art to add color to your web pages. Transferring all the files to the web can be done using a File Transfer Protocol (FTP) program. You can download shareware versions of FTP programs from web sites that feature shareware such as Paulspicks.com. (Shareware is software you can try before you buy it.)

Or, you can hire a web page developer to create a site for you. If you have little time and less patience to play with computer programs, finding someone to create your site is probably preferable.

In addition to the software and hardware that will be needed to produce the web pages, you will need content to put on the site. This will include general information about the name of the business, individuals to contact, phone and fax numbers, and it will also include information you want your visitors to see such as your catalog or articles you've written.

Q Where can I find a web hosting service?

You can find hosting services advertised in your local newspaper and advertised in various places on the web or in Internet magazines. You can also get some hosting services (but not hosting of your own domain name) free as part of an AOL account or free for joining many other communities on the web. The free web sites are good for practicing web building skills and getting some limited promotion; they generally won't let you use your own domain name. In addition, you may have more difficulty getting your set listed in search engines if you don't have your own domain name.

Q How can you sell products on the Internet?

To sell products on the Internet you'll need a merchant account (so you can accept credit card transactions) and a secure server (an encrypted area that makes it safer to send credit card information) and an order form or shopping cart software. (Shopping cart software lets you buy multiple things at one time.) Your hosting service can either provide the secure server and shopping cart software or suggest ways to get them. Once you have all those elements in place, you need to get living, breathing customers to find your web site and look through your offerings.

Q How do you get your web site found?

You will have to make an ongoing effort to let people know about your web site so they come visit. One way to do that is to tell everyone you know about the site and how to reach it. Another is to get the site registered in the key portal directories and search engines. In addition you'll want to include your web site on your business card, on your letterhead, and in your sales literature.

Another good way to get your web site found is to look for communities on the Internet and online services that match the demographic profile of the people you want to find your web site. Look for discussion areas and chats to participate in and places to send articles. Participate in these areas, join in discussions, and become a trusted resource. Whenever you sign your name, include your web site URL along with your signature.

Q How do you find a reliable hosting service?

The best way to find a reliable host site is to ask other businesspeople for recommendations. Make a point of asking people who have bought hosting services for themselves. You want to find someone who knows from experience what kind of service the company provides. What you don't want is to get a referral to a hosting company just because someone is a friend of the owner or owes him or her a favor.

Ask the people you talk to how often the site is down and for how long at any time. Find out about customer support, too. How quickly does the host company respond to routine questions? How soon to emergency situations? Is there anyone there in the middle of the night in case a server goes down?

If you are having someone create your web pages for you and they are also providing hosting, ask if they own the equipment on which the site will be hosted or if they outsource that to a hosting company themselves. If so, get the name of the company. Call the company and ask questions, such as how long they've been in business and how big they are. The last thing you want is your business web site hosted on someone's old PC in a damp basement. If you don't want your web site to suddenly disappear, be sure it's hosted on servers at a company that's not likely to go belly up in the night.

In choosing your web host, consider, too, how the site will be used. If you are having databases or other work programmed for you ask your programmer if you will need any special server or capabilities on the server.

Other considerations are how many Internet lines the server has coming in and whether they are redundant (if one route is down, will traffic be routed through another connection?). If your usage will be high, look for a place that has experience with other high traffic sites. Better, if you have someone designing the site, find out who his or her customers are and where they were placed and what their experiences were.

Q How do you get advertisers for a web site?

To get advertisers you generally need to have a lot of good content and have enough traffic to generate 50,000 or more page views a month at the very minimum. If you have fewer visitors than that, consider swapping ads with noncompeting web sites that sell to the same audience.

Q **Do companies that claim to get you good position in the search engines really work?**

They may, but there's not much that they can do for you that you can't do yourself—and probably do better because of your knowledge and enthusiasm about your business. To get started, take an hour or two to learn the basics of site promotion. You can find out what the search engines and directory services look for in sites by browsing through web sites such as selfpromotion.com, searchenginewatch.com, and clickz.com. Put suggestions you find there to work on your site, and once they are implemented then register your site with the leading search engines and directories. Those include:

Yahoo—http://www.yahoo.com
America Online—http://www.aol.com
Netscape—http://www.netscape.com
The Microsoft Network (MSN)—http://www.msn.com
The Open Directory Project—http://www.dmoz.org
Excite—http://www.excite.com
Lycos—http://www.lycos.com
Alta Vista—http://www.altavista.com
About.com—http://www.about.com
Snap—http://www.snap.com
Go.com—http://www.go.com

In addition, you may also want to consider a paid listing for your business name or keywords on GoTo.com (http://www.goto.com). Depending on how popular the search term you want is, this can be quite affordable since you pay only for click-throughs (when people actually click on your listing and go to your site).

Q **Can I send unsolicited e-mail to get customers for my business?**

Unsolicited e-mail (called "junk e-mail" or spam) has become a major problem for online services, ISPs, and for Internet users. The ease and low cost of e-mail made unsolicited mailings popular among people promoting X-rated web sites and questionable business opportunities, as well as people promoting legitimate business opportunities and products for sale. However, the volume of junk mail (along with the distasteful nature of some of it) clogs Internet gateways and wastes the time of recipients.

As a result several states have passed laws prohibiting junk e-mail, and most online services and ISPs forbid account holders from sending any unsolicited bulk mail. If you try to send it and get caught, you could have your e-mail account suspended. If you have a web site and send junk mail from your own web site, the hosting company may remove your web site and all records of it from their servers. Bottom line: don't send bulk unsolicited e-mail.

Q **Can I post ads for my product or service on message boards on online services or the web?**

Many online forums and web sites have specific areas set up to post classified ads. Restrict your postings to those areas and follow any rules or guidelines posted in such areas.

Q **How else can I promote my business on the Internet and online services?**

The best way to promote your business on a budget is by finding appropriate communities and participating in them the way you would in your local business networks. Be a regular contributor to the group, and when you post messages on boards be sure to include your e-mail address (if allowed) along with your name in a signature line. If the board or mailing list allows, include your phone number, but observe for a few days first. Many services such as BusinessKnowHow.com do not allow phone numbers or addresses to be posted as part of the Internet signature.

Q **Where can I find experts and other small businesses online?**

The Business Know-How forum (keyword Business Know-How) and the professional forums (keyword professional forums) on America Online have some of the best message boards for small and homebased business owners. You may also find mailing lists for your industry on the web (professional journals are often a good way to find the names of these mailing lists). Some of the other portal sites have busy bulletin board areas for small businesses as well.

Q **Is there any way to locate web sites that let me post free classified ads?**

You can go to any of the major portals and search for the term "free classified ads" and you'll be shown a list of web sites to visit. One to start with is http://www.freeclassifiedlinks.com, which contains links to hundreds of web sites that allow visitors to post free classified ads.

Q **How can I find someone to create my web site?**

The best way is to ask other small businesses for referrals to people they have used and liked. Find out what experience the web site developer has and ask for references. Ask to see sites they have created for other people. Consider whether you like the designs and how easy or difficult they make it to find information on the pages. Look for phone numbers of the companies the sites were created for (there is usually contact information somewhere on the site) and call and ask if the company was satisfied with the work.

Q **What will it cost me to have someone develop my web site for me?**

That depends on what you are doing with it, and whether you know yourself what you want on it. The more complex you want the site, and the more you change your mind once the developer starts, the higher your costs will be. Most web site developers who are experienced charge $50 to $75 an hour or more for their work, so indecision and changing priorities can get expensive.

If ongoing costs will be a concern, ask the developers you are considering if they can set up the web site so you can maintain it yourself without programming charges. There are ways to set up sites so routine changes can be made in pages and standardized new pages can be added without knowing any HTML. Adding that capability may be a bit costly up front, but if you expect to make frequent changes it's advisable.

Be sure you find out in advance from the developer who will own the designs and layouts. If you want to own them, get it in writing and make sure the developer delivers all the files to you before making the final payment.

III.

The Brass Tacks:
Finding Customers,
Getting Paid

13.

How to Find Customers
for What You Sell

Anyone can start a business. But to stay in business, you need a steady stream of customers who buy what you sell.

Finding those customers sometimes seems like a difficult, time-consuming, and expensive task. But it doesn't have to be. Although you may never learn to love sales and marketing (which is what finding customers is all about), you can learn to do it effectively and economically. Here are answers to some of the most frequently asked questions about how to win customers for your small business.

Q **Is there any secret to marketing products?**

The secret of successful marketing is to realize marketing requires you to do four things:

1. Get the word about your products and services out to as many potential customers as you can.
2. Remind those potential customers frequently about what you do.
3. Persuade them to buy from you rather than from the competitor.
4. Deliver a top-notch product with top-notch support so your customers will give you repeat business and refer new customers to you.

Q How do most small businesses get their customers?

Surveys that Attard Communications, Inc., have done over the years show that between 47 and 54 percent of small and homebased businesses get most of their customers through word-of-mouth advertising, referrals, and personal networking.

Q What is word-of-mouth advertising?

Word-of-mouth advertising is what happens when one person tells another about what you do. If the word of mouth is a glowing testimonial or even a neutral "I know someone who does that," it can bring customers your way. It will also make people more responsive to your ads or calls because they will have already heard positive things about your company. On the other hand, if the word of mouth is negative—if a customer complains you didn't satisfy his needs, screwed up a job, or didn't respond to his calls, word-of-mouth advertising will drive customers away.

Q What is networking?

Networking is making business contacts. It is you telling other people what you do. The contacts you make may be directly with potential customers, or they may be with individuals who will give you leads or refer customers to you. Your networking contacts may also be with people who can provide valuable information that will help you improve your business or gain industry knowledge.

Networking is what you do every time you:

- give someone you meet a business card
- shake hands and introduce yourself to others at chamber of commerce or professional association meetings
- participate in a formal or informal sales lead exchange group
- flip pancakes at the Lion's Club breakfast
- accept a seat on the board of a nonprofit organization
- exchange tips and business information with noncompeting businesses
- attend the professional association dinner dance
- introduce yourself to the person sitting next to you on the airplane or standing in line ahead of you at the bank
- offer to answer another business's questions

- ask another businessperson for suggestions or about experience in some particular matter
- donate a prize for a holiday bazaar

Q **How does networking lead to new business?**

Networking can boost business in several ways. One of its most important functions is to make your name familiar to prospective customers. If someone has met you or heard about your company from a friend he or she is likely to place more trust in you than in a stranger. This, incidentally, is the reason people buy name brand products instead of less expensive house brands, even though the house brands may have identical ingredients.

Networking puts contact information in the hands of potential customers. When you give people you meet your business card and they put it in their wallet or briefcase, you are making it easy for them to contact you. Even if a prospect loses your business card, he or she may remember your business name after meeting you and be able to get in touch with you by looking your name up in the phone book or calling information.

A single networking contact can, at times, give your business a tremendous, long-lasting boost. Barbara Robbie, who operated a formal gown rental service for many years in East Setauket, New York, was at a private party when she happened to meet a woman who was responsible for planning the annual spring fashion show at a local church. When Robbie described her unique business—renting out wedding party and prom gowns—she was asked if she would like to put on the show at the church that year.

Robbie accepted the invitation and then asked women from the church and girls from a local high school to model her gowns at the show. The models publicized the show to all their friends and the church publicized it in the weekly bulletin distributed among parishioners. On the night of the show, close to four hundred women and teenage girls packed into the church basement for the event. Robbie got dozens of new customers directly from the show and continued to get referrals and business from people who had attended the show for several years afterward. The church benefited, too: the fashion show proved to be one of the most successful fund-raisers it had that year.

Q **Won't people get annoyed if I talk about my business all the time?**

A little common sense goes a long way. For instance, no one really wants to "talk business" at social gatherings, but when a group of strangers happens to be seated at the same table or be standing in the same corner of the room at a cocktail party, it's natural for people to ask one another what they do for a living. If you are asked, there's nothing wrong with briefly stating what you do and sounding excited about it.

Many business functions are held specifically to allow business people to network. Others combine networking with association meetings. Such functions generally set aside a half hour or so for networking before the actual meeting takes place. The most difficult thing about networking at this type of meeting can be finding a way to shake hands with a new acquaintance and exchange business cards without spilling your drink.

Q **Is handing out business cards at business gatherings all I have to do to network and get new customers?**

Usually people who build the most contacts through networking are those who become actively involved in two or three organizations in which they have a sincere interest and which are somewhat related to their business. People who just show up to push their products and services and have little concern for the organization or little interest in what other members of the organization do are usually seen as opportunists and don't get much business tossed their way. Those who actively participate in a group, regularly attend meetings, contribute thoughts, and if needed pitch in and help plan events, maintain membership lists or even move chairs, or serve the organization in some other way are the ones most likely to land business.

Q **How else can I build business through networking?**

Asking for help when you need it can sometimes be extremely effective. Many successful businesspeople like being mentors to business owners who are just starting out. They will offer information, leads, and contacts to help a new business owner get off the ground. You can tap into this network through associations and business groups. Sometimes all it takes is to ask if anyone has any experience handling a problem that puzzles you.

Paul Mayer, author of several widely used shareware programs for IBM and compatible microcomputers, says his shareware sales were languishing along at one or two a month until he joined the Association of Shareware Professionals and learned about marketing shareware. A few years after joining the association, he was able to quit his full-time job and earn his living entirely from his shareware sales.

Be aware, though, that people don't like to be used. Don't expect people to do things for you that you could easily do yourself. And do remember to thank friends for their help. If you abuse people's generosity they will remember, and, like negative word of mouth, the memory will wind up driving customers away rather than attracting them.

Q **What other ways do home and small businesses find customers?**

Home and small businesses find customers in every imaginable way. Here are just a few:

- sending out personalized or mass mailings
- getting listed in the Yellow Pages and other directories
- using sales representatives
- calling prospects on the phone
- making personal visits to prospects' offices or homes
- using print or broadcast advertising
- exhibiting at and attending trade shows
- bidding on contracts from government organizations
- getting publicity in trade or other media
- speaking at meetings, on panels, etc.
- partnering with large corporations or becoming a certified developer, trainer, etc.
- participating in cooperative advertising programs with major manufacturers
- doing cooperative advertising with noncompeting small businesses
- getting products "advertised" in (included in) large mail order catalogs
- answering questions on online message boards, newsgroups, or chat rooms
- subcontracting or freelancing for larger businesses in the same field
- getting major distributors to take on and sell products

- getting products reviewed in publications
- getting certified by regulatory agencies
- being a member of one or more professional societies
- hanging up a sign in an area where business signs are permitted
- displaying wares (flowers, vegetables, antiques) on lawns, on sidewalks, or any other way visible to passersby
- selling at flea markets
- selling at juried craft shows
- selling products on consignment
- giving lessons (art, pottery, etc.) in a store or home and selling related products and supplies
- having an open house to sell products
- offering people free merchandise if they agree to host a "party" for their friends at which you sell your merchandise
- sending promotional newsletters to targeted customers
- getting work shown at galleries, banks, or restaurants
- having the business name professionally lettered onto the business car or van
- exchanging mailing lists with businesses that sell to the same customers but don't compete with you
- selling to federal, state, or local governments

Q **Will networking and word-of-mouth advertising be enough to get customers or should I advertise, too?**

Some small businesses never use traditional advertising; others would have few customers if they didn't advertise. Generally, businesses that sell consumer goods and services and require a high volume of sales tend to be the ones that benefit most from traditional advertising. Businesses that sell creative or consulting services to other businesses tend to benefit the least from traditional advertising.

Thus, car repair, catering, resume preparation, rental services, tutoring services, pizza parlors, hair and nail care salons, appliance parts stores, and similar businesses usually need to advertise regularly using the Yellow Pages, newspapers, magazines, TV, radio, or community mailers. Businesses selling creative services (writing or artwork, for instance), consulting services, programming services, or similar intangible services to businesses generally derive little benefit from traditional advertising, though they sometimes do well with direct mail.

Still other businesses find that their customers come from a combination of paid advertising and word of mouth. Barbara Robbie got the first customers for her gown-rental service by placing a very small ad in a popular weekly newspaper for 4 weeks as a trial. That ad brought her inquiries and customers, so she repeated it, and then she placed the same ad in a second weekly newspaper in the same community.

If you think your business will benefit from paid advertising, proceed slowly. Test small ads to find out which ads work best in which media. Doing so will help you avoid costly advertising mistakes and allow you to grow your business at a pace you can control.

Q **How do I find my first customer?**

Usually you find your first customers the same way you will find the rest of your customers: through personal contacts, ads, mailings, and so on. If you've researched your market before going into business, finding likely prospects for what you sell should be relatively easy. What some new businesses have trouble doing, however, is converting prospects to customers; in other words, convincing potential customers to actually purchase goods or services. Most often that difficulty occurs because the owner lacks self-confidence or dislikes selling.

Q **I always feel uneasy about pressuring people to buy from me if they don't want to. How can I overcome this problem?**

To overcome the problem, you need to think about sales in a different way. A good salesperson never pressures anyone into buying anything. Instead he or she *helps the prospect make a decision* that will solve a problem or achieve some kind of desirable benefit.

Thus, to overcome any dislike or fear of selling you may have, you must:

▸ *Believe in your product or service.* Would you buy what you plan to sell at the price you plan to charge and be satisfied with the quality of the product or service? If you can't immediately say "Yes!" don't expect to be able to convince many customers that your products or services are worth buying.
▸ *Know how the product or service helps customers.* Your customers don't really care whether you are starting a business or that you need their business.

All they care about is how well your products or services match their needs. Demonstrate how your goods fill real needs, how your services solve the customer's real problems or help the customer achieve some goal, and your products or services will almost sell themselves.

▶ *Learn not to take rejection personally.* Many times people are afraid to go out and sell their products because they fear personal rejection. They worry prospects won't want to talk to them, will complain about the call or visit, will slam the phone down, or won't like the product or service. Although such concerns are natural, you shouldn't let negative responses to your sales efforts get you down. No matter what you sell, there will always be people who don't want or need your product. No matter how good it may be, only a tiny percentage of people who hear about it (through calls, contacts, ads, or any other method) are going to be willing to buy and buy today. The rest are simply not going to be interested. Some may even be rude. You have to learn to roll with the punches.

▶ *Make sure you have capabilities to meet customers' needs.* Don't try to sell your services as a consultant, programmer, desktop publisher, auto mechanic, dressmaker, copywriter, or anything else unless you have the experience in the field. Without experience you will find it very difficult to convince people to buy from you. Your inexperience might also result in monetary loss or personal injury to your customer. If that were to happen, you could get sued. If you want to start a business in a field you know little about, get experience or hands-on training before you look for customers. Go to work for some other business, take training courses, volunteer your services to friends or community groups, or do whatever else may be necessary to build experience on your own time and at your own expense. Once you have the training and experience and can prove (to yourself as well as to potential customers) that you can do the work you say you can, selling will be much easier.

▶ *Don't sell yourself short.* If you are experienced and good at what you do, don't let the competition scare you off. If your research has shown there is room in the market for both you and your competitor, market to your strengths and don't worry too much about the competitor, even if they are much bigger or more widely known than your company. Your small size may actually be a hidden advantage if it lets you offer customers more personalized service or attention to details than your competitor can.

Q **How else can I convince customers to buy?**

There are a slew of techniques salespeople use, but the most important techniques for the small business person to remember are these:

- Qualify your prospect. Make sure he or she can afford what you sell and has the authority to make the purchase decision. You don't want to spend hours demonstrating your product to the manager of the marketing department if he or she doesn't make the buying decisions, or have any influence on them, for your type of product or service.
- Know what objections you are likely to hear and have answers ready to meet them.
- Know your product and your competitors inside and out.
- Give the customer a small sample of a product to test.
- Don't knock the competitor. Sell your product's benefits instead.
- Learn to ask for the order. Once you've interested a prospect in your product or service, ask them for an order. If you don't, he or she may just buy from your competitor instead of you. Tricks of the trade that make it easier to get the order are to ask what color the customer wants or when he or she needs the product delivered or the work completed. For products or consumer items, asking how the customer would like to pay for the product can work, too.
- Think of the word *no* as meaning "I need more information."
- Don't exaggerate. Have facts to support all your claims.
- Encourage your prospect to ask you questions and talk about his or her specific needs. Then explain how the feature of your product or service can meet those needs.

Q **Is there any way to make word-of-mouth advertising happen?**

The way to get positive word of mouth to circulate is to have a good product or service and bend over backward to please your customer. Calling customers to make sure they are satisfied with the product or service a short time after you've done the job is a good image builder and gives you an opportunity to ask for repeat business and/or referrals. When you get a referral, follow it up, using the name of the person who gave you the lead.

Q **Are there other ways to use the web or online services to get business?**

One way is to submit listings to any service that offers you a chance to be listed in a directory. Business Know-How has a free directory at http://www.business-knowhow.net. Member directories on online services such as America Online, Netscape, and Excite, may also lead to business. Be sure to enter a profile if you are allowed to.

Another option is to write articles about your area of expertise and submit those to web sites and online forums that focus on your area of expertise. If they publish them it helps get your name known and sometimes to bring in business. One consultant got a $4,000 speaking engagement because a seminar promoter had seen an article he had written posted in the Business Know-How forum on America Online. Others have gotten customers for services they provide.

Q **Do those little magnets, pencils, and other advertising specialties help?**

Like business cards, they are a good way to get people to remember your name and phone number. Another excellent tool for helping prospects remember you when they need you is to have Rolodex-type cards made up with your business name. The little tab on the card could have either your name printed or the nature of your business (printer, delivery service, etc.).

Q **Should I solicit business from a company I used to work for?**

Former employers frequently are the first customers of a new business. They are easy to sell to because they know what you can do from experience working with you.

Q **Can I solicit business from a former employer's customers?**

It depends on the circumstances. If you signed a noncompete agreement (an agreement preventing you from competing with the employer), or if the employer regards his customer list as a trade secret and you copied the list, you could be sued if you solicit business from the former employer's customers. If you haven't stolen a customer list and never signed a noncompete agreement, you might try calling some of those contacts or sending out an announcement that you are now in business for yourself.

Q **Can a home business use sales agents or distributors?**

If you can get a sales representative to take on your product or service, and if the sales agent is efficient, the relationship can be very beneficial since it will let you concentrate on producing the product or service while the sales rep concentrates on selling it.

Q **How can I find a good sales agent?**

The best way is to ask the stores you would like to see your products sold in or companies you would like to have sell your products which manufacturer representatives they order products from. If you have friends or business acquaintances who sell to the same market you do and use sales representatives, ask them for recommendations, too. Finally, you could ask around at industry trade shows about good sales reps.

Q **What do I need to do to convince an agent to represent me?**

You will have to have a quality product or service and often a line of products. You will also need to show you will be able to fill orders if the rep gets your product into a popular catalog or store and that you can handle the paperwork professionally. If you can't deliver the goods or don't handle the paperwork professionally, it will hurt the sales representative's reputation and ability to make good deals in the future; hence, good reps are often very choosy about the companies with which they deal.

Q **Should I tell customers I am homebased?**

It depends on who the customer is. Huge department store distributors or mail order companies may not want to deal with homebased businesses because they fear they may not have the resources to meet customers' needs. Your best bet, usually, is not to volunteer information about being homebased. But if asked, don't deny it either.

Q **Can a small business sell to the federal or state government?**

Yes. The federal and state governments have programs to encourage small businesses to bid on contracts or seek work as subcontractors on government work.

Among them are small business seminars, procurement (jobs) fairs, and outreach programs through community development organizations. The U.S. Air Force maintains two web sites to help small businesses learn about procurement opportunities and how to deal with government red tape.

Q   What does the government buy?

The government buys everything from food to computers to sophisticated electronic surveillance equipment. The Department of Defense alone buys billions of dollars' worth of goods and services each year. About 98 percent of the transactions (which equals about 20 percent of the total spending) are with small businesses.

Q   Can a home business or a one-person business sell to the government?

Home businesses that have the experience and capabilities do sell products and services to the government. The government, like any other customer, is primarily interested in a company's ability to perform the contract and meet deadlines.

Q   Is there a lot of red tape?

Yes, there usually is. In fact, the red tape is the leading deterrent to most small businesses who want to sell to the government. You generally can get some help dealing with the red tape through local offices of federal or state agencies or at Small Business Administration branch offices. Those can be found by looking in the federal government listing in your phone book distributed by your telephone company.

Q   How do I find out what the government wants to buy?

One way to find out what the government is buying is to read the *Commerce Business Daily (CBD)*. The *CBD* lists notices of proposed government procurement actions, contract awards, sales of government property, and other important procurement information. It is published every business day and contains approximately five hundred to a thousand notices each day. Each notice appears in the *CBD* only once. All federal procurement offices are required to place notices in the *CBD* about proposed procurement actions over $25,000 and contract awards over $25,000 that are likely to result in the award of any subcontracts. These notices are organized into categories to make it easier to find the ones that might apply to your particular business. The *CBD* is available in print and electronically. You can order a subscription by calling or writing:

Superintendent of Documents
Washington, DC 20402-9325
(202) 783-3238

If you have a computer and modem, the *CBD* can be downloaded in full from the Air Force Small Business web site at http://www.selltoairforce.org. A searchable version is online at CBD Net (http://www.cbdnet.gpo.gov).

You can get information about procurements that aren't published in the *CBD* by contacting local branch offices of government offices directly. Ask to have your name placed on bid lists and find out if there is a bulletin board (the traditional kind or an electronic bulletin board) you should read to find out about proposed procurements (purchases). It might also be a good idea to ask about possible subcontracting opportunities with prime contractors in your vicinity. Other sources of information that may be good leads to government contracts are cable TV, local newspapers, and state agencies.

Q **What's a prime contractor?**

A prime contractor is the contractor that has responsibility for a project.

Q **What are the benefits of subcontracting?**

Subcontracting work from prime government contractors gives small businesses the opportunity to participate in (and profit from) federal contracts by doing part of the work on big contracts. It is simply an indirect way of doing business with the government.

Q **How do I find lists of prime contractors?**

The Department of Defense and other agencies maintain lists of prime contractors. You can often get these lists at local government procurement opportunity fairs, through local branch offices of government agencies and through city, county, or regional economic or industrial development offices and on government web sites. Many of these offices have people specially designated to help small businesses wade through the red tape of selling to the government. If you have no previous experience working with the government, this help can be very useful, even if you will be subcontracting work from a prime contractor.

Q **Will my business benefit by exhibiting at major trade shows?**

Small companies that can afford the expense of the booth space, product literature, hotel accommodations, shipping costs for displays, and so on can benefit from exhibiting in trade shows if they have a product that works, is professionally packaged, and is ready to ship or be sold in quantity to customers at the show and afterward.

Q **What do you need to stand out in a trade show?**

You don't have to have the fanciest booth in the hall, but you do need a neat and attractive display in a good location for the booth to pay off. You also need to have the booth staffed. Empty booths with literature on the table but no one to explain it or demonstrate the product aren't going to bring in much business.

You will also need to have a sufficient amount of professional-looking literature to hand out. If you don't have literature or if it looks as if it was done by Aunt Tillie on her 9-pin dot matrix printer that needed a new ribbon, you aren't going to make many sales or impress many people.

In addition to the literature you have available at your booth, you should have press kits made up to hand out to members of the press or other important contacts who attend the show. Find out, too, if the show has a pressroom, and if so, if you can leave stacks of your press kits there for members of the press to pick up. That may get your literature to people who might not find your booth on the show floor.

Giveaways and gimmicks to attract passersby to your booth are useful, too. The giveaway doesn't have to be terribly expensive: samples of your product given away as contest prizes periodically during the show, T-shirts with your company name on them given away after each demonstration of your product(s), or even something as simple as a bowl of wrapped candies can attract people to your booth.

Q **How do I decide which shows to go to?**

Try to check out a show's history. Ask other vendors in your industry which shows have been most productive for them and which shows least productive. Ask which attract the most attendees and the most important contacts. Sometimes direct sale of your product from a booth isn't as important as the contacts you may make with businesses, distributors, or sales representatives who can help you bring in more business.

Q Is there any way to take advantage of trade shows without spending too much money for literature and booth space?

If your company is too small or new to comfortably afford its own booth at a trade show, you may benefit by helping someone else out in his or her booth, sharing a booth with another company, or simply attending the show and introducing yourself to large companies and distributors who could be useful contacts for you.

Q What about local trade shows? Are they worth participating in?

It can be cost-effective to exhibit at local trade shows if they attract the type of customers you want to attract. You may be able to get a booth at a local trade show for as little as $50 to $300 (depending on the size of the show and who's sponsoring it). Since the local shows are often specifically set up to encourage small business participation, the booth displays are often simple. Some companies will have nothing more than some brochures spread out on a table. A tabletop display of some sort—even makeshift—is preferable, though, since it will put your promotional material at eye level making it more easily viewable by passersby.

Q Can you go as an attendee and hand out fliers?

Doing that is frowned on (understandably) by vendors who have paid to work at the show. Bring business cards, introduce yourself, and hand out business cards, but leave your sales literature in your hotel room or home unless you are sharing a booth with another company.

14.
Publicity:
An Almost-Free Ride

How can you get out word about your product or services to your customers if you can't afford to advertise extensively? One way is through free publicity in newspapers, magazines, or on broadcast media. Here are tips and hints on how to get various types of publicity and on how to get the most mileage out of any publicity you do get.

Q **What is publicity?**

Publicity is making people aware of your business name and what you do. Usually that means getting the media to talk or write about you or what you do. The media can be television, radio, newspapers, magazines, or even books and newsletters. It may be local, regional, national, or specialized, such as a trade magazine. The nature of your business and what you sell will usually dictate which media will consider what you do newsworthy.

Q **Does publicity work as well as paid advertising?**

Favorable publicity often brings in more sales than advertising does. The reason: people tend to believe what they read in editorial copy more than they believe claims in ads. Thus, if you get positive publicity, your product gains a testimonial, and your business gains credibility in the eyes of your customers.

On the flip side of the coin, you have no way of controlling what the press says about your product or service. If they don't like it and publish something negative about it, you may lose sales.

Q How do I get publicity?

The way to get publicity is to *seek* it. You have to telephone and send press releases to appropriate editors, reporters, and broadcasters and tell them what you do and why they should write or talk about you. Rarely will they discover you on their own.

Q How do I find editors to contact?

First, make a list of publications and broadcast media your customers are likely to read. If you sell locally, include only the local newspapers, radio, and cable TV. If you sell on a more widespread basis, you'll want to include trade publications in your field and perhaps the mass media or large regional newspapers and popular magazines that cater to your customers' needs.

Once you have this list, call each publication or broadcast station and ask who covers the type of information you want them to publish.

Sometimes your call will be put through to an editor or reporter. Other times you will just be given the name of an editor or reporter to whom you can send a release. If you aren't sure about the spelling of the name, ask the receptionist to spell it for you. Editors and writers don't like to see their names misspelled.

If you do get to talk to an editor or writer, tell him or her briefly what you want to publicize, and answer any questions he or she may have. If you are asked to send or fax a press release, do so immediately. It would be a good idea to mark the release, "Here's the release you asked me to send," or something similar. Hundreds of pieces of paper cross an editor's desk every week. Your note on the release can help keep it from getting buried and forgotten.

Q Is there any way to contact many editors at one time?

Try to get a wire service to cover your story. Two to contact are:

Associated Press
50 Rockefeller Plaza, 6th Fl.
New York, NY 10020
(212) 621-1500
http://www.ap.org

Reuters
1700 Broadway
New York, NY 10019
(212) 603-3300
http://www.reuters.com

If your products or services are aimed at computer users or involve computers in any way, another wire service to which you might send your information is Newsbytes. Newsbytes distributes computer news to several of the major online computer information services. You can reach Newsbytes online by sending electronic mail to the address Newsbytes on most online information services. You can also write or call Newsbytes at this address:

Newsbytes News Network, Inc.
406 Olive Street W
Stillwater, MN 55082-4945
(612) 430-1100

If your business is big enough, another option is to subscribe to the PR Newswire. This is a membership news service that distributes company press releases and publicity stories for a fee to media throughout the country or to only selected media contacts. PR Newswire is affiliated with many professional organizations. If you belong to a professional association you may already be a member and have special rates available to you.

PR Newswire
810 Seventh Avenue, 32nd Fl.
New York, NY 10019
Phone: (800) 832-5522
Fax: (800) 793-9313
Editorial: (800) 776-8090
http://www.prnewswire.com

Q **How do I get editors to actually write an article or talk about my product or service?**

You have to have an interesting story, a "hook." The fact that you sell cellular telephones is neither exciting nor newsworthy. But if you tell a reporter about the interesting or new way your customers are using your portable cellular phone, you might make the news and get your company name in the press.

You also must know which media would be interested in the story you are presenting. "The major mistake people make is to propose stories that are not appropriate for the publication," says Ron Roel, *Newsday* business news editor/real estate. "Be familiar with the publications you are trying to pitch the story to. Know what kinds of stories they print, what the length is. Show that you have done some research and you have a particular reason to call about a particular story, not that you just want someone to write about you."

Q **There's nothing particularly newsworthy about what I do. Should I just forget about getting publicity?**

Not necessarily. If there is nothing truly new or newsworthy about your product, consider making news happen. One or several of these "gimmicks" might work well for your business:

▸ Conduct a survey about something related to your product or service. Send out a release announcing the survey and a second one announcing the results.
▸ Hold a contest. Send a press release out to announce the contest and another to announce the winners.
▸ Write a booklet about something related to your business and give it away free. Send a press release out to announce the free booklet.
▸ Conduct a free seminar or training class related to what you do. Send out a release to announce the seminar.
▸ Donate your product or service to a nonprofit organization that can use it. *Have the nonprofit organization send out the press release.* (They may have more name recognition and clout with the press than you do.)
▸ Tie your product or service to a trend and publicize the trend, showing how people are jumping on the bandwagon by using what you sell.

In addition, local publications or trade publications might also publish an article about you if you are doing something for the first time or have released a brand new product.

Q **How do you write a press release?**

Put whatever facts you think will most interest the editor (your hook) in the first sentence of the news release. The rest of the first paragraph should provide a little more detail, appealing directly to the editor's readers.

If the editor gets to the end of the first paragraph and doesn't know why the release is important, your information is not going to get used. Therefore, it is often *not* a good idea to start out your release with either your name or the name of your company. An opening paragraph like the following one, for instance, is not going to do much to spark anyone's attention.

> *George Anderson today announced the expansion of Anderson Widgets into the home gadget market. A leading seller of squeak-free garage door mechanisms, Anderson Widgets will begin selling automated stereo controls for home use this fall.**

Even if George Anderson or Anderson's Widgets were well-known in the community or industry, the information sounds humdrum and unimportant. Who really cares what Anderson is going to add to his line this fall?

Change that ho-hum first paragraph to one that emphasizes customers' needs, and the release becomes interesting:

> *Relief is just around the corner for parents who are tired of screaming at their offspring to turn down the stereo volume. Thanks to a new remote control device that can be hooked up to any stereo system, parents soon will be able to turn down the boom-box volume from anywhere in the house.*
>
> *The new gadget, introduced at a trade show today by Anderson Widgets, will . . .*

The paragraphs after the lead paragraph should give the editor any other important facts about your news. Be sure they include all the who, what, where, why,

---

*Large corporations often publish releases that start very much like this. They sometimes get their information used simply because the corporation, by virtue of its size, is newsworthy. Small businesses have to prove their newsworthiness to get mention by the press.

when, and how information that a news story normally contains. The release should be brief (about two to three double-spaced typed or typeset pages) but complete enough so the editor could write a paragraph or two without having to call you for additional information. The easier you make the editor's job, the more chance you have of getting publicized.

Q **Is there any special format I should use?**

You should follow these basic conventions in preparing your release:

- Use conventional typefaces and sizes. The editor wants information, not samples of your desktop publishing prowess.
- Print out your release on standard-sized paper that includes your letterhead. If budget permits, use letterhead-quality paper. If your budget is tight, standard bond paper will do.

TIP If you don't have letterhead, you can create your own on your computer by typing your business name on one line at the top left of the page and your address, phone number and fax number below that. Make the business name boldface type one or two point sizes bigger than the body of your letter. Make the address line about a point-size smaller than the body of the letter. Insert a rule line (or hold down the underscore key and make a line of underscores) below the address.

- If you wish, type "News Release" at the top of the page or just under your company name and address.
- Skip down a line or two and type "Release date:" followed by the date or "For Immediate Release" to tell the editor when to run the story. (A specific release date is generally used only if you don't want the information released before a particular date.)
- Skip another line and type "Contact:" followed by the names of one or more people (often this will be you) the editor should call if additional information is needed.

▶ Skip another line and write a headline that describes and summarizes the importance of the release. Usually this will be a variation of the material you have in the first paragraph of the release. Use bold-faced type for the headline if you can.

▶ Skip one line and start your release by typing a dateline. A dateline is a notation about the city and state from which your release is being issued and often the date the release was issued. If you will be mailing your release (rather than faxing it), you might want to leave the date out of the dateline. That way, if your release is late getting out or gets stalled in the mail, it won't look outdated when it hits the editor's desk.

See a sample of how the release might look below.

Sample Press Release

ANDERSON WIDGETS, INC.   **NEWS RELEASE**
123 4th Street
Hauppauge, NY 11788

For Immediate Release
Contact: G. T. Anderson
      (516) 987-6543

NEW DEVICE INTRODUCED BY ANDERSON WIDGETS
CONTROLS STEREO VOLUME FROM ANY ROOM

Hauppauge, NY—April 29, 2000—Relief is just around the corner for parents who are tired of screaming at their offspring to turn down the stereo volume. Thanks to a new remote control device that can be hooked up to any stereo system, parents soon will be able to turn down the boom-box volume from anywhere in the house.
The new gadget, introduced at a trade show today by Anderson Widgets, will . . .

Q   **Do I send identical releases to all editors?**

You could do that, but often it pays to change the headline and the first paragraph slightly to tailor the release for different audiences or markets. For instance, if news about the remote volume-controller for stereos was going out to local media, the headline might be changed to read "Hauppauge Manufacturer Develops Remote Control Device for Stereos." The copy (text) would be adjusted slightly to get the local angle in near the top of the release, too.

Q **Is a press release the best way to get publicity?**

The press release works best when used in conjunction with personal calls to editors or reporters. What often happens is that you alert the editor to the story in your phone call, and then if they are interested, they will tell you, "Send me a release," or "Send me some information." The personal contact isn't essential, but often it does help get your release and story noticed.

Q **Do I just send the release and forget about it?**

Usually it is best to follow up on the release by calling the editor or reporter a few days after you think a release should have arrived.

Q **Don't editors get mad at all these calls?**

Some editors get annoyed at phone calls. If you encounter an editor who doesn't want phone calls, be sure to make a notation on your contact list so you don't accidentally phone the next time you are sending out a release. Many, however, welcome them, provided you keep the following guidelines in mind:

- Keep the call brief. Reporters and editors very often must meet hourly deadlines. (Radio news personnel may be trying to squeeze in the conversation with you before the next broadcast goes on the air.) Your call will not be welcomed if you ramble and don't get right to the point.
- It's a good idea to outline in advance what you want to cover in your talk and to gather together any facts the reporter might ask for so you don't have to look them up or call back.
- Don't make a pest of yourself. Call only if you have news or information they may want.
- Never complain about a story the reporter did or about not getting publicity.
- If you have to call to correct an error the reporter made in a story, be polite and *never* make it sound like you think he or she made a mistake.

No one likes to be told they did something wrong, particularly if they think they were doing you a favor by giving you publicity. Besides, the error could have occurred in production.

▸ If your contact seems rushed or says it is a bad time to talk to him or her, don't keep talking! Ask when a better time might be and call back then.

Q How far ahead of time should I send a release?

The date you should send out the release varies with the type of media. Announcements of dated events should go out to newspapers, radio, and local TV stations about 2 to 4 weeks before the event. (It is a good idea to call the individual newspaper or broadcast station and ask how far ahead they want to get the releases.)

The lead time (time to allow) on magazines is 4 to 6 months for editorial copy. (Seasonal and some specialty magazines may be longer.)

Q Will the editor publish the press release as I wrote it?

In some small publications and in some trade publications, press releases are used as written. Usually, however, editors or reporters will select facts from the release and rewrite the information to suit their needs.

Q How often should I send out press releases?

Send out press releases as often as you have something newsworthy to publicize. The more frequently editors read your name, the more likely they are to remember having seen it before and to give credibility to what you have to say.

Q Should I send a photograph?

Sending a photograph is a good idea for all media, except radio, of course.

The reason a photo can be useful to newspapers and magazines is that they need "art" (to an editor, anything other than text) to break up the text and make the paper appear more readable. If there is a toss-up between two equally acceptable stories, and the editor is looking for some art to break up the page the story will be on, the story that came with the photo may get chosen over the one that didn't.

One problem, however, is that any photos you send out need to be good quality and should be 5-by-7-inch, or larger, black-and-white prints or color slides. Since there is no guarantee your photo or your release will be used, you will need to decide whether the extra cost of sending a photograph is practical, especially if you are only sending an individual release.

Q **What kind of photo should I send? Should it be a picture of me or the building my shop is in?**

A "head shot" (picture of you from the shoulders up) might be appropriate to send out if you have won an award, are writing a column, trying to get seminar or speech engagements, or are sending information about your business to TV stations. But usually what you should send out is a human interest picture showing how people benefit or enjoy what you sell.

Q **What about video news releases? Are they practical for small businesses to send out?**

If you are a very small business, the answer is probably no. TV newsrooms still get and read conventional news releases and will send their own reporter out to shoot a story if the story is sufficiently newsworthy and if it requires footage.

Q **What is a press kit and do I need one?**

A press kit (also known as a media kit) is a packet containing information about your company and its products or services. The purpose of the packet is to make it easy for reporters or others to find facts about you. It also makes it easy for you to respond to "send me something" inquiries.

From a practical point of view, whether or not you need a press kit will depend on how polished an image your customers or the media expect your type of business to present. If you are a small, one- or two-person operation, only sell locally, or get most of your business from word-of-mouth recommendations, you probably won't benefit by putting together a full-blown press kit. But as your business grows, or if your type of business requires you to present a polished, expensive "face" to the media and others, you may benefit by having press kits on hand and ready to pop in the mail.

Q **What goes into a press kit?**

The materials are generally enclosed in a good quality pocket folder. Often the name of the business is printed on the folder, but if you need to keep costs down, you might consider having stickers printed with your company name and applying the stickers to quality off-the-shelf folders. This "trick" works so effectively that many large corporations use it for press kits they hand out at trade shows. A brightly colored glossy folder with a professionally printed label works well.

Inside the folder you would put whichever of these items is appropriate for your business:

- an overview of the product or service
- current press release(s) about your products and services
- fact sheets with product specifications
- explanations of the technology involved if it is not widely understood
- photos of the product in use
- examples of how to use the product
- photos of what the purchaser will be able to produce using the product or service
- explanations of how to use the product if warranted
- company history
- testimonials
- copies of past publicity
- frequently asked questions and the answers
- background information about the principals if appropriate
- photo of the principal if appropriate
- your business card

Q **How do I get reporters to quote me in stories instead of my competitors?**

Become an expert on your industry. Then, when there's an event happening that you know about, call reporters and let them know you have information they may be able to use.

"Reporters don't have time to sit down and get to know you. Get in on a specific story. Let the reporter know you have something to say," advises *Newsday*'s Ron Roel. Make sure, he says, that you are available, easy to reach, and can explain things simply. "Too often experts get wrapped up in jargon and can't speak in less than a paragraph, making it hard to get the two-line quote that is often needed. Think in 'print bites.'"

Q **How else can I get my company name mentioned in publications?**

One of the best ways to get mentioned in publications is to write articles and get the articles published. If you are a consultant to a particular industry, for instance, try your hand at writing how-to articles on subjects related to what you do. A computer consultant might write a brief piece on how to choose a computer consultant, for instance, and submit it to the trade magazines that cater to the kind of customers he or she writes programs for.

Q **How do I get invited to speak at association meetings or conferences?**

If you are not well known enough for conference planners to seek you out, seek them out. Call and tell them what expertise you have or how your knowledge will be of interest to people attending their meetings.

Q **Will I get paid for speaking?**

If you are seeking to publicize a product or service or yourself, you probably won't get paid. On the other hand, if an organization thinks you will be a good draw for them, then you may get paid anywhere from a small honorarium to thousands of dollars for your time.

Q **How can I get more mileage out of speeches?**

There are dozens of ways to leverage your speech or panel participation into sales. Here are a few:

- If your speaking engagement is to publicize an event, be sure to have enough handouts about the event for all who might be there.
- Have sales brochures and business cards available for attendees to pick up.
- Use the speaking engagement as still another opportunity to get press coverage by sending out an announcement about your participation in the event.

- If you are publicizing a book, either have copies with you or have a form people can mail in to get the book.
- Add a line about your speaking engagements to your resume, capabilities brochure, or other information you send out to prospective customers. It adds credibility to your claims of being an expert.

Q **What other ways are there to publicize my business?**

There are probably as many low-cost ways to publicize a business as there are independent small businesses. If you think about what publicity really is—getting other people to talk about your business—you will think of dozens of ways to get publicity for your business. Many involve networking with other business owners or simply getting out and talking to potential customers. Here are some ideas that may work in your business:

- Make sure your business card gets into as many hands as possible. It is your calling card, the way people will remember who you are and what you do.
- Consider having an extra set of business cards made up in the form of Rolodex cards. If your potential customers can put your number directly into a Rolodex, they will see your name every time they flip past that part of the alphabet.
- Join the same associations, the local chamber of commerce, or other organizations to which your customers are likely to belong. Introduce yourself to people you meet and give them your business card. If you have sufficient expertise, offer to be a speaker at a future meeting. If you have time and sincere interest in the organization, offer to help with its projects. You can make both good business contacts and good friends that way.
- Make photocopies of any publicity you get and send it out with sales letters or other literature you mail to prospects.
- Do the monthly newsletter for an organization to which you belong. (This gets time-consuming, so be sure you have the skills and the time before offering.)

Q **Will it cost me anything to get publicity?**

Publicity is free in the sense that you don't pay media for space or air time as you would if you advertise. It is not a totally free ride, however. You still incur costs for printing and mailing releases, phone calls, product literature, and press kits you have to mail out, and it will take a considerable amount of your time to publicize your business on a regular basis. Still, publicity could be one of the most economical ways to spread the word about what you sell.

15.

Advertising Basics

If you ask a dozen small business owners about the value of traditional advertising, you are likely to get a dozen different answers. The owner of the limousine service will tell you he couldn't stay in business if he didn't run ads in the local papers; the person who runs the resume service may tell you newspaper ads don't bring many responses but advertising in the Yellow Pages does. One computer programmer may tell you paid advertising is a waste of money, while another will tell you the ads she placed in trade magazines allowed her to expand her business from a little home-based operation to a company that now employs twenty-five people.

Q **What businesses should use paid advertising?**

You should consider using paid advertising if you sell products or services that you can market to people with very specific interests (for instance, all hobbyists who have an interest in tole painting); need little explaining; must be sold to many customers to be profitable; or are traditionally advertised in newspapers, weekly shoppers, the Yellow Pages, or on TV or radio.

Q **Are there any businesses that shouldn't use paid advertising?**

Paid advertising may not be a good use of your money if you can only work for one or two customers at a time, if you are a consultant, if you sell creative services like writing or custom design, if your product or service needs a lot of explaining, or if no one else in your line of work advertises. In these cases the only type of paid advertising that might be worth considering would be ads or listings in trade directories or specialized trade publications.

Q **Is there any good way to determine whether or not I should advertise?**

One yardstick is whether or not your competition advertises. If the competition advertises, you probably should, too. And, you should advertise in the same publications the competition uses since your customers will expect to look in those publications for ads for your type of product.

Q **Where should I put paid advertising?**

There are numerous places you could advertise your products or service. You need to determine which places will help you reach the most number of likely buyers at the lowest cost. Among the places you may want to consider are:

- Regular or classified advertisements in daily newspapers, newsstand magazines, and weekly newspapers
- Ads in "weekly shoppers." These publications consist of almost all advertising and have little or no editorial content. They may be mailed or tossed on driveways or stoops and contain ads for plumbers, garage sales, hair salons, tire dealers, etc.
- Regular or classified advertisements in trade publications or special-interest publications
- Listings or advertisements in the Yellow Pages
- Listings or ads in trade directories
- Ads in card decks, which are ads printed on index-sized cards and mailed to subscribers of certain magazines or people who are known to buy a certain type of product or service through the mail
- Radio ads
- Network and cable TV ads
- Inserts in weekly papers or shoppers
- Classified advertising sections of web sites
- Text ads and sponsorships of Internet mailing lists

▶ Banner ads on targeted web sites
▶ Ads on the back of theater programs or church bulletins
▶ Coupon books or envelopes mailed to homeowners by a local mail service

Q **Why does paid advertising work for some businesses and not for others?**

Advertising is not an exact science. Response to advertising is affected by the words and pictures used in an ad, the location of an ad in a publication, and the business owner's skill at choosing the right media. The weather, the time of year, what's on a page next to an ad, or what comes on before or after a commercial on TV or radio all can have an effect on advertising response rates, too. Thus, to some extent, finding what works and what doesn't is a matter of trial and error for every business.

Q **Advertising is expensive. Is there any way to avoid wasting a lot of money on ads that don't work?**

There is no way to completely avoid advertising mistakes and no way to ensure that every ad you place will be a success. In fact, some may not bring in enough responses to pay for themselves.

You can minimize the risk of costly error, however, if you remember these seven secrets of successful homebased and small business advertisers:

1. Know the purpose of your ad.
2. Set a budget.
3. Make realistic estimates of the number of responses you will get to ads.
4. Know how many responses you will need to break even on your advertising costs.
5. Choose a target market and then put your ad in media aimed at that market.
6. Test on a small scale before launching an expensive large-scale ad campaign.
7. Expand the number and/or size of ads little by little, building on your successes, learning from the mistakes.

Q **Isn't the purpose of all ads to sell?**

Yes, but different ads sell in different ways. Advertising can be used to sell in any one of these four ways:

- Build name recognition (so the customer remembers the product or service and looks for it in the future when the need arises).
- Get inquiries that are followed up by sales calls or by sending sales literature.
- Sell products directly by getting people to call or send away for a product.
- Get customers to come to a shop or restaurant.

Generally, the more expensive a product or the smaller the ad the less likely it is that customers will buy directly from an ad. If you want to sell a product directly from an ad, you will need one that's large enough to give the prospective customer enough details to make a purchase decision. If you can only afford small ads, you will need to have sales literature made up to hand out to people who ask about your product or service.

Q **How do you target ads to specific markets?**

Different media appeal to different types of people for different reasons. Putting the ad where a lot of people will see it isn't necessarily as important as putting it where the *right kind* of people will see it. Place your ad where people who have a known interest or need in the type of product or service you sell will find the ad and respond to it.

For instance, an ad for candle-making supplies is likely to draw far more responses in *Crafts* magazine than it is in *Computer Shopper*. Although people who use computers might also make candles, they would never look in a computer magazine to find out about candle-making supplies. Similarly, while someone who makes candles or designs patterns may well use a computer, they aren't going to look for ads for drawing software or computer clip art in *Crafts* magazine.

Q **What do I need to know about my customers to choose the right advertising media?**

You need to know as much as you possibly can about customers' buying habits and interests. How old are they? Where do they live? Where do they shop? Where do they look for your type of product or service? Do they normally buy what you sell through the mail? What kind of publication are they likely to look in when they want information about what you sell? A phone book? A special interest or trade magazine? The ads in the Sunday newspaper or the weekly shopper?

Q **How many responses do magazine ads get?**

Advertising in the kind of magazines you see on the newsstands generates far fewer responses than most people imagine. Although response rates vary greatly, experienced marketers often find that a well-written ad placed in carefully chosen publications will get a response of about one-tenth of 1 percent of the media's audience—or less.

If the ad or the publication isn't right for the audience or what is being sold, the response rate can dip much lower. One entrepreneur placed an ad for a $39 item in a magazine that had a circulation of 600,000. The ad asked people to send for more information, rather than to place an order. He got only 72 inquiries, and although he immediately responded to each inquiry by mailing out a package of literature, only 3 out of the 72 people who responded to the ad actually bought his product. Needless to say, he didn't repeat his ad.

Q **Why do businesses advertise if the response rate is so low?**

Advertising is a numbers game. Some businesses can make a profit on a low response rate. Suppose, for instance, you spend $2,600 to purchase a full-page ad in a publication that reaches 250,000 people who are likely prospects for what you sell. You are charging $19.95 for your product and get 250 orders (a response rate of one-tenth of 1 percent, or .001), totaling $4,987.50 in sales ($19.95 × 250). Each product costs you $5.80, a price that includes manufacturing, packaging, and shipping costs. Thus, filling the orders would cost you $1,450 (250 × $5.80).

Your total costs would be:	$2,600 + $1,450 = $4,050
Your cost per customer would be:	$4,050 ÷ 250 = $16.20
Your profit would be:	$4,987.50 − 4,040.00 = $947.50

While $947 isn't going to make you unbelievably wealthy, if the ad brings in approximately the same number of responses every month, that one product would give you a profit of more than $11,000 over the course of a year.

Furthermore, people who use mail order to sell goods rarely have just one product. They have a line of products and use their ads partly to "buy" the customer, since every person who responds to one ad is a likely customer for other products a company sells. Most companies find that they make most of their profits by making repeat sales to their existing customers. Once they start to accumulate a lot of names, they also make money by renting their customer lists to noncompeting companies.

You must be able to afford to experiment, however. If either your ad or the publication is off target, you may get few or no responses to the ad.

Q Should I experiment with classified ads in magazines to save money?

Many businesses use classified ads in magazines to get new customers since the cost of these ads is much less than the cost of display (big) ads. But usually they use classified ads as a way to get inquiries, rather than a way to sell products directly. Since classified ads are too small to carry much information, people usually won't buy anything priced at much more than about $3 from such an ad.

Another drawback is that a classified ad may get fewer inquiries than a display ad, and your total cost per order is going to be higher because you have to send sales literature (or make a sales call) to follow up on the inquiries.

If the ad costs you $125 and you get 75 inquiries and send out a package of sales literature that costs you $1.00 each (including postage), your cost per inquiry will be $200 ($125 + $75). If four people who get your follow-up mailing actually buy your $19.95 product, you will take in only $79.80 ($19.95 × 4).* If the manufacturing of each product costs $5.80, your cost of filling those orders will be $23.20 ($5.80 × 4). Your total cost for getting the ad, responding to inquiries, and filling orders will have been $223.20, or $55.80 per customer. Thus, you would have lost $143.40 on that one ad. If, however, you sold each of those four customers another $100 in merchandise over the next year, you would—in the long run—make money as a result of running the original ad.

---

*Four responses in 75 would be a little over 5 percent. Although some people claim they get as many as 25 percent to actually buy the product from follow-up literature, most people usually get between 5 and 10 percent.

Q **Does advertising in newspapers work the same way?**

Newspaper advertising is harder to target than ads in magazines since newspapers are sold to a much more varied audience than are most magazines. In addition, newspapers generally aren't kept around as long as magazines, though people occasionally do clip ads from newspapers and save them for several months.

You can target potential customers through a particular newspaper or weekly shopper by choosing certain distribution areas. Weekly shoppers, and even some large dailies, will sell advertising by region, charging varying fees depending on the number of people in each region and the total number of regions in which you want your ad to circulate. Weekly newspapers sometimes are put out by a publishing company that allows you to buy advertising more or less the same way—you pay one rate for one publication, another if you add a second weekly, and so on.

In choosing newspapers in which to advertise, think about the demographics of the distribution area. If you are selling in-ground swimming pool maintenance services, most of your customers are likely to be affluent, so you would want to be sure to advertise in publications distributed to affluent areas.

Not all products sell well from newspaper ads. An ad for point-of-sale software might do well in a magazine aimed at retailers, but the same retailers might not see or respond to that ad in your local newspaper.

Q **Can I tell from one ad whether or not I should continue my advertising?**

Running one ad isn't really a good way to determine whether or not you should advertise. All you can learn from the response to a single ad is whether that one ad worked in the media you chose. For instance, one woman who wanted to start a one-person cleaning service put a small ad in the smaller of two weekly newspapers in a well-to-do community on Long Island, New York. She got no responses to the ad. She tried the identical ad in the competing newspaper and got all the customers she could handle.

The same thing could happen to you. Or, if the ad doesn't bring as many responses as you'd like, it could be that the ad doesn't have a good headline, doesn't make clear what you sell (a very common problem when people try to be creative when writing their ads), isn't in the right media to reach potential clients, or neglects to give a phone number. People who are most successful at advertising track responses and test different ads, changing one thing in an ad at a time (either the headline, copy, media in which they advertise, etc.), until they are satisfied they are getting the best possible results.

Because of the number of advertisements competing for readers' attention, potential customers may gloss over your ad the first few times they see or hear it. Experienced advertisers say customers often need to encounter your ad or hear your name a minimum of six to nine times before they pay much attention to it. Furthermore, a prospect might not want your service this week, but might need it three months from now. If he sees your name in an ad now and then sees it again in three months, you will seem somehow familiar to him and therefore more trustworthy than someone whose name he hasn't seen before. He may call you instead of a competitor.

Of course, a lack of initial response could really mean you shouldn't bother advertising.

Q **Should I advertise in the classified sections of newspapers?**

Certain kinds of businesses gain a lot of benefit from classified ads or small display ads in the classified section of publications. Many people turn directly to the classified ad section when they are ready to buy a product or service. That means you don't have to sell them on buying the product or service; you just have to convince them to buy from you.

One indicator of whether you should advertise in the classified section of a particular publication is if it has a classified heading, such as "Plumbing" or "Music," that seems appropriate for what you sell. If you find such a heading and see that many people advertise under it regularly, you can probably figure readers look for that type of product or service in that paper.

The most successful classified ads in newspapers and weekly shoppers tend to be those for services people can't do themselves or don't want do themselves, or for products or services they can't find anywhere else. Usually plumbers, electricians, those who repair appliances, tutors, cleaning services, rental services, and the like do well with this type of small ad.

Q **What should I put in my ad?**

What goes into an ad will depend somewhat on the size and nature of the ad; however, whether you are placing a full-page ad or a small classified ad, it should:

- get the reader's attention
- make clear what is being sold
- build interest and desire for what is being sold
- tell the reader what action to take and persuade the reader to take that action

You should also be sure the ad:

- states how the reader can contact you
- states the name of the product or service
- includes your business phone number and, preferably, your address, too. If you don't want to give out your address in an ad that has your phone number in it, at least include the town if the publication circulates throughout several towns.

Q **Do I need an ad agency?**

You probably do not need an advertising agency to create ads for local media until you've been in business for a while and are spending $50,000 or more a year on advertising. Newspapers, weekly shoppers, and even some radio and TV stations will offer some help and advice if you are creating ads for use in their publications or on their stations. Although a good advertising agency might be able to produce better results, your business may not be big enough to interest them. As your business grows, however, you may want to look into getting ad agency help. If you just need someone to create a brochure or other product literature, you might want to use a freelance commercial artist rather than an ad agency.

Q **How can I judge how well ads are working?**

If you are running several different ads at one time you will need to ask people where they got your name, or code ads in some way so you know which ads produced how many responses. Otherwise you have no way of determining which ads are working for you and which aren't, which should be continued and which dropped.

If you are using coupons in your ads, you can put a distinct number or letter in tiny print in a corner of each coupon to indicate which publication the coupon came from. If people will be responding to you by mail, you could key the responses to the publication by changing something noncrucial in the mailing address or adding something like "Suite 5" or "Dept. A" to your mailing address. You might also key an ad by using or not using your middle initial or using a nickname. For instance, if I had three classified ads running for the same product in three different publications, one might say to reply to Janet Attard, another to J. Attard, and another to Jan Attard.

Q **How do I track the ads?**

You need to keep a list showing which ads people responded to in which publications. If you have a computer you can keep this list in a database or a spreadsheet program for easy sorting. When you have only a few orders it may seem silly to do this, but as your business grows, you will need to know exactly which ads and which media produced the most orders so you can plan your advertising to get the most mileage for the least money.

Q **How often do I have to advertise?**

If your testing shows advertising does bring you customers, then you will probably want to advertise on a regular basis unless your business is seasonal. How often "on a regular basis" is will depend in part on your budget and in part on the media in which you advertise. If weekly publications bring you good results, however, you should probably advertise every week. If you are advertising in a daily publication, you may want to pick certain days of the week to advertise and always run your ads on those days so prospects know to look for your name and number on those days.

Q **Should I advertise on radio or TV?**

You will need to compare the costs and results of TV advertising to that of other media. TV advertising must be repeated several times a day for several weeks in order to be effective. It also needs to be aired at a time customers are likely to see or hear ads and respond to them. A tuxedo rental store in one town, for instance, did well with TV advertising right around prom time.

Q Should I advertise on the web?

If your customers are likely to look for what you sell in ads on the web, advertising on the web may be beneficial if you can find a cost-effective way to deliver ads to a targeted audience. Banner ads on the web are a little like billboards on highways. You'll need a lot of people passing by to get any to act immediately on the message they see. The average click-though rate for banners on the web is less than ½ of 1 percent (1 in 500 people). Once someone does click on your banner and reach your web site, you still have to convert them to a customer. Thus if your goal is primarily brand recognition, and if you have the money to advertise widely enough and frequently enough to make your name remembered, banner ads can pay off.

If your budget is limited, as most small and homebased business budgets are, buying banner ads on popular general interest web sites isn't likely to pay off. But if you can find popular small web sites that are targeted directly at your audience, banner ads, classified ads, or ads in the site newsletter may pay off. Like all other forms of advertising, you'll have to test each ad and compare the cost of acquiring customers this way to the overall profitability of the customer. But, if you find the right sites, it can pay off.

TIP

Some small web sites are amenable to bartering ads in lieu of cash payments. Thus, if you have a web site or newsletter of your own, you may want to suggest a barter arrangement to sites that sell noncompeting products to the same market you do. If your usage is about equal, a one-for-one swap of ads would be appropriate. If one site has more usage than the other, then work out an appropriate deal.

Q Does pay-per-inquiry advertising work on the web?

The answer depends on how the program is set up and what a customer is worth to you. If you are paying for inquiries from a banner advertising network that distributes your banners to many web sites and then pays each web site for each time someone clicks on your banner and goes to your site, the answer is probably no. The reason is because there are some web site owners who abuse the system and develop automated programs that will click on banners just to drive up the number of clicks they get paid for. Although the companies that run such networks may try to prevent such fraudulent activity, they can't catch all of the perpetrators. If your budget is limited and your banner gets picked up by one of the fraudulent operators before the network realizes it and takes steps to lock them out of the system, your money will be wasted.

On the other hand, paying for click-throughs can be a good way to advertise when there is little or no chance for fraud. For instance, GoTo.com (http://www.goto.com) is an Internet search engine that lets companies buy their position in search results. When a visitor searches on a keyword that the business is listed under, the order of the companies listed in the results is based on the amount each company chose to pay for click-throughs. For instance, suppose three companies choose the word *fax* as a keyword they want to be found under. Company A agrees to pay 10 cents per click-through; Company B agrees to pay 25 cents a click-through; and Company C agrees to pay 15 cents per click-through. Search results for the term *fax* would then show up with Company B's listing first, Company C second, and Company A third. The closer one comes to the top of the list, particularly for keywords where dozens or more companies might be listed under a keyword, the more likely it is that their listing will actually get seen by people interested in their product or service. Since only the corporation running the search engine gets paid for click-throughs (instead of many different web sites, as in the example) fraud is unlikely. The risk of fraud is further reduced because the company has several layers of fraud protection built into their system to ensure that mistaken or fraudulent clicks are not charged to the advertiser.

Similarly, if you work out a deal with individual targeted web sites to pay for click-throughs, and you watch your web site logs to see where the click-throughs are coming from, you should be able to benefit from pay-per-click advertising. Although not all web sites accept pay-per-click ads, if you search around and network with other small companies you should be able to locate opportunities for this type of advertising. As your company grows and can afford to spend more on advertising, you might want to have an advertising agency place the click-through ads for you.

Q **Should I get a listing or ad in the Yellow Pages?**

Some businesses get many customers from their Yellow Pages ads or listings, and others get no calls. To decide whether or not you should use the Yellow Pages, you need to consider carefully where your customers look for your type of product or service. You should also consider whether there is a clear-cut heading under which to put your ads. If there isn't, you might not get many customers from your listing.

If your service or product can be easily depicted in a small picture or if you can add some kind of textual information that will build confidence (for instance, "board certified"), then a display ad might be worthwhile. If you are just starting out, however, you may want to make the ad small. If it is successful, consider getting a slightly larger ad the next year, as long as you can be sure the ad will stay on the same page with other listings for your type of business.

Q **Will color help in the Yellow Pages ad?**

Opinions differ on how effective color is in a Yellow Pages ad. Some people say it increases response and some say it doesn't. One of the problems with using color in your ad is that the salespeople may have talked everyone else into buying an ad with a color border, too—so yours won't stand out.

Q **Do I need to offer a money-back guarantee?**

It is a good idea to offer a money-back guarantee for at least two reasons: it builds customer confidence and it can help lower your chargeback rate if you accept credit cards. Often customers won't buy from a store or a mail merchant unless they can return merchandise for a full refund if they aren't satisfied. Although there will always be some who take advantage of money-back guarantees and attempt to return a product after using it, the majority of customers are honest, and the goodwill you create by offering the guarantee will usually outweigh any losses due to people returning goods they've broken, copied, and so on.

Q **Do I need to be able to accept charge cards?**

Being able to accept charge cards as payment can boost sales. However, it can also increase your costs and risks. Securing merchant status may be difficult, too. See chapter 18 for additional information.

Q **Should I use special offers?**

Special offers can increase your response rate and help you determine which media gets responses. However, special offers can also bring out the tire kickers and freebie hunters, too. You need to test special offers to see which attracts the most paying customers. If you use a special offer, make sure it has a cut-off date or people will be pulling out the coupon or ad for months to come and demanding your product at the special rate. Also, if your cut-off date is at 9 P.M. Friday, don't be surprised if a lot of people wait until 8:30 P.M. on Friday to order or to walk into your store.

Q **What kind of special offers can I use that won't cost a lot?**

Discounts on products work well (the need to offer discounts should be considered when developing your pricing strategies), free information, and giveaways of inexpensive items, such as balloons, markers, pens, and magnets, may be useful in certain circumstances. For kids, free samples of your product or a free trial period are typical types of promotions.

Q **Can I say my product is better than that of the competition?**

The only safe way to indicate that your product is better than the competitor's is with indisputable facts. Size, weight, retail price, and number of pieces, for example, could be compared without problem to show your product's benefits over that of the competitor. But if you say your competitor's products are ugly or shoddy, you could be setting yourself up for a costly lawsuit. The same is true if you say your products are healthier or longer-lasting if you don't have hard facts to back up your claims.

Q **Should I advertise in card decks?**

Card decks can bring your sales message to a large group of potential customers at once (typically 100,000 prospects), and the prospects can be well targeted, such as all readers of a particular trade magazine. Response rates are low—typically one-tenth of 1 percent—though they may be higher or lower depending on how well your items match your target audience. As with mail order ads in magazines, however, there are companies that can make a profit despite the low response rate. Those companies seem to be ones with high-ticket products, products that lead to repeat sales, and products that are one of a line of products sold by the company who places the ad. If you only have one product to sell, it is probably unwise to try to use card deck advertising unless the product sells for at least $40 or $50 or more and you will be following up leads from the card deck with sales calls or additional literature.

Q How do I get into card decks?

Many magazines do card deck mailings periodically. In addition most card decks you receive will contain contact information for the publisher of the deck. Thus, if you see a deck that seems to be addressed to your target market, just call the publisher of the deck and ask for their rate card. You can also find the names of card deck publishers in directories available in the library. *Standard Rate and Data Service* directories are among those that list card deck publishers.

Q Are there any ways to cut the high costs of advertising?

Here are several ways you may be able to cut costs:

- Barter your product or service for space or air time. (Barter is taxable. Ask your accountant about tax implications.)
- Ask for a lower rate than the one advertised on an advertiser's rate card—the rates may be printed in black-and-white but aren't necessarily carved in stone.
- Ask about remnant space, which is space left that hasn't been sold at the time a publication is ready to go to print. If you have your ad ready to go, you may be able to purchase the remnant space for much less than the price of the space listed on the rate card.
- If you sell retail products, ask manufacturers about cooperative advertising programs. These can reduce your advertising costs.
- Do cooperative advertising with other small businesses. You may be able to advertise in their catalogs or have your product literature inserted into their merchandise packages in return for inserting theirs in with mailings going out to your customers.
- Trade lists with other noncompeting businesses, or trade your list for ad space or air time.
- Rent out the mailing list you accumulate to bring in extra income.
- Send an ad or a catalog of products along with every order you fill to encourage additional sales. The ad or catalog rides free with the order if it doesn't increase the shipping weight enough to raise the cost of shipping.
- Tack up business cards in stores, beauty shops, print shops, universities, and other public places if appropriate.

- Post computer shareware or text files with contact information in electronic libraries on commercial services and private bulletin boards. If you don't have a modem or don't have access to these online services, you can get people to upload your shareware and files for a fee.
- Send disks with your shareware to companies that sell shareware through catalogs.
- Consider placing inserts in weekly shoppers rather than doing a residential mailing.
- Consider doing small direct mail campaigns instead of advertising if you don't need to sell to a lot of people at once.
- Have your business card or other business information printed on a Rolodex card and mail the cards to your customers and prospects.

16.
Mail Profits: Using the Mail to Build Your Business

Each day the United States Postal Service collects, processes, and delivers approximately 550 million pieces of mail. A large percentage of that volume is made up of business mail designed to get new customers or make repeat sales to existing customers. Here are tips on how you can use the mail to bring in business.

Q **How can businesses use the mail to market their products or services?**

There are probably as many ways to use the mail as a marketing tool as there are ways for you to communicate with prospects and customers. Here are just a few ideas:

▸ Send out traditional direct mail packages (several pieces of sales literature in one package—typically a letter, brochure, and response card or return envelope aimed at getting the prospect to place an order immediately).
▸ Send out sales letters designed to get the prospect to call and make an appointment to talk to you about some product or service you sell.
▸ Send out a newsletter to prospects to demonstrate your expertise and drum up sales for your business.
▸ Send out invitations to an open house or other event designed to drum up business.

- Send reminders about services people need to purchase periodically (oil change or health checkups, for instance).
- Send a package of coupons for items in your retail store to people in your local area.
- Send catalogs listing new and old products.

Q What kind of response does direct mail get?

Most mailers are satisfied if a mailing to a rented list of targeted prospects gets a 1 percent response (in other words, if 1 person out of 100 responds to the mailing). That figure goes down to one-tenth of 1 percent or less if the list you mail to is a residential mailing list (rather than a list of people who share a specific interest). It goes up—often to 5 percent or more—if you are mailing to a list of customers who have purchased from you in the past.

With a mailing, as with advertising, response rates are important for planning and estimating; however, what really matters is the cost of getting the customer and the long-term profitability of the customer. If you are selling one item by mail, you will need to look closely at how many responses you will need to make a profit in order to determine if the mailing is worth doing.

Q Is it less expensive to use the mail to get customers than it is to advertise in magazines or newspapers?

It depends on what kind of mailing you are doing. If you are trying to sell products that compete with commercial items, and you will be mailing out expensive sales literature, you could easily spend as much to reach 5,000 people with a direct mail piece as you would spend to put an ad in a publication reaching tens of thousands or even hundreds of thousands of people. However, your mailing might have a better chance of being seen and read than an ad would, thereby getting more responses and orders.

If you are a freelancer or a small service business that sells to other businesses, you could send out a simple sales letter to a hand-picked list of 50 or 100 likely prospects for less than $50 and possibly land one or more clients who will give you thousands of dollars' worth of work.

Q **Is one mailing enough to get new customers?**

Often, no. Just like with ads, people have to see your mailings many times before ordering from you. Some mail marketers prepare a series of six or seven different letters and mailings and automatically send out a different letter in the series every few weeks until the customer buys, or until they reach the end of the series of letters. Each successive mailing brings in new customers that the preceding mailings didn't attract.

Q **Where do I get mailing lists?**

You can get mailing lists from companies called mailing list brokers. You can also get lists directly from some magazines and associations, or you can create your own lists from contacts in your industry or by calling companies likely to need your product or services and asking for the name of the purchasing agent, a department head, or whoever would be responsible for making purchasing decisions. Among the companies that rent mailing lists are:

Best Mailing Lists, Inc.
7505 East Tanque Verde Road
Tucson, AZ 85715
(520) 885-0400 or (800) 692-2378
http://www.bestmailing.com

Database America
470 Chestnut Ridge Road
Woodcliff Lake, NJ 07675
(800) 431-2914
http://www.databaseamerica.com

Edith Roman Associates, Inc.
Blue Hill Plaza, 16th Fl.
P.O. Box 1556
Pearl River, NY 10965-3104
(914) 620-9000 or (800) 223-2194
Fax: (914) 620-9035

InfoUSA.com
5711 So. 86th Circle
Omaha, NE 68127
(402) 593-4593 or (800) 321-0869
http://www.infousa.com

MyProspects.com
MySoftwareProducts
ClickAction, Inc.
2197 East Bayshore Road
Palo Alto, CA 94303
(800) 325-3508
http://www.myprospects.com

Teleconnect, Inc.
2701 South Coliseum Blvd., Suite 1167
Fort Wayne, IN 46803
(888) 420-1126
http://www.teleconect.com

In addition to large national lists such as these companies provide, you may be able to find small specialized mailing lists by searching the web. For instance, one such company, Demand Research, sells a database consisting of the names and contact information for the CEOs and CFOs of 6,700 U.S. publicly held corporations. The company also has specialized lists of human resources, MIS, marketing, and sales executives; comptrollers; manufacturing and R&D executives available. The company can be reached at

Demand Research
4587 Morse Centre, Suite 325
Columbus, OH 43329
(614) 891-5600
http://www.demandresearch.com

You can find many others in the Yellow Pages of your phone book or in the *Standard Rates & Data Services (SRDS)* directories available in your public library.

Q **What kinds of lists can I get?**

There are two broad categories of mailing lists: compiled lists and response lists. Compiled lists are created by getting names, addresses, and phone numbers from phone books, industry listings, and government lists of business names. Each name on the list may be verified by a phone call and, in some cases, names of contacts (if a business) can be added to the compiled information.

A response list is a list of people who have responded to some appeal—a mail order ad, a subscription offer, etc. These lists generally cost more and produce better responses than a compiled list.

Q **How often can you use a mailing list you get from a mailing list broker?**

It depends on the company and the list and on the form in which you buy it. It used to be that you could only rent mailing lists for one-time use. Now, however, you can purchase some lists on CD-ROM and use the list as often as you want within the time frame specified in your agreement with the mailing list company. Response lists generally aren't available on diskettes.

Q **How does the list broker know if you reuse the list?**

Lists are "seeded" with names of people who get and track mailings to prevent unauthorized reuse of lists.

Q **What does it cost to buy or rent a mailing list?**

The base prices for compiled lists average about $75 to $100 per thousand names to rent for one-time use. The fee to purchase a compiled list may be about triple the rental fee.

The base price for response lists generally range from $10 to $25 additional per thousand names. Usually response lists can only be rented for one-time use.

On top of the base prices for compiled or rented lists, you normally pay extra for selecting names by zip code and for pressure-sensitive (self-sticking) labels. You also pay extra if you want phone numbers in addition to addresses or if you want names and titles of contact people at various organizations.

In many cases there are minimum fees or a minimum number of names you must rent at once. One company, for instance, requires a minimum order of five thousand names for response lists.

Q **How do I choose a list?**

You choose a list that matches as closely as possible the characteristics of your customers or expected customers. For instance, you might be able to get a list of all female executives who have purchased some type of mail order product in the last six months. If you can describe your typical customer to the list broker, he or she should be able to help you identify and get the best list for your needs. You could also compile your own list from your knowledge of an industry or from the local phone book.

Q **Can I use e-mail to find new customers?**

Many people have used—or tried to use—e-mail to find new customers. Unfortunately, many of the people who have done so used unsolicited e-mail (called junk e-mail or spam) to promote opportunity scams, pornographic web sites, and other fraudulent or unacceptable material and sent their mailings to millions of people. As a result there has been a tremendous outcry against the use of unsolicited e-mail, and many legitimate businesses who have tried to send it found their messages were never delivered (in many cases because the online services and ISPs blocked the incoming junk e-mail) or that they got few or no responses. In many cases, too, businesses that sent unsolicited e-mail have had their e-mail accounts and/or their web sites closed down by their ISP.

A number of big corporations are developing e-mail services that they hope will allow businesspeople to us e-mail legitimately and effectively to bring in customers. These services base their mailing lists on something known as opt-in lists—lists of names compiled from people who have indicated they want to receive commercial mailings on particular topics. Thus the opt-in lists are not only composed of people who want to receive mail but are targeted—so you can purchase lists made up of people who want to receive information about your industry or type of product or service.

As these big corporations fine-tune their offerings—and if they develop to a price point that makes it affordable for businesses with limited budgets to rent their mailing lists, then it may become practical to use a mass mailing to build your business. At the time this book was written, however, those companies that had legitimate opt-in mailing lists were charging 13 to 22 cents per name or more. Some had steep start-up fees or minimum purchase requirements of $10,000 to $22,000. Others could only target by general interest—not by geographic area, limiting the number of small businesses that find the services practical or affordable.

You could use e-mail to build your business, however, by developing your own opt-in e-mail list. To do this you'd need a web site and a means for getting people to sign up to have you send them mail. See chapter 16 for additional information.

Q **How can I be sure that if I rent an e-mail list, I won't be renting a list that was compiled by stripping names off an online message board or chat room?**

Ask how the names on the list were compiled, and check any sites the service claims to use to get opt-in names. Search the web for the name of the company and see if there have been any news stories implying the company or its owners have been involved in sending out spam. Check the Federal Trade Commission (FTC) web site at http://www.ftc.gov to see if the company name or the owners have ever been sued by the FTC. Finally, consider how big the company is and whether it has a reputation of its own to maintain. Large corporations with many shareholders to please are more likely to have procedures in place to help ensure that the name on their lists really are willing to receive mail.

Q **Can I buy e-mail lists?**

Most legitimate sources of e-mail services will only rent e-mail lists.

Q **What established companies rent e-mail lists?**

There will be an increasing number of companies that do. Three of the initial players in this field are:

ClickAction, Inc.
2197 East Bayshore Road
Palo Alto, CA 94303
(800) 325-3508

Teleconnect, Inc.
2701 South Coliseum Blvd., Suite 1167
Fort Wayne, IN 46803
(888) 420-1126
http://wwwteleconect.com

Edith Roman Associates, Inc.
Blue Hill Plaza, 16th Floor
P.O. Box 1556
Pearl River, NY 10965-3104
(914) 620-9000 or (800) 223-2194
Fax: (914) 620-9035

Q **What's a house list?**

A house list is the list of your own customers. If you sell a line of products or the type of service that is needed periodically, your house list will often produce more customers than any other list.

Q **How important is it to have the name of a person on the mailing?**

Usually you will get a better response if you address your mailings to particular people. A letter addressed to "Occupant" or "Sales Manager" or "President" or "Purchasing Agent" immediately tells the recipient that what is inside is an ad from a business or individual they don't know. That makes that letter less important to read. Overworked businesspeople and home owners who don't like getting junk mail often will throw out such letters without ever opening them.

Q **What should I put in a mailing to find new customers?**

It is usually best to include a sales letter, brochure, and a response card or return envelope. Some people just send out a brochure or a sales letter, but using both gives you more opportunity to explain what you sell and show the recipient of your mailing the benefits of your product or service.

Q **How do I write a sales letter?**

The purpose of a sales letter is to sell—in other words, to convince someone to take some specific action, such as order a product, call you for an appointment, visit your store—and to take that action immediately.

Although that might seem obvious, many small business owners send out sales letters that don't sell. A typical letter reads something like this:

> *We are pleased to announce the opening of the George Jones Bookkeeping Service. The service, which is designed to help small businesses meet their bookkeeping needs, uses the latest computer equipment to store all customer records. You can reach us from 9 A.M. to 5 P.M. at 555-1234.*

The problem with a letter like that is that the recipient really doesn't care that *you* have opened a bookkeeping service or anything else, What might interest them, maybe enough to call you, is information about what your service will do for them. Tell them how you can save them time, minimize errors, or perhaps help them reduce their income tax bills by making sure they have all the records they need to take all the deductions they are entitled to—then you are much more likely to catch their attention and attract their business.

Q **How do I write a brochure?**

Use the brochure as an expansion of your sales letter. The brochure should give further details about your product or service, but it should still *sell*, not tell. The cover of the brochure should highlight the key benefit of your product or service, and the text and headlines inside the brochure should build on that benefit and add one or two additional reasons to buy or call you immediately. Finally, the brochure or a separate response card should ask for the order or the phone call and, if possible, give the recipient an incentive to do what you have asked immediately. That incentive might be a discount for ordering before a certain date, a free gift for calling within the next 5 days, or something similar.

Be sure the brochure includes your business name, address, and phone number in several places. You also need to make sure people who see the brochure for the first time can immediately tell what the brochure is all about and what you want them to do. Studies have shown that you have between 3 and 7 seconds to capture a prospect's attention with your mailing piece. If the prospect can't figure out what you are selling or why it should interest him or her, your brochure will wind up in the garbage.

One good way to test the clarity of your brochure is to have someone who knows nothing about your business read it and tell you what he or she thinks the brochure says. If the person can immediately tell you what you are offering and why it's a good idea to buy what you are selling, then your brochure probably will accomplish your goals. If there are questions about what you are selling or about the information in the brochure, you probably have not conveyed your sales message as well as you could have. In that case, consider rewriting the brochure or have a professional help you write it.

Q **Do I need pictures in my brochure?**

Photographs or drawings can be useful in your brochure if they help get your sales message across. If the pictures are just there to satisfy your ego or sense of pride, they probably don't belong. You may be thrilled about the new building you are moving into; your customers probably don't care, however. Thus, including a picture of your new building is likely to be a waste of space and money, since it costs extra to put a photo in a brochure.

Q **What kind of information should go in a brochure?**

You will want to make sure your brochure includes all the main features of your product or service and that it expresses those features as benefits. For instance, instead of saying your database software stores customer data, you'd talk about how the software saves time by automatically printing customer addresses on shipping labels or improves cash flow by making it easy to spot overdue accounts.

In addition to features, you would want to include facts, statistics, and perhaps testimonials that would help the reader make a decision to call or place an order. If you are using the brochure to make a special offer, the nature of your offer and how the recipient can take advantage of it, as well as a cut-off date for the offer, should be very clear.

Q **How do I get testimonials?**

Satisfied customers will often write or call you and tell you how great they think your product or service is. These people, if asked, often don't mind letting you include their comments about your product or service in your sales literature. You should get a signed statement from them indicating you have their permission to use their comments in your sales literature.

Q **Can I make up testimonials?**

No. That is a violation of truth-in-advertising laws.

Q **Can I rent my mailing list to other companies?**

Renting mailing lists is a good source of extra income for many companies; however, you will usually need to have at least 5,000 to 10,000 names for your list to be rentable. The information also must be current and accurate. If your information is much more than 6 or 9 months old, it may have too many address or name changes (for business contacts) to be useful to others.

Q **Do I need a bulk mail permit from the post office to send out mailings?**

Mail permits let you take discounts on large mailings if these meet certain post office specifications. These specifications include the number of pieces mailed at one time, the uniformity of the pieces mailed, the destination of the mail, and the method of sorting, bundling, and depositing the mail at the post office. Since you have to pay a one-time permit fee plus an additional annual fee for each class of mail for which you want discount rates, you will need to be mailing at least several thousand pieces of mail each year in batches of at least 200 to make getting a permit worthwhile. (At this writing the one-time fee and the annual fee are each $85.)

If you are going to use a letter shop to prepare your mailings, they should be able to send out your mailings using their permit.

Q **Should I use first-class or third-class mail?**

That depends partly on your budget, partly on how soon you need the mail to arrive, and partly on whether you want your mail to look like a letter rather than an ad so that it will get opened. If you are mailing a piece that must reach everyone on the list by a certain date, and that date is a week or two away, or if you want your mailing to look like a regular letter, use first-class mail. Sending the mailing third class immediately alerts recipients that it is not a personal letter. In addition, third class gets sent only after all other mail goes out. If a post office is particularly busy, as it is during certain times of the year, third-class mail sits on the side until someone has time to get to it. That means it can sometimes take more than two weeks for third-class mail to reach its destination. A brochure urging readers to visit your trade show booth isn't going to do any good if your customers get it a week and a half after the trade show is over.

Q **How can I make my mailing stand out among all the other junk mail people get?**

One way to make your letter stand out is to use real stamps on it rather than using a meter. Using a lot of small denomination stamps instead of one first-class mail stamp may make it stand out, too. Still another way to make your mail stand out and get people to open it is to put a message on the outside of the envelope telling people that the contents will benefit them or save them money.

17.

Getting Paid

One of the biggest drawbacks of being your own boss is you no longer collect a paycheck at the end of the week. Instead, unless you run a cash business, you are likely to have to wait weeks or even months to collect for work you've done or products you've delivered.

Sometimes such delays are unavoidable. It may be standard practice for a particular company or most of the companies in a particular industry to take 60 to 90 days or longer to pay. Other times, though, your customers will give your bills low priority because money is tight or because you are a small business and unlikely to damage their credit rating or be much of a pest if they pay you late or don't pay you at all.

Regardless of the circumstances, unusual or unexpected delays in payment can put a crimp in your business and gray hairs on your head, particularly if you have a payroll to meet or a family to feed, clothe, and shelter. The strategies in this chapter should help you avoid some common collection pitfalls.

Q **How long could it take to collect from customers?**

If you don't get paid at the time products or services are delivered, it can take anywhere from a few weeks to 90 days or more to collect on your invoices. While some companies pay within 10 to 30 days of delivery of work or a product, it is not unusual for payment to take 45 to 60 days from the time your invoice reaches your

271

customers. In some industries, or with some individual companies, you can expect to wait 90 days or more for payment.

Q **When should I consider a payment late?**

Consider a payment late if it does not arrive within about 10 days of the time you would normally expect it to arrive. For instance, if a business normally pays in 30 days, you should have payment in hand within 40 days of the date you mailed the invoice.

Q **What should I do if I don't get paid on time?**

If you sell to businesses, call your contact at the company and make sure they got your invoice and that the invoice has been signed off and forwarded to the accounting department for payment. If you sell to consumers, send out a friendly reminder asking if the customer has misplaced or overlooked the bill.

Q **What should I do if the customer says he never received the invoice or that he mailed the check?**

Although there are some businesses that will use such ploys to delay payment, occasionally invoices, checks, and mail do get lost or misplaced. As long as the loss is an isolated incident, the best thing to do is give the client the benefit of the doubt. Send a new invoice if the client tells you the invoice has been lost. If accounting says the check has been cut, ask when it was mailed. If the company is local and more than a week has elapsed since the check was supposedly mailed, ask them to put a stop payment on the old check and issue you a new one. If you suspect the company is not being honest about mailing the check, tell them you will stop by in person and pick it up.

Q **What can be done to speed collection?**

In some types of businesses there may be nothing you can do except to plan ahead for the delay in payment. This is one reason accountants and experienced business owners warn neophytes not to quit a job to start a business unless they have or can raise enough cash to cover business and living expenses for 6 to 12 months. But for many businesses one or more of these suggestions may help.

- Discuss payment terms before the work is done. Be sure you and the customer are each clear about when payment will be expected.
- Ask who should get your invoice when the work is done. It may or may not be the person who assigns you work. If your invoice is misdirected, payment is likely to be delayed.
- Put everything in writing. If you don't have a formal contract with your customers, summarize details of any verbal discussions in a letter (commonly called a letter of agreement), and send it to the customer. The letter should include enough details about prices, delivery, and payment to avoid disputes later on about your fee, what you are supposed to do for that fee, when you are supposed to do it, and when and how much you should be paid.
- If the customer has the right to accept or reject work, make sure any contracts or letters of agreement specify a time frame within which the customer must make that decision. If you don't, the customer could hang on to your work and/or delay payment for months just by neither accepting nor rejecting what you've delivered.
- Consider retainer arrangements with some or all of your customers if it is customary in your field. These can be set up on a per job basis or on a long-term basis. If the retainer gives the customer a certain number of hours of your time each week or month, make sure the contract is worded so that your customer can't "save up" (carry over) unused time. Otherwise you could get stuck with two or more customers each demanding at the same time that you make good on the time you "owe" them and do their projects immediately despite other commitments you have made.
- Get part or all of your money up front. If you can't get the entire fee in advance, arrange for progress payments for the balance. Set up the arrangement so you have covered all costs and at least some of your profit before you finish a job or deliver the final product. That way if the company stalls, "loses" the invoice for your final payment, runs into a cash flow problem of its own, or decides not to pay you for any reason, the loss will be minimal.

DIRTY TRICKS WARNING

From time to time you will run into a business that has no intention of playing fair with small business vendors. Such businesses are often surprisingly large and regularly chisel vendors or subcontractors out of anything from a few dollars here and there to a few hundred dollars, knowing full well the small vendor won't do much more than raise an eyebrow or kick a tire because (a) the amount is too small to be worth pursuing legally, or (b) their business is too important for the small vendors to jeopardize by insisting on full payment. If you run into one of these businesses, you basically have three choices.

- make a fuss and risk losing the client
- waste your time and money going to court and, later, try to collect on any judgment you are awarded
- swallow pride, your tongue, and a little gall, and accept the lower fee as yet another cost of doing business

Unfortunately, the last option is usually the most practical from a purely business point of view since it wastes the least amount of time and money—which is why the bigger company knows it is likely to get away with its tactics.

- If you are working for a federal or state government agency or a prime contractor to a government agency, ask if they have a program to pay small businesses within 30 days. If they do, find out what you have to do to be part of that program.
- If you are working for other businesses, consider offering a discount for payment within 10 days. A common discount is 2 percent for payment within 10 days.

DIRTY TRICKS WARNING If you offer a discount for early payment, you will find some companies will take the full 30 days or more to pay and then still take the discount. You can argue with them, insist on payment, or ignore the "mistake." What you do will probably depend on whether or not you want to do business with the company in the future.

- Send out invoices as soon as jobs are finished. The sooner your invoices go out, the sooner they are likely to be paid. If you deal with businesses that run payables only once or twice a month, and your invoice reaches accounting the day after the company ran payables, your invoice could take 15 to 30 days longer than it should have to get paid.
- Look into the possibility of getting merchant status and accepting credit cards. If you are approved, depending on your agreement with the company, you will usually get paid by the credit card company within 2 days to 2 weeks.
- Decide, based on industry norms and your experience with individual vendors, how long it should take to get paid. Any time you do not receive payment within the time limit you set, send out a reminder or overdue notice immediately. Follow up with repeat notices at regular intervals until you get paid. The longer you wait to collect on late accounts, the harder it may be to collect.
- Be persistent if you have trouble collecting. The adage about the squeaky wheel getting the grease holds just as true for collecting from accounts as it does for other situations.
- If possible, don't start a new job for a company until you get paid for the previous one.
- If you sell to businesses and have a computer and modem, consider checking the credit rating of potential business clients. You can check business credit ratings quickly and at relatively low cost on the Credit FYI web site at http://www.creditfyi.com. The cost is only $14.95 for a detailed record or $4.95 if little credit history is available.

Q I've done a lot of work for a company that always seems pleased with my work and pays on time. Now, they are more than two months late paying me and won't return my phone calls. Could it be they were displeased with the last two projects I did for them?

When a customer who appears to be pleased with your work stops paying on time and won't talk to you about the problem, there is good reason to suspect the company is having a cash flow problem and that the missing payments are a result of their cash crunch, not the quality of your work.

Q What can I do to get them to pay me?

This is always a difficult situation for a very small business. On the one hand, if the customer is big and has provided a lot of business in the past, you may not want to lose their future business. Thus, you may not want to be too aggressive in your collection efforts. On the other hand, you can't stay in business if you don't get paid for your work in a reasonable amount of time. If you are a freelancer or a very small business, very late payment for just one or two large jobs can affect your ability to pay your own bills if you don't have much spare cash.

Therefore, the first thing you have to do is decide whether you want to keep this customer's business and if the business is worth keeping. If you sell to businesses rather than consumers, one thing that may help you decide if a customer's business is worth keeping is to talk to other business owners who sell to the same company. Find out what their experiences have been with the company.* Trade or business associations are a good place to make such contacts. If you start hearing things like "They do that to everyone" or if you learn several other suppliers or freelancers have stopped doing business with the company, you may well want to consider crossing the company off your customer list. Networking with other business owners can also help you avoid losses and payment delays by alerting you in advance to companies that are known to be slow or late payers.

If the business is worth keeping, about the best you can do is send statements with polite reminders of the unpaid bill each month and continue to try to reach

---

*You have to be careful that you don't say anything that could be considered libelous or slanderous to the client company. For instance, you don't want to imply the company is about to go bankrupt or never pays its bills to anyone. You could mention the company seems to be taking a long time paying you, and ask others if they know how long the company usually takes and/or what their experiences with the company have been.

your contact at the company. If you do succeed in reaching your contact, try to find out the reason for the holdup. If the company is having cash flow problems, suggest they pay you part of the outstanding balance every 2 weeks until the invoice is paid.

If you don't want to deal with the customer in the future, send a series of firm (but not threatening) collection letters. Phone call reminders may also help pry money loose from the company. If the company doesn't respond to your letters or calls, you might consider suing them in small claims court if the amount involved is within the limits set in your region. Occasionally you will find that a company will pay what it owes shortly before the day they are told to appear in court.

Q **What should I do if the customer keeps calling me but isn't paying?**

Basically, you have only four choices:

- Thank them for thinking of you but tell them you can't ship merchandise or start new projects for them until they pay part or all of what they owe you.
- Refuse to do business with them at all.
- Ship goods on a COD basis or get up-front payment for services.
- Take the order or the job and add it to their bill—and risk having their cash flow problem become yours.

Q **I don't want to be bothered going to court because of the amount of time it will take. Would it do any good just to send a letter telling the company I'll sue if they don't pay?**

No, you can't do that. Threatening to sue a company (or a consumer) when you have no intention of doing so could cause you to be sued yourself. If you are unsure of what you can and can't do to legally collect from your customers, ask an attorney for advice. For a relatively small fee, you could save yourself a bundle if the advice prevents you from getting sued or helps you collect debts.

Q **Should I sue if I can't sue in small claims court?**

That's another sticky situation for very small businesses. Unfortunately, in some cases, despite the loss of the income, the most practical thing to do is accept the loss and go about your business. Unless the company owes you a lot of money and you could recoup your costs of suing, legal and court costs and the time you have to devote to the lawsuit may make it impractical for you to sue. Your best bet in a situation like this is to ask your attorney for advice and consider all possible outcomes before making your decision. Remember, too, that should you win and your customer can't pay, your victory will be a very expensive one.

Q **The company claims I didn't do part of the job so they aren't going to pay me. What can I do?**

The first thing you should do is sit down and talk to your contact at the company to determine the cause of the misunderstanding. If you had a contract to perform the work, ask them to pinpoint how the company thinks you failed to live up to your responsibilities. If the problem revolves around a misunderstanding over terms in the contract or over the nature of the work to be delivered, see if you can work out an equitable solution. If not, discuss whether the company might make partial payment (if you are willing to accept partial payment) in settlement of the contract.

If you can't work out your differences, you will have to sue the company if you want to collect the money you are owed. If the amount is larger than the maximum claim allowed in small claims court, the cost of your legal fees might make the lawsuit impractical to pursue. Thus, if you can reach any kind of compromise with the company, you are likely to come out ahead. (You will also learn, albeit the hard way, to make sure your contracts let the customer know exactly what you will and won't do for your fee.)

Q **Do I have to have a written contract with my customers to get paid?**

Under something known as the Uniform Commercial Code (UCC), contracts for the sale of goods worth $500 or more must be in writing to be legally enforceable. (Items you can move or ship are generally considered "goods.") Although personal services and goods valued under $500 are not covered by that law, it is always a good idea to get contracts in writing. Without a written document there is generally no way to prove whose version is correct if a dispute arises.

Q **How should I go about notifying people that their account is past due?**

It would be a good idea to develop a series of letters notifying the customer of the past due amount and requesting payment. Each of these letters should be slightly more emphatic than the previous one about the importance of paying the past due amount *now*.

If you send out computer-generated statements, the reminder could be printed directly on the statement instead of being mailed as a separate letter. If you use multipart forms, an alternative to a form letter might be to put a sticker saying essentially the same thing as the form letter on a copy of the original bill and mail it to the customer. Still another alternative (a little less friendly, though) is to send the customer a copy of the original bill and, using a rubber stamp, mark it "Past Due."

Q **Are there any regulations about what I can and can't do to collect bills?**

The Fair Debt Collection Practices Act set down a number of guidelines governing the collection of consumer debt by third-party bill collectors. While the provisions of the act may not apply to you unless you retain a collection agency to collect outstanding consumer bills, you would still be wise to abide by the provisions of the act.

Among the actions you should avoid are:

- making threats
- using harassing or abusive language
- accusing the debtor of being a liar or deadbeat
- making the debtor's name known publicly (reporting late or defaulted payments to credit bureaus is not illegal, however)
- making false, misleading, or deceptive statements about what will happen if the debtor doesn't pay (such as saying you will sue if you have no intentions of doing so)
- implying that the originator (person who is requesting payment) of a collection letter is an attorney if he or she is not
- making a collection letter look like a telegram
- implying that the debtor has committed a crime
- making dunning calls more frequently than once a week
- making calls at very early or very late hours (after 8 P.M. is considered very late for dunning calls in some states)
- calling a consumer who is a debtor at work if his or her employer forbids it

Q **What should I say in past due notices?**

The first reminder should be very polite, suggesting the customer has merely forgotten or misplaced the bill. The tone should be friendly and indicate you assume the customer will pay it immediately now that he or he has been reminded. It might read something like this:

Dear Mr. Southard,

Bills sometimes get misplaced or overlooked, and we have not yet received your payment for our invoice #1234 dated April 25. Please check your records, and if payment has not gone out, mail a check today.

If a check was recently mailed, please disregard this notice. Thank you for your attention to this matter. We appreciate your business.

Sincerely,

If you don't get payment within two weeks of sending the first reminder, send a second notice. This second notice should be worded a little more strongly than the first. In addition, it should also ask the customer to call you if there is any problem related to the bill. This may flush out customers who aren't paying because they dispute a charge or aren't satisfied and those who might need to pay the bill in stages instead of all at once.

Dear Mr. Southard,

We have not yet received your payment of $230 for invoice #1234 that was mailed to you on April 25. Would you please take a minute to check your records now and forward payment so we may bring your account up to date? If there is some problem with your bill that you would like to discuss with us, please don't hesitate to call.

Thank you for your immediate attention to this matter.

Sincerely,

The third letter should be a little firmer:

Dear Mr. Southard,

We still have not received your check for $230 for invoice #1234 dated April 25. Since you have not questioned previous statements we assume our records are correct. To preserve your credit *privileges, please forward us your check for $230 today so that we may bring your seriously overdue account up to date. If you cannot pay the full amount at this time, please call our main office to work out a payment method you can abide by.*

Thank you for your speedy cooperation in this matter.

The fourth letter should specify what you will do if you do not receive payment by a specific date. You must be careful not to make such letters threatening or to misrepresent what you will do. Don't say you will report the customer to credit bureaus or sue unless you plan to do those things, and don't say or imply anything that could otherwise be construed as threatening. To be sure your collection letters don't violate any laws, it would be a good idea to have an attorney review and approve them. Here is a sample of what your fourth letter might look like.

Dear Mr. Southard:

Over the last two months we have sent you several reminders about your overdue payment of $230 for invoice #1234. At this time, your bill is still unpaid.

Please remit your payment of $230 within 5 days to prevent further collection action.

Sincerely,

Q **Can I send postcards instead of letters to alert people to past-due accounts?**

No. By law, there can be no marks or visible indication referring to collection efforts on anything you put in the mail. If you use envelopes with see-through windows allowing the address to show through, make sure nothing about late payments shows through the envelope window.

Q **How should I handle phone calls to collect money owed me?**

Collection phone calls should pretty much follow the procedures described for letters. The one thing you will need to do, however, is make sure at the outset that you have reached the right individual. Even if the person's last name is unusual, you could have phoned the wrong person, particularly if you looked up his or her phone number in a telephone book. As noted in the list of collection practices to avoid, you also should avoid making your calls at unusual hours.

Q **Does it pay to use a collection agency?**

Most people do not like to be contacted by collection agencies, and some will pay up when they see their account has been turned over to one for collection. Additionally, the agency may be more persistent and routine in its collection efforts than you are. However, a collection agency doesn't have any methods available to it that you don't. They can't threaten, harass, or mislead the customer into paying the debt, and they have no legal means of forcing payment. Nothing short of a court order can force your customers to pay up.

Q **What do collection agencies charge?**

Collection agency fees range from one-third to one-half the amount collected. Be sure you know in advance all the fees you will be charged. For instance, will you have to pay a fee for each letter the agency mails on your behalf or just give the agency a percentage of the amount collected?

Q **A customer owes me a lot of money and seems to have skipped town. Is there any way I could track this person down and collect?**

If the amount owed is significant, you might want to consider hiring a private investigator to do the search.

Q **My customer is from out of state. Where do I file the lawsuit?**

In most cases you have to file suit for collection in the legal jurisdiction where the customer is located.

18.
The Charge Card
Dilemma

Credit cards are the payment method of choice in an ever-growing number of sales transactions each year. In June 1999, VISA, which claims a 60 percent market share, was processing 64 million transactions a day for an annual sales volume of $1.4 trillion. Consumers and businesses alike use credit cards to purchase equipment, clothing, office supplies, medical and dental services, car repairs, travel, and a wide range of products and services. In fact, businesses that don't accept credit cards often find themselves at a competitive disadvantage.

As one business owner puts it:

> *The more I sell the more I make. . . . Because I am so much like everybody else, I need to place myself so that I can sell more than the guy down the street. . . . Or, if I cannot beat them I have to at least join the "me too" club. Accepting credit cards falls into the "me too" category.*

As convenient as it may be for people to charge purchases on credit cards, the widespread use of credit cards presents three major problems for small businesses:

- Banks often won't grant a merchant account (what you need to accept credit cards) to new businesses, Internet, or conventional mail order businesses.
- Small and homebased businesses often don't realize there are a number of third-party providers that will work with new and mail order businesses.

Thus, they are easy prey for providers who charge high transaction fees and try to lock new businesses into expensive, noncancellable leases for equipment.

▸ Very small businesses are at risk for catastrophic losses if they are hit by a rash of charges on stolen credit cards.

Although there are no guarantees, by arming yourself with the facts in this chapter you stand a good chance of avoiding the pitfalls in obtaining merchant status and processing charge sales.

Q Won't it cut into my profits if I accept charge cards?

Accepting credit cards will increase your cost of doing business since you will have to pay the credit card company a percent of each sale and are likely to also have to pay an additional flat transaction fee plus some flat monthly charges. Thus, if you have a low profit margin, you may want to increase your prices overall to offset the credit card fees. You may find, however, that your sales volume and the dollar amount of each sale increases more than enough to offset the fees you pay the credit card company. In addition, if you have been used to billing customers and waiting 30 or more days for payment, letting customers charge purchases could reduce your billing costs and improve cash flow. You shouldn't expect to clear up outstanding bills by gaining merchant status,* however. It is against credit card company rules to let customers charge unpaid bills to their cards. Only new purchases can be charged.

Finally, keep in mind that after achieving merchant status, some businesses find little improvement in sales, and a few actually lose money due to credit card fraud or consumer abuse.

Q How long does it take for the credit card company to pay me when I accept charge cards?

How soon you get your money will depend on whether funds are transferred to you electronically, held for a time against possible chargebacks, or mailed to you in a paper check. Generally, however, you can expect to get paid in 2 to 14 days.

Merchant status is the term used to indicate a business is authorized to accept credit cards in payment for goods and services. A business with merchant status will have the charges processed through their merchant account with a bank or other credit card processor. Credit card companies and banks use the term *merchant* to denote any business that accepts credit cards.

Q How do I go about accepting credit cards?

To accept credit cards, you will have to apply for merchant status (also called a merchant account) through a bank or other financial institution, an authorized Independent Sales Organization (ISO), or the credit card company itself for certain cards. Once you are granted merchant status, you will need to buy or rent a device for imprinting or electronically processing the credit cards. If you are selling on the Internet, you'll also need a secure method of accepting orders and/or "shopping cart" software which lets customers enter orders on an order form, adding or deleting things from their cart (order form) as they shop.

Q Do I need a separate account for each credit card I want to accept?

No. Your merchant account provider should be able to arrange for you to accept all major credit cards. You may pay a different rate for charges processed through some cards, however.

Q Where do I go to apply for merchant status?

If you have been in business for two years or more, your business is not home-based, and you don't sell mail order, you may be able to get merchant status through the bank with which you normally do business. If you are a small mail order company, run a homebased business, are new in business, or operate certain types of businesses, your regular bank may turn down your request for merchant status, or not even be willing to talk to you about it.

Q Can I get merchant status without going through a bank?

You don't have to get a merchant account through normal banking channels. In fact, most start-ups get their merchant account through a third-party merchant services provider. These providers, which are also called independent sales organizations (ISOs), are intermediaries between merchant banks (banks that process credit cards) and businesses that want to accept charge cards from their customers. As the word *sales* implies, these companies sell credit card processing services and within certain limits can sell their services for whatever the market will bear. Most also sell, lease, or rent credit card processing terminals and provide other services such as check verification.

Q **Why is it so difficult to get merchant status? Don't the banks or other companies want my business?**

Banks want business, but they don't want risky business, and home businesses, new businesses, Internet businesses, and mail order operations all look like high-risk operations to credit card processors. Here's why: Federal laws give credit card users broad protection against unauthorized use and unfair credit practices.* As a result of these laws, credit card issuers act as intermediaries in disputes between the consumer and the merchant. If a consumer claims she did not make a purchase or that a purchased item was inferior and the merchant won't replace it or refund their money, the credit card company refunds the cardholder's money in most cases and charges back (bills) the merchant for the amount of the refund. While merchants are supposed to be given a chance to prove the purchase was actually made or the goods were satisfactory, merchants say that doesn't always happen.

If the merchant is very small (as homebased operations often are), the company may not be financially able to make good on chargebacks, particularly if they are hit with someone buying merchandise with one or more stolen credit cards. If they go bankrupt (or simply close their doors and disappear, as some fraudulent businesses do), the credit card issuer has to absorb the loss. In addition, under VISA regulations, if the percentage of VISA chargebacks to a merchant account goes over one percent, the merchant bank may face stiff fines or possible loss of their ability to process VISA cards.

Q **Why do banks object to giving legitimate Internet and mail order businesses merchant status?**

Mail order businesses are particularly risky from the credit card processor's point of view because the company selling the merchandise never sees the customer, does not get the customer's signature at the time of the sale, and has no way of determining for sure that the person calling in the order is actually the owner of the card.

---

*The Truth in Lending Act and the Fair Credit Billing Act both contain regulations affecting credit card use and billing.

Q Are there any other circumstances that might prevent me from getting merchant status?

Credit card processors are not going to want to give you merchant status if you have a bankruptcy on your records, tax liens in effect, or accounts that have been written off by a lender.

Q I've heard stories about business owners paying steep applications and other fees and sometimes still not getting merchant status. Does that happen a lot?

It used to. Several years ago Dennis Mulgannon opened a pizzeria in California and wanted to accept credit cards. His bank turned him down for a merchant account because his business was too new. But then one day, he relates, "this guy came into the store and asks to see the owner. He says he can get me not only merchant status but also an electronic reader and printer.

"Well, I saw the clouds part, and heard the Mormon Tabernacle choir singing the *Hallelujah Chorus*. But it must have been just a recording . . . $300 and four weeks later I was 'regretfully informed' that I'd need to reapply after I had been in business longer."

Today, businesses find it much easier to get their applications accepted, but that doesn't mean the abusive practices have stopped completely. Small start-ups with limited knowledge of retailing and the merchant card industry are easy prey for sales agents and service providers that charge high fees and/or lock the new merchant into noncancellable equipment leases.

Q How much should I expect to pay to apply for merchant status?

Application fees vary considerably. Most were charging $100 to $200 in 1999, but at least one (Merchant Warehouse in Brighton, Massachusetts, didn't charge an application fee). If the service provider you plan to submit your application to charges a fee, ask if it's refundable if you are not accepted.

Q How much should it cost to buy or rent the terminals to process the cards?

Fees vary with the type of terminal, but average prices for up-front purchase of electronic terminals or software used to process credit card purchases range from

$300 to approximately $700. (Mobile equipment is higher.) Some of the terminals include a printer, others require you to purchase a separate printer that is about the same price as the terminal.

Terminals and software can also be leased, but the leases are noncancellable and can quadruple your cost. A terminal that cost $500 to purchase outright would typically be leased at $40 a month for 48 months, for a total of $1,920. If the business wanted to keep the equipment at that time, they'd have to pay an additional sum to buyout the equipment at the end of the lease term.

One woman who had gotten a referral from her banker to an ISO (independent sales organization) was talked into leasing a terminal. After signing the lease she discovered she could have purchased the terminal for $385. She wanted out of the lease, but the lease was noncancellable.

"They told me I could send the machine back with a check for $1,725 or keep it and send them a check for $1,913.94," she says.

Q   **Why is there such a large discrepancy in fees?**

Independent sales organizations have to order and pay for credit reports on applicants and have to pay employees to review applications and credit reports. Thus, they often charge an application fee to cover these costs and to discourage applications from people who have little real interest in achieving merchant status or who know they are unlikely to get merchant status because they have many delinquent accounts or have defaulted on loans.

However, since an ISO's actual costs to process an application should be well under $100, fees much over $100 are likely to include a fair amount of "profit" being made on the application process itself. Much of that profit is likely to go to the independent sales agent, rather than to the company the sales agent represents.

Sales agents also make a commission on the sale or lease of terminals or software.

They make considerably more money when you lease equipment or software than they do if you purchase it outright. Thus many encourage leasing even though it is very expensive over the long term.

Q Besides the application fee and the cost of the terminal or software to process the cards, and Internet shopping cart fees if I sell on the web, what other fees will I have to pay?

You generally have to pay several fees. Typically they include some or all of the following:

A "discount" fee. A percentage of the selling price of the goods purchased, usually 2.5 to 3 percent for mail order transactions, but some providers were charging 5 percent or more. The fee for in-person retail sales is usually under 2 percent.

A per-transaction fee. The amount varies from as little as 10 cents a transaction to as much as 56 cents or more. It is always in addition to the discount rate or fee.

Monthly minimum. The minimum amount of processing fees you have to pay each month. Typical amounts for this minimum run from $10 to $25.

Statement fee. Yes, that's right. ISOs charge you for the "privilege" of seeing a statement each month showing what you've bought or sold. The fee runs $10 and up.

Gateway fee. If you are selling on the Internet and want incoming orders to be processed in real time (immediately processed from the information entered by the customer), you usually have to pay either a gateway fee each month or extra fees for each transaction. One company for instance was charging a $20 gateway fee in 1999. Another didn't have a gateway fee, but charged 56 cents per transaction. This fee was double what the transaction fee was if the orders were manually keyed in.

These fees are all in addition to any fees you have to pay for a web site or for online shopping carts (online order-taking software). Between fees such as these and the cost of noncancellable licenses, some business owners find it cost them a minimum of $60 to $70 a month or more to accept credit cards even if they make few sales. So, shop around and get rates from several providers before signing on the dotted line.

Q How do I get paid?

With most merchant accounts you have to give the provider access to your bank account. The way most work is that they transfer money from transactions to your account about two or three days after each sale. They can also transfer money out of your account if necessary to cover monthly minimum fees and any chargebacks.

Q Is it ever worth paying much higher than normal fees?

Certain kinds of businesses find it particularly difficult to get merchant status because of the nature of the product or service they sell. One ISO mentioned not dealing with limousine services, escort services, or companies selling "adult" products. Another mentioned not accepting multilevel marketing companies and certain kinds of telemarketing services because they tended to either disappear or have a high customer dissatisfaction rate, and therefore a high chargeback rate. In addition, many ISOs won't grant merchant status to a small business if the owner has a poor personal credit history.

If you fall into any of these categories you may have to pay high rates to find a third-party processor willing to take on the risk of your business. However, you shouldn't be willing to do so until you have first approached several other sources for merchant status. What one company won't accept, another may. Additionally, what your bank considers a poor credit history may not be considered "that bad" (as one ISO representative put it) to a third-party processor.

Q Couldn't I avoid all these hassles by having a friend process my charges for me with his number and giving him a percent of each sale?

No. This practice is forbidden by credit card companies because of the potential for fraud. Even though your operation may be totally legal, if the credit card company discovers what's going on, your friend could lose merchant status.

Generally only two kinds of companies want to have their cards processed this way: (1) those that can't qualify for merchant status on their own because their business is risky and (2) fraudulent businesses. The way the latter type operates is that a con artist will pose as a new merchant and will make contact with existing merchants in town, saying how difficult it is to get merchant status, and offer the other merchants a percentage of each charged sale. The con artist will then submit phony orders, duplicate orders, or advertise some kind of bargain and have the calls go to the established merchants. He or she collects the money from the merchant, then skips town before the scam is discovered. The result: the helpful merchant has to make good on all the chargebacks to his or her merchant account.

On the flip side, once you do achieve merchant status in your own name, you should never let anyone talk you into processing their charges through your merchant account.

Q **I've seen companies advertised on the Internet that let you accept charge cards without having a merchant account. Are these legal? And if so, does it make sense to use them?**

Some companies do have authorization from merchant banks to accept credit cards on behalf of others. Companies that operate this way charge 20 percent or more of the purchase price to take orders for you. Additionally, customers may not recognize the name of the fulfillment company and may dispute the charge. In most cases that fee on top of your other costs of doing business would make it impractical to use them. The cost of doing business this way and the potential for confusing customers makes this an impractical arrangement for most small businesses.

Q **How does having another merchant process your charges differ from what an ISO does or from what a fulfillment service does?**

The primary difference is that the bankcard company knows about the arrangement and has authorized the company to act as a third-party processor or to take orders. If you are unsure whether a company is legitimately able to process charges for you, ask whose name will be on the bill the customer receives. If it is the other company's name and they do not store your inventory and ship your product to the customer, you would be wise to try to get the name of their merchant bank and verify through the bank that the company does have authorization to process charges for other merchants.

Q **Where can I get names of companies offering merchant accounts?**

Start with your own bank, since some banks in some communities will work with small and homebased businesses if the business owner has a longstanding relationship with the bank. If the bank won't offer you a merchant account, ask them if they can recommend a third-party processor who will.

TIP

If your bank does offer merchant accounts, be sure to compare their fees to the fees you will pay using a third-party provider. The third-party provider may be less expensive to use. If the bank can't refer you to anyone, ask other business owners in your area who their merchant card processor is and what their experiences have been with the company. Other good sources of information may be associations or business groups to which you belong.

Q **I really don't know any business people in my community and I don't belong to any associations. Where else can I get names of companies offering merchant status?**

If none of your local contacts can help you, you may want to contact one of the bankcard companies or third-party processors in the list below. Each of these companies has some restrictions, and each has different fee structures and requirements. Make sure you read and understand all details of any agreement you sign with these or other companies:

NOTE

When I checked around for my own merchant account in 1999, I found the best rates for my purposes came from Merchant Warehouse and Authorize.Net. Be sure to check several sources, however, since rates could change and your needs may be different from mine. If you need shopping cart software, and an easy-to-create Internet storefront as well as merchant account services, you may find a company that offers a combination of shopping cart software, merchant account and real-time processing would be better for your needs.

Merchant Account Sources
Card Service International Headquarters
26775 Malibu Hills Road
Agura Hills, CA 91301
(800) 456-5989
http://www.cardservice.com

Costco Wholesale Corporation
P.O. Box 34535
Seattle, WA 98124-1088
(800) 774-2678
http://www.costco.com

EMS Global (ECHO network)
Electronic Merchant Systems—Global
E. 9212 Montgomery, Suite 202
Spokane, WA 99206
(509) 924-6812 or (800) 757-5453

First Data Merchant
6200 South Quebec Street
Englewood, CO 80111
(800) 762-6663
http://www.firstdata.com

MerchantWarehouse.com
60 Birmingham Parkway
Brighton, MA 02135
(800) 941-6557
Fax: (617) 782-6604
http://www.MerchantWarehouse.com

Novus Network Services
P.O. Box 28545
Columbus, OH 432281
(800) 347-6673
http://www.novusnet.com/merchant/
data/main.htm

Teleflora Credit Line
11444 West Olympic Blvd.
Los Angeles, CA 90064
(800) 321-2654
Fax: (310) 966-3547
http://www.creditline.com

U.S. Merchant Services
611 South Federal Hwy., Suite A
Stuart, FL 34994
(561) 220-7515 or (800) 783-3664
http://www.backup.retailbusiness.com/usmer
chantserv

Automated Real-Time Processing (for Internet sales)

Authorize. Net Corporation
3311 N. University Avenue, Suite 200
Provo, UT 84604-4445
(801) 818-3311, ext. 100
Fax: (801) 818-3312

Authorize.Net has a list of merchant account providers and shopping carts compatible with its system on its web site at http://www.authorizenet.com/pages/reseller_list.htm.

CyberCash
2100 Reston Parkway, 3d Fl.
Reston, VA 20191
(703) 620-4200
Fax: (703) 620-4215

To find merchant accounts that work with Cybercash see the list on the Cybercash web site at http://www.cybercash.com/fi_display/home.html.

You can find many other merchant account providers by searching the web for the term *merchant account*. E-commerce web sites such as Netscape, Icat, Yahoo, Lycos, and any others that offer storefronts will be able to refer you to merchant account providers as well. Compare what each has to offer, and don't deal with any company that won't answer all your questions and provide you copies of agreements it expects you to sign. Go over all contracts and agreements carefully making sure you understand every word in them. Finally, be sure to ask other merchants what rates and fees they are charged for processing cards and what bank or merchant account provider they deal with. Compare what you are being offered with their experiences, and proceed with care.

Q **Are there any dangers in accepting credit cards?**

The biggest danger is getting hit by crooks who are buying goods with stolen credit cards, stolen credit card numbers, or counterfeit credit cards. By law, the credit card holder is liable for only the first $50 in losses if their card is lost or stolen, or if someone gets their number and makes unauthorized purchases to their account. All purchases above that amount, once the unauthorized use is discovered, get charged back to the mail order and Internet merchants, who have to cover the loss even though they shipped the merchandise.

Q **How can that happen? If I ship the merchandise, and it hasn't been returned, why should I absorb the loss?**

The merchant is always responsible for verifying that the person using a credit card is legally authorized to do so. You are supposed to compare the signature on the credit card to the signature on the sales slip at the time of purchase to verify the person using the card is the person to whom it belongs. You are also supposed to compare the number imprinted on the card to the number that shows up when a card is passed through an electronic verification terminal, since there are some counterfeit cards being used that have one number printed on the card and a different number encoded into the magnetic data strip on the back of the card.

If you are taking orders over the telephone, it is impossible to verify a signature or match numbers in this way. You have no way of knowing if the caller is the actual owner of the credit card and authorized to use it or if he or she is using a stolen card or has obtained the number fraudulently. Until the person to whom the card was issued discovers the loss or unauthorized use of the card and reports it, all charges are likely to go through up to the limit of the card. But once the cardholder discovers the unauthorized charges and challenges them, all the unauthorized purchases will be charged back to each merchant who accepted the card in payment for sales.

Q **How much would I stand to lose?**

The amounts can be substantial if you sell high-priced merchandise or if you sell the kind of products people order in quantity. California business owner John Ferguson, whose small company takes orders over the telephone and then ships merchandise to customers, had to borrow from friends and family to make good on $14,000 worth of fraudulent charges made on stolen cards, He implemented procedures to screen out possible fraudulent orders and during the following year refused to ship $25,000 in orders that seemed suspicious. Says Ferguson, "I don't believe I have refused any legitimate sales. If I had, the customer would have called to complain that they never received their order and not one has."

Q **Is there any way to tell if an order placed over the phone is legitimate or not?**

Based on his experiences, Ferguson says people ordering goods on stolen credit cards often share some of these characteristics:

- They will usually be placing large orders.
- They might request/insist their order be shipped by overnight delivery. This is so they know exactly when the package arrives (UPS guarantees 10:30 A.M. delivery) so they can be waiting to pick it up.
- They don't seem to care what the cost is. They want the item at any price.
- They hesitate to give you a daytime phone number.
- They request the item be shipped to an alternate address than the one listed for the cardholder.

Q **What should I do if an order does sound suspicious?**

Under any of the above circumstances you should be particularly cautious and do everything possible to ascertain the person ordering the merchandise is actually the cardholder.

These tips, though not infallible, may help you decide if an order is legitimate:

- Get a complete name, address, and phone number of the cardholder. Then, verify the information you are given by calling the merchant bank or using whatever other address verification system is in place through the ISO that processes your charges. If the address you were given doesn't match the address of the cardholder, don't ship.
- Only ship to the address of the cardholder. People ordering with a stolen card generally request the merchandise be shipped to a vacant house or apartment. (Some shipping companies leave packages at the door if no one is home.)
- A person using a stolen card won't give you their real phone number. Find an excuse to call the customer back, using the phone number he or she gave you, and ask to speak to the cardholder. If you can't reach the cardholder, don't ship the merchandise.
- Look up the address and phone number of any local orders in the phone book.
- If the address and phone number check out but you still have doubts, ship the merchandise AOD (acknowledgment of delivery) or certified mail. That way, you get a signature back that may help you fight your bank if the customer has signed but claims to have never received the merchandise.
- Hold on to signed sales slips and orders for at least a year.
- Send a reminder letter to people when you ship an item telling them the item has been shipped and when they can expect it to appear on their bill. This type of letter can reduce complaints and chargebacks from people who simply forget what they ordered or from whom.

NOTE Don't automatically discredit an order that looks suspicious. I once had someone place an order and ask that it be shipped to Mickey Mouse. The address verification feature on Authorize.net didn't find any problems with the address.

My order form includes a place for an e-mail address, and the person had included their e-mail address, so I sent them a note to ask about the order. The individual, who had used his real credit card data and real address for shipping had used the name Mickey Mouse, because he was afraid to use his real name on the Internet.

Q **How does a chargeback differ from a return, from the bank's point of view?**

A customer who wants to return something goes to the merchant, and the merchant issues the credit. A chargeback is when the customer can't get satisfaction or when there has been unauthorized use of the account, and the customer complains to the credit card company. The credit card company then refunds the money to the customer, and in turn has to get the money back from the merchant. Too many chargebacks could cause a merchant to lose merchant status.

Q **A friend told me he has a fulfillment service that lets him use their 800 number and their merchant account to take customer orders. Is this OK to do?**

If the company is a legitimate fulfillment service and stocks and ships merchandise for you, the benefits of their order-taking services and your ability to give your customers the option of paying with a credit card may be worthwhile—if you can afford the cost.

If the company is going to take orders, bill customers under *their names*, and then send the orders to you to fill, your best bet would be to contact someone in authority at the card issuer or merchant bank and make sure that company is authorized to process your charges.

IV.

The
Business Side
of Business

19.
Your Business
and the Law

If you are like most small business owners, you don't ever expect to become involved in a lawsuit. However, whether you sign a $100,000 contract to remove asbestos from a school building or sneeze and scare the cat (who leaps up off the windowsill and spills your open bottle of Yoo Hoo onto the turn-of-the-century heirloom family Bible you were restoring for a customer), as a businessperson, your actions have potential legal consequences.

While there is no way to anticipate or avoid all possible legal entanglements, you can learn to steer clear of some common pitfalls. This chapter should help you get through the school of hard knocks with fewer bruises.

Q **Does every business need an attorney?**

In a word, yes. While it isn't practical for a small business to call in an attorney to dot every *i* or cross every *t* in every business transaction, sooner or later every small business can benefit from an attorney's advice.

Q **When do I need an attorney?**

Kent Seitzinger, a California attorney who frequently works with small business clients and who has taught business law at California State University, Sacramento, says:

The easy answer is [to retain an attorney] before a problem ever arises. In law, as in most endeavors, the proverbial ounce of prevention is worth a pound of cure. Translated into the legal arena, what this typically means is that you can pay an attorney a few hundred dollars to advise you before entering into a matter or pay the attorney several thousand dollars to help bail you out later on.

Therefore, among the times when your business should seek an attorney's advice are:

▸ when a contract must be signed and the terms or clauses in the contract are difficult to understand
▸ any time you sign a contract for a significant sum of money or that obligates you to do something over a lengthy period of time
▸ any time you buy a business or franchise
▸ when you need to structure an agreement to discourage employees from starting their own businesses to compete with yours
▸ any time you are sued or are threatened with a lawsuit
▸ when you have an invention to protect
▸ when you form a partnership or corporation

Q **How can I find a good attorney?**

The best way to find an attorney is through a referral, whether you get the referral from another business owner or through an industry association to which you belong. Although your sister's husband's uncle might be a great divorce attorney, he or she may not be the best person to represent you when your client claims your rewiring job was responsible for the fire in his office.

If you don't know anyone who can refer you to a business attorney, you might try calling the local chamber of commerce, Rotary, or a local industrial association in your area and ask for referrals. If you can't get a specific referral from one of these groups, call the local bar association, or look in the Yellow Pages of your phone book. If you want to get biographical information about an attorney you see in the Yellow Pages, go to the public library and look him or her up in the *Martindale-Hubbell Law Directory*. You can also use the Internet to find attorneys. The Martindale-Hubbell web site (http://www.martindale.com) has a search capability as does http://www.findanattorney.com.

Q **How do I know an attorney is the right one for me?**

An attorney is no different from any other person you hire. You must be able to communicate with him or her, and he or she must have the background and experience to handle the work you need done. Ideally, your attorney should have experience handling matters for other businesses with similar legal needs and problems to those of your business. To determine how closely the attorney's experience and personality mesh with your needs and preferences, ask the attorney questions like these:

- Is there a charge for an initial consultation?
- What is your background and experience?
- What type of clients do you have?
- Do you have a specialty?
- How big are the businesses you typically serve?
- What do you charge?
- How much experience do you have with ——?
- Are you the person who will do most of the work, or will a paralegal or someone else be involved?
- Could the legal fees exceed any settlement costs?*

Q **How much does it cost to hire an attorney?**

You may pay anywhere from $75 to $300 an hour or perhaps more for legal help. Geographic location, experience of the attorney, and area of specialization will all influence the fee. Depending on the situation, you may have to pay the attorney a retainer up front to take your case. This money is held in an account, and the attorney takes his or her fee and costs out of this account as the work progresses. If you are paying an hourly fee, get an estimate in advance of what the total costs may be and how long the legal work may take or how long it is likely to take for the case to come to trial.

In some instances, an attorney may work on a contingency basis. In this case he or she will take a percentage of the settlement (what you win). The contingency fee will generally be at least 25 percent and often higher.

---

*In Minnesota, two law firms claimed $208,733.67 in legal expenses for representing four clients. They won the case for the clients, but by law, the maximum damages their clients were entitled to were $750 each for a total of $3,000.

Q **Is there any way to keep legal fees down?**

If the work you need done is routine, consider reading up on the subject before you talk to the attorney. Always do whatever preliminary work you can. You might do a preliminary trademark or trade name search, for instance, before retaining a trademark attorney. Another way to keep costs down is to use boilerplate contracts for some jobs. The boilerplate could be either one created initially by your attorney or one adapted from an industry-standard contract. If you adapt a standard contract, have the attorney look it over to see if it needs any changes to fit your individual circumstances.

If you are being sued or will be suing another party, collect and organize all the pertinent data or documents that may be necessary to put together your case. If your attorney will need industry statistics, information on government regulations affecting your business, or other information you have or know where to get quickly, let the attorney know and gather the information yourself, rather than have the law firm do the research. Remember, the less time the attorney spends on your behalf, the lower your bill will be. While the value of your own time always has to be considered, chances are if you are running a small business your hourly billing rate is going to be a lot lower than the attorney's. Furthermore, you may have more knowledge of your industry and be able to hunt down the facts or pertinent regulations more quickly than the attorney could.

If you have to call the attorney for anything, gather all your facts and list the points you want to cover in the call before you lift the receiver. When you reach the attorney, get right to the point. Since attorneys bill for phone time, the less time you spend on the phone, the lower your bill will be.

Q **When should I ask customers to sign a contract?**

You should have a written agreement with your customers whenever the amounts of money or work involved will be substantial. A written agreement is also advisable whenever you want to avoid misunderstandings about the terms of a sale or agreement.

Oral contracts are enforceable up to one year only if you are selling services and only when the amount of the sale is $500 or less if you are selling goods. Whichever you sell and regardless of the amount, it can be extremely difficult to prove who agreed to do what if you don't have a written contract.

Q **What should I do if my customer and I agree to a deal over the telephone?**

You should put the details of the oral discussion into a letter confirming the deal and send the letter to your customer. That way you and the customer both have something to refer to in case a dispute develops about what was agreed to. Be sure the letter includes everything you discussed, including details of the job, fees, and due dates.

Q **A supplier sent me a letter summarizing details of a deal we had discussed, but he seems to have left out a couple of points I thought we agreed on. What should I do?**

Let the supplier know immediately in writing that you dispute what he has summarized in his letter to you. If it is a sale of goods, under the Uniform Commercial Code you could be bound by the supplier's letter if you do not object to the terms within 10 days.

Q **Can I write my own contracts?**

You can write your own contracts and probably will in many situations. If the contracts are for large sums of money or will obligate you to do anything for any length of time, you should have your attorney review them to be sure they cover your needs.

Q **Where can I get copies of contracts and agreements to use?**

Professional or trade associations you belong to may have samples of industry-standard agreements. There are also numerous books and software programs containing sample contracts and agreements. These are often grouped by industry or subject (legal contracts for consultants, or legal contracts for the advertising industry, for instance). You can find printed copies of common forms at office supply stores, and you can even find some legal forms to download online, free.

Among the books that can be of help:

Graphic Artists Guild Handbook Pricing and Ethical Guidelines, Graphic Artists Guild (1997), 11 West 20th Street, 8th floor, New York, NY 10011-3704, (212) 463-7730.

The Partnership Book: How to Write a Partnership Agreement by Denis Clifford and Ralph Warner, Nolo Press (1997), (415) 549-1976.

Write Your Own Business Contracts: What Your Attorney Won't Tell You by E. Thorpe Barrett, Oasis Press/PSI Research, 300 North Valley Drive, Grants Pass, OR 97526, (503) 479-9464.

Selling Through Independent Reps by Harold J. Novick, Amacom (1999), American Management Association, 135 West 50th Street, New York, NY 10020.

Software Development: A Legal Guide by Stephen Fishman, Nolo Press (1998).

Keep in mind that sample contracts and legal forms are general in nature. They are not a substitute for talking to an attorney and may not apply to your specific circumstances. They will, however, help familiarize you with the terms and issues involved in various business situations and can give you some idea of possible conditions or special considerations your attorney will need to know to prepare your agreements or contracts.

You also can buy legal forms on disk from large computer stores and catalogs.

Nolo Press: Small Business Legal Pro 3.0
http://www.nolo.com
Available through online retailers as well.

In addition to books and software several web sites have free forms available. Two of them are:

http://www.adlaw.com/RC/rf_forms.html
http://www.findforms.com.

Q **What if I want to change something in a contract I've been asked to sign?**

Changes have to be agreed to by both parties, so call or contact the other party (or your attorney) before you make the change. If you make the change on the contract instead of printing out a new contract with the change in place, you and the other party both have to initial and date the changes.

Q **Can a letter be a contract?**

A letter, a letter of agreement, or even a memo could be a valid contract if it contains all the elements of a contract.

Q **What are the elements of a contract?**

To have an enforceable contract, the contract must be for an activity that is legal and should contain these elements:

- an offer to do something in return for something else by one party
- an acceptance of the offer and terms of the offer by another party
- a consideration (an obligation to do something you don't legally have to do, such as write a manual in return for a sum of money)

The terms of the contract should be carefully spelled out so there is no misunderstanding. Points covered in the terms should include:

- a description of the job
- the date by which the job should be completed
- the location at which the job will be performed
- the method and timing of payment(s)
- a clause stating how attorney's fees will be handled in the event of a dispute

Q **Is there any problem dealing with customers in another state?**

There's nothing wrong with dealing with customers out of state; however, it can be extremely difficult to collect payment on out-of-state accounts. If the customer decides not to pay and you decide to sue, you are likely to have to file suit and go to court in their state. Thus, if you are dealing with a one-time sale or a customer you don't know well, consider getting all or a large part of your money up-front or in progress payments.

Q **How do I decide if I should sue another company?**

Decisions about whether to bring a lawsuit against any business or individual should be made just like any other business decision: on the basis of what you stand to gain or lose by following the particular course of action. Going to court is not something to do to get even. Generally, however, the decision about whether to sue will be based on how much the lawsuit will cost you.

If the amount is small enough that the dispute could be brought to small claims court (where you don't need an attorney), you would decide to proceed or let the matter drop based on the time it would take you to prepare your case and file the papers and the time you would spend at the courthouse waiting for your case to be heard.

If the amount involved or the nature of the dispute precludes using small claims court, you have to weigh the costs of the suit against what you stand to gain if you win the case or what you will lose if you don't sue. Unfortunately, when you add up the cost of the attorney's fees and expenses, court costs, legal stenographer's fees, expert witness fees (which may exceed $20,000 alone on a relatively simple matter, according to one attorney), and other incidentals, you may find it impractical to sue anyone unless the amount of the dispute is large and you have a clear-cut case.

Q **What alternatives do I have?**

The most expedient solution, of course, would be sitting down and talking to the company or individual with whom you have the dispute and trying to work things out on your own. Before you make up your mind not to budge or give in to anything the other party says, remember that standing on your principles may be a lofty ideal, but it may not get you anywhere. The goal in settling a dispute should be to come to some kind of win-win compromise that will let both you and the other party return to the business of doing business.

If you and the other party can't work out your differences on your own, you may then want to consider some type of alternate dispute resolution such as arbitration or mediation, which let you bring your dispute before an impartial third party trained in negotiation methods. You should realize that arbitration may be binding and mediation is not.

Q **What is a nondisclosure agreement and when do I use one?**

A nondisclosure agreement (also called a confidentiality agreement) is a contract used to protect client lists, methods of doing business, proprietary processes used in a business, designs, formulations, and similar intangibles from being used by anyone without your authorization. You might use one when you are presenting a patentable idea to a manufacturer or when you are hiring employees or contractors who will have access to information you do not want made available to others or used for any purposes other than your own.

Q **Is there any way I can prevent employees from leaving and starting a business like mine?**

Depending on laws in your state you may be able to prevent former employees (or businesses you buy out) from opening up a competing operation by having them sign a covenant not to compete. However, it is likely you will only be able to do so in a limited geographic area and for a limited amount of time. If you want employees or a business you buy out to sign a noncompete agreement, you should be sure to have the agreement drafted or at least reviewed by an attorney familiar with your state's laws regarding covenants not to compete.

Q **Can I get sued if a customer doesn't like my work?**

Possibly. It will depend on what the customer doesn't like about your work, what your original agreement was, and whether the customer has time and money to pursue a lawsuit.

Q **How can I protect myself?**

To protect yourself against unwanted lawsuits you should be cautious and honest in all your business dealings. Be realistic about the capabilities of your company, and have an attorney look over important documents before you offer or accept them.

In addition, to protect yourself against financial loss, make sure you have adequate business insurance. Although you may take every precaution to avoid a lawsuit, someone may still sue you, and even if he or she loses the case and you don't have to pay one cent in settlements, you could literally go broke paying the costs of defending yourself. The right business insurance policies can protect against that kind of loss.

Q **What are statutory damages?**

Statutory damages are monetary penalties specified by law. Frequently they will be a multiple of something else, such as three times the financial loss incurred by the plaintiff.

Q **What are slander and libel, and when should I be concerned about them?**

Slander and libel both involve damage or injury to someone's reputation or business through disparaging remarks. Usually slander refers to verbal remarks and libel to published (written) remarks that are malicious or harmful. Attorneys often refer to the two (slander and libel) collectively as defamation. As a businessperson you might be accused of libel or slander if you imply your competition makes shoddy products, is not professional in their business dealings, or if you write or say anything that could be construed as tarnishing their reputation. You could also be sued for libel, or slander if you wrongfully accuse or imply customers or employees are bad credit risks, thieves, or something similar.

Q **Can't I tell people the truth if asked for credit or employment references?**

By definition, truthful remarks cannot be defamatory. However, credit and employment information is protected under privacy laws in many states, and you could unintentionally violate these laws by giving out information. Furthermore, whether you actually could be found in violation of privacy or defamation laws, paying the court costs to defend yourself can be extremely expensive. To stay out of trouble, never say or imply anything about competitors, employees, or customers that you can't back up with facts. Furthermore, never make any kind of detrimental information available to the public or say or do anything that could hold the person or business up to ridicule. If ever questioned, say, about an employee you fired, for your own protection verify only dates and names. Do not say he or she was a lousy worker or a thief. The same holds true for customers who are credit risks. Report the facts to credit bureaus, but avoid saying anything else to anyone else.

20.
Intellectual Property:
How to Protect What
You Create

Whether you realize it or not, your creativity may be one of your most valuable business assets. The products you invent, the artwork you design, the words you create, and the name and logo you use to represent your business all have monetary value. Under law, these products of your creativity are considered intellectual property and, like any other property you own, can be protected against theft or unauthorized borrowing if you take the proper precaution at the proper times. This chapter will help you gain a better understanding of how and when to protect your creativity.

Q **What is intellectual property?**

When you hear the word *property* you probably think of things you own, like buildings, cars, televisions, jewelry, equipment, and other kinds of tangible property you can see, touch, buy, and sell. There is another kind of property, however, that may be even more valuable to you as a business owner. It is intellectual property—property such as names, inventions, artwork, writing, music, computer programs, designs for products, formulas, processes, business plans, and anything else that results from creative endeavors.

Just like any other property, intellectual property has value under the law and can be bought or sold. Unlike other property, however, the value of intellectual property lies in its uniqueness and often in its reproducibility. The design for a new product, for instance, may be used to produce hundreds of thousands of items worth millions of dollars. Thus, if the design is illegally copied and used to manufacture a similar product, the individual or company that created the original product could sustain a significant loss of a money-making opportunity.

Q **How is intellectual property protected under the law?**

The laws that can be used to prevent others from illegally copying and profiting from your creative efforts are called intellectual property laws. Among them are the laws covering copyrights, patents, trademarks, and trade secrets. These laws are specialized, often quite complex, and to some extent are being defined or redefined on a case-by-case basis as the law struggles to catch up with the information age and the technology that drives it.

Q **How do the various intellectual property laws differ from one another?**

The division lines aren't always cut-and-dried, but as a general rule of thumb:

> ‣ copyright laws help protect written, drawn, photographed, and artistic works
> ‣ patents and trade secrets laws help protect inventions, new machines, and new processes
> ‣ design patents help protect the way a product looks
> ‣ trademark and trade name regulations help protect the distinguishing identity of goods and services

Q **Can a product be considered more than one type of intellectual property?**

Yes, sometimes you can get protection for your intellectual property under more than one law. Gerry Elman, an intellectual property attorney who heads the law firm of Elman & Associates in Media, Pennsylvania, says that some software, for example, "embodies patentable ideas, and can be protected by copyright as well." This, he says, is like having belt-and-suspenders protection for your property.

Q **What is a copyright?**

Copyright gives the owner of a work the exclusive rights to:

- reproduce the copyrighted work
- prepare derivative works based on the copyrighted work
- distribute copies or phono records of the work to the public by sale or transfer of ownership or by rental, lease, or lending
- perform or display the copyrighted work publicly

Q **Can I copyright my idea?**

No, you can't copyright an idea. Copyright protects only the means (words, a drawing, etc.) you use to *express* the idea. It doesn't prevent others from adopting your idea and using it themselves. For instance, if you drew a picture of a uniquely shaped computer desk, you would own a copyright on the drawing, but your copyright on the drawing would not stop someone from actually building and selling thousands of desks based on your picture. However, the copyright law has been extended to protect "architectural works," so you could use it to prevent someone from building the skyscraper from plans you'd created.

Q **Is there any way to protect ideas?**

You may be able to protect your ideas with patent or trade secret laws, which are explained later in this chapter.

Q **Can I copyright my business or product name?**

A name cannot be protected by copyright. You may be able to protect your name as a trademark, however. And you may have rights protecting your unique business name as a "trade name."

Q **What can be copyrighted?**

The copyright law covers "original works of authorship that are fixed in a tangible medium of expression." Among the types of works that can be covered by copyright are:

- literary works
- computer programs, which are classified as literary works under the copyright laws

- musical works, including accompanying words
- dramatic works, including accompanying music
- pantomimes and choreographic works
- pictorial, graphic, and sculptural works
- motion pictures and other audiovisual works
- sound recordings

Q **How do I get a copyright?**

Under copyright laws in the United States, work created on or after March 1, 1989, is *automatically* copyrighted the moment you create it in a fixed form that others can perceive.

Q **What does *fixed* mean?**

Fixed in a tangible medium of expression is a rather broad term designating a variety of material objects. Essentially, putting something into fixed form simply means putting what's in your head onto paper or disk or audiotape or some other format that others can read, see, or listen to. Among the things regarded as fixed formats are paper manuscripts, books, phono records, audiotapes, computer disks, sheet music, and films.

Q **Don't I have to register the work or put some kind of notice on it?**

Works published before March 1, 1989, had to bear a copyright notice or the copyright was lost. Works published on or after March 1, 1989, do not have to carry a copyright notice and don't have to be registered. Registering the copyright and putting a copyright notice on your work are both advisable, however. Putting the notice on the work alerts people to your copyright claim to the work and identifies the owner and year of the copyright. Registering the work adds these advantages:

- It establishes a public record of your ownership of the work.
- It permits infringement suits to be filed (you can't file an infringement suit until a work is registered).
- Registration made within five years of publication establishes prima facie evidence in court of the validity of the copyright and facts stated on the copyright certificate.

▸ Registration made within three months after the publication of the work or before infringement allows you to collect statutory damage and attorney's fees if you sue for infringement and win. If the copyright wasn't registered before infringement, all you can collect are actual losses related to the infringement. (Statutory damages are a penalty that can be levied in place of or above the dollar amount of any actual loss.)

Q **If I put a copyright notice on the work how should I do it?**

The copyright notice normally consists of the following three things:

▸ the symbol © (the letter *c* in a circle) or the word *Copyright* or the abbreviation *Copr.*
▸ the year of first publication
▸ the name of the copyright owner

For phono records of sound recordings, the symbol ℗ (the letter *p* in a circle) should be used instead of the circled *c*.

Q **Where do I put the notice?**

The notice should be put in a place that gives "reasonable notice" of your copyright. The first page of a manuscript, the label of a record, somewhere in the front matter (traditionally the back of the title page) of a book.

Q **If I want to register the copyright, how do I do it?**

To register a copyright you will need to send a properly completed registration form, a nonrefundable fee of $30, and a nonreturnable deposit of the work to the Copyright Office. All three of those things must be in the same package. The requirements for the deposit of the work vary with the type of work being registered, but it is usually one or two complete copies of works that can be easily duplicated. To get application forms, information about deposit requirements, or other information about copyright, write the Copyright Office, Library of Congress, Washington, D.C. 20559-6000, or call the office at (202) 707-3000. Or, visit their web site at http://www.loc.gov/copyright and download forms and booklets.

Q I'm a freelance programmer and technical writer. If a company pays me to write a program or manual for them, who owns the copyright on the work I produce?

You generally own the copyright on work you create as an independent contractor (freelancer) unless you sign an agreement assigning the copyright to your client.

This, too, is a change from the way things were done in the past. It is a result of a 1989 Supreme Court decision in a case between Baltimore sculptor James Earl Reid and the Community for Creative Non-Violence (CCNV). Prior to that case, some companies hiring contractors to do work for them assumed they owned the copyright under work-for-hire provisions of the copyright law. In the case between Reid and CCNV, the Supreme Court found that CCNV's commissioning and supervision of Reid were not enough to make him an employee and, therefore, work-for-hire rules did not apply. As a freelancer, he owned the copyright to his work.

If you are not the only person working on the program or manual, the work would probably be considered a joint work, and you would co-own the copyright if there were no agreements specifying other arrangements.

Q What is work for hire?

Work for hire is a term used in copyright law to denote transfer of copyright ownership to an employer, organization, or person other than the individual who created the work. Such transfer leaves the originator of the work with no rights and no future interests in the work. He or she will have no say in how the work is used by the owner and will get no fee or royalty for future use of the work.

Under the U.S. copyright law, a work may be considered a work for hire is if it is done by an employee of a company as part of his or her regular employment, or if an independent contractor signs a formal contract giving away rights to certain categories of works such as contribution to collective works, work done as a supplement to work of another author (illustrations for a written text, for instance), translations, compilations of works, tests, or systematic instructional text.

Q If I hire an ad agency to design ads for me, who owns the designs?

Based on the Reid decision, the ad agency might be able to make a case for owning the copyright on anything it writes or designs for you unless you have an agreement stating otherwise. It would be a good idea, therefore, to have the agency sign an agreement assigning the rights in the work to you.

Q **If I revise a work, what year should I put in the copyright notice?**

The year of original publication. Years in which the work was revised may be included, too, but the significant date is the date of first publication.

Q **How long does copyright last?**

The copyright on works created on or after January 1, 1978, is in effect for the author's life plus 70 years. If the work is a joint work, the term of copyright extends until 70 years after the death of the last surviving co-owner. Works made for hire have a term of 120 years from creation or 95 years after publication, whichever is less. The copyright duration for anonymous and pseudonymous works is the same as that for works made for hire unless the author's name is revealed in Copyright Office records.

Q **How long does it take the Copyright Office to process registrations?**

It can take up to 120 days to get a certificate of registration or, if the application cannot be accepted, a letter explaining why it has been rejected. If you want to be sure the Copyright Office received your registration packet, send it by Priority Mail with delivery confirmation, and you could also enclose a stamped, self-addressed postal card with pertinent information identifying your copyright application.

Q **Do I need an attorney to get a copyright, or can I do it myself?**

Registering a copyright is just a matter of filling out some forms and sending the proper fee, so you probably don't need an attorney to register it. However, if you are copyrighting catalogs, advertising materials, programs or other works that were not created by you or one of your regular employees, you have to be sure you own the rights (see above).

If you are copyrighting computer software, you might want to consult an intellectual property attorney to determine if your program has patentable material and about how much of the source code might be considered a trade secret and can be blacked out when the source code is submitted to the copyright office for registration. Be sure to get Copyright Office Circular 61, *Copyright Registration for Computer Programs*, if you plan to copyright your own software.

Similarly, if the work you are copyrighting contains any kind of trade secrets or could be used in patentable items or processes, you should consult an attorney who specializes in these things.

Q **What does it cost to register a copyright?**

The registration fee is $30.00.

Q **If I don't register the copyright, should I mail myself a copy of the work and save the sealed package to prove the date and authorship?**

That's a waste of time and effort. As attorney Gerry Elman explains, "It's a myth that you can date something by sticking it in an envelope and mailing it to yourself. That's because you could send an empty envelope to yourself, sealed lightly with rubber cement, keep it safe, and then when the time comes that you want to ante-date something, stick your newly created letter inside and seal the envelope shut."

Instead, Elman recommends having a friend with no interest in your work or a notary sign and date your document as a witness. For works in digital form, there are companies online that offer a "digital notary" service that time-stamps and locks a computer file.

Q **I publish a monthly newsletter. If I register the copyright, do I have to register each issue of the newsletter separately, or can I register a year's worth on one form?**

Since each issue is separately copyrightable, you have to register each one separately. A group registration is available, but it is for registering groups of works by the same author. Copyright Office Circular 62, *Registration for Serials*, explains the regulations for newsletters, bulletins, and other periodicals. Circular 104, *Group Registration of Contributions to Periodicals*, explains group registrations.

Q I forgot to put a copyright notice on my program. Will I lose my copyright on it?

If the program was published after March 1, 1989, no, you won't lose your copyright. It would be a good idea to add your copyright notice to future copies, though it isn't necessary.

If the program was written after January 1, 1978, and registered within 5 years of publication, the copyright may still be valid. See Copyright Office Circular 3 for more information.

Q Do I have to give the Copyright Office a copy of the source code if I register my software?

Not necessarily, but if you don't, you have to ask the Copyright Office for special relief from the strict application of the law. They will respond with a letter saying that they can't determine whether there is copyrightable authorship in the materials you sent but that they will issue a certificate under the "rule of doubt." If you do provide at least some of the code, portions containing trade secret material may be blocked out if you request another form of special relief. For additional information, get Copyright Office Circular 61.

Q Is there any other way I can protect my software?

You might be able to patent your software or use trade secret law, trademark laws, or unfair competition laws to protect it. An intellectual property attorney would be the best source of information if you plan to market your software to a large commercial market. Whether you plan to hire an attorney or not, however, a good book to read for additional information on software and legal issues is *Software Development: A Legal Guide*, by Stephen Fishman, especially if you plan to market your own software. It is published by Nolo Press.

Q Can I copy phone listings?

According to a March 1991 Supreme Court ruling in the case of *Feist Publications v. Rural Telephone Service Co.* you can safely copy the white pages in the phone book. In the decision that was handed down in the case, the court said copyright is not awarded for sweat-of-the-brow work but for originality. Listings in the white pages of a phone book, the court ruled, are facts with no originality in organization or expression and therefore cannot be protected by copyright.

The ruling did not automatically negate copyrights on other kinds of compilations. It would seem from the wording of the decision that compilations showing originality of organization and expression would still be protected by copyright. What is likely to be tested in future court cases is just what constitutes originality of organization and expression. Congress also continues to study this issue and may enact legislation specifically protecting compilations of information.

Q **Can I reprint things I find in online databases?**

Generally, no. An online database usually consists of more than a listing of mere facts; databases are usually specialized and involve some originality in selection, arranging, and often writing and editing. Thus, unlike the white pages in the phone book, their ability to be copyrighted would probably be upheld if challenged.

Q **I found a lot of information in an electronic library that I'd like to include in my newsletter. Am I allowed to do that since I paid to download them from the online service?**

No. The author of the text in the files you downloaded owns the copyright, and reprinting the file in your newsletter without his or her permission is an infringement of the author's rights.

Q **I found some nice holiday artwork on the web that didn't have a copyright notice. I want to put them on my web site on a page that plays "Rudolph the Red-Nosed Reindeer." Can I do this?**

Not without getting permission of the copyright owners. "The fact that the owner of the photographs is not identified does not change the answer," says Thomas O'Rourke, an attorney who specializes in intellectual property. "If a car were parked in a parking lot without license plates, you wouldn't have the right to use the car just because it was there. Copyright ownership is no different.

"Bear in mind also, that music may be covered by several copyrights. One person may own the copyright on the words, a different person own the copyright on the music, and still others may own the rights on the arrangement or performance, making the rights to use the song difficult to obtain."

Q If I upload text or shareware to an online information service, do I give up any rights in my work to the online service?

No, you wouldn't lose your rights in the work. You would still be the owner of your copyright. The service might claim a compilation copyright, which is simply a copyright on the particular collection of material available on the service. That doesn't take away your individual copyrights in your work, though. You are still the sole owner of your work. Of course, by making it public, you would give up the right to claim that your material is a trade secret and it could also affect your right to patent the subject matter.

Q I have a hand scanner and want to scan some artwork I found in a book and use it in my publication. Is this OK to do?

If the book is old enough that the copyright has expired or if the artwork included in the book is in the public domain, you should be able to scan in illustrations to use in your publication. If you are scanning from a new book of clip art or a book that is a collection of old prints, look in the front of the book to see what the company says about reuse of the material in the book.

Q What does being in the public domain mean?

When a work is in the public domain, it means the work is not covered by copyright protection. It can be used freely by the public without permission from the creator or his or her heirs. Among the types of work that are in the public domain are federal government publications and works for which the copyright has expired. In the past, some works wound up in the public domain inadvertently because they were published without a copyright notice. Under the current law, however, copyright notice is no longer required on published works.

Q A magazine wants to buy my craft design for reprint in the publication. The agreement with the letter they sent me reads: "I hereby agree to sell all right of copyright." Does that mean I can't resell the design to a British publication?

Yes, it does. By signing that agreement, you give up all copyrights in the material the magazine is buying. If you want to have the design published, but don't want to sell all rights, you could try calling the publication and asking if they would be willing to change the rights clause—for example, to "first North American serial rights." If you are unfamiliar with the rights that can be offered, check your library for books about selling writing. These books generally have information about the different types of publication rights.

Q **How much does a drawing have to be changed to be considered a new drawing? If I traced the outline and filled in my own details, could I sell the new design as my own?**

What you would be doing is creating a derivative work, and under the copyright law, only the copyright holder or someone the copyright holder authorizes may do that. Even if your design looked somewhat different from the original, if any of the author's expressions were copied, rather than just the idea, you would be infringing on his or her copyright.

Q **What about "fair use"? How much of a copyrighted work can I reprint without getting permission?**

The answer depends on many factors, including your intended use. The fair use rule says portions of works may be reproduced for educational, news, commentary, or research without infringement under certain circumstances. The circumstances are decided on a case-by-case basis using all four of the following criteria:

- the purpose and character of the use, including whether such use is of a commercial nature or is for nonprofit educational purposes
- the nature of the copyrighted work
- the amount and substantiality of the portion used in relation to the copyrighted work as a whole
- the effect of the use upon the potential market for or value of the copyright

In addition, a number of more specific guidelines are published for reproduction of text, music, and other works by educators and librarians. These are discussed in Copyright Office Circular 21, *Reproduction of Copyrighted Works by Educators and Librarians.*

Q **Where do I get forms to copyright my work, and what do they cost?**

You can get the forms free from the Copyright Office. (You pay a $30 registration fee when you return the completed form.) You can order them by phone by calling (202) 707-3000 or download them from the Copyright Office web site at http://www.loc.gov/copyright. Be sure to get the right forms for the type of work you are registering. The forms and what they are used for are as follows:

For Original Registration
- Form TX—for published and unpublished nondramatic literary works
- Form SE—for serials, works issued or intended to be issued in successive parts, such as periodicals, newspapers, magazines, newsletters, annuals, and journals
- Form PA—for published and unpublished works of the performing arts (musical and dramatic works, pantomimes and choreographic works, motion pictures and other audiovisual works)
- Form VA—for published and unpublished works of the visual arts (pictorial, graphic, and sculptural works)
- Form SR—for published and unpublished sound recordings

For Renewals
- Form RE—for claims to renew copyright in works copyrighted under the law in effect through December 31, 1977 (1909 Copyright Act)

For Corrections and Amplifications
- Form CA—for supplementary registration to correct or amplify an existing registration

For a Group of Contributions to Periodicals
- Form GR/CP—for registration of a group of contributions to periodicals; gets filed in addition to application form TX, PA, or VA

Q **How old do works have to be before I can assume they are in the public domain?**

Anything published before 1922 should be in the public domain and safe to reprint.

Q **If I copyright my work here in the United States is it protected in other countries, too?**

Many foreign countries abide by the same international copyright conventions that the United States does, and your work would be protected under their local laws if you comply with the provisions of the conventions. You can get a list of countries that honor U.S. copyrights from the U.S. Copyright Office. If someone in another country infringed on your copyright, you probably would have to sue in that country.

TRADEMARKS AND TRADE NAMES

Q **What is a trademark?**

A trademark is a word, group of words, name, device, or symbol used to identify goods you sell and distinguish them from similar goods sold by other businesses. It can consist of words, graphics, or letters and is used to identify a product, line of products, or all the products produced by your company. A brand name like Coca-Cola or a symbol like the multicolor striped apple that identifies Apple Computer products are both trademarks. Trademarks and service marks are protected under federal law and may also be protected under state law.

Q **Can I trademark a service?**

Yes. It is called a service mark.

Q **Is my business name a trademark?**

Your business name is a trade name. It is protected at the state or local level. If you opened up a lawn-care company called The GreenCarpet Lawn-Care Service, your next-door neighbor couldn't open a business with the same name or one confusingly similar, but there would be nothing to stop a company in another state, or depending on your state laws, another part of your state from opening up a company with the same name even if it was in the same business. If you obtain a federal registration for this term as a service mark, you could protect it from being used by other lawn-care companies in the country, something you might want to do if you want to franchise your lawn-care service, or expand the business to another state.

Q **If I want my business name to be my trademark, do I have to register it locally and also register it as a trademark?**

Registering your business name is a state or local process and is completely separate from registering a federal trademark. So if you want national protection for your name you would have to register the name locally and apply separately for trademark protection. If you don't need national name protection, registering the name locally may stop other local businesses from using the name. If you want statewide protection for the name but don't need national protection, you could register a trademark with your state. Your secretary of state's office should be able to direct you to the proper source of information for registering a name as a trademark in your state.

Q **Are there any restrictions on what can be used as a trademark?**

Your trademark or service mark can't be confusingly similar to others for a similar product or service, and it must do more than just describe a product or service. It has to give it a unique identity. You could not register the term *Lawn Service* as a trademark, for instance, but could probably register terms like *LawnMaker* or *Greenlawn* if those terms aren't already trademarks for similar products and services. In addition, your trademark can't be a generic term for a kind of product. Terms like *photocopier* or *tissue* can't be trademarks but *Xerox* and *Kleenex* can. In fact, you can lose your mark if it starts to be used as a generic term as in *xeroxing* a document or getting a *kleenex* to blow your nose. In the past Aspirin and Escalator were trademarks, but now they're generic terms for the kind of product. Major corporations wind up spending a lot of money to keep the names of popular products from becoming generic terms.

Q **Should I invent a nonsense name or use something that reminds people of what the product or service does?**

Your choice of trademark should be based on marketing factors as well as the ability to register the term. A truly unusual coined name will be far easier to protect as a trademark, since there will be little likelihood of there being similar names or marks in use. Xerox and Exxon are two familiar examples. A potential drawback of using a coined term, however, is that prospective customers may not immediately be able to identify the nature of your goods and might bypass your ads or sales literature.

On the other hand, a name that is too descriptive of your product or service may present problems, too. You may discover someone else is already using the clever name you chose, or that the name really won't be suitable if you expand your business in the future. Got It Message Center may be the ideal name for an answering service but would be inappropriate if you later decided to expand the business into a full-fledged order fulfillment service.

Thus, you might want to choose several possible names and test them out on friends and acquaintances and do some preliminary searches to see if they are already in use. If preliminary searches and feedback show the name sounds promising, then you can decide to search further if you want to use the name widely or just adopt it if it is not in use in your immediate geographic area.

Q **How do I get a trademark?**

If your mark is not confusingly similar to any others, you can acquire rights to it by using it in commerce and continuing to use it. If you can prove you were the first company to use a mark, you might be able to prevent others from using it in direct competition with you, even if you haven't registered the mark. Like copyrights, though, it is much better to register your mark.

Q **What are the advantages of federally registering a trademark?**

You gain federal nationwide protection, and if your mark was infringed, you could get federal court orders to prevent continued use of the mark. In addition, you might be able to collect money if you sued and won.

Q **Is there anything I have to do before I start using my mark?**

Before you start using your mark, you should do a trademark search to be sure no one is already using it.

Q **I'm only going to sell to businesses in my state. Do I have to do a national name search, or can I just do a search of local business names?**

If you are only going to be using your mark locally and won't be investing a lot of money in name recognition, check federal trademark registrations and search locally. Search of Yellow Pages listings, county and state business name listings, and ads for products or services similar to what you sell will probably be sufficient to tell you if there are companies marketing products or services in your area with confusingly similar names or logos. Be aware, however, that if your name should conflict with similar products sold nationally or with a federal trademark registration, you could be forced to stop using your name if theirs existed first. Similarly, if you later expand to other geographic regions and into international markets you might run into name conflicts you didn't discover on a local search.

Q **When should I search a wider geographic area and how do I do it?**

Your best bet for doing a national and international search is to hire an intellectual property attorney or a trademark search firm or information broker familiar with doing trademark searches to search for you. If you want to do the search yourself, or do a preliminary search before retaining an attorney, several electronic databases will simplify the search process. The U.S. Patent and Trademark Office has a web site that contains a database of federal trademark registrations and applications at http://www.uspto.gov. Note that this database is not updated frequently, so it may need to be supplemented by a search in a fee-for-service database as well. The primary ones are Thomson & Thomson's Trademarkscan Federal and Trademarkscan State, which list trademarks registered at state and federal levels. Both of these databases are available on the web through various online services. You can find them on America Online by searching for keyword *trademarks*. Since not all trademarks are registered, it's a good idea to search other directories and databases. Similar information is available using various web search engines such as Alta Vista, Yahoo, and InfoSeek.

Yellow Pages and industry directories available in public libraries are valuable search tools, too.

The Patent and Trademark Office in Washington, D.C., has a library that is open to the public. In addition, public and university libraries throughout the country have been designated patent and trademark depository libraries. These libraries have copies of patents and federal trademark records you can search. To get information about the patent and trademark depository libraries, call the Patent and Trademark Office at (703) 308-3924.

Q **If I hire an intellectual property attorney or trademark search company to do the search, and they don't find anything similar, can my trademark be challenged?**

Yes, your mark, even once it is registered, could be challenged as being merely descriptive for up to 5 years. Additionally, while an attorney or search firm is likely to do a more extensive and knowledgeable search than you would on your own, there is no guarantee that they will turn up all unregistered uses of your mark. Your mark, even after it is registered, could always be challenged by a prior user of the mark. If your mark starts to be used as a general term to describe a class of products, you can lose your rights to it as well.

Q **What does it cost to register a trademark?**

The federal filing fee for registering a trademark is $245. If you have an intellectual property attorney do the search for you and prepare the applications, you can plan on paying an additional $700 to $2,500 in addition to the filing fee, depending on the extent of the searches done, the results of the searches, the amount of time it takes to write a response to any Trademark Office correspondence, and the attorney you retain. Be sure you ask about fees in advance if budget is a major consideration.

Q **Must I have an attorney to register a trademark?**

No, you don't need an attorney to register your trademark. Depending on your plans for the business or product, it may be advisable, however. The extra fees buy you better searches (unless you happen to be an expert at electronic searches and other search techniques) as well as the attorney's expert judgment on whether or not the mark could be considered confusingly similar to others in use for the kind of product or service you sell. Whether retaining an attorney or registering your trademark are worthwhile at all will depend on your budget and plans for what you sell.

Q **I have a trademark I want to use, but I'm not ready to start the business. Is there a way I can keep others from using the mark?**

Yes. A 1989 amendment in the trademark law allows you to apply to register a trademark you intend to use by filing a special form and paying a $245 fee.

Q When do I use the ™ symbol and when do I use the ®?

If you are claiming trademark rights and haven't federally registered the trademark or the registration hasn't yet been approved, you would use the symbol ™ to denote your claim to a trademark or ^SM to denote a service mark. Once registration is granted you use the symbol ® to denote the registered trademark.

Q How do I protect my trademark?

To protect the trademark you have to continue using it, and you have to keep it from becoming a generic term to describe a class of products. To maintain the distinction, your mark should be used as an adjective, as in Band-Aid adhesive bandages or WordSmith writing services. To further protect your mark, you should make sure it is always printed in the same way and that your trademark notice is used at least once in each printed piece containing your mark.

Q How do I actually register the trademark?

To register the trademark, you need to submit to the Patent and Trademark Office a written application, a drawing of your mark, and three identical specimens showing the mark in actual use.

You can get the application form and instructions by writing the U.S. Patent and Trademark Office, Washington, D.C. 20231 (mark your envelope "Trademark Information Requested"). If you have questions about trademarks or patents call (800) 786-9199. Or you can apply for a trademark online through the Patent and Trademark Office web site at http://www.uspto.gov.

Q What if another company starts using my trade name or mark?

If you decide it is worth the cost of fighting the unauthorized use of your name or mark, you should contact an attorney. If you've registered your mark or name, he or she will send the company a letter demanding they stop using the name. If you haven't registered the name, the attorney can help you find out if you have common law rights to the name through first use and if it is worth the time and cost to pursue the matter.

Q **I'm setting up my business on the web. The .com name I wanted to use is already taken. Is it OK to register the name as a .net or .org domain?**

The answer depends on how strong your trademark rights are in the name versus how strong the .com company's rights are, how similar your line of business is to the .com company, and how much money either of you are willing to invest to fight for the name.

Thomas O'Rourke says, "As a general rule, if the dot.com name you would like to use is not a famous name that has strong trademark rights or if it is one that you have been using in your business for some time, you may be able to use the dot.net or dot.org domain name. For example, using the name McDonald's as a domain name for any commercial business would be risky unless the business is so removed from the food business that the public would not believe that you are licensed, endorsed or otherwise approved of or connected with McDonald's." (O'Rourke is a partner in the law firm of Wyatt, Gerber, Meller & O'Rourke located in New York City.)

However, if the .com company is bigger than you, has registered their mark nationally, and has an attorney on staff or on retainer, they might sue you. If they do, you'd have to decide whether keeping the name is worth the cost to fight the suit, or give up the name and possibly lose web site traffic or business as a result. Yet another consideration: .com is the more common domain. You could lose business just because people type in .com instead of .net with the name you want. From a business perspective, therefore, choosing a different domain name might be a better decision.

TIP When you register your domain name, consider registering at least the .net and .org domains as well as the .com domain. Doing so will keep other companies from using those variations of your name. To get added hits from search engines and to give yourself a work area for your company, you might want to actually set up all three domains, too. Store some of the site on the .net domain, register it in search engines and link it to your main site for additional traffic. Use the .org area as a test area. Don't register it in search engines if testing is its intended use.

Q Are all domain names considered trademarks?

No. "The mere existence of a domain name in the absence of use by a business, such as in connection with the advertising and promotion of goods and services, or registration of intended use, does not necessarily create trademark rights," says O'Rourke. Thus if someone registered a domain name, but hasn't used it and doesn't use the name in business elsewhere, they may not have any trademark rights in it.

Q Do I need to check domain names before I choose a name for my business?

From a practical point of view, yes. Having a web site is becoming as common as having a business card. Even if you don't plan to put your new business on the web immediately, you may want to do so in the future. "Before you invest money and time in developing the goodwill in a company name, you should check the availability of both your company name and your domain name so you don't have to make changes after you've begun to use the name," advises O'Rourke.

Q I've been doing business under my name for several years and wanted to register it as a domain name, but someone else already took it! What can I do?

The answer goes back to the issue of how well established your name is, how widely established it is, and how much money you have to fight for the use of your name. If you have only operated locally, the company using your name as a domain name is located in a different state, and you have a limited budget, from a practical standpoint there isn't going to be much you can do if they are actually operating the site. If they have registered the domain name but haven't set it up, contact them and ask that they turn it over to you. But be prepared for a price tag with the name. As the Internet was first becoming popular, many people bought up domain names they thought might be in demand. They now try to sell those back to people who want them.

On the other hand, if the use of the domain name "would be likely to cause confusion, mistake or deception leading the public to believe that the owner of the domain name is sponsored, endorsed or otherwise approved by you, you could have a cause of action for trademark infringement," says O'Rourke. "Your chances of success depend on how strong your trademark has become."

Q How much does it cost to file a lawsuit to force someone to stop using my trademark as a domain name?

Filing the lawsuit is only a small part of the total cost, and that alone can cost you $2,000 to $5,000. To actually bring a suit to court can easily cost $20,000 or more.

Q Does a U.S. trademark give me any protection in foreign countries?

No. If you want trademark protection in other countries you will have to determine their laws and apply there.

Q How long does trademark protection last?

Trademark protection can last indefinitely; however, to retain trademark registration, you will have to file an affidavit of continued use between the fifth and sixth year of use saying you are still using the trademark. Additionally, at the end of the tenth year and every 10 years thereafter you have to renew your registration.

Q Does it cost anything for the affidavit or the renewals?

Yes. There is a $100 fee when you file the affidavit of continued use, another $100 for the affidavit of incontestability, and a $300 fee each time you renew the registration.

Q It sounds like a lot of work and money. Should I bother?

That is a decision only you can make, and it should be based on your budget and your future plans, If you plan to stay a small local business, it probably isn't necessary to go to the time and expense of registering your name as a trademark. If you expect to grow and sell in wider geographic areas, it may be very worthwhile to apply for trademark registration.

PATENTS

Q What kinds of things can be patented?

Patents are granted in these broad categories:

- products, machines, processes, or compositions of matter
- major variations of existing products, processes, or compositions of matter
- new varieties of plants
- new, original designs for manufactured items (design patent)

Q **What makes an invention qualify for a patent?**

To qualify for a patent, an invention has to meet these qualifications:

- It must be new, which means it can't be patented or described in a printed publication in any country, and it must not have been used publicly or placed on sale in the United States.
- It must be useful.
- It cannot be something obvious to someone having ordinary skill in the relevant technology.

Q **How does the Patent Office interpret the terms "obvious" and "ordinary"? How can I tell if my invention is obvious?**

That's one of the sticky parts of patenting inventions. Explains intellectual property attorney Gerry Elman, "If you've got more than ordinary skill, what's possibly 'obvious' to you, may not be obvious to someone with ordinary skill and may be legally patentable. If you've got a good idea, talk with a patent attorney if you think it's a moneymaker."

Q **Is there anything that can't be patented?**

Printed material, general business ideas, methods of doing business, scientific theories, mathematical formulas, useless devices, and obvious changes to existing devices cannot be patented.

Q **How do patents differ from copyrights?**

A copyright protects the form of expression of an idea—one specific drawing, one set of words, etc. To get a copyright, your work only has to be original. A patent protects the conceptualization of an idea and has to be not only original but also *not obvious*. For instance, if Thomas Edison had copyrighted a written description of how to make a light bulb, no one would have been able to reproduce his description without infringing on his copyright. However, people could have used his description to make their own light bulbs. By patenting the light bulb, Edison prevented others from manufacturing and selling the light bulb unless they licensed the rights to do so from him.

Q **What rights does a patent give me?**

A patent protects new and original inventions or processes from being copied, produced, or sold in the United States and its territories and possessions. It gives you the right to prevent other companies from making, using, or selling your invention and the right to sue if anyone infringes patent as defined by the claims (in other words, if anyone copies or uses or sells your invention without your permission). A patent makes it possible to get a court order to stop an infringement and to sue for and be awarded money for past infringement.

Q **Does a patent give me the right to sell my invention anywhere in the United States?**

No. That's a common misconception. A patent does not give you any rights to *sell* your invention. It only gives you the right to *stop others* from selling it. The right to actually sell your product may be controlled by the FDA or some other regulatory agency or could be limited by existing patents. Suppose, for instance, you fiddle around with one of the pocket electronic organizers and devise a way to make a new plug-in card that will let the pocket organizer double as a remote control for the TV and a garage door opener. You might have a patentable invention but might not be able to sell the invention because of prior patents on the machine and/or its plug-in cards.

Q **How do I find out for sure that no one else has already patented my idea?**

You should search industry publications and catalogs and have a search of Patent Office records done to determine what patents might exist for inventions similar to yours.

Q **Where can I do such a search?**

You can search the patent records at the Patent and Trademark Office in Washington, D.C. (see page 457). Or, you can search records in the PTO depository libraries located throughout the United States. Information from U.S. patents issued since 1974 are online at http://www.uspto.gov and at http://patent.womplex .ibm.com. See Appendix 1.

Q **How long does a patent last?**

Patents on inventions last up to 20 years from the date the patent application is filed, provided periodic maintenance fees are paid to the government. Design patents are granted for 14 years.

Q **Can a patent be renewed?**

No. When the patent expires, you can't use the patent to prevent anyone from using the invention.

Q **When do I file a patent?**

If you plan to patent an invention, do so as soon as possible. A good time is as soon as you can describe the invention in enough detail to enable someone else to make and use it. In the United States you have to apply for a patent within one year of the time you first disclose the device or offer it for sale. In other countries, you have to apply for the patent before it is publicly disclosed. Since disclosure includes showing your plans to others without first making them sign a confidentiality (nondisclosure) agreement, it is a good idea to get nondisclosure agreements signed by anyone you show the device to before it is patented and make marketing decisions early on.

Q **What does the Patent Office charge to patent an invention?**

The Patent and Trademark Office fee depends on the number of claims in the patent application and the size of the company filing for the patent. The minimum fee is $380 for small businesses and $760 for big businesses and covers applications with no more than three independent claims and no more than twenty total claims.

Q **Do I need an attorney to file for a patent?**

You will very likely need the services of a patent attorney or a patent agent. (Patent agents don't have to be attorneys to practice before the U.S. Patent Office, but they do have to pass a difficult exam.) While you are technically not prohibited from submitting an application yourself, it is usually foolish to try to do so unless you are very well versed in patent law. In fact, a form letter the Patent Office sends out to inventors whose applications are rejected reads in part:

> *An examination of this application reveals that applicant is unfamiliar with patent prosecuting procedure. While an inventor may prosecute the application, lack of skill in this field usually acts as a liability in affording the maximum protection for the invention disclosed. Applicant is advised to secure the services of a registered patent attorney or agent to prosecute the application, since the value of a patent is largely dependent upon skillful preparation and prosecution.*

Furthermore, an attorney can help you plan the right strategy for your purposes. Explains attorney Gerry Elman,

> *The first thing to think about is—why do you want a patent? Is it because you are about to sell a product and want to make sure nobody else can ride your coattails into the marketplace? Or is it because you have an idea for a product and want to sell this idea to some company that would make and sell the product, paying you a fee for each one sold? Or do you want to be able to say you have a patent pending so that investors will fund your business? Or do you just want to put it on your resume and your Who's Who listing? These different motivations would give rise to differing strategies in the expenditure of time and money.*

Q **How much will it cost me to have a patent attorney file the application?**

If you do retain a patent attorney, expect to pay $2,000 to $6,000 or more. If your invention has potential for significant profit this would be money well spent, since the value of your patent could hinge on the way the patent disclosure and claims are written.

Q **Where do I find a patent attorney or agent?**

Look in the Yellow Pages of your phone book under "Patent" and/or under the lawyer listings. You can also get a list of attorneys and agents registered to practice before the Patent Office from the Superintendent of Documents, Government Printing Office. The list is also available online at http://www.uspto.gov. While you may file for a patent without using an agent or attorney, if you pay anyone else to prepare your application, they must have passed the Patent Office examination and must be registered to practice before the Patent Office.

Q **What about companies that say they will patent and market your products? Are they any good?**

Some are better at marketing their services than marketing other people's products. Check around carefully before using one of these groups. Try to find other inventors and ask what their experiences have been and who they know to be truly helpful. If you can't find any inventors organizations, try calling local SCORE, SBDC, SBA (see Appendix 1 for addresses and information), or university or college business school offices, and ask for references. There is also a magazine for inventors called *The Dream Merchant,* where you can get marketing information for your invention. The magazine maintains a database of inventors' groups around the country and provides referrals for subscribers. For information about *The Dream Merchant,* write the magazine at 2309 Torrance Blvd., Suite 201, Torrance, CA 90501, call (301) 328-1925, or visit their web site at http://www.dreammerchant. net.

Q **When I file a patent can I leave out information that is a trade secret?**

No. You must disclose your invention in full so that anyone of ordinary skill in the relevant technology would be able to make and use the invention.

Q **How can I see if there is interest in my idea and protect it from being stolen by a manufacturer?**

The best way is to file for a patent on your invention before showing it to manufacturers.

Q Can I patent a variation of a product?

Only if the variation is not an obvious change. In addition, if your variation is patentable, the patents on the original invention—if they have not expired—might prevent you from selling your invention without the consent of the inventor of the original item.

Q Can I patent a novel idea for using existing products?

Only rarely. The idea would need to be an unobvious process to be patentable.

Q Will the patent I get here protect my invention from being copied and used in other countries?

No. You will have to file patent applications in the foreign countries in which you want protection. Gerry Elman points out that the Patent Cooperation Treaty allows you to file a single application within one year of your U.S. patent filing that can start the chain of activity to protect your invention in up to 103 countries in which you may later seek patent protection. But this process generally works only if your U.S. patent application was filed before you made any public disclosure of the invention.

Q Are there any books I can read that will help me understand the patent process?

A book you may find useful is *Patent It Yourself*, by David Pressman (Nolo Press). You may still need to hire an attorney, but by reading this book and using the information in it you could possibly save several hundreds of dollars in attorney fees.

Q What happens if someone does infringe my patent?

As stated previously, you have the right to sue and could be awarded money for past infringements. However, suing can be a lengthy and expensive process, pitting "little you" against the money and legal staffs of giant corporations. If you are determined and have a valid patent you might win the lawsuit in the long run, but the monetary and emotional costs can be draining. It took Robert Kearns, the inventor of the intermittent windshield wiper, 12 years to win his battle against auto companies for infringing his rights. Eventually he won a $10.2 million settlement, $8 million of which went to legal fees, and he was planning to use the remainder to bring still more infringement suits. It is possible, however, to get patent owner's insurance to pay an attorney's fees for such suits. Gerry Elman suggests that if you shop around you might find a lawyer willing to bring your patent infringement suit on a contingency basis.

Q **How do I protect the idea for an invention?**

If you are working on an invention and want to document your progress and the dates of your work, you could have your log signed and dated by a notary or a friend who is not involved in any way with the invention. If you are working by computer, you might use a digital notary to time-stamp your files.

Q **I have already started to market the product—can I still get a patent?**

In the United States you can apply for a patent within one year of the time it is first offered for sale or disclosed publicly, so if you have been marketing the product for less than a year, you may be able to get a patent in this country. Most other countries require you to apply for the patent before disclosing your invention; thus, you cannot qualify for patent protection in those countries. For specific information, consult a patent attorney.

Q **How can I protect a design for a new product?**

There is something called a design patent that lets you protect things such as designs on jeans, the shape of an object, and other designs used for manufactured goods.

Q **What is a nondisclosure agreement and when do I need to use one?**

A nondisclosure agreement prohibits others from using your confidential information or trade secrets for their own benefit or divulging that information to anyone else.

You would use one if you have employees who have access to confidential information, such as your customer list or plans for an invention, or if you have to show confidential information to others outside your company. Pay special attention to this if you haven't yet filed a patent application for the subject matter.

Q **What is a trade secret?**

A trade secret is business information you have that gives you a valuable edge over your competitors. This information may be a recipe for a cookie, an invention, the unique part of the code for a program, your customer list, plans to introduce new products, or almost anything else that is generally not known and gives you a competitive advantage.

Q **What kind of protection is there for trade secrets?**

If what you have is not generally known, and if you have taken care to maintain secrecy, you can sue the individual who disclosed your secrets. You may also take legal action to stop use of your trade secrets by others and recover damages if warranted.

Q **What do I have to do to maintain secrecy?**

Generally you have to limit access to what you consider a trade secret, be it your customer list, your recipes, or formulas. If you need to give people access to your trade secrets, you should make them first sign a nondisclosure agreement, preventing them from using or passing on what they learn. If you have employees, don't leave important papers lying out on desks or in unlocked drawers where someone working late could easily get at them. Avoid giving suppliers or bankers or anyone else you deal with access to your trade secrets, too.

Q **How can trade secret laws help me?**

Trade secret laws can protect your invention or your software in the development stages and can help you prevent others from profiting from your business procedures, lists, processes, or other unique parts of your operation. Some companies that have products with short lives or short budgets take their chances on trade secrets and speedy commercialization rather than go to the expense and time to apply for and get a patent. However, if another company develops on their own what you have, if you don't have a patent you have no recourse against them.

Q **What is licensing and how does it work?**

Licensing allows you to make money from other people's use of something you have created or you own. For instance, when you license a design you have created or software program you have authored, you give the licensee the right to use that work under specific circumstances that are spelled out in detail in a written agreement. The agreement will usually specify such things as how, when, and where the licensee may use your work, how you will be compensated for the work, and whether the licensee has exclusive or nonexclusive rights to use your work.

Q **Can any attorney help me with patents and other intellectual property?**

Only a patent attorney or patent agent may represent an inventor applying for a patent. An attorney in a general practice often won't have the background and experience in intellectual property law to help you protect or defend your rights to intellectual property. If the matter is something more or less routine (like registering a copyright), a general practice attorney may be able to process the paperwork. (In all probability, the attorney will "job out" the routine paperwork to a firm set up specifically to handle it.) He or she probably won't have the expertise to counsel you on how an intellectual property law (such as the copyright law or patent law) relates to your specific situation and how that situation is generally handled in contracts and in courts. Your best bet is to locate an attorney who specializes in intellectual property, and is familiar with your industry.

Q **How can I find an intellectual property attorney?**

The Roster of U.S. Patent Attorneys and Agents is on the web at http://www.uspto.gov. You can search the authoritative Martindale-Hubbell Law Directory on the web at http://www.lawyers.com. Patent attorneys are specifically identified, and the lawyers may also list in the directory their specific areas of expertise. If you can't find one who knows your field, call the bar association or a trade association and ask for a recommendation. If you are in the arts (music, painting, writing, for example) you can get information and referrals by contacting the Volunteer Lawyers for the Arts, and ask where you can get the information you need. If you can't find a branch of Volunteer Lawyers for the Arts in your phone book, call the main office at 1 East 53rd Street, New York, NY 10022, (212) 319-2910, and ask for information and/or reference to a branch nearer to you.

21.

Health Insurance:
Protection You Can't
Afford to Do Without

One of the biggest drawbacks to self-employment is the high cost of health insurance. If you are working for a company that offers health insurance and quit to start your own business, you lose not only the steady paycheck but also the company's contribution toward your health care insurance. If you aren't married, if your spouse is unemployed, or doesn't have health care benefits, you can expect to pay hundreds of dollars a month for coverage.

And the coverage isn't what it used to be. According to a study released by the Kaiser Family Foundation, the percentage of American workers enrolled in conventional insurance plans (also known as indemnity or fee-for-service) declined from 73 percent in 1988 to 9 percent in 1999. The nonconventional plans apparently have done little to make health insurance affordable for small businesses and the self-employed. Rate increases tend to be 1 to 2 percent higher for small businesses than big, and forty percent of small businesses do not offer health insurance plans to their employees. As a result, many self-employed simply don't purchase insurance. In fact, 25 percent of self-employed individuals have no health care insurance. But despite the high cost of insurance, gambling that you won't need health care benefits is risky business. Read on to find out why, and what your various options are.

Q I'm only 27 and never get sick. Is there any reason I can't wait a few years to get health insurance?

Just because you seldom get sick doesn't mean you couldn't develop some type of long-term illness or be involved in a serious accident. A single illness or accident could put you in the hole with doctor and hospital bills totaling $20,000 to $30,000 in just two or three weeks if you don't have health insurance.

Q I'm planning on quitting my job to start my own business. Can I convert my company health insurance policy to a personal one?

If your present employer has twenty or more employees and you become ineligible for insurance under the company group plan due to a "qualifying event" (see below), you may be entitled to continue the plan for up to 18 months* under the Consolidated Omnibus Budget Reconciliation Act of 1985 (COBRA). If you become disabled, the continuation period is extended to 29 months. You will have to pay the premiums out of your own pocket, however. At the end of the continuation period you have the option of changing it to an individual conversion policy under the health care policy's regular conversion options.

Q Does the COBRA law apply to all companies that have twenty or more employees?

No. Some government, church, and self-insured plans are exempt from the COBRA law, so be sure to check before assuming you can continue coverage.

Q What are qualifying events?

The following five events are considered qualifying events under COBRA:

1. You cease to be an employee for any reason other than gross misconduct.
2. You change from full-time to part-time employment and no longer qualify for the company's health care plan due to the reduction in hours you work.

---

*A dependent spouse who loses coverage because of the death of the insured, or due to separation or divorce and children who become too old for coverage under the insured's plan, or lose coverage in some other way may continue coverage for up to 36 months.

3. You are the spouse of the insured and lose coverage due to divorce, legal separation, or the death of the insured.
4. You are a child who ceases to be eligible for group plan benefits.
5. You become entitled to Medicare benefits.

Q How long do I have before I have to decide whether to continue the coverage under COBRA?

Your group plan administrator is supposed to notify you within 14 days of a qualifying event of your right to continue the coverage. You then have 60 days to elect coverage, which will be retroactive to the time you became ineligible for your employer's plan. You then have up to 45 days to pay the first premium.

Q If the employer changes insurance plans, what happens to my coverage?

Although you, personally, pay for the continuation coverage, it is under the employer's policy. Thus, if the employer changes to a new carrier and/or plan, your coverage changes to the same carrier and/or plan. If the employer should stop offering health insurance, your coverage would be terminated along with all the others that were under the company health plan.

Q What will it cost me to continue my present coverage?

The rate for the coverage is the same rate your employer is charged plus a 2 percent administrative cost. If you pay part and the employer pays part of the cost now, the amount you pay will be the combined amount (your share plus the employer's share).

Q Can I lose this coverage in any way?

The continuation coverage terminates at the end of the continuation period or if any of the following occurs:

▸ You don't pay the premium when it is due.
▸ You become covered as an employee under some other plan.
▸ You remarry and become included under the new spouse's group health insurance.

- You become eligible for Medicare.
- Your former employer ceases to provide group health care for all employees, terminating the plan.

Q **Can the insurance company refuse individual coverage for me or my family at the end of the continuation period?**

If you haven't let the policy lapse, they can't refuse to insure you; however, rates may be higher and coverage not as good as the group plan.

Q **Suppose my employer has fewer than twenty employees. Is there any way I can continue my health insurance if I lose my job?**

Some states have continuation laws that are similar to the federal COBRA law. Your state insurance department or an insurance broker should be able to tell you if there is some type of health insurance continuation law in your state.

Q **Is it advisable to use the conversion option in the group plan?**

The conversion option will give you continuity of insurance. It is also useful if you or your dependents have health problems that might make it difficult to get a new health care policy. If you and your dependents are healthy, however, a policy may be less expensive and better than the conversion plan. Shop around.

Q **Should I join an association to get their group health insurance?**

If you will be joining an association only to get their group health plan, ask to see a copy of the policy and ask about the rates for coverage for yourself and your dependents. Not all group or association plans are created equal, and some may not give you the coverage you need.

Q **What will a good health insurance policy for myself and my family cost?**

That figure varies greatly according to where you live, how old you are, how many dependents you have, and whether you or family members have had previous health problems and what type of plan you choose. As a rough guide, the average premium paid by a business with fewer than 10 employees to cover a family of four was $520 a month in 1998. A single, 58-year-old woman living in California reports she paid $250 a month for insurance from a health maintenance organization in 1999. Meanwhile, a New York resident was paying more than $800 a month to cover his family.

Those who opt for early retirement packages or who are laid off by their employers may be able to get insurance bargains, however. A computer programmer in his mid-fifties who was laid off when his company merged with another firm took advantage of retiree insurance offered as part of the severance package. He was paying only $140 a month for health and limited dental coverage for him and his wife. Coverage was through an HMO.

Q **Is group health insurance cheaper than individual coverage?**

Not necessarily. In fact, an individual health insurance plan may cost less and offer more than small group plans. The only way you can be sure which would be best for your circumstances is to compare rates and features of a group policy to an individual policy. Make sure you read policy brochures carefully since some plans that say they are for individuals are really small group plans in disguise. One insurance company, for instance, has one plan it bills as being an "economical health insurance program for individuals" and describes another as "an opportunity for individuals to enjoy group benefits and group rates." The two plans are identical and both are small group plans. The only differences between them are the name of each plan and the artwork in the brochures describing them.

Q **What should I look for in a health insurance policy?**

Most people choose insurance based on rates and deductibles. But rates and deductibles are less important than your ability to continue coverage, warns health insurance expert Hal Zoller. Zoller, who owns Resource Equity Group, an insurance firm in Greenville, South Carolina, specializing in health and life insurance, says it's important to "know what you are buying up front. Get information about what kind of policy you are buying . . . and under what conditions it can be canceled," Zoller says. "Make sure you are not vulnerable to losing coverage. If you have group coverage tied to employment and you go out of business or are unable to work, you will lose coverage and you won't be able to get insurance elsewhere if you have any kind of medical condition at that time."

If you are buying insurance for only yourself and your dependents or are buying it for yourself and one or two other employees, Zoller suggests you look for a policy that:

- is a true individual policy, not a small group plan being sold to individuals
- does not tie eligibility to employment
- offers comprehensive major medical coverage in or out of the hospital
- is offered by a company that is committed to health insurance as a speciality, has an A or A+ rating by A. M. Best & Co., and at least $100 million in assets
- offers you some flexibility in tailoring coverage to your needs

Q **I haven't had any health problems so I don't think any insurance company would turn me down. Why do I need to be concerned with the eligibility requirements in a policy?**

Eligibility requirements govern more than just your initial eligibility to get the insurance. They also govern whether you can *keep* the insurance. For instance, if your policy pegs eligibility to employment or self-employment and you become disabled and unable to work, you would become ineligible for the insurance and could lose it at the very time you need it most. Finding new insurance at a reasonable price would be impossible because of your disability.

Q **What is the Health Insurance Portability and Accountability Act and who does it help?**

The Health Insurance Portability and Accountability Act (HIPAA), which went into effect in 1997, was put in place to improve the "portability" of health insurance when workers change jobs or convert from a group plan to an individual policy. Before the law was enacted, a change of jobs or a shift from COBRA coverage to an individual policy could result in being denied coverage, asked to pay a higher premium, or accept a policy that excluded coverage for a preexisting condition as defined by the policy.

HIPAA provides guaranteed continuity of coverage for those who are eligible. A terminated employee must first exhaust all of his/her group continuation coverage (COBRA, etc.) before HIPAA eligible coverage is available, and there can be no more than a 63-day gap between coverages.

What that all means to you if you're leaving an employer to start a business is that if you were covered under an employer-sponsored plan, you cannot be turned down for individual coverage once you have exhausted your group "continuation" options (that is, COBRA, etc.) if your new coverage takes effect within 63 days. You may be asked to pay a higher premium, however, due to a health condition.

HIPAA also mandates that small group plans (2 to 50 employees) be required to issue coverage without regard to the health status of the employees; however, rates may be higher than standard. Zoller advises that "renewal" is a legal term found in the policy that describes the conditions under which the insurer may cancel, or non-renew coverage. All policies are guaranteed renewable under HIPAA. But that doesn't mean you are protected from losing your coverage. Your present plan may not continue if you lose eligibility due to a change in your circumstances such as unemployment or disability. (If you lose your job, you are no longer part of the group, and therefore no longer eligible for the group plan, even though it would have been renewed if you hadn't left the company.)

You can find some additional information about HIPAA on the web at http://www.hcfa.gov/regs/q&a-con.htm. The rules are complicated and some of them are still being formulated, and some of the rules vary from state to state. So if you or a spouse has a medical condition that might be considered uninsurable, be sure to seek advice from an insurance broker who is familiar with the HIPAA rules for your state.

Q **I let my insurance coverage lapse and now an insurance agent tells me I might be uninsurable due to a medical condition I have. What can I do?**

First, find out if the agent you are using deals only with one or two companies. If so, find an insurance broker who is experienced in handling health insurance and who is familiar with insurance offered by many companies. Since each company has its own underwriting requirements it is possible that what makes you uninsurable to one company might not make you uninsurable to another. If you do have a condition that would make you uninsurable to all companies, ask about health insurance risk pools and open enrollment options in your state. Risk pools, which accept people who have been rejected by other insurance companies, are available in 27 states. Open enrollment periods are another option for insurance offered in 13 states by Blue Cross/Blue Shield. During open enrollment, everyone who applies for insurance and can pay the premium is accepted. Policies obtained through one of these options are likely to be expensive but at least should provide some coverage. Be sure to read the policies carefully to see what they say about coverage for preexisting conditions.

Q **How can I tell whether something is a true individual policy or small group insurance being sold to individuals?**

"Make sure the person selling you the insurance leaves you literature about the insurance you are considering and read it carefully," suggests Zoller. "If the coverage is described as a policy, and you are described as the policyholder, chances are it is a true individual policy. If it is referred to as a plan or program, it is probably some type of group plan."

Pay particular attention to the legal-sounding descriptions in the policy literature, too. These descriptions should explain what the document is and what parties are involved. Says Zoller, "If there are more than two parties involved (the insurance company and you), it probably is not an individual policy but some sort of a group policy with the other parties being an administrator, association, trustee, et cetera." Still another giveaway that a policy is not a true individual policy is any statement requiring continuing employment or participation in an association for eligibility.

Q **Is individual insurance the only kind of insurance I should consider?**

It depends on circumstances. If you have employees you will cover, you must purchase group insurance to meet legal requirements for maternity coverage and underwriting. Group insurance may be preferable, too, if you can't get an individual policy due to previous health problems, or can get better maternity or other benefits under a group plan. Additionally, if you have more than a couple of employees, individual plans are likely to be impractical for providing coverage for all of them. In that case, you might want to consider group insurance to cover the employees and individual coverage for yourself and your dependents. No matter what your circumstances, however, differences in policies from different insurance companies and even differences in policies by state or region of the country make it imperative for you to understand exactly what kind of protection you are buying.

Q **Do I need separate coverage for doctor bills, hospital stays, and/or surgery?**

Those coverages are usually all rolled into one comprehensive major medical policy. Policies that offer only in-hospital and surgical coverage or daily indemnity policies and policies that over certain illnesses (such as cancer) are of questionable value. If you have a comprehensive policy, cancer and other "dread diseases" will be covered under the policy, making supplemental "dread disease" insurance superfluous.

Q **What about policies that say they will pay back premiums minus any claims when you reach a certain age?**

Read them carefully to make sure you know exactly what you are getting. One such plan covered only in-hospital care and had a very high deductible. Since it is quite easy to pile up thousands of dollars in medical bills without ever stepping foot inside a hospital, plans like this are not good substitutes for having comprehensive major medical coverage.

Q **What benefits should I look for in a health insurance policy?**

Make sure the policy protects you against burdensome out-of-pocket expenses for inpatient and outpatient care. Find out:

▸ What the deductible is on the policy (how much you have to pay per year out of your own money before the insurance company pays anything).

▸ What percentage of bills the insurance company pays after you reach the deductible.

▸ Whether the deductible is applied to each illness or injury or is figured on a calendar-year basis. A calendar-year basis is much better since you could be struck with two separate illnesses or injuries that are costly in one year.

▸ What the maximum out-of-pocket expense will be. (In other words, how much do you have to pay before the company will pick up all covered medical expenses instead of just a percentage of them?)

You also need to look at how the insurance company determines the amounts it will pay. Will they pay all usual and customary charges for your medical and hospital bills in the geographic region where you are treated, or do they pay according to a schedule of fees? If payments are according to a schedule of fees you might find that the schedule allows only $2,000 for a surgical procedure you need but that all the doctors in your area charge $5,000. If that were the case, you would have to pay the additional $3,000 out of your own pocket.

Check for limitations and exclusions on coverage, too. For instance, some plans or policies limit intensive care to two or three times the regular room rate or pay only for a limited number of days. Find out what the policy says about preexisting conditions: Will it deny any claims for preexisting conditions? Will it pay claims if there is no recurrence within a set period of time? Warns Zoller, "Read the definition of a preexisting condition first, and then read when they will be covered. For example, under one policy, a preexisting condition might be a condition for which you have received treatment in the last 12 months. Under another, preexisting conditions might be defined as having *symptoms* (with no treatment). Usually preexisting conditions will be covered within 12 to 24 months, and in some states, unless excluded by a special rider, all preexisting conditions disclosed on the application are covered immediately."

Other things to look into include maternity benefits, if needed, requirements for second opinions or approvals prior to surgery or to hospital admission, and your own preferences or individual needs. Does the policy cover holistic or chiropractic care? Psychologist or psychiatrist fees? Alcohol and substance abuse? Are you likely to need these things? What about yearly checkups or routine preventive screening tests such as mammograms or bone density scans for osteoporosis?

If you choose some type of health maintenance organization or preferred provider group plan, find out what doctors, hospitals, and testing labs belong to the plan and how far away you would have to travel to use them. Find out, too, if the plan pays for care that is performed outside of the organization's member doctors and hospitals and if so, under what circumstances. You don't want to find out after you get a bill for $10,000 or $20,000 in medical bills that the insurance company won't cover them because the hospital and/or doctor wasn't part of its network.

Q **What are preferred provider and health maintenance organizations?**

Preferred provider organizations (PPOs) and health maintenance organizations (HMOs) are two forms of something known as managed care plans, which are plans designed to reduce health care costs.

HMOs are both the insurance company and the health care provider. With HMOs, insured individuals usually *must* use the HMO health care providers unless there is no suitable HMO specialist or other provider available within the HMO. If that is the case, the individual will be referred to an approved provider outside the system. The primary advantage to the insured is that actual out-of-pocket expenses can be just a couple of dollars for each doctor's visit or prescription. The disadvantage is that it may not have any coverage for health care services performed by doctors or facilities that are not part of the HMO, which can be a major problem if you should be dissatisfied with the doctors or treatment plans offered through the HMO.

Preferred provider organizations operate a little differently. Typically, health care providers who participate agree to accept payment at fees specified by the PPO and charge the patient a slightly higher copayment than the patient would pay at an HMO. (Copayment in one preferred provider plan is $10, for instance.) If the insured would rather choose his or her own health care provider, however, he or she can and will be reimbursed for out-of-pocket expenses the same as under traditional health care (fee for service) plans. The benefit of a PPO is that the premiums may be 10 to 15 percent lower than traditional indemnity health care premiums, and the out-of-pocket expenses for routine checkups and tests may be lower, too. Potential disadvantages could be lower benefits if you choose doctors who are not part of the system.

Q **Would I be better off trying to get coverage for my employees through an HMO or PPO instead of through more traditional group plans?**

Only you can make that decision based on your needs and the needs of your employees. Look at the plan details, coverages, list of preferred providers, and premiums. Then compare to more traditional plans before making your decision.

Q **An insurance broker who called here tells me he can get insurance for my employees at a much lower rate than I am paying now. Is it wise to switch companies just for rates?**

"One of the things small businesses need to watch out for is the difference between new business rates for group insurance and the in-force rates," warns Hal Zoller. It is not uncommon for companies to be notified of rate increases of as much as 50 to 100 percent when their policies renew. At the same time the insurance company may be advertising the very same plan at a very low "new business" rate.

"If continuity of coverage can be maintained, the new plan appears to have a successful record and you can save more than twenty-five percent, the switch might be worthwhile if benefits are comparable to what you now have," says Zoller.

Q Do I need to get disability insurance?

Long-term disability insurance is often overlooked because it is expensive and because no one likes to think about the possibility of becoming disabled. Nevertheless, if you should be unable to work for a long period of time due to accident or illness, you would have long-term living expenses. Long-term disability insurance can help cover those needs.

Q How much disability insurance do I need? Enough to replace all my salary?

Usually people get disability insurance to cover 50 to 65 percent of their salary. Insurance companies usually will not give you coverage for your full salary since they feel a greater percentage would be a disincentive to rehabilitation.

Q What should I look for in a disability policy?

Look at what the policy pays, when it pays (how long the waiting period is, how long you would continue to receive benefits), and look at the policy definition of disability. Some policies will pay if you are unable to work in any occupation; others pay if you are unable to work in the trade or occupation you were pursuing when you were disabled. A policy that pays if you can't work in your own trade or occupation would be best.

Q Isn't it difficult for homebased business owners to get disability insurance?

If you are just starting out in your own business, it might be difficult to get adequate disability insurance, since the amount a policy will pay is based on your previous earnings.

Q Is there any other insurance I might need?

If you don't have life insurance, you should look into getting a simple term or low-cost universal life policy. Other insurance you may need will depend on your individual circumstances. A good insurance broker who is familiar with the needs of businesspeople and your type of business can help you identify potential risks. You may find it beneficial to deal with two insurance brokers, one for health and life insurance and one for property/casualty insurance. Once you know the risks, you will have to assess the potentials for financial loss to determine what types of insurance protection to buy.

Useful Web Sites

http://ehealthinsurance.com

Compare costs for many different types of policies, see doctor lists and policy details. You can even apply online. (Not available for all states.)

http://netquote.com/kindex.htm

Quote comparisons for life, health, and business insurance.

http://www.healthinsurance.org

Offers information and quotes. Targets small businesses and the self-employed.

http://www.healthaxis.com (also available through BusinessKnowHow.com)

Offers quotes, doctor look-up, tracking of benefits. Several insurance companies participate.

22.

How to Protect Your
Business and Personal
Assets from Loss

Business insurance is something few people like to discuss and no one likes to buy. After all, who really wants to pay for something they can't see or touch and hope they never have to use?

Like it or not, however, insurance is a necessary evil. A fire or theft, an accident involving a customer or employee, or a lawsuit brought against you or your company could destroy your business and eat up your life savings if you don't have adequate insurance. This chapter alerts you to some of the risks you may face and gives you the basic facts you need to make informed decisions about what kind of business insurance you should consider buying to protect your business and personal assets from financial loss.

Q **I'm always careful in my work and fix things if customers have complaints. Am I really likely to be sued?**

No matter how knowledgeable or careful you are, you could suddenly find yourself the defendant in a lawsuit. Typical is the case of an independent consultant who recommended specific hardware and software for one of his business clients. When the software didn't work properly with the hardware configuration, the client sued and won a $100,000 judgment against the consultant. In another case a small company offering data storage and list management services as a sideline sustained a $2 million loss after it inadvertently mixed up two lists, substituting a list of credit risks for a list of prime customers.

Professional negligence is just one type of risk you may face as a business owner. Other possible exposures (risks) include product liability, personal injury (if a client or employee tripped and broke a leg in your home office, for instance), vehicular accidents involving an employee, and loss of equipment due to fire or theft.

Q **I operate my business from my home. Won't my personal insurance policies protect me against losses?**

Personal insurance policies offer little or no coverage for business-related losses. Homeowner's insurance usually excludes liability coverage for business pursuits and may exclude computer or other business equipment used in the home. If electronic equipment is not excluded, it may be limited to only $2,500, an amount far below what many home business owners have invested in their computer software and peripherals.

Q **Is there any way I can get protection for my home office without getting a separate business policy?**

You may be able to gain some protection by purchasing riders or endorsements for an incidental office in your home. (A rider or endorsement is an add-on to your policy.) When available these add-ons give you a limited amount of property coverage for losses to home office equipment and furnishings and a limited amount of liability coverage for personal injuries to clients or employees* on your premises. Sometimes these add-ons are combined into one endorsement, and sometimes they are sold separately. They typically cover only businesses with $5,000 or less of annual sales.

Q **Can I get endorsements to my home policy for professional or product liability protection?**

No, product liability and professional liability (which is a form of malpractice insurance) are not available as endorsements to homeowner's insurance.

---

*Home office liability coverage for employees in your home office is separate from workers' compensation insurance, which you also need.

Q I'd like to run a day-care center from my home. Will an endorsement to my homeowner's policy cover my insurance needs for that?

Sometimes you can get an endorsement if you provide day care for only a handful of children; however, the regulations vary from state to state. Find out what the regulations are in your area, then ask an insurance agent or broker to find you an appropriate policy.

Q What insurance companies offer endorsements for an office in the home?

Many companies that offer homeowner's insurance now have riders for businesses in the home. Among them are Allstate, the Hartford, and State Farm.

Q Are the endorsements or add-on policies expensive?

The actual cost depends on what you do, how much insurance you need, and where you are located, but usually they are quite inexpensive. The additional amount you pay to add one or more business endorsements to your home policy could be as low as $20 per year.

You could pay more for an endorsement, too, and not get the best possible coverage for your needs. An insurance agent in Long Island, New York, told me about getting one home business owner an endorsement for his homeowner's policy to cover $20,000 worth of computer equipment. The endorsement added $400 a year to the cost of the businessperson's homeowner's policy. When I asked the agent to look up the cost of a businessowner's policy that would provide the same amount of coverage for the computer equipment, he found the cost was $275 ($125 less than the endorsement) for a policy that would have covered the computer equipment and given the person a million dollars in liability protection against business-related personal injury claims.

Moral: get comparison prices from several insurance brokerages and ask about all options that might be available to you. Work with the insurance agent or broker who is most willing to help you find the right insurance for your needs and budget.

Q **Will the extra casualty and liability insurance from an endorsement be enough?**

It all depends on what kind of business you run. For instance, if you have an endorsement to your homeowner's policy, the limit of coverage (the most the insurance company will pay) for injury to clients or employees will be the same as the limit stated in your home policy. This is usually quite a bit less than the limit in a commercial policy. If you rarely have business clients come to your home office and don't have employees, however, it may be adequate for your needs.

If you don't have much data processing or other specialized business equipment and don't store equipment that belongs to other people on your property, the added endorsements may give you all the casualty insurance you need. On the other hand, if you *do* have a lot of money invested in data processing equipment, the additional fire and theft and data processing protection you can buy this way may not be adequate.

The limits and the premiums vary from company to company, too, so be sure to ask what they are. Make the agent or broker look up the figures and give you something in writing (preferably a copy of the policy and endorsements). If you don't, you may not be getting the coverage you think you are buying.

In researching this chapter, for instance, I called the local office of a nationally known insurance company three times on different days. On each call I spoke to a different agent in the office and asked the identical question: What are the limits for equipment coverage on your company's incidental office in the home rider? *Each agent gave me a different answer.* One said she thought it was $5,000; another said he thought it was $2,000; and a third said he thought it was $8,000. None of them bothered to look up the actual value. They expected me to accept the figure they "thought" was right.

Be aware, too, that endorsements usually cover only specified perils and will generally be limited by the same deductibles that are applied to your homeowner's policy.

Q **My sales are a lot higher than $5,000. What kind of insurance would I need?**

There are so many home businesses in the country that the insurance industry has developed a product to fill needs such as yours. It's a home business insurance policy. It costs about $200 and lets you insure your business property for $10,000 and includes general liability and coverage from losses to income if you can't work due to a loss.

Q **What happens if I don't tell the insurance company about my home office?**

If you suffer a business-related loss or are sued for a business-related accident, they may refuse to pay the claim. The cost of business endorsements is usually so minimal that if you have a business in your home it would be foolish not to at least get endorsements to cover your business activities. If the insurance company you use now doesn't have such endorsements available, shop around for one that does.

Q **Will an incidental office in the home endorsement pay to replace my computer system if I drop it and break it while moving it from one place to another?**

No. The endorsement will only give you the same kind of insurance protection you have for other household goods: namely fire, theft, and other specified perils. To cover accidental breakage, spills, and so on, you need a special form policy for the computer equipment.

Q **What is a special form policy?**

Special form policies cover you for everything except situations specifically excluded in a policy. A named perils policy protects you only for named (listed) exposures or hazards. For instance, if you had a named perils policy that states it protects against fire and theft but does not mention accidental breakage, you wouldn't collect if you accidentally broke some piece of property that was covered by the policy. However, if you have a special form policy that says the property is covered for all risks except earthquakes, you could recoup your losses from accidental breakage or damage that was not caused by an earthquake. *Special form policies* is the term now used for what used to be called "all-risk" policies. The name was changed because they do exclude some perils, and the name was therefore confusing. As with any policy, be sure to read the policy and make sure it covers the risks you want covered. If anything is unclear, ask your broker for an explanation.

Q A friend told me he had bought computer insurance real cheap from a company that sells it mail order. Is it really wise to buy computer insurance that way?

Like anything else you will need to comparison shop; however, you might save money buying computer coverage through mail order. A company called Safeware, which has been in business for more than 10 years, offers a good, all-risk policy at a reasonable price and has an excellent reputation for handling claims. The insurance covers most losses, including accidental breakage, spills, and power surges. A few risks are excluded (not covered). These include earthquake damage and theft of computer equipment left in an unattended car; however, endorsements can be added to cover those two and other special situations.

The rates on the Safeware policies are based on the replacement costs of your computer system. In 1999, the company was charging $129 for a replacement value policy that protected $11,001 to $14,000 in computer equipment. Policies for computer systems with lower or higher replacement values were available as well. If you have or are considering buying a businessowner's policy (BOP), ask if it includes all-risk computer coverage and coverage for equipment out of the office if you travel and carry a computer with you. You might want to compare Safeware's rates and coverages with endorsements available to your BOP.

Q Does Safeware sell insurance where I live? I didn't see them in the phone book.

Safeware sells insurance in most parts of the United States. To find out if their insurance is available in your area and to get current rates, you can contact the company at (800) 800-1492 or (614) 781-1492. Or visit their web site at http://www.safeware.com.

Q I write about computer equipment and have a little repair business on the side, so I often have equipment that doesn't belong to me in my home office. Does my insurance cover loss of those items if there's a break-in or fire?

If you do not have a commercial insurance policy, you probably would not be covered for that type of loss. You need either a businessowner's policy with coverage for property of others or separate bailees' insurance. (Bailees' insurance has nothing to do with bail for criminals. The term *bailee* means anyone who has temporary possession of someone else's property.)

Q I'm a professional musician and use my truck to transport equipment from one engagement to another. My insurance broker says I need commercial insurance because my regular insurance might not cover my equipment if it's lost or damaged on one of these moves. Is he just trying to make extra money?

No, he's not just trying to make an extra buck, he's giving you good advice. If something got lost or stolen in transit neither your homeowner's nor your truck insurance would be likely to cover the loss. To cover losses in transporting equipment you need inland marine insurance. Despite the term *marine* in the name, inland marine insurance has nothing to do with ships, recreational boating, or bodies of water. Instead, the name was originally associated with the concept of insuring goods after they are taken off the boat and are in transit to some other location. Today, however, inland marine insurance offers protection against a broad range of perils including the transportation of equipment.

Q When do I need regular business insurance?

You will need regular (commercial) business insurance if your business office is not located in your home or if you are a homebased business with insurance risks that aren't covered by endorsements to your homeowner's policy or a home business policy. You may also be required by your state, regional, or local governing bodies to have some specified kind and amount of insurance to get a license. A carpenter might be required to have $500,000 worth of liability insurance, for instance. These regulations vary from one locality to another, so you will have to check with your town, city, county, and state governments to determine what rules apply. You may also have to be bonded for some types of work.

Q My business office is not in my home. Will I need separate insurance policies to protect me against robberies, theft, injury to customers, and the like?

You will probably be able to get one comprehensive policy called a business-owner's policy or businessowner's packaged policy (BOP) that will cover your business for a variety of perils. Be sure to give your broker enough information so he or she can evaluate what risks you may be exposed to, search for the right policy, and let you know if other insurance is advisable.

Q **Under what conditions might a home business need a separate business policy?**

Some examples of when you might need businessowner's coverage for a home business include:

- if you store other people's property in your home office
- if you have more computer equipment than your homeowner's fire and theft provisions will cover
- if you need business interruption insurance
- if you frequently have customers or independent contractors who come to your home
- if you generate more revenues in your home business than allowed by an endorsement add-on to a homeowner's policy

Policies and individual business needs vary, so read the policies you are considering and make sure you understand what you are buying.

Q **What does a businessowner's policy cover?**

A businessowner's policy gives you coverage for a variety of property and liability risks. These policies are available for many small offices, stores, and apartment houses and may be either named peril or special form (all-risk) policies. Businessowners' policies are usually tailored for specific businesses but are likely to offer:

- liability coverage against slips and falls and other physical injuries to customers
- accidental libel or slander* and similar nonphysical injury to individuals
- casualty insurance (fire and theft)

*The protection against accidental libel and slander available in most BOPs does not apply to publications. If you publish newspapers, magazines, books, or other written media, you will need to get separate coverage if you want protection against libel and slander. Your insurance broker should be able to find an appropriate policy for you.

- business interruption insurance (replaces business income and pays for extra expenses after a fire, theft, or other insured loss so you can pay the rent, equipment leases, and other ongoing business expenses plus extra costs incurred to get the business running again)
- insurance for property of others while it is on your premises

Don't just assume a BOP will meet all your needs, however. Get specifics. "Each insurance contract is unique," explains Ed Coyle, a former property and casualty insurance broker from Wheaton, Illinois. He warns that the variations can be confusing: "There is no generic policy. Each company tends to add their own bells and whistles to make their policy different."

Depending on circumstances, you may need extra protection against employee theft, glass breakage, machinery or boiler breakdown, or other perils. Computers and computer equipment would be covered as other property but may not be covered against losses due to brownouts, spikes, and so on. If you want that type of protection you might get a separate computer policy.

Q **Is a businessowner's policy expensive for a home office?**

No. A businessowner's policy suitable for a home office will probably cost about $250 to $350 a year, an amount that is quite reasonable for the extra insurance coverage you get. The businessowner's policy would be completely separate from and in addition to your homeowner's policy.

Q **How do I know I have enough of the right kind of insurance?**

The most important thing you can do is find a good insurance broker who understands your business and will help you understand what your risks are and how to protect against them. If you don't have an insurance broker and don't have friends who can recommend a good one, look in the Yellow Pages under "Insurance." When you call agents, explain what kind of business you are in and ask what they recommend. Be sure they understand the way your business operates and be sure you know exactly what the policy or policies they suggest will or won't cover.

Q **What's the difference between an insurance agent and a broker?**

The definitions vary somewhat from state to state, but in general an insurance broker represents the customer and finds the right policy or policies from among the offerings of many different companies. An insurance agent may represent only one insurance company (such as Allstate or State Farm) or may be an independent agent who represents many companies and functions like a broker.

Q **What is errors and omissions insurance?**

Errors and omissions insurance is malpractice insurance for professionals who aren't medical practitioners. Often called E & O insurance or professional liability insurance, it protects professionals from financial loss due to claims involving negligence, errors, omissions, and wrongful acts. Traditionally, coverage included all legal fees, court costs, and settlements up to the limits of the policy. Some policies now being written have first dollar exclusions (deductibles) on legal fee coverage or reduce the maximum the policy will pay in settlement by the cost of the legal fees. Therefore, be sure to read your policy very carefully.

If you are involved in a traditional profession, such as accounting, real estate, or personnel recruiting, you may be able to get a policy or references to companies that offer suitable policies through your professional association. If you are in a profession with few practitioners, finding a suitable policy can be quite difficult.

Q **Don't businessowners' policies include professional liability coverage?**

Professional liability is different from and usually purchased separately from other kinds of liability insurance. Several companies offer E & O insurance as an add-on to their businessowner's policy for printers.

Q **What does errors and omissions insurance cost? Isn't it expensive?**

Unfortunately, we live in a society where people like to sue one another. That makes E & O insurance quite expensive for many businesses. Rates are based on a variety of things, including the type of business, dollar volume of the business, the number of customers, and experience in the field, and often start at $1,000 a year or more. In 1999 one company was charging a computer consultant $1,600 a year for a million dollars in liability coverage. The consultant had annual sales of approximately $190,000. A human resources consultant found that errors and omissions policies in his field ranged from $1,500 to $3,000.

The high price of professional liability insurance means many people who run small homebased businesses feel they can't afford E & O insurance. They find it difficult to justify the cost because it is a struggle for them to pay for basic health insurance and automobile insurance.

Q **A friend of mine who is a consulting engineer says he doesn't need liability insurance because he put the house and everything else in his wife's name and he is careful in his work. Is that a safe way to avoid buying errors and omissions insurance?**

If you need E & O insurance there really is no completely safe way to avoid the cost. Many very small companies do choose to go without E & O insurance because of the cost; however, doing so is a gamble. You have to understand what your risk is and be willing to live with the risk and the consequences should you be sued. If your friend has put everything in his wife's name without the advice of an attorney he may not have the protection he thinks he does. State marital laws might consider his wife a partner in the business and equally liable for the business. Furthermore, even if his current assets were covered, the plaintiff may be able to collect the judgment from future income.

Q **I have errors and omissions insurance now but plan to retire soon and will be discontinuing the insurance then. Will my current insurer still cover me if someone sues me 5 years after I retire for something they claim I did before I retired?**

It might not. Be sure to have your insurance broker review your policy and advise you.

Q **I'd like to switch insurance companies. What happens after I do? Who covers professional liability claims made in the past? The present company or the old one?**

If you switch companies, you should ask about something called prior acts coverage, which will extend your present level of protection backward to years past at present levels of coverage.

Q Can't I incorporate to protect my personal assets in case I'm sued for professional malpractice?

Contrary to popular belief, incorporation does not automatically protect your personal assets from liability in malpractice (or other) lawsuits. Although incorporation makes the business a separate legal entity from its owners, there are numerous circumstances that can cause that status to be lost. In fact, a good attorney could probably find a way to strip away corporate status of almost any small business based on criteria such as these:

- the business failed to keep corporate financial affairs distinctly separate from personal financial matters
- the business didn't hold required shareholders' and directors' meetings or keep adequate records
- the business was undercapitalized
- the business didn't file an annual report or filed it late

Even if you were able to maintain your corporate status and/or were found not guilty of any personal negligence, you could still lose a tremendous amount of money due to the high cost of legal fees. In 1989, for instance, the average cost of legal fees to defend a corporate director in a liability suit was $1.2 million. While the costs for a liability suit against your small business might not come up to those average costs, you would still be looking at five- or six-figure bills for legal and court costs if you were sued.

Q I went to a seminar on starting a business and heard someone mention being bonded. What is bonding and how does it protect me?

There are two basic types of bonding that businesses sometimes need to be concerned with: surety bonds and fidelity bonds. Surety bonds don't protect you. They protect the customer by guaranteeing something will be done in a certain way. Bid bonds and performance bonds that are often required on construction projects are an example. Essentially they guarantee that the work you contract to do will be completed and that suppliers will be paid. If you default on the contract, the bonding company becomes responsible for completing the job and paying suppliers and will come after you to make good on their losses. Other types of surety bonds are those required of pawnbrokers to protect owners of property from loss and bonds required of liquor stores to assure the state will be paid if the liquor store breaks any laws.

Fidelity bonding is honesty insurance. Fidelity bonds are purchased to protect businesses from financial loss due to fraud, theft, embezzlement, or other dishonesty by their employees. If there is a loss the bonding company pays the business and goes after the employee. Banks and other concerns where employees handle money or the equivalent often bond employees. There are also fidelity bonds to protect your clients from fraud, embezzlement, or other dishonest acts committed by contractors or contractors' employees. Your insurance broker can help you find the right kind of bonding for your needs.

Q **How do I get bonded?**

If a municipality or other governing agency requires you to be bonded in order to get a license to practice your business they should be able to suggest names of companies to contact. You can also get names of companies to contact by looking in the Yellow Pages under the heading "Bonds."

Q **Can I get bonded if my business is a start-up?**

Bonding works a little like credit. If you are a start-up company with little or no history of completed jobs you may have to build up gradually to the point where you can be bonded for major projects. For instance, at first $50,000 might be the largest bond you can get, and you might be able to get it only if you put up collateral. As you gain experience and build a history of successful completion of projects, the amounts of bonding you will qualify for will increase. If you need to be bonded to do work for a municipality or government agency, ask if they have programs to help you get the bonding you need. Your local SBA or SCORE office (see Appendix 1) or state or regional economic development agency may also provide help.

Q **I'm planning to hire someone to work for me part-time. Is there any kind of insurance I have to get?**

You will have to get workers' compensation insurance. You will also have to pay the employer's share of Social Security insurance and withhold the employee's share and taxes. (See chapters 23 and 24 for tax requirements.)

Q Who and what does workers' compensation cover?

Workers' compensation compensates employees for work-related injuries and illnesses. It also provides liability coverage to pay the employer's legal fees if the employee or employee's family file suit against the employer for an injury, illness, or death.

In most states employers are required to get workers' compensation for most types of employees. Domestic workers, farmworkers, and casual laborers are sometimes excluded from those requirements. Workers' compensation compensates employees for medical bills, a percentage of lost wages, funeral expenses, and survivor's benefits as appropriate due to work-related injuries or diseases. The amounts and percentages and length of time benefits are paid are regulated by state laws.

The specific illnesses or accidents a worker may be compensated for are also regulated at the state level; however, loss of limbs, back injuries, and other typical and easily identifiable work-related injuries are generally covered. In some states, less easily identifiable conditions such as stress-related or psychological illnesses are considered compensable conditions as well.

Q Do I have to get workers' compensation if I have just one employee?

Some states only require businesses to provide workers' compensation when there are three or more employees. Other states require it for all employees. If your state does not require you to carry workers' compensation if you only have one employee, you should consult an insurance broker and/or attorney to determine how best to protect yourself against possible work-related injury lawsuits.

Q What does workers' compensation cost?

The cost of workers' compensation depends on the industry, the classification of the individual workers, the size of your payroll, and something known as experience rating. The cost of premiums can be as little as $1 or less per hundred dollars of payroll or as high as $25 or more per hundred in high-risk industries.

Q Can I avoid getting workers' compensation by having employees work for me as independent contractors?

Many companies are attempting to cut costs by calling their employees independent contractors. By using independent contractors instead of having employees, employers also eliminate their share of Social Security and some other payroll taxes, the need to pay for health insurance and other benefits, plus a lot of book-keeping.

If the people who work for you are really employees, however, treating the employee as an independent contractor is risky at best. If the contractor is injured working for you, he and the courts may consider the relationship to be an employee/employer situation, and you would not only be liable for the costs of medical care and lost wages but also be assessed statutory damages (a penalty) for not having workers' compensation. Calling an employee an independent contractor is also risky from a tax standpoint. The IRS and state tax departments are cracking down on abuses. (For a list of guidelines the IRS uses to determine whether someone is an employee or independent contractor, see chapter 23.)

Q | **Is there any way I can keep workers' compensation costs down?**

The most important thing a small business owner can do to keep workers' compensation rates as low as possible is to make sure your business is classified property. "Most businessowners don't realize their workers may actually fall into several different rate categories," says Linda Jasper, president of Suffolk Sidewalks, Inc., a construction company in Miller Place, New York. "Most insurers will automatically lump your entire payroll into one classification: the highest one. But not all work your employees do will actually fall into that higher classification."

In the construction business, Jasper explains, the rate for a concrete worker who does foundations is higher than the rate for a concrete worker doing flat-work since there's more danger of injury with the foundation work. "If you are aware of these categories and keep good records showing what percentages of man-hours go into high-rate and low-rate jobs, you can save money by having some of your workers classified in low- or medium-rate categories instead of having them all lumped together into the highest rate categories."

If you pay more than $5,000 a year in workers' compensation, another way you may be able to cut costs is with experience rating. This is a system that set rates based on actual claims history of your company compared to others in the industry in the previous year. Dividend insurance plans might be another option. Dividends are paid on premiums but are not guaranteed. They are dependent on the insurance company's claims experience, with all the companies it insures. Your insurance agent will be able to advise you about the best policy for your needs.

Q My office is in my home. Won't my homeowner's insurance cover me if an employee trips in my home office and gets hurt?

No, homeowner's policies and home business endorsements usually don't cover injury or work-related diseases of employees of your business. Household workers (people who come in and clean your home, for instance) may possibly be covered by your policy, however.

Q I have an employee who drives his own car to do errands for me. Do I need special auto insurance for that or will his own insurance cover it?

You need to get insurance. Even if your employee were driving his car, if he was on a business errand for you and injured someone you could be sued. The kind of insurance that offers you protection is called employee nonownership and hired car liability, which protects the owner of the business for the actions of the employees while they are driving their personal autos. Depending where you live, it may cost as little as $75 a year.

Q How much will business auto insurance cost?

The cost will vary considerably according to the following factors:

- the number of vehicles insured by the business
- the type of use and cargo of the vehicles
- the size of the vehicles
- the business location (where the vehicles are garaged)
- the area (radius) of operations

Q Where can I get business automobile insurance?

The company from which you buy your personal vehicle insurance might also sell business vehicle insurance. It would be advisable to call several brokers and get information, or better yet, call several businessowners in your area and ask them which broker they use for insurance and how satisfied they are. You can find names of insurance brokers in the Yellow Pages of your phone book.

Q If I rent equipment and it is damaged while it is in my office, will my insurance cover it?

Probably not. You may be able to purchase a floater (special policy) to cover the potential risk, however.

Q I'm testing a new product for woodworkers. Do I need to get product liability insurance if I put clear instructions and warnings in the package I sell?

Yes. No matter how clear your warnings are or how the user abuses a product, you could be sued if someone suffers an injury as a result of your product.

Q Won't all my other insurance protect me?

No. Product liability is one type of insurance, like professional liability, that usually must be purchased separately.

Q It sounds like I could spend every cent I earn just buying insurance. How do I decide what kinds of insurance I really need and how much I should buy?

Keeping insurance costs under control is something that concerns businesses of all sizes. Key to the process is something known in the insurance industry as risk management. Coyle explains that risk management is a four-step process:

1. Identification of sources from which losses may arise.
2. Evaluation of the financial risk involved in each exposure based on expected frequency, severity, and impact.
3. Treatment of risk by elimination, reduction, control, or transfer to others (such as an insurance company).
4. Monitoring the results of your efforts.

Q Isn't risk management just for big businesses?

Even very small businesses can put risk management techniques into practice. Begin by making a realistic determination of all the ways you might possibly suffer financial losses. On your list should be all possible business-related losses. Include casualty and theft losses, embezzlement (if you have employees), injury to others from products or services you sell, personal injury to customers or employees due to a fall or some other accident while on your business premises, libel or slander (knocking the competition or talking about customers with bad credit ratings can get you sued), and even things such as the loss of income from your business if it should be interrupted by a fire or theft or some other insurable catastrophe.

Decide which are most likely to occur and which of those would be most devastating to your business or personal assets. Cover what you can with insurance, and at the same time try to reduce risks of the loss and the cost of any insurance coverage.

Q   **How can I reduce risks of something happening?**

There are literally hundreds of different ways to reduce risk. Among them:

- Don't accept work you aren't qualified to perform.
- Be meticulous about labeling, dating, and backing up all client work.
- Make backups or copies of important documents, records, and data, and consider storing them off premises. A large customer list, your receivables, work in progress, and other important documents might be difficult or impossible to recreate should a fire, computer system outage, theft, or other disaster hit your place of business.
- Remove or correct any obvious hazards in the workplace. For example, get rid of anything people are likely to trip on, repair broken banisters or railings, make sure stairways and walkways are kept free of snow or ice or other slippery substances.
- Learn how to lift boxes and heavy items without putting excessive strain on your back and teach employees to do the same.
- Set and enforce safety rules, such as not opening all the file drawers in a cabinet at a time.
- Make sure electrical circuits aren't overloaded.
- Protect computer equipment at minimum with surge protectors.
- Consider shutting down small home computer systems (unplugging them) during severe electrical storms. Even a good surge protector isn't likely to withstand a lightning strike on an electric line.

- Check references before hiring employees.
- Make sure employees who will be driving for you have in-force driver's licenses.
- Make sure your employees are properly classified in your workers' compensation policy.
- Deposit receipts nightly.
- Don't let any one employee have unsupervised control of the books, cash, or any aspect of your business.
- Have regular health checkups and encourage your employees to do the same.
- Live a healthy life-style.

Q **How will reducing risks cut costs?**

Reducing risks helps you avoid or reduce losses, which in turn keeps rates down on policies that are based on your claims history. Reducing your risks also will keep out-of-pocket expenses down for uninsured losses.

Q **Where can I get more information about business insurance?**

The Insurance Information Institute is an excellent source of information about business property and liability insurance. They have a consumer information hotline you can call if you have questions about any kind of insurance except health and life insurance. They also publish a book called *Insuring Your Business* by Sean Mooney that offers clear explanations of various types of insurance businesses may need. The book is $22.50 plus a $2.50 shipping and handling fee. The Insurance Information Institute is located at 100 Williams Street, New York, NY 10038. Their telephone number is (212) 669-4290.

Helpful Web Sites

http://www.iii.org
Insurance Information Institute web site.

http://www.insure.com
Consumer Insurance Guide web site. Reporting, information, and resources on all aspects of insurance. Excellent resource.

http://www.independentagent.com
Information for consumers and businesses on purchasing insurance. Includes a search function for finding insurance agents.

http://www.insure.com/home/compq.html
Information on computer insurance.

23.

Taxing Issues

Few things in life are quite as taxing as having to pay taxes. For starters, you know you are going to have to pay the IRS a painfully large chunk of your hard-earned income. Then, to make matters worse, you know you will have to give up a healthy chunk of your time to collect the receipts you need and read up on the latest changes in tax laws.

To add insult to injury, you are likely to stumble on the estimated preparation time in the instructions to Form 1040 and realize: (1) The estimated time figures couldn't possibly be accurate, and (2) the IRS used your tax dollars to pay someone to tell you how long it should take to prepare your tax return.

While nothing may dispel your aggravation with the system, this chapter and the next one will help you gain a better understanding of tax regulations governing self-employment and home offices. In them you will find dozens of answers to frequently asked self-employment and home office tax questions. The subjects covered run the gamut from the most basic "Do I have to report it" questions to what you should do if you inadvertently run afoul of the tax laws.

The information in this chapter applies only to questions arising from Schedule C or Schedule C-EZ self-employment income. Schedule C is the sole proprietor business return; Schedule C-EZ is a simplified Schedule C designed for use by businesses with business expenses of $2,500 or less. While every attempt has been made to insure the accuracy of the information, neither this chapter nor any book or source of general information can substitute for your own personal tax adviser. Tax laws change frequently and the interpretation of the laws, in some instance, can vary according to specifics of your individual situation.

INCOME AND TAXES—SORTING THEM OUT

Q **I sell handicrafts at flea markets and just make a little extra spending money. Do I have to report this income to the IRS?**

Yes. The income has to be reported on your tax return. You will have to pay income tax and possibly self-employment tax on your profits (net income). In addition, if your state has a sales tax, you probably should be collecting sales tax on the items you sell.

Q **Do I have to report *all* income I make on my own to the IRS?**

Yes. Whether you make money from full-time self-employment, from moonlighting, from a hobby, or from work as an independent contractor or freelancer, the IRS expects you to report the income and pay taxes on it.

Q **Suppose I don't get paid in cash. Do I still have to report the income?**

Yes. If you barter what you sell for other people's goods and services, or for credits toward goods and services, the IRS expects you to report the value of the trade. If you run a business, the income from bartering (value of goods and services received) is also subject to self-employment tax.

Q **My records show one of my clients reported less on the 1099 form they submitted to the government than they actually paid me. Can I use their figures in reporting my income on my tax return?**

No. You should report the actual income you received, and ask the company to file a corrected 1099.

Similarly, if a company reports too much income on a 1099, checks off the wrong box on the 1099 (marking your earnings as lotto winnings, for instance), or makes any other mistake, you should ask them to file a corrected information return.

Q I did work for a company based in another country. They paid me but didn't send a 1099 to the U.S. government. Do I have to report that income?

Yes.

Q How will the IRS know whether or not I report all my income?

There are any number of ways the IRS can and does find out about unreported income. Here are a few of them:

▸ 1099 information returns filed by companies are matched against your income tax returns by computer.
▸ Jealous neighbors or associates you have a falling out with could report you.
▸ One of your customers could be audited and trigger an audit of companies with which it does business.
▸ Your return could be kicked out at random for a compliance audit.
▸ Some other circumstance could cause the IRS to audit part of your return and, due to your answers or some discrepancies, cause the IRS to dig deeper, getting bank records and/or examining the way you live to determine if you are hiding income.
▸ Your return might have attracted notice because you made a large (over $10,000) bank deposit or cash purchase.

No matter what the mechanism, if the IRS discovers you have purposely underreported income (or misrepresented facts on your return) you could be charged with fraud.

Q Do I have to file a business return to report my spare-time income, or can I just include the income on Form 1040?

The answer depends on how regularly you make money at what you do and whether or not you carry out the income-producing activity in a businesslike way. If you regularly seek customers and regularly make money, you will need to report the income as business income on Schedule C or Schedule C-EZ. You will also have to pay self-employment tax if you make more than $400 profit. (See the questions on self-employment tax in this chapter.)

If you seldom make money from the activity and it is something like scuba diving or tole painting that could be considered a hobby, you may not have to file a business return.

You will need to report the income, though, and may benefit from reporting the income on Schedule C or Schedule C-EZ (see below).

Q **I wrote and sold three short novels this year. All of my self-employment income came from advances against royalties on those books. Since the payments were royalty, can I report the royalty payments as supplemental income (Schedule E) and avoid the self-employment tax?**

No. Writers, photographers, artists, and others who create books, dramatic works, artworks, music scores, and other creative works have to report royalties on Schedule C as business income.

Q **Are there any benefits from reporting part-time self-employment income as business income.**

Yes. Here are several:

- Almost all ordinary and necessary business expenses are fully deductible on Schedule C. If you use Schedule C-EZ you can deduct up to $2,500 in business expenses. The same expenses, if reported as a miscellaneous deduction on Form 1040, Schedule A, are subjected to the 2 percent floor on miscellaneous expenses, which means they are only deductible to the extent that they exceed 2 percent of adjusted gross income (AGI).
- If you are running a business and your expenses exceed your income, you can use the loss to offset other income. If you don't file a business return, deductions for expenses for hobbies or other income-producing activities will be limited to the amount of income from the activity.
- If you report income on Schedule C and have a room that qualifies as a home office, you may be able to take a substantial home office deduction. The IRS does not allow a home office deduction if what you do is termed a hobby.

▸ Interest on personal loans is no longer deductible. However, interest on business loans *is* deductible. Thus, if you borrow money to buy a computer for your home business you can deduct the interest on the loan on Schedule C prorated to your business use of the computer. You could not deduct the interest on a personal loan for a computer to use in conjunction with your hobby. If that same computer were used more than 50 percent for business, you could also expense or depreciate the cost. (See "Can I deduct the cost of my home computer and car phone?" on page 392 in the next chapter.)

Q Who should use Schedule C-EZ?

Schedule C-EZ is aimed at those who have few business deductions and a limited amount of income from a small business. To use this schedule to calculate your taxes you may have no more than $2,500 in business expenses for the year. In addition, you cannot use the form if you take the home office deduction, show a loss for the year, have more than one business that you run as a sole proprietor, have employees, have to File Form 4562 (for depreciation and amortization expenses), or have unallowed passive activity losses from the business from a previous year. Having inventory at any time during the year also disqualifies you from using Schedule C-EZ.

Q Can I have a full-time job working for someone else and file a business return, too?

Yes. If your income-producing activity qualifies as a business, you can file a Schedule C return even if you have a part-time or full-time job working as an employee in another business.

Q Do I have to have a separate business checkbook to file a business return?

The IRS doesn't require you to have a separate business checking or savings account to file either a Schedule C or a Schedule C-EZ. However, having a separate business account will simplify record keeping for you and help prove your business intent to the IRS should you ever need to.

Q **Do I have to be registered as a business or have a business name to file a business tax return?**

For IRS purposes, you do not have to have a business name or be registered as a business with any government authorities. Some states and some municipalities do require anyone who operates a business to get a business certificate or license. Such laws, where they exist, have nothing to do with federal income tax laws, however.

Q **Don't I need an employer identification number to file a Schedule C?**

You don't need an employer identification number (EIN) unless you hire employees or start certain types of pension plans.

Q **How many hours a week do I have to work for myself for the IRS to consider what I do a business and not a hobby?**

The IRS doesn't set any minimum number of hours. Instead, it wants to know if you have a profit motive for pursuing the activity and if you are carrying out the activity in a businesslike way.

Q **How do I show a profit motive?**

The easiest way is by making a profit. If you make a profit pursuing the activity in 3 of the last 5 years including the current one, the IRS will assume the activity is a business. If the activity you are involved in is raising race horses, the time frame for making a profit is extended to 2 of 7 years.

Q **What happens if I don't make a profit within the specified time? Will the IRS automatically declare my business a hobby?**

Not necessarily. The 3-out-of-5-year guideline (known as the hobby-loss rule) is a major factor, but not the only one the IRS will look at in determining if something is a business or a hobby. Other things they will consider are:

▸ Do you carry out the activity in a businesslike manner? (Keep good records. If you don't keep copies of receipts, correspondence, etc., you aren't going to look very businesslike.)

▶ Does the time and effort you put into the activity indicate you intend to make the activity a profitable business?

▶ Do you have the expertise necessary to carry on the activity as a successful business?

▶ Do you depend on income from the activity for your livelihood?

▶ Are losses due to circumstances beyond your control, or are they normal for the start-up of your kind of business?

▶ Have you changed your methods of operation to attempt to improve the profitability of that activity?

▶ Have you previously been successful making a profit in a similar business?

▶ Will you be able to make a profit in the future from appreciation of assets?

▶ Do you materially participate (take an active part) in the business?

Q **Is any activity that makes a profit considered a business?**

No. Occasional profit-making transactions (say, the sale of your childhood stamp collection) would not be considered a business. Additionally, the IRS does not consider you to be in business if what you do is manage your own stock or investment portfolio.

Q **What about independent contractors? I do a lot of work as an independent contractor for one company. Could the IRS call me an employee and deny my business deductions?**

The independent contractor issue can be complicated. Many companies try to call employees independent contractors to avoid the hidden costs of having employees. Those hidden costs can easily amount to one-third or more of the actual salary paid to the worker. They include such things as the unemployment taxes, employer's share of FICA, and workers' compensation, as well as things like medical insurance, sick pay, vacation and holiday pay, pension plans, and so on.

To prevent this kind of abuse, the IRS has tried to establish criteria to distinguish employees from independent businesspeople. Generally speaking, these criteria say that if you are a writer, attorney, speaker, consultant, or other professional or tradeperson who operates independently and offers services to the public (in other words, to multiple clients), you are not an employee. However, the IRS also says you will be considered an employee if the client company has the right to control and direct the means and methods of accomplishing the work you perform for them.

To clarify these two broad rules, the IRS has developed a list of 20 factors it considers on a case-by-case basis to determine whether an individual is an employee or independent contractor. The importance of each factor—according to the IRS—varies with the occupation and the individual circumstances under which the services are rendered. Here are the factors and how the IRS views each:

1. *Instructions:* An employee is told when, where, and how to do the work; an independent contractor performs work without being told when, where, or how to do the job.
2. *Training:* Training is for employees; independent contractors would use their own methods, receiving no training from the client.
3. *Integration:* If an individual's services or job is integrated into the daily business operations (the business can't operate well without the service), the person performing the service is considered an employee.
4. *Performance:* An employee is expected to personally perform the job hired for; an independent contractor may assign others to do the work.
5. *Assistants and cost of goods:* An employee would not bear the cost of hiring and training assistants or employees and does not pay for cost of goods out of his/her own pocket. An independent contractor would be responsible for hiring, training, supervising, and paying assistants and for paying the costs of materials as part of the job contract.
6. *Work relationship:* An employee performs work frequently at recurring intervals as part of a continuing relationship with a company; independent contractors don't maintain similar continuing relationships.
7. *Schedule:* The employee must keep hours set by the employer; the contractor chooses his/her own hours.
8. *Hours worked:* An employee is likely to work full-time for only one company; a contractor is available to work for multiple companies.
9. *Location of work:* An employee works on the employer's premises or on a route specified by the employer; the contractor is not restricted to working on the client's premises.
10. *Sequence of work:* The employee follows company instructions and routines; the independent contractor does work in whatever sequence he/she deems best.

11. *Reports:* The employee must account to the employer for daily actions and activities; the contractor does not account to the client for his/her daily activities.

12. *Method of payment:* Employees are usually paid by the hour, week, month, or year; contractors are usually paid by the job or on straight commission.

13. *Expenses:* Employees have business and travel expenses paid for them by employers; independent contractors pay their own business and travel expenses.

14. *Tools:* The employee is often (but not always) furnished with significant tools or equipment to do a job; the contractor supplies his/her own tools or equipment.

15. *Investment:* Employees have no significant investment in what they do; independent contractors put significant investment in equipment or facilities used to perform services.

16. *Profit or loss:* The employee gets paid and is not subject to losses. Independent contractors do not get salaries; they make a profit or suffer losses.

17. *Number of business customers:* The employee works with one business or one primary business at one time; contractors may perform services for multiple companies at once.

18. *Availability:* An employee is not available to others for work; a contractor is available to work for multiple companies.

19. *Ability to be fired:* An employee can be fired; a contractor has to be paid if he/she produces the results specified in the contract.

20. *Right to quit:* An employee can quit without incurring liability; a contractor is legally obligated to meet contract terms or risks financial loss.

In summary, if you look like you are an employee (work a regular schedule in the client's office and never work for anyone else), chances are the IRS would call you an employee if you or the company was ever audited.

Q **What about programmers and others who take on long-term contracts on government or other projects requiring work be done on-site? Does the IRS consider them employees or contractors?**

Many such occupations fall into a category the IRS calls "technical service specialist," which is defined as an individual who is an engineer, designer, draftsman, computer programmer, systems analyst, or in a similar line of work. These technical service specialists are considered employees if they are working under contracts arranged by a third party such as a job shop or temporary employment agency.

The IRS says, however, that the designation technical service specialist doesn't automatically doom someone to be an employee. Someone considered a technical service specialist can be an independent contractor if he or she contracts directly with the client firm and doesn't appear to be an employee based on the criteria described above.

Q **What happens if the IRS says I'm an employee?**

A company that wrongly classifies you as an independent contractor would have to pay unemployment taxes on your earnings and might also be liable for a penalty of 100 percent of the tax they didn't withhold. You would lose any home office deductions and deductions for payments to pension plans. Business deductions would have to be reported on Schedule A rather than Schedule C and would thus be subject to the 2 percent limitation on miscellaneous deductions.

Q **What taxes do I have to pay when I work for myself?**

You have to pay federal income tax and, if your profits from self-employment amount to more than $400 for the year, self-employment tax. You may be liable for state and local income taxes as well.

Q **What is self-employment tax?**

Self-employment tax is a combination of Social Security and Medicare taxes. When you are an employee in someone else's company, Social Security and Medicare contributions are withheld from each paycheck you receive. These withholdings are called FICA (Federal Insurance Contributions Act) and are matched by equal amounts your employer must contribute on your behalf.

When you are self-employed, you have to pay both the employee's share *and* the employer's share of these taxes. To compensate somewhat for this double whammy, you get a slight break on Schedule C (in the form of an adjustment to self-employed income), and you can subtract an amount equal to one-half of your self-employment tax from your income on line 27, Form 1040 (adjustments to income).

Like FICA withholdings, self-employment tax is calculated on Schedule SE separately from and in addition to any income tax you owe.

Q How much is the self-employment tax?

The self-employment tax rate is a percentage of income based on two separate rates—one for Social Security and one for Medicare. For the 1999 tax year, the Social Security rate was 12.4 percent on the first $72,600 of net self-employment income. The Medicare tax rate was 2.9 percent of all net self-employment income. Thus the total self-employment tax rate works out to be 15.3 percent of the first $72,600 of net self-employment income (12.4 percent + 2.9 percent) plus 2.9 percent of all additional net self-employment income.

The rules and income ranges change periodically, so be sure to check the actual rates each year you have self-employment income.

Q I have a full-time job and work for myself on the weekends. My full-time employer withholds FICA from my salary. Do I have to pay self-employment tax, too?

Yes. Here's how it works. If the wages from your full-time job are under $72,600 you will have to pay self-employment tax on the difference between the wages from your job and $72,600. You have to pay the 2.9 percent Medicare portion of the tax on all of your self-employment income.

For instance, suppose you earn $45,000 at your full-time job, and have additional net self-employment earnings of $30,000. The maximum income for the 15.3 percent self-employment tax rate is $72,600. The $45,000 in wages (which have had FICA withheld) is applied toward that maximum first. You pay the 12.4 percent rate Social Security portion of the tax on combined income up to the $72,600 Social Security income maximum; you pay the 2.9 percent Medicare rate on all of your net self-employment income. Thus:

> $72,600 (maximum subject to self-employment tax)
> − 45,000 (wages)
> ———————
> $27,600 (amount of net self-employment earnings
>   subject to the 12.4 percent Social Security
>   portion of the tax)

The total self-employment tax you would owe on the $30,000 you made on your own would be:

$27,600 \times 12.4\%$ (Social Security portion) = \$3,422.40
PLUS
\$30,000 (total net self-employment earnings) $\times 2.9\%$ (Medicare rate) = \$870
Total self-employment tax due: \$3,422.40 + \$870 = \$4,292.40

Q **Do I have to pay self-employment tax if I'm retired?**

The same rules apply whether you are retired or not. Thus, if you make more than \$400 in profit from self-employment you are liable for self-employment taxes even if you are already collecting Social Security.

Q **Do I just put aside the money and pay the income tax and self-employment tax when I file my income tax return each year?**

The answer depends on your personal tax situation. If you expect to owe more than \$1,000 over and above any withholdings or tax credits for the year, you will probably have to pay estimated tax payments. These tax payments are usually paid in four equal installments on April 15, June 15, September 15, and January 15.

As a general rule, you will have to pay quarterly estimated taxes if you expect to owe more than \$1,000 in income and self-employment tax *and:*

 ▶ your withholding and credits for the year will be less than 100 percent of your previous year's tax liability

or

 ▶ your withholding and credits will be less than 90 percent of the tax liability for the current tax year

Q **My income is never spread out evenly during the year. Some quarters I make a lot of money and some I make almost nothing. Do I have to pay the estimated tax in four *equal* payments?**

No. You will need to annualize your income and then calculate what percentage of the total you made in the present quarter. Then calculate your estimated taxes based on that percentage. If you plan to use this method you will need IRS Publication 505 and Form 2210.

Q All my income is from self-employment, and it looks like it will be a lot less this year than it was last year. Will I have to pay a penalty if I pay less than one-fourth of last year's taxes for each quarterly payment?

As long as you have paid in 90 percent of the tax due for each quarter you shouldn't have to pay a penalty.

Q How do I go about sending in the payments?

Use IRS Form 1040-ES. The form includes a worksheet for your records and vouchers you fill in and submit with each payment so the payments are credited to you.

Q What happens if I miss an estimated tax payment or don't pay in enough during the year?

You pay a penalty for amounts you owe on each separate installment. The IRS method for calculating the penalty is complicated. If you miss an installment, the IRS suggests you divide what you owe among remaining payments (so you don't underpay for the remainder of the year) and then use Form 2210 at the time you submit your taxes to annualize your income and calculate any penalty you may owe. Alternately, the IRS will calculate the penalty for you.

Q Do I have to pay estimated taxes to the state, too?

If your state has an income tax, chances are you will need to pay a separate estimated tax to the state. Your local IRS office may have state tax information and forms. If they don't, call or write your state tax department for information. The addresses and phone numbers are listed in Appendix 4.

24.

What Can I Deduct?

One of the benefits of being self-employed is you can take a variety of deductions you might not otherwise qualify for. If you keep good records and are aware of what you may and may not deduct as a business owner, owning your own business can help you lower your taxes substantially. Here are a number of questions and answers to get you started considering ways your business can cut your personal taxes.

Q **What expenses for starting my business are deductible?**

Start-up expenses (expenses you incur before you are ready to take work from customers) are considered capital expenses and have to be either included in basis (the starting value of your business and its assets) or amortized (spread out over several years). To be amortizable, the expense has to be something that would be deductible if you were already in business and paid before the business started operation.

Such start-up costs include costs of studying a prospective business and the costs for actually launching it such as initial advertising expense, employee training, equipment, etc.

Q **From a tax standpoint, when does my business actually begin? Is it with the first customer?**

You can be in business if you are ready to accept customers. The actual event that triggers you being in business (as opposed to starting a business) will vary by the type of business and your own personal way of operating. Something as simple as registering a business name, having business cards made up, or even accepting money for something you have done for free up to now (teaching friends to use computers, for instance) can be the grand opening of a homebased business.

Thus, from a tax standpoint, you might want to consider putting off as many business purchases as you can until after you are actually in business. But remember: while you don't have to have acquired any customers or made a profit to be in business, if you don't make a profit in 3 out of 5 years you could trigger the hobby-loss rule as discussed in the previous chapter.

Q **Once I'm in business, what expenses can I deduct?**

Any product or service purchased for use by or in your business is deductible if it is ordinary and reasonable for the type of business you run. Schedule C filers will generally find their deductions fall into these broad categories:

- deductible business expenses
- depreciable business property
- the home office deduction
- cost of goods sold (if you are a manufacturer or sell products)

Q **What kinds of expenses are deductible business expenses?**

The specific expenses that will be deductible for your business depend on what you do and what would be ordinary and necessary for your business. Some typical examples of expenses follow.

Business Expenses

Deductible the Year in Which the Expense Is Incurred

advertising expenses	association dues
advertising giveaways	auto mileage or car expense*
airplane and cab costs on business trips	bad debts

*Items discussed in more depth elsewhere in this chapter.

bank fees
beeper service
blank computer floppy disks
books related to your business
business cards (if you are in business already)
business gifts*
business insurance fees
calendar
cellular phone service
college courses to improve business skills*
commissions
consultant fees
copy paper
copyright registration fee
employee salaries*
file folders
hotel/motel fees*
industry directories
ink cartridges
interest on business loans
interest on business credit cards
Internet access and online service fees,
    prorated to business use
licenses
meals
notepads
paper daybook/scheduler
pencils
pens
postage
professional fees (attorney, CPA, etc.)
professional journals and trade magazines*
publicity expense
repairs of business property or equipment
ribbons for typewriters or printers
seminars*
stationery
telephone call expenses*
tolls and parking fees
toner for copier, fax, printer
trade show and conference fees

trade show booth fees
training tapes (audio and video)
travel*
voice mail or answering service
wages paid to employees

Home Office*
Rent, real estate taxes, mortgage interest, and utilities are fully deductible for nonhome-based businesses; home businesses may allocate part of these expenses to business.

Assets to Depreciate or Expense*
answering machine
beeper
bookshelves
car*
cellular telephone
computer*
computer memory
desk
facsimile machine
fax boards
filing cabinets
hard drive
improvements to business property
in/out baskets
label printer
modem
office chairs
office drapes, blinds, decorative pictures
other computer boards
telephone handsets
tools
trucks
workbench

Amortizable Costs
computer software
customer list

printers	legal fees prior to opening
scanner	other start-up costs
shrink-wrap machine	patent purchase
storage cabinet	research to start a business
storage racks	

Q **Can I deduct the sales tax on supplies I bought for my business or only the actual price of the supplies?**

You can deduct the sales tax you paid on the price of supplies used in the course of business. You can't deduct sales tax or freight on capital assets used in your business, however. The sales tax on those have to be capitalized in the cost of the asset.

Q **I translated some documents for a small company, but the company never paid me and is now out of business. Can I deduct the money the company owed me as a bad debt?**

Not if you are a cash basis taxpayer as most homebased and very small businesses are. A bad debt only qualifies as a deductible expense if there is a true creditor/borrower relationship, if there has been an actual loss of money (you lent the customer money, for instance), or if you are an accrual basis taxpayer and have already reported the debt as income.

Q **I run my business from my home and only have one phone line. Can I deduct anything for all the business phone calls I make?**

If you have only one telephone line coming into the house or apartment, you cannot deduct any part of the line charge (basic service charges) for having the phone in the house. You can deduct the cost of any long-distance or other calls you can separate out from your bill and verify as business calls. Voice messaging, call waiting, or other special services would be deductible if you can prove the business purpose.

If you have a completely separate telephone line coming into the house and use it exclusively for business, *all costs* including the line fee and basic monthly charges could be deducted. The second line is also advisable to make sure business calls are always answered professionally. Despite the growth of homebased businesses, customers don't appreciate hearing a five-year-old pick up the phone and say, "Daddy's in the pool" or hearing spurts of rock music every time your teenage daughter picks up the extension to see if you are still on the telephone.

Q **Can I deduct the cost of my home computer and car phone?**

Computers, computer peripheral equipment, car phones, and other property that might be used for entertainment value as well as for business are called listed property and must comply with special rules. If you can provide the business purpose, you can deduct the business portion of their cost using one of two methods: the first-year expense method (Section 179 deduction) and depreciation. If your business is classified as a hobby by the IRS (see pages 380–81 in chapter 23), the Section 179 expense may not be allowable in full due to the limitations of the hobby-loss rule.

Q **What is the Section 179 expense deduction?**

The Section 179 expense deduction lets you write off certain equipment costs in one year instead of spreading them out (depreciating them) over time. To take the deduction you must:

  ▸ use the equipment more than 50 percent of the time in your business and be able to prove it
  ▸ prorate the cost to your business usage (if you use the equipment 60 percent of the time for business, you can expense 60 percent of the cost)
  ▸ recapture (pay back) a portion of the deduction if you dispose of the property or stop using it for business before the end of its useful life (the IRS considers computers, copiers, etc., to have a useful life of 5 years)

Additionally, these limits apply:

  ▸ For the year 2000, the total amount of equipment you may expense in one year is limited to a maximum of $20,000, or your net income, whichever is lower.
  ▸ The $20,000 limit is per taxpayer, not per business. Thus, if you have more than one business the maximum you can expense is $20,000.
  ▸ Married individuals filing separate returns are treated as one taxpayer (together their expense deduction may not total more than $20,000).

Members of partnerships or S corporations must follow special rules and should consult their accountants or a good tax guide before taking the 179 expense deduction.

▸ Automobiles may be expensed only up to certain IRS stated maximums. In 1999, the maximum expense deduction you could take for an automobile placed into service for your business was $3,060.

▸ If you put more than $200,000 of equipment into service in the year, the amount you may expense is reduced by one dollar for each dollar over $200,000. Thus, no expense deduction may be taken if you put $220,000 of equipment into use.

NOTE The total amount you can deduct under the Section 179 rules is scheduled to increase to $24,000 for tax years 2001–2002 and to $25,000 after 2002.

Q What do I have to do to prove the business use of a computer, car phone, or similar equipment?

To prove the business use of equipment, you must keep a log of usage if you use the equipment partially for business and partially for personal use. For computers and other office equipment you would need a log showing when each thing was used, the amount of time it was used, and the purpose of the business use. For automobiles you would need to keep track of the date of each use, the business purpose, the mileage for each trip and the total car mileage for the year. (See Table 24.1.) If you have a computer and modem and subscribe to any of the online services, you'll find templates and/or programs for logging expenses in on-line electronic libraries. Some of the files you find will be free for the price of the download; others will be try-before-you-buy shareware.

Q Can I deduct any equipment expenses if I don't use the equipment more than 50 percent of the time for business?

You could depreciate the business portion using the IRS tables for straight-line depreciation.

Table 24.1: Mileage Expense Log

| Date | Destination/Purpose | Mileage | | | Tolls/Parking |
		Leave	Return	Total	

Q **Can I use the Section 179 deduction to offset income from my daytime job if my business shows a loss?**

Under the rules that were in effect at the time this book was written, you can use the 179 expense deduction to offset other earned income such as wages from employment, earnings from rentals, royalty income, and farm income.

Q **What's the difference between a business asset and a business expense?**

A business asset is something you buy or acquire or develop that has or is expected to have monetary value and will use in your business for more than one year. Examples of assets are land, equipment, patents, buildings, and franchise rights. For tax purposes, a business expense is money a business pays out for products or services that will be used within the current year.

Q **Are they treated differently for tax purposes?**

Yes. The cost of business expenses is immediately deductible from income. The cost of an asset has to be spread out and deducted over a period of years or be added to the value of the asset and not deducted at all.

Q **How are amortization and depreciation different?**

Amortization means spreading out the cost of an intangible asset, such as a patent or goodwill; depreciation refers to spreading out the cost of tangible business property (things you can see or touch), such as machinery, buildings, etc. Generally, expenses that have to be amortized have to be spread out over a longer time period than expenses you can depreciate.

Q **How do I know whether to consider a purchase a deductible expense or to depreciate it?**

Generally, equipment or anything else you buy that has a useful life of more than a year has to be depreciated. Cost of things like bank fees, legal fees, advertising costs, office supplies and postage, and other costs that are incurred repeatedly would be expenses that are deductible in the year they were incurred for cash-basis taxpayers.

Q **How do you know what the useful life is of something?**

The IRS publishes tables showing the allowable useful life of various classifications of business assets. You'll find these lists in IRS Publication 534, *Depreciation*.

Q **Is it a good idea to expense the car I just bought?**

For most home businesses, it probably isn't a good idea to expense a car. (For additional help read the information on deducting car expenses in this chapter.)

Q **What automobile expenses can I deduct?**

You can take a depreciation deduction for the use of your car in business. This may be done in one of three ways:

▸ Calculate the business mileage driven and take a deduction based on this number. For 2000, the business mileage rate was 32.5 cents a mile. Thus, for every 1,000 business miles you drive you would get a $325 deduction using this method.
▸ Calculate the business mileage as a percentage of the personal mileage and prorate the value of the automobile at the time it was placed in

service to the business usage. Then use the MACRS 5-year property rules to depreciate the car. (If you bought a new car for $20,000 and used it 50 percent of the time for business, you would depreciate $10,000 of the purchase price. The other $10,000 would be a personal expense and is not depreciable.)

▸ Use the Section 179 deduction to expense the business portion of the car in the first year of use. The amount you may expense was a maximum of $3,060 in 1999. Thus, for many taxpayers, expensing the car is not a wise decision.

Q Can I deduct the cost of business travel?

Yes. If you are making a trip primarily for business you can deduct the costs of traveling to do business or to attend trade shows, conventions, and conferences that are related to your business. You can deduct the full cost of your airfare or train fare; cab fare while away; room charges; incidentals (laundry, dry cleaning); tips; baggage fees, including insurance; and telephone, telegraph, and fax calls. Additionally, you can deduct 50 percent of the cost of your meals while you are traveling and 50 percent of business entertainment costs if you are meeting clients and taking them to the theater or a ball game. If you drive your own car rather than take an airplane or train, you can deduct your auto mileage at the business mileage rate allowable in the year you take the trip.

Q Can I deduct the cost of a business trip to another country?

Rules get stricter for out-of-the country travel for self-employed people and major shareholders of small corporations. If you are outside of the United States for a week or less (counting the day you return, but not counting the day you leave on the trip), your travel expense will be fully deductible even if you spent some time on nonbusiness activities. If you are outside of the United States for more than a week and spend less than 25 percent of your time on nonbusiness activities, your travel expenses will be fully deductible, too. However if you are out of the United States for more than a week and spend more than 25 percent of your time on nonbusiness activities, you will have to allocate the travel costs based on the percentage of time spent on business. The rules for allocating the expenses can be found in IRS Publication 463, *Travel, Entertainment and Gift Expenses*.

Q **What about conventions held in other countries?**

If the convention is held within North America, the general business tests for foreign travel apply. If the convention is held outside of North America, the convention must be directly related to your trade or business and you have to show a reasonable explanation why the convention was outside North America.

Q **Is travel or conventions on cruise ships deductible?**

If you use a cruise ship to reach your business destination, the deduction for travel is limited to twice the allowable per diem federal travel rate. If meals and entertainment are paid for separately, these have to be calculated first at 80 percent of cost. The cost of the journey other than meals is then added on to the meals up to the maximum allowable amount for the trip.

If you are attending a convention on a cruise ship, numerous rules apply involving the ship's ports of call, time spent on business activities, and so on. You will need to document and submit records for hours spent at onboard business meetings, schedules of activities, etc. If you meet all the rules, then you are allowed up to a $2,000 deduction per year for a convention on a cruise ship.

WARNING If you plan foreign business travel or conventions overseas or on a cruise ship, be sure you understand all the rules governing deductibility of your trip before you make the arrangements. If you don't, or if you don't save all the necessary documentation, your deductions could be denied.

Q **I took the vice president of an out-of-town company I do business with on a tourist boat trip around Manhattan. Can I deduct both our fares?**

You can deduct 50 percent of your expenses if the entertainment was ordinary and necessary for your business *and* if the entertainment was directly related or associated with business *and* if the expense isn't considered lavish or extravagant. Essentially, if you discussed business with the visiting VP before, during, or after the trip, the expense would probably be allowable.

Q Could I deduct expenses for taking the VP's spouse and mine along on the excursion?

If the two of them were traveling together and it was impractical for you to entertain the client without the spouse, and your spouse goes along because the customer's spouse is there, the cost of tickets for both spouses would be considered ordinary and necessary and be deductible as entertainment expenses.

Q If I travel into the next state on business, can I deduct the cost of my lunch?

Not if you return home the same day. There's no such thing as a tax-free (or 50 percent tax-free) lunch unless you are away from your "tax home" overnight or long enough to require sleep.

Q What is my "tax home"?

Your tax home is your place of business. To be away from your tax home, you have to be away from the area or city surrounding your tax home. If you regularly work in two or more widely separate areas, your tax home is the area you select as your principle place of residence.

Q Suppose I want to combine a vacation with a business trip. Can I still deduct my trip?

If the primary purpose of the trip is business and the trip is within the United States, you can deduct all your costs to and from the location plus the hotel and other business-related costs described above for the business part of the trip. Money you spend on transportation, meals, or entertainment during the vacation part of the trip are not deductible. If, however, the primary purpose of the trip is vacation or personal, no part of your transportation costs from your tax home to your destination are deductible. The transportation costs after you arrive that relate to the business activity would be deductible.

For example, say you travel to Disneyland for a vacation for a week. While there, you drive to the next county to visit a client and, because of the distance, return to your hotel the next day. You could deduct the costs of reaching the client and the overnight hotel fee plus 50 percent of food costs as business expenses, but the rest of your expenses for the week plus your airfare to Disneyland would be nondeductible personal expenses.

However, if you were attending a week-long business convention at Disneyland and spent a day visiting relatives before returning home, you could deduct your entire plane fare plus the hotel cost and meals (at 50 percent) and other incidentals while at the hotel. The costs of traveling to your relative's town and expenses you incurred that day would not be deductible.

Q Can I deduct the cost of college courses I take?

You can deduct the costs of educational courses you take if you can prove they maintain or improve the skills you need to run your present business; however, you cannot deduct the cost of any education that would qualify you for a new trade or profession even if it also improves the skills you need for your current line of work. For instance, a psychiatrist was allowed to deduct costs of studying to become a psychoanalyst since that was regarded as upgrading her skills. A computer repair person with no college degree who returned to college to become a computer programmer would be considered to be taking classes to qualify for a new occupation and the deduction would be disallowed.

Q What about seminars? Are they deductible?

If there's a sound business reason for attending a seminar or other short-term course, you can deduct the costs. If you have to travel to get to the seminar and the majority of your trip is spent attending the seminar, you can also deduct your travel costs as a business expense. If you spend more time on personal activities than attending the seminar (say, take a four-week vacation after you attend a one-week seminar on the opposite side of the country from your business), your travel would be disallowed but the seminar cost allowed.

Q Can I deduct subscriptions to trade and business magazines on Schedule C?

Yes, if they are necessary for your business, they are fully deductible on Schedule C. List them under the miscellaneous deductions below travel and entertainment.

Q Can I deduct the cost of using the Internet?

You can deduct the business use of the Internet. If you use the services partly for business and partly for pleasure, you can only deduct the time spent online for business. You should keep a log recording the amount of business time spent online and the charges.

Q · What is the home office deduction?

The home office deduction is a deduction you can take for the costs of operating the business portion of the home. If your office space qualifies and if you have a net profit from your business, the home office deduction can lead to a significant tax savings. It is separate from and in addition to deductions for everyday business expenses such as pens, paper, legal fees, etc., and must be deducted from income after all other business expenses. It allows you a deduction for a portion of your mortgage interest, real estate taxes, gas, electric, water, garbage disposal, and home repairs. And it allows you to depreciate (take a deduction spread out over a period of years) the business portion of your home. You cannot use the home office deduction to show a business loss, however.

Q · What are the qualifications for the home office deduction?

To qualify, your home office:

- must be used exclusively and regularly for business, and
- must be an ordinary and necessary expense for the business
- your business may *not* be a hobby or passive activity such as managing investments

If you are an employee of a company rather than self-employed, you may be able to take a home office deduction if the use of your home is for the convenience of the employer and you are not renting your home office to your employer.

Q · Are there any exceptions to the exclusive use rule?

Yes. The area you use for your home office does not have to be used exclusively for the business if:

- your home business is a day-care center or
- you use part of your home to store inventory you sell in your business

If you store inventory, however, the space you use must meet all five of these criteria:

> - your business is selling products wholesale or retail
> - the inventory is kept for use in your business
> - your home is the only fixed location of your business
> - you use the storage space regularly
> - the space you use is separately identifiable and suitable for storage

For instance, suppose you sell novelty items at an indoor flea market. You store your inventory on shelves in your basement and use it to stock your booth as needed. You also have a Ping-Pong table in the basement that the kids use occasionally. The space used to store the inventory would be deductible even though the room is not exclusively used for your business pursuits.

Q **I use part of my den to run a word processing business from my home. The family uses the other part as a family room. Can I take a home office deduction for the part of the room I use?**

The answer is probably not, but it would depend on circumstances. If you work at a little desk squeezed in between the TV and the sofa, your office would not pass the exclusive test and would be disallowed. If the area you use for your business could be easily separated from the rest of the room by a panel or wall or other divider and your part of the room is furnished with office equipment, your deduction might be upheld if you were audited, but there is no guarantee.

Q **What about other businesses for which paperwork is done in a home office, but services are performed (and income actually made) in other locations?**

Starting with tax year 1999, this type of home office is deductible provided it is used regularly and exclusively for business.

Q **How do you determine the amount of the home office deduction?**

The amount you can take as a home office deduction will depend on:

- the percentage of your home used for business
- the direct costs of operating your home office
- the indirect costs of operating the office
- your income after business expenses have been subtracted on Schedule C

You calculate the deduction on Form 8829. Start by calculating the percentage of your home used for business. To do that you divide the square footage of your home office by the total square footage of your home. The directions for Form 8829 say you can use any other "reasonable method" of calculating the percentage of your home used for business. However, when you fill out Form 8829, you are asked to record the total area of your home and the area occupied by your office.

For example: If you use a 10-by-15-foot room for your home office (150 square feet), and the total square footage of your home is 1,500 square feet, the percentage of space used for business would be 10 percent.

Then, you complete a series of calculations step by step on Form 8829 that lead you through the process of deducting allowable expenses in the order they are allowed. First comes mortgage interest, real estate taxes, casualty losses, and any carryover from previous years; then, if you still show a profit, you can deduct utilities, maintenance, and repairs; finally, if you still show a profit, you can deduct an amount for depreciation on your home office.

Q **What is the difference between indirect and direct costs?**

Indirect costs are any costs you split between your home and home office, such as the 10 percent of your first mortgage interest if your office uses 10 percent of your home space, for instance, or 10 percent of your real estate taxes.

Direct costs are those related only to the business portion of your home. For instance, if you built an addition onto your home to accommodate your office and used it for no other purpose, the interest on a second mortgage you took out to pay for the addition and the extra real estate taxes that would be assessed on the addition would both be direct costs.

Q **Do I include my office phone bill in utilities or are they a Schedule C expense?**

Phone bills go on Schedule C. Remember, you can't deduct any portion of the basic line charge for the first phone line coming into your home (your home phone). (For additional information, see the question on telephone deductibility on page 391.)

Q **What utility expenses are deductible?**

Electricity, heating, air-conditioning, water, and garbage removal, if separate from your real estate taxes.

Q **Can I deduct the cost of the lawn service and the ornamental trees we planted?**

Landscaping costs are not allowed as home office deductions unless your office is located in a separate building on your property. Then you may deduct whatever landscaping costs apply to the separate building.

Q **Our roof was leaking and we had a new roof put on the house. Can I deduct a portion of that cost?**

No. A new roof is considered a permanent improvement because it adds to the useful life of the property. Thus, the cost has to be capitalized and cannot be deducted. The business portion of the cost could be depreciated though. In addition, you would add the expense to the basis of the house.

Q **What is basis?**

Basis is the base or starting point for figuring depreciation, amortization, gain, loss, or depletion. You use it in determining the value of assets you place into service in your business. If you buy a piece of equipment you depreciate, your basis in that piece of equipment is the cost of the equipment. If you convert personal tangible property to business property (a computer you bought for home use, then later decided to use in your business), the basis is the fair market value of the property at the time you put it into business use.

Q **Can I use the current fair market value of my house for determining depreciation?**

Probably not. Basis for figuring depreciation on your home is either the fair market value at the time you placed it in service or the adjusted basis, whichever is lower. To find the adjusted basis, you subtract the cost of the land the house is on from the total purchase price of the house. Add in the cost of any permanent improvements made to the house, and subtract any casualty losses that have occurred.

Thus, if you purchased your home for a total purchase price of $325,000 and if the land the house sits on is worth one-third of the total purchase price of the house, and you made no permanent improvements to the house since you bought it, your basis in the house is:

purchase price   *land value*   *basis of the house*
$325,000   − $107,250 ($325,000 × .33)   = $217,750

If the home office occupies 10 percent of the house, the basis of the home office would be $21,775. It would be this amount on which depreciation is calculated.

Q   **How do I calculate the depreciation on the home office?**

Under current rules, a home office placed in service from 1993 on is depreciated over 39 years under something known as the straight line MACRS rates. These rates (as well as rates for other depreciation methods for other property) are published each year in the free IRS publication called *Depreciation* (Publication 534). To figure your depreciation, use the worksheet for Form 8829.

Q   **Suppose you rent an apartment instead of owning a home. If you use a room exclusively for business can you deduct a portion of your rent?**

Yes. You would calculate the square footage used for business purposes (your office space in relation to your total apartment living space) and then include the cost of your rent in the "other expense" section under indirect expenses on Form 8829.

Q   **If I deduct 10 percent of the mortgage interest and real estate tax costs on Form 8829, can I still deduct mortgage interest and real estate taxes on Schedule A?**

Yes, but only the unused portion. In other words, if you deducted 10 percent on Form 8829, you would deduct the remaining 90 percent on Schedule A.

Q **What is the advantage of deducting the business portion of the mortgage interest and real estate taxes on Form 8829 instead of Schedule A?**

The advantage is that the home office deduction lowers your net business income, which in turn lowers your self-employment tax and your adjusted gross income (AGI). Since several personal deductions and one possible penalty (see discussion on estimating taxes on pages 385–87) are tied to the AGI, the more you can legally reduce your AGI, the better off you may be from a tax standpoint.

Q **Are there any business expenses I can't deduct, depreciate, or amortize?**

Expenses that are considered capital expenses cannot be written off. Neither can expenses for intangible property if the useful life can't be determined. In some cases the deductibility of an expense depends on how the transaction is set up. Here is a list of some items that either cannot be deducted or that can only be deducted under certain circumstances. You should consult your accountant before spending any substantial sums on these transactions to assure the transaction is set up in the best possible way for your business.

- Land. (Land can never be depreciated. Clearing, grading, and landscaping usually cannot be depreciated either; however, they could be added to your basis.) If you are using the land for mining or logging, it can be depleted, however.
- Trademarks and trade names.
- Goodwill (not depreciable).
- Franchises, designs, drawings, and patterns (depreciable only if they have a useful life that can be determined).
- Customer lists, subscriber lists, etc. (depreciable only if you can separate their value from the value of goodwill that goes with the business).

Q **Won't taking the home office deduction increase the risk of audit?**

That is a possibility, but the number of returns audited each year for any reason is relatively small, and if you have all the documentation and receipts you need to prove your deductions there is no reason to not take all the deductions you are legally entitled to take.

Q **What happens when I sell the house? Won't I have to pay capital gains tax on the business part of the house even if I buy a more expensive house?**

If it is a qualified home office, meeting the exclusive and regular tests, you have to split the sale price between the business and personal use of the house. You have to pay tax on the recapture of depreciation even if you purchase a home that costs enough to defer all the gain.

Q **How do I value property I bring into a business?**

You have to determine the value of the property at the time it was placed into service. For most equipment this will be less than the purchase price if the equipment is not new.

Q **Can I deduct the cost of health insurance I pay for myself?**

For 2000–2001, self-employed individuals are allowed to deduct 60 percent of the premiums they pay for health insurance for themselves and their family if they are not covered by a spouse's or any other employer's health care plan. That rate is scheduled to go up to 70 percent in 2002 and to 100 percent by 2003. The rule allowing this deduction was not permanent at this writing, however. You will have to check current tax regulations before taking the deduction.

Q **My children work for me. Can I deduct their wages as a business expense?**

Yes, you can deduct wages you pay your children. You must be able to prove the work your children did was work for the business and that the wages you paid them were ordinary and reasonable for the type of work performed.

Remember, too, that in hiring your children or spouse you become an employer and will have to comply with additional IRS requirements.

Q **What additional IRS requirements will I be subject to if I hire my children?**

Any of your children who work for you will need a W-4 form filled out, and you will have to withhold income taxes from their salary and remit it as you would for any employee. If your business is a sole proprietorship, you do not have to withhold or pay the employer's share of Social Security or federal unemployment tax for any of your children under the age of 18 who work for you in your business. Be sure, however, to check state employment regulations, since they may be different. If your business is a partnership or corporation you will have to withhold Social Security and federal unemployment tax. In either case, you will need to be able to prove the children really did work for you if challenged by the IRS.

Q **How do I prove my children and spouse worked for me?**

Have them keep a log showing when they worked and what they did, pay them by check, and have them deposit the checks in their own bank accounts.

Q **Do I have to pay Social Security for my spouse if he or she does some work in the company?**

You have to withhold Social Security and income tax but not federal unemployment tax.

Q **Under what circumstances do I have to report money I pay to other free-lancers or independent contractors?**

If the total amount you pay to anyone who is not an employee and not operating as a corporation amounts to $600 or more during the year, you have to report the total to the IRS at the end of the year on Form 1099, which is called an information return. You need to file a separate 1099 for each individual whom you have paid $600 or more during the year.

Q **What happens if I don't file a 1099?**

You will have to pay penalties both for failing to file the return with the IRS and for failing to send the copy to the recipient. The IRS penalty starts at $15 per return (up to 30 days late) and increases to $30 (return filed before August 1) and then $50 for returns filed after that or not filed. The penalty for failing to send the recipient a copy is $50. For both the IRS and the recipient statement, the penalty applies if you send the statements but not all the required information or if you report the information incorrectly.

Q Can I deduct contributions to a pension plan?

Yes. There are several types of pension plans available to you when you are self-employed. The amount you may contribute depends on your income and the type of plan you choose.

Q What types of pension plans are there, and which is the best for a one-person business?

It depends upon your goal. A defined benefit plan will let you choose the amount of money you want to receive each month when you retire and then specify how much you have to put in the account each year to meet that goal. Administering this type of plan is difficult, says CPA Jack Slick, because it requires the use of actuaries and mortality tables.

"The simpler plans such as money purchase plans, profit-sharing plans, and simplified employee pension plans (SEPs) are much easier to administer, and contributions to the plans are discretionary," says Slick. Most people opt for the simpler types of plans.

All of the plans allow you to defer taxes on the income until you reach retirement. Unfortunately, contributions to the plan on your own behalf are not deductible for self-employment tax purposes.

The SEP, often referred to as a SEP IRA, is the easiest to implement. Slick explains that it is similar to a normal IRA but has higher contribution limits. Contributions to a retirement plan can't exceed $30,000 on behalf of a self-employed individual. In addition, the simpler plans place a limit on the deduction based upon a percentage of income. For money purchase plans this limit is 25 percent of business income; for profit-sharing plans and SEP IRAs the limit is 15 percent of business income. The actual rate is lower, however, since you have to reduce your income by half of the self-employment taxes paid before calculating your contribution and calculate the contribution using a formula that lowers the rate. The formula is the contribution rate divided by one plus the contribution rate. So in the case of a money purchase plan with a 25 percent income contribution rate, the maximum actual rate that is applied equals 0.25 divided by 1.25, or 20 percent. That 20 percent rate would be figured not on the total business income, but on the business income minus 50 percent of the self-employment tax.

Money purchase plans and profit-sharing plans are generally referred to as Keogh plans. These plans must be in place and approved by the IRS by the end of your tax year in order for you to make a contribution to them for that year. SEP IRAs can be opened and money contributed to them for the tax year anytime before your return for that year is actually due. This period also includes any valid extensions you obtained on your return.

Q **If I decide to hire employees, do I have to include them in the plan, too?**

If you have full-time employees they must also be covered under your retirement plan. In some cases this can substantially reduce the amount of money you were expecting to put away on your own behalf. If you are thinking about starting a retirement plan, it's worth your trouble to talk to a person that specializes in this area so that you can implement a plan that matches your needs and concerns and doesn't overly stress your business.

Q **My spouse does not have a pension plan where he works. If I have a Keogh or a SEP IRA, can he keep contributing to his IRA?**

Yes, as long as your spouse is working, but, because yours would be a qualified pension plan, his or her IRA contributions would only be fully deductible if your combined income is under $150,000. Limited deductions would be allowed between $150,000 and $160,000.

Q **What if I can't pay my taxes?**

If you can't pay federal or state income taxes, you should complete your return and mail it on time without payment. (If you can make a partial payment, by all means do so.) You will have to pay both a penalty and interest on the unpaid amounts, but the penalty and interest if you file and don't pay will be less than if you don't file.

Q **What are the penalty and interest charges if I file a return without sending in the money due?**

If you file but don't pay the tax, you will be subject to a penalty of one-half of 1 percent of the unpaid tax for each month or part of a month the tax is unpaid up to a maximum of 25 percent of the tax. This penalty is avoidable only if you can show failure to pay is due to a reasonable cause. (Not having the money is not a reasonable cause. Neither is not knowing you had to pay taxes. You were supposed to have known the laws and put aside enough money to cover your tax liability.)

You will also have to pay interest on the unpaid amount. The interest is the short-term Treasury bill rate plus 3 percent and is adjusted quarterly.

Q What is the penalty for not filing a return at all?

Failure to file a return brings steeper penalties. 1f you don't file a return the penalty is 5 percent of the unpaid tax for each month or part of a month the tax is unpaid, up to a maximum of 25 percent of the tax. Failure to pay penalties may also apply. If your return is more than 60 days late, the failure to file penalty will be at least $100 or the tax due, whichever is lower.

Q My business got some publicity and we have been so busy I don't know where I'll find the time to get my personal tax return done on time. I'll only owe a couple hundred dollars in taxes for last year and don't want to get hit with stiff penalties, but I don't see how I can possibly get the return done on time. Is there anything I can do?

Yes. File Form 4868, which is an application for an automatic four-month extension of the filing deadline. If you can't get to a tax office, your public library or post office is likely to have copies of this form. Or you can download it from the IRS web site. Filing the form only extends the deadline for filing. It does not extend the deadline for getting your tax payments in to the IRS. All taxes have to be paid by the due date of your return, which is generally April 15, or you will be assessed applicable interest and penalties.

Q How many years after I file a return can the IRS come back and challenge it?

The IRS normally can come back and ask for more taxes within three years from the due date of the return. However, if you neglect to report an item of income that amounts to 25 percent or more of your income the IRS has up to 6 years to tap you on the shoulder. Additionally, if fraud is suspected, the IRS can come after you at any time. There is no statute of limitations on prosecuting and collecting extra taxes due in the case of fraud.

Q **What are my chances of being audited?**

It depends partly on what your income is. In general only about 1 percent of all returns are audited. But many factors affect the likelihood of an audit, including income. Schedule C filers with incomes of more than $100,000 are more likely than the average taxpayer to get audited.

Q **What should I do if I get audited?**

If you are audited, be sure you understand what information the IRS wants. Gather that information and arrange it neatly, making photocopies of any receipts or documents the IRS asks for. Mail the information or appear at a scheduled appointment as requested. (If you can't make the appointment, call well in advance and reschedule it.) If you are asked any questions during the audit, answer them directly, politely, and succinctly. Don't volunteer any information.

If the amount in question is large or if you are the nervous or talkative type, you may want to consider having your accountant go to the audit in your place.

Q **What tax records do I have to keep and how long?**

Keep tax returns forever.

Keep all papers regarding the cost of your house and mortgage and improvements to it for at least 5 years after you sell the house.

Save the supporting documents for income tax returns (expenses, income) for at least 5 years.

Q **What happens if your deductions are disallowed during an audit?**

You will have to pay interest and, depending on the reason and amounts involved, perhaps penalties. If the IRS suspects fraud, the penalties can be steep.

PULLING IT ALL TOGETHER:
RESOURCES TO HELP

Q **Are the income tax guides sold in bookstores and on newsstands every year any good?**

Yes, the major tax guides available each year can be helpful if you do your own taxes. They can help clarify instructions or regulations that are unclear and will alert you to tax law changes effecting the current year's return. Although each of the books provides the same basic information, you may find one better than another for your personal needs since each organizes and presents the facts in slightly different ways. Since tax laws change almost yearly, if you use such tax guides, it is wise to buy a new one each year.

Q **Does the IRS offer any help?**

Yes. Local IRS offices generally have representatives available to help you figure out how to fill out forms or how to handle different types of deductions. This help is free, friendly, and nonthreatening (since you are asking for information, not being audited). However, don't wait until a couple of days before your taxes are due if you think you will need help. The office will be busy then, making the wait for help lengthy and the time representatives can spend with any individual somewhat, limited.

The IRS publishes numerous help booklets, too. These are available in print or on the IRS web site. Some are instructions for specific forms; others are general guides on specific topics. Some of these have quite clear and easy-to-follow explanations. Among the IRS publications that may be of use to you are:

Name	Publication Number
Business Expenses	535
Business Use of Your Car	917
Business Use of Your Home	587
Depreciation	534
Miscellaneous Deductions	529
(covers what you can deduct for hobbies if your income producing activity doesn't qualify as a business)	

In addition to the help available to the general public at IRS offices, the agency also sponsors a program called the Small Business Tax Education Program (STEP), which teaches business owners and others some of the intricacies of dealing with IRS forms, record-keeping requirements, deposit of withholdings, and other business tax issues. For information, call the IRS at (800) 829-1040.

Q   **Where can I get copies of forms I need?**

You can pick up copies of forms and publications at your local IRS office, or you can order them for free by calling (800) 829-3676. You can also find forms on the IRS web site. Software programs for preparing your taxes have the forms built in.

Your public library will also have forms available. If don't see the forms you need where other forms are located in the library, ask the reference librarian for help. Often they have reproducible copies of every form in existence in a book that remains (for safekeeping) at the reference librarian's station. The post office may have forms as well.

Q   **Where can I get copies of state tax forms?**

If you need state tax forms, go to the Federation of Tax Administrators (FTA) web site at http://www.taxadmin.org/fta/FORMS.html and choose the link to your state. You can also find many tax forms in your public library.

Q **Are the computer tax programs any good? Do they really save any time?**

Yes, they are very useful. They automatically copy the data you enter or import it to the right places on each form or schedule you have to complete and automatically update all of them if a change is made in any one.

They also help prevent you from making mistakes in the way you fill out the return and in the calculations.

However, the programs are not a substitute for being aware of the tax laws and how they apply to your personal situation. But if you have some familiarity with the laws, they can be of tremendous help.

Q **Is there any other place I can get tax help?**

Local community groups and libraries occasionally offer tax help. If you have a computer and modem, check the online computer information services for tax help. The Business Know-How forum on America Online is one of many resources that offer tax help. In addition, you can find shareware programs and spreadsheet or database templates online to help you complete your taxes and online help from publishers of major commercial tax software packages such as ChipSoft (TurboTax and MacInTax) and Parson's Technologies.

Q **Now that I've read this chapter, am I aware of everything I need to know about taxes for self-employed individuals?**

This chapter only touches on the basics for self-employed taxpayers. Depending on your situation, rules that haven't been discussed here such as passive loss rules, alternate minimum tax, and others may apply. Be sure to check the IRS instructions and other tax publications to determine what rules do apply to your situation, and if necessary, get help from a tax adviser or the IRS itself. When it comes to taxes, what you don't know can hurt you.

V.

Managing
It All

25.

How to Gain Control
of Your Time

It's ironic. One of the biggest attractions of self-employment is the opportunity it offers to free up commuting time and simplify life. Yet, rather than looking for things to do with all their spare time, people who start their own business quickly gain new insight into the meaning of words like "cope" and "juggle," particularly if they work at home. They become adept at talking to clients on the phone while simultaneously gesturing at squabbling offspring and mouthing, *Cut it out or I'm going to wring your neck when I get off the phone!* They also become the master of the white lie, being able to devise a plausible business reason for putting a client or customer on hold the instant they spot bubbles oozing out of the dishwasher and realize it wasn't a good idea to substitute laundry soap for the dishwasher detergent they forgot to buy.

Fortunately, there are ways to make time management easier even if you don't have any employees to whom you can delegate work. The following pages contain dozens of ideas for managing your time more efficiently and improving your productivity.

Q **Why is managing time so difficult for the self-employed?**

When you are self-employed you don't have the support staff you'd have in a corporation. There's no switchboard operator, no secretary-typist, no file clerk, and no bookkeeper. Neither are there salespeople, copywriters, or a public relations department. You do it all. You wear all the hats.

To make matters worse you are likely to have to do it all in relative isolation. Without the benefit of daily contact with business associates, it is easy to lose sight of your goals and spend far too much time chasing rainbows or doing nonproductive busywork.

Q **Most mornings I boot my computer before I start making coffee. By the time my neighbors are leaving for work, I've already been at work for an hour or more. And I'm still working long after they return home. What am I doing wrong?**

Sometimes long hours are unavoidable. I was printing out labels on a dot matrix printer at about 7:30 A.M. one day when I got a call from Tom Gabrielli, a self-employed commercial artist. Tom was doing a rush job for one of my clients and needed some information before he could send the work off to the printer. Knowing I work from home, Tom wasn't surprised that I answered the phone at that hour instead of letting my answering machine pick up the call. But when he heard the clatter of the printer in the background, he aid, "Oh no, not you, too! I've been working since six A.M. What time did you start?"

As a commercial artist, Tom's work is somewhat cyclical. During the busy times of the year he is likely to start early and work late; but in summer, when his business tends to slow down a bit, he gets to travel or relax on sunny beaches while his corporate counterparts are watching the car temperature gauge inch toward hot in a rush-hour traffic jam.

If your business has busy seasons, you may find there are times when there is no good way to avoid long hours of work. But if you are regularly overworked or regularly behind schedule, chances are you need to gain control over the way you use your time.

Q **What can I do to control the way I use time?**

There are dozens of ways to control the way you use time. Some involve doing very simple things such as keeping a list of office supplies that are running low. Referring to such a list and replenishing your stock before you run out will help you avoid frantic last-minute races around town to pick up some supply you need to finish a job. If some of the supplies you use are hard to find (colored printer ink or transparency film for an inkjet printer, for instance) ordering them ahead of time could save your neck as well as your time. A client wouldn't be very happy to hear her job won't be delivered in the morning because you ran out of some crucial supply last night.

Other time and clutter management tips may require willingness to change lifelong habits and attitudes. If you were born to clutter, procrastinate, and start umpteen projects at once, you may need to manage your time more efficiently by focusing your activities and/or restructuring your environment for productivity.

Gaining control of your time is a three-step process:

1. Decide what you want to achieve with your time now and in the long run.
2. Pinpoint activities or interruptions that interfere with what you want to achieve.
3. Implement appropriate changes to eliminate or minimize the obstacles to attaining your goals.

Q **How do I get started?**

Getting in touch with yourself doesn't have to be a long, involved or unduly emotional project. It simply means thinking about the things you most want to do and what you need to do to accomplish those things. You can break the process of getting yourself more organized into these four simple steps:

▸ Make a written list of long- and short-range goals.
▸ Keep a time log to monitor the way you now use your time.
▸ Evaluate how the way you use time relates to the goals you want to achieve.
▸ Restructure your activities environment, habits, and/or workloads one by one to eliminate inefficient habits and time-wasting routines.

Q **This all sounds like a lot of busywork. How is it going to help me get more done in less time?**

Effective time management isn't a matter of completing more activities in less time. It is a matter of using your time efficiently (managing it) to achieve your goals.

For example, suppose Mary Jones offers word processing and mailing list maintenance services to small businesses near her home. She has a couple of steady customers and gets sporadic business from several shopkeepers in the area. Now that the twins have started junior high school, she has more time to work and realizes she'll probably need extra money in a few years to help pay for their college tuitions.

Which of the following should she do?

▶ look for new customers by sending a mailing to all local businesses telling them about her services
▶ create a newsletter or flier to demonstrate her skills and have it distributed with the local chamber of commerce mailing
▶ advertise resume preparation and word processing in the Yellow Pages and local weekly newspapers
▶ look for a job teaching word processing
▶ try to get typing jobs from bigger businesses or organizations
▶ start a temporary employment agency specializing in providing highly skilled word processors to industry
▶ get a "real" job during the day and type resumes at night

Almost any of these options might bring in some additional income. In fact, Mary might be tempted to try all of the above activities once to bring in more work. The new work she brings in might make her very busy, but if it all comes from one-time customers or requires her to spend a lot of nonbillable time talking to new clients or learning new skills, she might be very busy but still not meet her income objectives.

If Mary wants to make the best possible use of her income-producing time, she will need to focus on her goals and plan around them. First, she should decide how much money she wants to earn or needs to earn, how many hours she is willing or able to work to bring in that amount of income, and what kind of work she likes to do. Then she should look for the best ways to produce the amount of income she needs in the number of hours she can allot to income-producing activities.

Thus, if she needs an extra $200 a week, and local shopkeepers tend to have only small, one-time jobs—and quibble over the price of those, to boot—doing a mailing to small shopkeepers will be a waste of Mary's time and money. However, if she has some background working in a legal or medical office, she might do well to focus on soliciting business from attorneys in a 20-mile radius.

If Mary has the time, energy, and desire to expand her one-person business and can raise sufficient capital to start a temporary employment agency, the best way for her to spend her time at the moment might be researching whether the community could use another employment agency and what she would need to do to start one.

The same kind of carefully thought-out approach can help you better manage your time to meet your goals.

Q **I've heard a lot about goal setting. Does it work? Do I really need to write goals down?**

Goals are a lot like vacations. To make them happen you have to pick a destination and map out a route to reach the destination. Writing your goals down and asking yourself what, specifically, you need to do to achieve each goal can give you the focus and direction you need to reach them.

Q **I want to be rich, and I also want to finish writing my customer's program by the end of the week. Which do I write down on my list of goals?**

Start by listing your long-term goals, but be as specific as possible. Getting rich is not specific. Boosting personal net income to $500,000 a year within three years is a specific goal. Once you have a specific goal, determine the steps necessary to reach that goal and set a date for doing so. If "buy a house" is your long-term goal, write down the amount of the down payment you are willing to pay and how much money you'll need to earn to keep up with the mortgage payments, maintenance, utilities, and other bills. Consider what steps you need to take to make your business grow to achieve that level of income and set realistic target dates. See the sample goal-setting worksheet on page 422 (Table 25.1).

Q **I've heard it is a good idea to keep a time log. How does keeping a time log help me manage my time more efficiently?**

Keeping the log will let you quickly detect patterns in the ways you use and abuse time. For instance, your log may show you that, like your corporate brethren, you are wasting anywhere between 35 and 45 minutes a day just looking for things on your desk or in your files. Or it may show that you are spending a lot of time making or accepting phone calls that have nothing to do with reaching any of your goals. If you waste even 5 minutes on each of a dozen calls during the day, you have wasted an hour of your time—plus the cost of any calls you made.

Table 25.1: Sample Goal-Setting Worksheet

Goals to Achieve

Writing out your goals and the steps to achieve them makes them more attainable. A form such as this can help organize your thoughts.

Long-term goal:
Buy $300,000 home

Achieve by: 6/04

Requirements	Actions	Do By (date)
$100,000 cash down payment		6/04
have net income of $150,000	hire 3 employees	12/02
	add microcomputer repair services to increase income 30%	12/01
	bring in 2 corporate accounts to increase income 20%	4/02

In addition to helping you spot patterns in the way you waste time, a time log can help you identify patterns relating to the profitability of various jobs or contacts. When you look over your log, you may be surprised to see it takes you only three hours to complete a $250 job you do weekly for Smith & Sons, but you spent five hours on work for Rainbow City that also brought in $250. If the cost of doing each job is the same, you don't have to be a mathematical genius to figure out which produces more income for your time.

Q Can most people find such patterns in their workweek?

Yes. In fact, the 80/20 principle or the Pareto Principle (for the Italian economist who first expounded it) holds true for most businesses and individuals. In essence the principle says that 80 percent of your business will come from 20 percent of your customers or, alternatively, that 20 percent of your efforts will produce 80 percent of your income.

Your time log will help you pinpoint the customers and activities that produce the bulk of your income. To streamline your business and increase profits, focus on finding more customers like the 20 percent who now provide the bulk of your profit, and spend less time doing work for the type of customers whose work is marginally profitable.

Q **How do I keep a time log?**

It's simple. just record all your activities for a week. Every time you start or stop an activity, get interrupted by a phone call, stop working to throw a load of clothes in the washing machine, make a brief notation about what you did. Try to write these notes at the time you start or stop an activity, not later in the day when you may forget what you did, or how long it took. You can use a format like the one on page 424, or just keep a running tally of start and stop times on a pad of legal paper or in a notebook. Or use the time log function in Quickbooks, Gold Mine, or some other computer program you own. The important part is to keep the log.

Q **How long should I keep recording my activities?**

Keep the log for at least a week. (See Table 25.2.)

Q **My work varies a lot from week to week. How can I see patterns?**

While the type of work you do may vary, chances are the way you deal with your workload and interact with customers won't change much from day to day or job to job. Here are some questions to consider that may help you spot time-wasting activities or inefficient ways of dealing with your workload:

- Did you start each day with a plan of what you wanted to accomplish?
- Did you try to do too much?
- Did you usually finish one task before starting the next?
- Did you get a lot of incoming phone calls that weren't important?
- Were all the phone calls you made necessary?
- Did you spend too much time making unimportant decisions?
- Have you developed standardized letters and procedures for dealing with recurring situations?

Table 25.2: Time Log

Here is a very simple time log to use. Every time you start, finish, or change activities, write down the time and the nature of the activity.

Keep the log for at least a week. At the end of the week, look at your patterns of activity. How many jobs did you start? How many did you finish? What kept you from finishing the jobs? If you've written down everything you did during the week, you should be able to see at a glance how you are spending your time and when and how you are being interrupted or change activities.

Activity	Start Time	Stop Time	Completed? Y	N

- Are you grouping jobs for maximum efficiency?
- Are your methods or equipment up-to-date and adequate for your needs?
- Did you tend to spend time daydreaming instead of working?
- Did you spend a lot of time looking for things?
- Did you spend more time organizing your work or your work space than doing work?
- Did you delegate business or personal chores to others, or did you let others delegate their chores to you?
- Did you put off starting big, important jobs while you got lots of little chores out of the way?

- Did you have to run to the store frequently for business or personal items you forgot to buy?
- Did you do things for other people you really didn't want to do?
- Did you spend a lot of time worrying about problems?

Q What do I do with the log after I've made it?

At the end of the week review your notations. Consider which things helped you to achieve long- or short-range goals and which didn't. Determine what kinds of activities or interruptions got in the way of reaching your goals. Among the things to watch for: How many jobs did you start? Did all of them have to be done? How many did you finish? What kept you from finishing the jobs? If you've written down everything you did during the week, you should be able to see at a glance how you are spending your time and when and how you are being interrupted or change activities.

Once you identify time-wasting activities, you can improve your efficiency by adapting some of the suggestions in the next chapter.

26.

Practical Ways to Save Time in Your Home Office or Small Business

Even if you were a good time manager when you worked for a corporation, you may find that managing your time in a home office or other small business is extremely difficult. One reason is that corporate time-saving strategies just aren't practical for businesses with low budgets and few if any employees. Another is simply that your workload is likely to be heavier when you work for yourself than it is when you work for other people.

In either case, managing your time is something you must learn to do if you expect to succeed. Here are dozens of time management tips you could put to work in your home office or small away-from-home business.

GETTING THE WORK OUT

Q I start off each morning with good intentions but somehow get side-tracked. By the end of the day I find I haven't accomplished anything. What can I do?

Make sure you start off each day with a schedule. If at all possible, make the first task on your schedule the most important thing you have to do. At the end of each day, write out your schedule for the next day, allowing yourself reasonable time limits for completing each task or portion of a task. Get everything together to start the

426

next day's work, and leave it where you'll see it first thing in the morning if you find you have trouble getting down to work when you first enter your office.

Q **My projects tend to be long term. It could take me a month or two to develop an inventory control system for a big customer, for instance. How can I schedule something like that?**

Keep a master project calendar. Break the task down into steps (or milestones), and then schedule each step according to when it has to be completed.

Q **How does keeping a To Do list help?**

Listing tasks on a sheet of paper offers these benefits:

- reminds you of jobs to be done
- helps keep your desk free from clutter (a list of five things to do takes up a lot less room on your desk than five stacks of papers and folders)
- makes it easier to prioritize tasks
- gives you a feeling of accomplishment when you cross off items on the list as you finish them

Q **Is a To Do list different from an appointment calendar?**

They can be the same, but often a To Do list will contain things that can be done at any time, while the appointment calendar is for meetings with other people or things that have to be done at specific times, such as calling a client between 10 and 11 A.M. on Friday. You can keep both the To Do list and the appointment schedule on the same sheet of paper, however (see the illustration on page 428), or you can use a computer program such as Microsoft Outlook or a handheld device like the Palm Pilot.

Q **What if I can't do everything I scheduled?**

Consider whether you can cancel a task or activity, give it to someone else to do, or simply work extra hours this week and learn not to take on so much next week. If you routinely have more work to do than you have time to do it, it's time to either hire help or be more selective in the type of work you accept.

Table 26.1: To Do List and Appointment Schedule

Day: _____   Date: _____

Appointments		Things To Do		
		Item	Time to Complete	Priority
9:00				
10:00				
11:00				
12:00				
1:00				
2:00				
3:00				
4:00				
5:00				
6:00				

Notes:

Q **I make schedules but can't seem to stick to them. What could be wrong?**

You may be scheduling too many things for each day or not allowing yourself time to account for occasional interruptions or delays. One solution is to schedule a block of time to do catch-up chores. This could be one hour a week or one day a week. It should be used only to finish jobs that haven't been completed or to do those non-income-producing tasks you keep putting off, like filing, bookkeeping, etc.

Another possible reason you find it difficult to get everything you've scheduled done is you may be scheduling activities that don't fit into your long-range plans.

For instance, you may be teaching a programming course one night a week, doing the bookkeeping for your uncle once a month, and selling advertising special-ties as a sideline, all while you try to keep up a computer consulting business. As a result, you may be torn in so many pieces you simply can't devote the time needed to any one activity. If this is your problem, choose what is most in line with your goals and focus your attention on that activity and eliminate any that don't help you accomplish your goals.

Q **I'm having trouble getting started on a big project. What should I do?**

The best procedures to follow when you can't seem to get going on a project are these:

- Break the job down into small pieces and tackle one piece at a time.
- Set deadlines for yourself. Work often expands (and slows down) to fill the time allotted for it.
- Establish milestones and reward yourself with a trip to the beach or the movies, or by doing something else you enjoy each time you reach one of the milestones.
- Delegate less important jobs to others, or if you have no one to delegate the work to, consider subcontracting the work out to a helper.
- Be sure you have all the information you need to proceed with the project. If you don't, get the needed facts and the job may start to fall into place.

DEAL WITH DISTRACTIONS

Q **I never seem to get one thing finished before I have to start another. What can I do?**

List tasks you need to perform on a To Do list. Assign priorities to work you have to do. If you have trouble finishing tasks or tracking multiple projects, put the most important thing you have to do at the top of your list, make that the first thing you do, and continue working at it until it is finished; then, tackle the next item on your list. At the end of the day, leftover tasks—if still important—get moved to the next day's To Do list.

TIP If you spend a lot of time at a computer, learn to use a program such as Outlook, Act, or Time and Chaos. These will organize your contact information, appointment calendar, and To Do list. They can be set up to send reminders to you as well. You can set options to tell the program how far ahead of a meeting or a deadline you want to be notified. As long as the computer is on, you won't be able to forget about important projects.

Other methods that may work for you are assigning the most difficult tasks you have to do to the hours of the day you tend to be most productive or when you are least likely to be interrupted.

Q **I'll be working, remember something I wanted to do, and before I know it, I'm in the middle of doing the new thing and have put aside the project I started earlier. How can I keep from interrupting myself?**

That's a common problem. To solve it, keep a notepad near you when you work and write down all the things that you remember you have to do. Then, do the tasks all at once near the end of your work day if they still seem important. You will be surprised how many of those little things you thought were important earlier in the day are no longer important near the end of the day.

Other ways to handle distracting tasks are to set aside one day a week to finish projects you've started during the week or one day a week as the only day you'll start new projects or pursue new ideas.

Q But isn't that procrastinating? Isn't it better to do things right away?

Procrastination is putting off things because you don't want to or don't know how to get started on them. Grouping tasks lets you concentrate on one thing at a time and accomplish each more efficiently. It can also help you spot unnecessary or marginal chores and eliminate them.

If you have employees, you may also find you can delegate some of the tasks to one of your employees.

Q Usually an interruption is a customer or a family member who needs something done right away. How can I avoid those interruptions?

Learn to distinguish between urgent tasks and important ones. An urgent task is one that demands to be done *now!* An important task is something that furthers your longer-term objectives. Some tasks seem pressing because someone else wants you to drop what you are doing so you can help them immediately accomplish their goals. A spouse who calls home and expects you to stop working to go out and pick up a part they need or a customer who calls and expects you to answer grammar and usage questions because you write their advertising copy (and of course does not expect to be billed for your time) are two examples of urgent tasks that don't foster your goals.

TIP If you have one or more people you don't want to anger but who frequently make such urgent calls, letting the answering machine pick them up may avoid unwanted confrontations. If you are unavailable, the person trying to reach you might take care of the problem himself or herself. If not, be assured the person will call back.

If you have customers who make a habit of calling you for free advice or information, consider billing for phone time or charging a retainer fee. Warn the customer a little in advance, and ask which they'd prefer: a retainer contract or to be billed for each call.

Q You can't put off a baby that needs a diaper change or the parcel post guy at the door. What do you do when you are frequently interrupted by family obligations or household duties?

Don't try to play superman or superwoman. You may need to hire household help. If you can't afford household help on a regular basis, consider having someone come in once every other week to help out, and try to get more cooperation from other members of your family on a daily basis. In addition, schedule work that needs a lot of concentration for times when someone else can attend to the baby's needs or when the doorbell isn't likely to ring.

Q Are those personal organizers and planning systems any good?

Sure—if you use them. Their benefit is they let you keep all your notes and records about projects, people, appointments, and expenses in one place. They can serve not only as an appointment reminder and scheduler (daybook) but also as a tickler file and record of business activities for tax purposes.

Generally, they have pages on which you can list daily or weekly appointments and To Do lists; a monthly and/or yearly planning calendar; sections for addresses and phone numbers, expenses, and notes. Some offer project planning sections, graph paper, a ruler, miniature envelopes for receipts, trip records, and other forms, and miscellaneous information guides. Since the planners are usually loose-leaf format, forms or sections may be added or removed to customize the planner to your own use.

The main problem with such systems is the human one. If you don't use the diary regularly or make legible entries in the diary or if you overschedule appointments for yourself, it won't do you any good.

Q Where can I find these planning books?

Several companies make planners. Among them are Rolodex, Day-Runner, Day-Timers, and Franklin Covey. The Rolodex and Day-Runner systems are sold in many office supply stores. The systems from Day-Timers and Franklin are generally not available in stores. You can get additional information about the various products from these contacts:

Rolodex:
http://www.rolodex.com
(800) 446-5652

Day-Runner:
http://www.dayrunner.com
(800) 643-9923

Day-Timers:
http://www.daytimer.com
(800) 805-2615

Franklin Covey:
http://www.franklincovey.com
(800) 654-1776

Q How much do these planning systems cost?

The initial cost can run anywhere from around $30 to $250 depending on the size of the binder, the type of binder (zippered or non-zippered, for instance), the quality of the covering (vinyl, simulated leather, real leather), and what types of planning tools you want to put in it (To Do list forms, expense records, daily calendar, etc.).

Q What about electronic organizers?

If you buy one of the better ones they, too, can be invaluable—if you use them and if you don't lose or misplace them. They can store names, addresses, phone numbers, appointments and can be used as a calculator, clock, and memo pad. Some of the better ones can transfer information to and from a computer (with the purchase of cables and software) and have memory cards available that allow you to use the organizer as a dictionary, for financial planning, or even for a limited amount of word processing if you can type on the tiny keys.

TIP Be sure you read the directions and understand how to change batteries in the electronic organizer without losing data.

Q **Are there similar time management systems for computer users?**

Yes. Both Day-Timers and Franklin Covey have developed software for Windows and Macintosh computer users that functions like the paper planning systems. Other companies make software (often called personal information managers or PIMs) that perform similar tasks. Computer magazines and catalogs should have ads for this type of software. Check back issues of computer magazines for reviews of the products if the prices are high.

Q **How do I know which system is best?**

Think about how you work and where you work. Do you need something small and portable? Do you travel a lot? Could you discipline yourself to make regular entries in a planner? (If not, they will all be a waste of money to you.) Do you need something that can transfer data to your computer system?

Send for catalogs and brochures and look at the planning guides in the stores. Try to determine how much space you need and how you want to organize appointments and notes. Then choose the one that seems most suited to the way you want to work.

Q **How can I motivate myself to get more done?**

If you tend to plod along without the stimulation of someone looking over your shoulder to see if work is done, give yourself deadlines and make yourself stick to them. Make it a contest with yourself, or a race with the clock (actually set an alarm clock), or program your computer to alert you at a certain time.

Q **It takes me a long time to make decisions. How can I quicken the process?**

Learn to look at the big picture. What do you want to achieve? What is the relative importance of the decision you are about to make? If it makes little real difference whether you choose A or B, choose either and move on to something else. (Flip a coin if you have to, but make the decision and move on to your next task.)

Q **What if the decision *is* important or could cause a big loss?**

If you can't make a decision any other way, take out a sheet of paper and divide it into two columns. On the top of one column write "Pros," and at the top of the second column, write "Cons." Put the reasons for making a positive decision under the pros, the reasons for a negative decision under cons, and compare the two. Sometimes just writing it all down can help you clarify your thinking.

Q **It's one thing to know what I *ought* to do to get organized and quite another to make myself do it. How can I motivate myself to get more organized?**

If reminding yourself of your long- and short-term goals doesn't help, try reminding yourself how much your time is worth. If you bill at $60 an hour, every minute you waste doing unproductive tasks or making unnecessary phone calls costs you a dollar.

GAIN CONTROL OVER TELEPHONE CALLS

Q **I don't have anyone to screen or place calls for me. How can I reduce the amount of time I spend on the phone?**

Here are a few suggestions that work for even the one-person home office:

Use an answering machine or voice mail system to answer phone calls. The advent of voice mail has given telephone answering systems new respectability. Where once an answering machine message was a good indication the business you had called was very small and probably located in someone's kitchen, now companies of all sizes use voice mail to answer calls.

If you have your own answering machine, set the answering machine to let you monitor calls and cut in only if the call is important. If you don't need to monitor calls, however, don't. Monitoring them may disturb your concentration on a project, defeating one of the purposes of having the machine pick up the calls in the first place.

Use caller identification (Caller ID). Pick up only those calls that further your goals.

Make all outgoing phone calls at one time. Set aside a specific block of time (say 11.00 A.M. to 11:30 A.M.) to make phone calls, and stick to it. Instead of reaching for the phone each time you think you need to make a call, make notes to yourself about who you want to call and why. When the time you've set to make calls rolls around, place those calls you still think are necessary.

Grouping calls this way will help you reduce or eliminate the number of unimportant impulse calls you make. Since you have a specific time frame in which to make and complete all calls, you will be less likely to waste time chitchatting about nonbusiness matters.

Q **Is there any way to avoid chatting about inconsequential things during phone calls?**

To keep business calls more focused, make mini-agendas for your calls. List the key points you want to discuss and check off each point as you go over it, noting any items that will be followed up at a later time. When you have gotten to the end of your agenda for the call, sum up the main points covered, and if both parties agree everything has been covered, say good-bye and hang up. You'll save your own time, the time of the person you were talking to, and cut your phone bill as well.

Q **How else can I reduce the time I spend on the telephone?**

Here are several ways:

Use electronic mail. How many times has something like this happened to you? You need to talk to your contact at a client's office for information about a project you are doing. You call but your contact is out of the office. Your contact calls you back, just after you leave for an appointment elsewhere. You return the call when you get back and the contact is in a meeting.

If you use computers and modems, this kind of phone tag could be eliminated with electronic mail (e-mail). E-mail is simply a way of sending information from one computer to another without the computers having to be hooked up. Much like regular mail, when you send electronic mail it gets deposited in the recipient's electronic mailbox and waits there for the recipient to pick it up at his or her convenience any time during the day or night. Unlike regular mail, delivery to the recipient's mailbox is usually immediate.

Another time-saving benefit of using electronic mail is that it can help avoid aimless small talk if you have a client who can't stop talking once on the telephone. If you need to get information to a customer in a hurry, e-mail can also cut down on the delivery time and avoid busy or turned-off fax lines. Finally, if your customers live in other countries and you choose a service with international access, you and your customers can communicate at the hours you are each most alert.

TIP Many people use e-mail as a way to control their time. E-mail lets you avoid lengthy conversations with talkative customers or friends, and it helps you avoid telephone tag. You and the people with whom you correspond can read and answer at whatever time of the day or night they wish to. But e-mail can also be a big time-waster, too! The faster you respond to some messages, the faster the person who sent them will come back at you with more questions or comments. Worse, some people will send the same message to you through multiple channels. They might send a message in e-mail, leave one on voice mail to tell you to check your e-mail, and just in case send a copy of the e-mail in the mail or through interoffice mail.

If you find e-mail takes too much time, consider unsubscribing to mailing lists you joined and don't read regularly. Also, don't answer e-mail the second it comes in. The faster you answer a letter the sooner the person who sent it gets it, reads it and responds to your response. If it's junk mail that's taking up your time, consider creating more than one e-mail address for yourself. Use one for business-related activities. Use the other for all nonbusiness e-mail. Check each of them only once or twice a day. After all, how often do you read and respond to mail that comes to you from the post office?

Send a fax instead of calling. Most businesses have fax machines and leave them on constantly. If you have frequent dealings with certain businesses, ask for their fax number and ask if it is OK to send messages by fax. Besides using fax for messages, you can order parts and supplies, send for and receive literature, and even order your lunch or enter radio contests.

CONQUER CLUTTER

Q **I waste a lot of time looking for things. Either I put things away and don't remember where I put them, or they get buried under something on my desk. What can I do?**

If you frequently misplace things in your office, consider these solutions:

▸ *Make sure you have adequate storage space.* It's hard to keep things organized and neat if you don't have any place to keep your business files, equipment, supplies and tools, etc.

▸ *Work out orderly and convenient storage and filing systems.* Think about what you need to do your work and how you can organize your work space efficiently. It is likely that you actually use only 20 percent of the files, equipment, tools, or other items in your work area on a regular basis. Make sure those are located close to where you work so they are easy to put away or file as soon as you are done with them. Could you install shelves in your work area? Put up pegboards or racks to store frequently used tools near your working area? Look around the home improvement stores and discount department stores as well as office supply stores for ideas about storage furniture and supplies.

▸ *Do filing and straightening regularly.* Set aside 10 minutes at the end of each day to put away anything you've taken out. Make sure you always put things back in the same place, too. If you group your phone calls and have a speaker phone or a phone with a long cord, you can do your filing and straightening while you are making your phone calls.

▸ *Cross-reference your files.* Could a piece of paper be filed in two places? Put the paper in one file and put a note about where to find it in the other.

▸ *Use your computer to store names, phone numbers, and reminders.* A database program or a personal information management (PIM) program can put names, numbers, and notes where you can find them quickly. If you don't have a database program or a PIM, put the names of all contacts in one word processing file and use the search feature of your word processor to find the information when needed.

Q **What's the best way to clear the clutter off my desk?**

Rediscover your wastebasket. Unless you have already trained yourself to toss out all but important documents and mail, some 50 to 75 percent of the items on your desk are outdated or refer to things you don't need to do. Set aside a half hour to an hour to clear your desk of everything you no longer need. If you have several months' worth of accumulated clutter to sift through, set aside a little bit of time each day for the project, tackling one part of the area at a time, or even one corner of the desk or workbench at a time.

If you keep magazines and newsletters because you might need a name or number or the information in an article, copy down the name and number or tear out the article from the newsletter and file those things in appropriate files. Then throw out the remainder of the publication. Not only will it save room, it will make it possible to find the names, numbers, or information you were saving without having to go through stacks of old publications.

Don't leave things out so you'll remember to do them. Instead, put a description of what needs to be done and a due date on a To Do list, and put the associated paper, materials, or other paraphernalia away until it is time to do the job. If you think you will forget where you put the things you were going to leave out, include a notation on the To Do list about where you put the materials you'll need.

Q **How do I decide what to keep and what to throw out?**

If you are trying to organize a home office that has become so cluttered it would make a typical 10-year-old's room look neat, the best approach is to clear desks, bookcases, and work surfaces of *all* stacks of papers, magazines, newspapers, etc. Pile the stacks into cardboard boxes, keeping them separated as they were on your desk if you worry about losing things you might need.

When all is clear, start putting items back in place. Start with essential equipment and tools first (computer or typewriter, Rolodex, desk calendar, telephone, etc.). Then start sorting piles of paper you think contain the most current items. Toss out any piece of paper you don't have a specific need for.

Leave all the other piles of paper in the boxes you put them in, and move the boxes to a storage area away from your office (a basement, closet, or garage would do). Retrieve papers or items from the boxes only as you need them over the next several months. After six months, consider tossing all the papers and files you haven't needed into the recycling bin since it is unlikely you'll ever look at them again.

WARNING If you are so unorganized that your business certificate, tax returns, or other documents that must be saved might be buried in the piles of clutter, beg or pay a friend or spouse to sort through it all for you before tossing it out.

439

Q **How can I deal with my "pack rat" tendencies?**

Do you save mail, odds and ends of supplies, scraps of material, notes to yourself, magazines, newsletters, etc., just *in case* you need them? If you absolutely can't bring yourself to throw out those odds and ends, try this: Keep a cardboard box under your desk or elsewhere in your work area. Throw in all the things you are afraid to throw out but don't have a specific use for now.

Once a month, go through the box and throw away everything that is outdated or no longer seems important. Do not add a second box when the first is filled. Force yourself to take the time to go through the box. If you never seem to find the time to do it, consider doing this: Take the top half of the materials out of the box and set them aside. *Remove the remaining items from the box and throw them out without looking at them*. If they were buried in the box for over a month because you weren't sure if you needed them you will never miss them. Put the items you set aside (the newest ones) back in the box. Repeat the procedure each month.

Q **What can I do with all the business cards I accumulate? I wind up moving them from one place to another on my desk for weeks and then can't find the one I want when I need a contact.**

Get a Rolodex with plastic sleeves to hold business cards. Ask people to give you *two* business cards. Store one under their name in your Rolodex and the other under an industry or other classification. For instance, John James, a computer consultant, might be filed under J for James and under C for consultant. Alternately, type the name and contact information into a searchable computerized database. Print out the database and store a paper copy so you will be able to find contact names if your computer has to be repaired or can't be used due to a power outage.

Q **I don't have enough room to add more storage space. What can I do?**

Empty file cabinets of old or outdated files. Although we live in the information age, it's not necessary to save every piece of information that comes into your office. According to a 1987 report published in *Personnel Journal*, Americans create 30 billion original documents a year and ignore 85 percent of what they keep on file. If you purge your file cabinets of material you no longer need, you will free up storage space and make it easier to stay organized. If you aren't sure what documents you should keep and what you can safely throw out, see the Records Retention Chart beginning on page 467. The chart lists typical office and business documents and suggests a length of time such items are normally stored or useful.

Q **My housemate is always hounding me about the mess in my office, but I find structure stifles my creativity. Is there a way to be a free spirit and be neat, too?**

There are a couple of things that might work. First, try organizing your space a little. Take a few hours to put away things you seldom need or use and arrange the rest into some kind of order. You may find that just organizing things a little actually lets you be more creative because you can concentrate on your work rather than going crazy looking for some tool or piece of information you need.

The other possible solution is to try to close off your office area from your house-mate's view. If you have a separate room for it, close the door. If you don't have a separate room, look for ways to screen off your corner so the clutter isn't visible to your companion or can be hidden when you aren't working in the office. Inexpensive folding screens from discount department stores are one possibility, decorating magazines might offer other ideas.

TIP If you use a computer system and your desk or filing cabinet is cluttered, your computer hard drive is likely to be cluttered, too. You can speed up file searches by periodically removing unneeded files from your hard disk and by running a hard disk optimization program. These programs "pick up" after you, fitting your files into orderly patterns on the hard disk so the head (something like a phonograph needle) that has to read the data doesn't have to constantly jump from one part of the disk to another to retrieve or store information.

Q **What about old tax records and other files I have to save? What can I do with them?**

Move inactive files you can't throw away to some other location. If you do not have to refer to them often, move them to some other storage area such as a basement, attic, garage, or rented space in a storage facility. Use suitable storage containers to protect the records from being destroyed by moisture or by mice if either are a problem. Metal or plastic garbage pails (clearly marked so they aren't thrown away) make inexpensive home storage containers.

Q **Is there any good way to deal with all the mail I get?**

Some of these techniques will help:

▶ Set aside a specific time each day to take care of your incoming mail. If practical, schedule mail chores for mid-afternoon. The change of pace late in the workday will be welcome. A mid- or late-afternoon slot for reading mail will also ensure you won't blow the whole day on unimportant tasks if you get distracted by something you spot in a piece of junk mail or magazine article.

▶ Open, read, and handle all of your mail in the allotted time.

▶ Open your mail over the wastebasket or the recyclables container, immediately discarding envelopes, ads, or catalogs you don't need. Unless you have a very specific reason for not doing so, throw out all mail you are tempted to save "just in case" you want to refer to it later.

▶ If you have been sitting for most of the day, stand while you open and read the mail. The change of position will be good for you, plus you are likely to take less time opening and reading the mail if you are standing up.

▶ File mail you need to save *before you sit down again*. Once you sit, inertia is likely to set in, and the piece of mail you were going to file later will still be on your desk the next day.

▶ Ask to be taken off the mailing lists if you don't use the products in mail order catalogs you receive or if you don't read the newsletters or trade publications you get. You'll be helping to reduce landfills as well as the clutter on your desk.

Q **How else can I save time?**

If you think about the way you work and the jobs you do, you will probably be able to discover dozens of ways to save time. Here are some ideas to spark your own creativity:

Group jobs in batches and automate the work as much as possible. If you have a computer, learn to use it to speed multiple mailings, do your accounting, or cut down on other tedious chores. If you are cutting out fabric for craft items, cut the material for numerous items at once, rather than one at a time.

Delegate some business chores to family members. Even 5- and 6-year-old children can stuff envelopes, fill bean bag frogs, or sort things by size or color. A 7- or 8-year-old could probably file, staple, sort, and make photocopies, too. Older children or a spouse can proofread your letters, enter data in a mailing list, or do any number of other tasks if you show them how.

Learn to do two things at once. If you have to do something boring or repetitious or that doesn't require much concentration, try to do something else at the same time. Here are just a few examples:

▶ Do your filing while you talk on the telephone. A telephone with a built-in speaker will not only let you move about the room while holding a conversation but it can also keep you from getting a stiff neck if you do a lot of calling.

▶ Hook up a portable phone to your business line and fold laundry or do the gardening while making routine business calls.

▶ Take a tape recorder or a Dictaphone with you when you travel any distance in the car, and dictate letters, outline client proposals, or develop ideas for your own marketing plans.

TIP A remote microphone hooked up to a standard tape recorder makes it easy to control the recorder without taking your hands off the steering wheel or eyes off the road.

▶ Use a car phone to make routine customer calls while you are stuck in traffic jams.

▶ Use the tape deck in your car radio to listen to instructional tapes or books on tape. It is a great way to acquire certain types of information and training you wouldn't have time to get any other way.

▶ If you use a computer and don't have a print spooler for your printer, get one. A print spooler is a program that lets you queue up and print one or more documents while you continue to work on the computer. Without a spooler, printing documents may prevent you from doing any work on your computer until the printer is finished.

- If you can't perform spool printing, let your computer print out work while you do other business or personal tasks.
- Relax and work at the same time. You can fold and stuff and label envelopes, insert business cards in folders, and do other rote tasks while watching your favorite TV shows at night.

Carry reading material or small jobs with you when you have an appointment away from your office. That way, if you get stuck waiting, you can accomplish something productive during the delay.

Devise standardized letters and product literature to send in response to routine situations. If you have the kind of business that requires you to send out capabilities statements or other promotional material, assemble packages in advance so you can just add a cover letter and mail out the material quickly instead of hunting through various file folders to find press releases, brochures, resume testimonials, or magazine articles.

Devise standard formats for computerized documents. That way, every time you have to type a letter you can open a file and with one or two keystrokes insert all the margin settings, type size and font specifications, the date (if your software has a function that automatically inserts the date), etc.

Learn to use the mail merge features of computer software to add addresses to mass mailings or to call up and insert boilerplate paragraphs if you frequently need to create documents containing certain standard information.

Schedule breaks or changes in your routine to eliminate fatigue. You can get far more work accomplished when you feel up and ready to tackle it than you can when you are overtired or burned out. If your work keeps you cooped up or isolated for long periods of time, force yourself to take a break. Schedule lunch with a friend, take the baby for a walk in the park, do the shopping daily, go for a walk or a swim, etc. You'll feel refreshed, get more done, and feel better about yourself, too.

Try to limit the number of hours you work each week. Productivity slips when you work long hours on a regular basis.

Learn to say no. Don't let the whole family give you their errands to do because you are home. If you are running a business from home, establish a schedule and stick to it just like you would have to if you were going out to work.

Be forewarned: your spouse, children, relatives, and friends who have been used to you always being willing to do anything they want on a moment's notice won't appreciate your change in attitude. But unless you set priorities and stick to them you won't stay in business very long.

Learn to cut a deal. If Johnny wants you to drive him to Billy's house on the other side of town (picking up three other friends on the way), make sure (1) he first finds someone else to commit to driving the crew home, and (2) he does a specific chore (dust or vacuum a room, clean a bathroom, etc.) before you take him to the friend's house. If hubby wants you to take his car in for inspection, have him do the grocery shopping on the way home from work. If your neighbor Bill asks you to type his resume as a favor, ask if he'll drop your books off at the library. And if your wife gets upset that you are typing Bill's resume when you *still* haven't put together the book-case she bought last month, have *her* type Bill's resume while you take care of the bookcase.

 If you have your children work for you, structure what you give them to do according to their age and abilities, and take the time to show them how to do jobs properly. In addition:

> ▸ Remember that a child is likely to take longer than you to accomplish a task, and plan accordingly.
>
> ▸ Break jobs up into pieces they can accomplish in reasonable amounts of time.
>
> ▸ Let them have their friends help with chores. Three or four 10-year-old girls can turn an occasional stint at stuffing and sealing a couple thousand envelopes into a game and get the work done in record speed. One child faced with stuffing and sealing a bunch of envelopes on her own is likely to think of all sorts of reasons she can't do it today.
>
> ▸ Consider whether you need to lower your standards for housework somewhat. If the living room looks neat and picked up, does it really matter whether or not Mark vacuumed under the sofa this afternoon?

Learn to make effective use of mail delivery services. You can order almost anything you need and have it delivered to your door these days. You can also have almost anything picked up at your door for shipment by any of a number of delivery

445

services, including the U.S. Postal Service. Shipping supplies such as envelopes and labels are often free, too. Airborne Express, for instance, picks up parcels for free and will even bill you if you have an established business. The post office will pick up parcels for a small fee, charging one fee whether they are picking up 1 package or 50 at your location.

Courier services can also be a tremendous time-saver for local or regional deliveries. You can avoid having to spend hours traveling to a client's location just to drop off a package. They offer same-day delivery service to many areas, and if your package is heavy, it may cost less to use a courier service than it would to ship the same package by overnight mail.

For information about the services of the post office, call (800) 222-1811, or write U.S. Postal Service, Marketing Communications, 6 Griffin Rd. N., Windsor, CT 06006-0833. Airborne Express can be reached by writing to Airborne Express Customer Assistance Center, P.O. Box 662, Seattle, WA 98111-9926. Check the Yellow Pages in your phone book for contact information for other delivery services.

27.
Expanding Your Business

What makes the difference between businesses that fail and those that grow and prosper?

Opportunity-chasers and dream-seekers will tell you it takes luck, timing, and plenty of money to succeed in business. But people who have built small businesses usually have a different story to tell.

Although luck and money are nothing to sneer at, people who have created viable businesses know that what it *really* takes to succeed is vision, not dreams; hard work and industry knowledge, not luck; careful planning and persistence, not untold wealth.

Combine those ingredients with a little bit of business smarts and a sincere desire to satisfy customer needs, and most businesses will thrive and grow in time. But with growth can come a whole new set of problems, often involving cash flow and personal satisfaction with the business.

Q **What's the best way to expand a successful business?**

The first thing to do is to stop and consider what you want to achieve. Often businesses that are profitable and satisfying when they are small turn into cash-gobbling, ulcer-producing monsters when the owner tries to expand the business without considering all the implications of growth.

Therefore, before plunging ahead, take a realistic took at your own motivations and preferences. Ask yourself:

- Why do I want to expand my business?
- How big do I want the business to grow? (What sales volume do I want to achieve? How much profit will that bring me?)
- How long will it take (realistically) to reach that goal?
- Am I willing and able to devote the time and money to reach that goal?
- Am I ready to hire employees, delegate authority, and manage the business instead of work at it? Or am I willing to hire a business manager to make decisions for me?
- Will what I have to do to expand the business make it worthwhile personally as well as financially?

Your answers to those questions will help you decide how fast and how big to grow your business and if you should expand at all.

If you are sure you are ready and willing to expand your business, take the time to update your business plan. Work out all the market data and financial information, being sure to consider these points:

- Which of your products or services are most profitable to sell?
- Could you sell more of them to the same customers?
- Are there related products that might sell well to your customers?
- How could you increase the number of customers for what you sell now?
- What will it cost to produce or buy more of what you sell?
- What will it cost to market more products or to market to a wider area?
- How many employees will you have to hire, and what will it cost you not only for salaries but also for benefits and for workers' compensation, employer's contribution to FICA, etc.?
- Will you need to rent office or warehouse space? Move to bigger quarters? Add on to the house?
- Will you need to borrow money or give up ownership to raise money to expand or to maintain cash flow? What will it cost to borrow the money?

Plug all your figures into your business plan, and then ask your accountant to look it over. His or her input can be valuable in helping you spot problems or opportunities you may not see.

Q **Is there any way to expand the business if I don't want to borrow a lot of money or give up ownership control?**

You can grow the business slowly out of your profits. It may take you longer, but if you aren't in a hurry and plan carefully it can work.

Q **Should I hire temporary workers to fill in during work overloads?**

If your business is not located in your home, using temporary workers is one good way to handle work overloads—one that many small and big companies alike find valuable. However, if your office is located in your home, you are likely to find it difficult or impossible to get temporary workers through an agency. Large agencies, for insurance reasons, generally make it a policy not to send temps to homebased businesses.

Q **Should I hire family or friends?**

A family business often turns out to be a satisfying team effort. While Mom may no longer be whipping up egg creams at the soda fountain as Pop sweeps the floor, the mom-and-pop shop is not dead. It's just moved home. In many cases Mom takes the orders while Pop produces the product, or Pop may do sales while Mom does customer support. Or Pop may bake cookies while Mom makes arrangements for packaging, shipping, and distribution.

And when it works it can be one of the most satisfying ways to run a business. But sometimes family or friends just don't make good employees or business partners. Sometimes they don't have the needed skills, and other times they just don't have the desire to work as hard at the job as you would like them to. Although it can be difficult to do, before hiring or agreeing to work with family or friends, evaluate their capabilities and attitudes using the same standards you would for anyone else. And if your spouse is the one you will be hiring, be sure you can do without his or her income from another job and that you can also pay for the health insurance that he or she will be giving up by quitting.

Q **How can I keep good employees when I find them?**

Treat your employees with respect and consideration, and pay them what they could expect to earn elsewhere. If you have an employee who is of crucial importance to your operation, consider offering him or her some kind of sweat equity deal, trading ownership in the company for his or her efforts in building the company. Your accountant should be able to help you work out an equitable arrangement.

Q **I lost my biggest customer. Now what do I do?**

Pick yourself up, brush off the dirt, and see what you have to do to get back in the race and stay there. Do the best you can to determine what caused the loss of the customer, but don't dwell on the loss. What you want to know is why you lost the customer and, what, if anything, you can do to prevent a similar problem from arising in the future.

If you lost the work because the customer is having cash flow problems or went out of business, consider whether other customers you have in the same industry might also go belly-up. Be realistic. Times change. Needs change. Industries change. The small business that stays in business is the one that looks to the future as well as the present. If an industry or the local economy is changing, the time to take steps to deal with the change is before the bottom falls out, not after.

Finally, try never to let one customer be the primary source of your company's income.

Q **Should I hire someone who's retired?**

There's no reason not to hire someone who is retired if the person wants to work. Along with the gray hair will come years and years of experience and often a work ethic that can be hard to find in younger employees.

Q **How do I keep employees from stealing my customers or ideas?**

If the possibility of an employee quitting to start a competing business is real, ask your attorney about drawing up a noncompete agreement that would be effective in your state, and then make sure all employees sign it. If your customer list is crucial, try to make sure only trusted employees have access to it and, if possible, that no one employee has access to all of the list.

Q **What if I have to fire someone?**

If you have to fire someone, try to let them know what the reason is, but don't let them talk you out of firing them. They'll always resent the fact you intended to fire them and could try to sabotage your business.

Q **Is there any way to avoid the high costs associated with hiring employees?**

If the work you need done doesn't have to be performed in your office, consider using a reliable independent contractor to do the work. The fee you pay the independent contractor would be deductible on your income taxes, but if the individual works from his or her own home using personal equipment and is free to offer services to other businesses, you can probably avoid having to pay payroll taxes. If you are the only business the individual works for, you might be considered an employer by the IRS, so ask your accountant for guidance if you have any doubt about the nature of the arrangements. You will also avoid the need to buy extra equipment and office furniture.

Another option is to subcontract out jobs to other businesses as the opportunity arises. You could subcontract out an entire job to one or more people (hire one person to write a product brochure and another to do the graphic design and layout) or subcontract out just part of it (you do the writing and hire someone else to do the design). In fact, if you find several reliable independent contractors you might be able to greatly expand the services you offer and the number of clients you can handle.

Q **How can I keep costs down as I grow my business?**

If you work at home, keep the business in the house as long as it is feasible to do so. If you need more space, see if there is a place within the house to expand. An attic or garage or part of the basement might give you the space you need to breathe until the business is making enough money to allow you to move into bigger quarters.

Whether you work at home or away from home, try to determine why you need more space, too. Is it to store files, books, equipment? If so, do you really need to save everything? And if you do, must you retain it in your office? Self-storage facilities might be able to hold what you don't need regularly and allow you to avoid moving to more expensive quarters.

If you do need more space, could you sublet office or warehouse space from another business? Could you rent warehouse space and use it for an office to cut costs? If you will be buying furniture or equipment, consider whether used items might be just as good as new for your purposes.

Another option if you need more space is to add on to your home or to buy a bigger house. If you can do neither, consider whether any relatives might have storage space in their home that you could use. Pay them rent for the space, and you get a business deduction and provide them with some extra income. If the rent you pay them is less than you'd pay for storage space or a larger office, you both benefit.

Q **Where can I get help if I run into problems I don't know how to handle?**

Small businesses today have a wealth of inexpensive or free resources available to them. The appendices in this book contain just a small sampling of the many places you can turn for information and help.

These organizations include the Small Business Administration (SBA), the Service Corps of Retired Executives (SCORE), Offices of Women and Minority Business, the small business specialist at the Department of Defense and other government offices, Small Business Development Centers (SBDCs), Small Business Investment Corporations (SBICs), and state, city, or county offices of economic development (see Appendix 1). Business and industrial associations, college and university business schools, adult education courses, and online information services can also help your business flourish.

In addition to these resources there is the one resource that will always be close at hand: you.

In the long run it will be *your* vision, *your* ingenuity, and *your* ability to learn from others, work with others, and even help others reach their goals that will carry you and your business into a prosperous future.

Afterword

You can find more answers to your business questions on my web site (http://www
.businessknowhow.com) and in my Business Know-How forum in the WorkPlace
Channel on America Online. (The AOL keyword to reach the forum is Business
Know-How.)

If you have a story to share or questions you'd like to see answered in future
books, please send e-mail to AnswerBook@businessknowhow.com, or write to me in
care of Attard Communications, Inc., P.O. Box 223, Centereach, NY 11720.

Appendix 1

KEY GOVERNMENT RESOURCES

SMALL BUSINESS ADMINISTRATION (SBA)

The U.S. Small Business Administration, established in 1953, provides financial, technical, and management assistance to help Americans start, run, and grow their businesses. With a portfolio of business loans, loan guarantees, and disaster loans worth more than $45 billion, SBA is the nation's largest single financial backer of small businesses. Last year, the SBA offered management and technical assistance to more than one million small business owners. The SBA also plays a major role in the government's disaster relief efforts by making low-interest recovery loans to both homeowners and businesses. The SBA has an extensive web site at http:// wwwsba.gov. You can find the local office in the federal government listings in your telephone directory.

SMALL BUSINESS DEVELOPMENT CENTERS (SBDC)

The U.S. Small Business Administration (SBA) administers the Small Business Development Center Program (SBDC) to provide management assistance to current and prospective small business owners. SBDCs offer one-stop assistance to small businesses by providing a wide variety of information and guidance in central and easily accessible branch locations.

The program is a cooperative effort of the private sector, the educational community, and federal, state, and local governments. It enhances economic development by providing small businesses with management and technical assistance.

There are hundreds of SBDC offices around the country. You can locate offices for your state on the SBA web site at http://www.sba.gov/gopher/local-information/small-business-development-centers. Or, call your nearest SBA office and ask for help locating an SBDC office.

SCORE (SERVICE CORPS OF RETIRED EXECUTIVES)

The SCORE Association is a national nonprofit association with 12,400 volunteer members and 389 chapters throughout the United States and its territories. SCORE is a resource partner with the U.S. Small Business Administration. You can locate SCORE offices from their web site at http://www.score.org.

OTHER AGENCIES

U.S. COPYRIGHT OFFICE

The U.S. Copyright office maintains U.S. copyright registrations. It also provides information about copyrights to the public. Forms and information about copyright law are available on its web site at http://lcweb.loc.gov/copyright.

THE INTERNAL REVENUE SERVICE (IRS)

In addition to collecting your taxes, the IRS is an excellent source of information about what you need to do to comply with federal tax laws. The agency publishes numerous guidelines written in plain English that will explain the rules you need to follow. The publications can be downloaded from the IRS web site at http://www.irs.ustreas.gov.

U.S. DEPARTMENT OF LABOR

The U.S. Department of Labor provides information on labor laws, employment trends, safety and health standards, and other matters of interest to small businesses. The office has an extensive web site at http://www.dol.gov.

U.S. PATENT AND TRADEMARK OFFICE (USPTO)

The USPTO is responsible for registering trademarks and patents. They provide free access to their databases of trademarks and patents through their web site at http://www.USPTO.gov. For additional information phone (800) 786-9199.

FEDERAL TRADE COMMISSION (FTC)

The Federal Trade Commission enforces a *variety* of federal antitrust and consumer protection laws. The FTC seeks to ensure that the nation's markets function competitively, and are vigorous, efficient, and free of undue restrictions. The FTC also works to enhance the smooth operation of the marketplace by eliminating acts or practices that are unfair or deceptive. Their web site contains numerous guidelines for consumers and businesses and is a good source of information about potential scams. It's located at http://www.ftc.gov. Phone (202) 326-2222.

Appendix 2

250 BUSINESS IDEAS

The ideas below are presented to get you thinking about the many different types of businesses you might start. The list includes businesses that could be homebased and businesses that would not normally be run from the home. It also includes products or services that might be incorporated as additional profit centers into existing businesses. If you don't see anything in this list that interests you, browse through the Yellow Pages of your phone book, the classifieds, and the "back of the book" advertising in local newspapers and trade magazines and other specialty publications.

AUTOMOTIVE

auto detailing

body shop

car wash

custom painting/pinstriping

quick oil change and lube

repair shop

window tinting

used-car dealer

BUILDING/HOME SERVICES

carpet cleaning

chimney sweeping

closet organizing

house and office cleaning service

inspection service

landscaping

lawn maintenance

moving company

tree spraying

lawn care

upholstery/drapery cleaning

water damage cleanup

yard cleanup services

BUSINESS SERVICE

advertising agency

answering service/voice mail service

billing

bookkeeping

collection agency

computer software training

concierge services

coupon mailer service

database entry and maintenance

desktop publishing/design

desktop publishing/typesetting

employment agency

executive recruiting service

fax broadcast service

freight broker service

gift basket sales

job shop

legal transcription

mailbox service

mailing (lettershop) services

mailing list maintenance

market research consultant

medical billing

medical transcription

meeting planner service

newsletter publishing

promotional product sales

public relations agency

resume printing

resume typesetting

resume writing

secretarial services

sign shop

temporary employment agency

translation

word processing

COMPUTER AND INTERNET-RELATED

computer programming

computer repair

computer support services

computer systems analyst

computer training

content provider

home computer setup

interactive advertising agency

Internet banner creation

Internet banner management services

Internet consultant

Internet database programmer

Internet employment agency

Internet marketing service

Internet radio producer

Internet retailer

multimedia producer
network installation
online community management
web artist

web designer
web hosting service
web page maintenance

CONSULTING

audiovisual consultant
broadcast consultant
cultural diversity consultant
drug-free workplace
human resources consultant

pollution control consultant
recycling consultant
telecommuting consultant
time-management consultant
toxic waste consultant

CREATIVE

artist
cartoonist
fashion designer
photographer

writer (see "Writing and Editorial" below)
songwriter/composer
bandleader
web design

CRAFTS

computer crafts
craft instructor
custom framing
decorative painting
decorative wood accessories

doll making
jewelry design
pattern design
pottery design

ENVIRONMENT

asbestos inspection
hazardous waste control

hazardous waste inspection
radon testing

FOOD

bed and breakfast inn

candy distributor

catering service

convenience store

delicatessen

delivery services

gourmet café

gourmet lunches

grocery shopping service

meal delivery service

personal chef

pizza parlor

specialty cookies

FOREIGN TRADE

import-export agent

INFORMATION

information broker

online newsletters

private investigator

self-improvement seminars

seminar promoting

web site (see "Computers and Internet")

MAIL AND SHIPPING

courier service

lettershop (fold, stuff, meter, prepare mail for
   bulk mailings)

mail list broker

mail list rental

packaging store

MISCELLANEOUS

annual plants sales

auctioneer

clown

disc jockey

farm stand

home carpentry

home inspection

home painting

laundromat

piano tuner

special events promotions

tax preparation

TV producer

vending machine route

videocassette rental and delivery
   service

MOBILE SERVICES

ambulette transportation to doctors' offices
car detailing
mobile car wash

pet grooming
traveling auto repair

PERSONAL SERVICE

astrologer
airport taxi
balloon delivery service
beautician
child care
companion to sick
computer dating service
day care for elderly
dry cleaning pickup and delivery
financial planner
fitness trainer
gift shopping
hair salon

interior design
limousine service
medical claims processing
nursing service
personal coach
pool cleaning
pool parlor
referral services
shopping service
singing telegram service
tailor
wedding planning

PETS

mobile pet grooming service
pet boarding
pet shop

pet sitting
pet supply mail order

PROFESSIONAL

accountant
anesthesiologist
attorney (general practice)
dentist
doctor
financial manager
franchise attorney

insurance broker
intellectual property attorney
investment banker
orthodontist
physical therapist
sports medicine clinic
veterinarian

PUBLISHING

booklet publisher
local small business directories
newsletter publisher

(also see "Writing and Editorial" and "Computer and Internet")

RENTAL

car rental
equipment rental

prom and wedding gown rental
tuxedo rental

REPAIR

appliance repair
computer repair service
electrician
heating and air conditioning repair

office machine repair
oil burner repair
plumber
TV and VCR repair

RETAIL

antiques dealer
collectibles dealer
consignment shop
fashion boutique
flea market vendor
florist

health food
jewelry
motorcycle and lawnmower parts
sports merchandise
T-shirts

SALES

advertising specialties
business brokerage
business machines
candles
computers
custom T-shirts
direct mail catalog sales
discount phone services

health supplements
household goods
independent distributor
independent sales representative
insurance
makeup
natural products
pet supply mail order

print broker

real estate broker

recharged laser cartridges

shareware sales

telecommunications services

telemarketing company

TEACHING/INSTRUCTIONS

business writing

computers for kids

crafts

creative writing

dance

drawing/painting

driving school

horseback riding

music

painting

sewing

skiing

spreadsheets

swimming/diving

tennis

tutoring

word processing

WRITING AND EDITORIAL

book reviewer

computer hardware or software reviewer

copy editor

copywriter

financial writer

health writer

nonfiction feature writer

novelist

proofreader

publicist

science writer

script writer for TV

script writer for audiovisual productions

technical writer

web site writer (see "Computer and
    Internet")

Appendix 3

SUGGESTED RETENTION SCHEDULE
FOR BUSINESS RECORDS*

The retention schedule below was compiled by Fellowes Manufacturing Company and is based on a combination of record storage experts' recommendations and a survey of actual business practices. The list is reprinted courtesy of the Fellowes Manufacturing Company.

The schedule is presented here as a general guideline only. It may have to be adapted to meet legal requirements of your state and/or of any federal agency regulations** with which your business must comply. Be sure to check with appropriate state and federal authorities or with your CPA for any specifics for your business. In addition, there may be a very good reason to keep records longer than legally required for historical reference purposes.

 KEY The letter *P* means Permanently, *O* stands for Optional; otherwise figures represent the suggested number of years for retaining the records.

*Fellowes Manufacturing Company, © 1986. Reprinted with permission of Fellowes Manufacturing Company.
**For retention requirements established by federal laws and regulations, see the current "Guide to Record Retention Requirements" published annually in the Federal Register, which can be obtained at nominal cost from the Superintendent of Documents, U.S. Government Printing Office, Washington, DC 20402.

ACCOUNTING AND FISCAL RECORDS

Accounts, charged off	7
Accounts payable ledger	P
Accounts receivable	10
Accounts receivable ledger	10
Balance sheets	5
Bank deposit record	6
Bank reconcilement papers	8
Bank statements	8
Bills collectible	7
Bills of sale of registered bonds	3
Bill stubs	7
Bonds canceled	3
Bonds registered	P
Bonds, sales or transfer	15
Budget work sheets	3
Building permits	20
Capital stock bills of sales	P
Capital stock certificates	P
Capital stock ledger	P
Capital stock transfer records	P
Cash books	25
Cash receipts and disbursement records	10
Cash sales slips	3
Charge slips	10
Check records	7
Check register	10
Checks, dividend	10
Checks, expense	10
Checks, paid and canceled	9
Checks, payroll	7
Checks, voucher	6
Checks, warrants	P
Correspondence, accounting	5
Correspondence, credit and collection	7
Cost account records	7
Customer ledger	P
Donations	7
Drafts paid	8
Earnings register	3
Entertainment, gifts and gratuities	3
Estimates, projections	7
Expense reports, departmental	5
Expense reports, employees	5
Financial statements, certified	P
Financial statements, periodic	P
Fixed capital records	P
General cash book	25
General journal	10
General journal supporting papers	P
General ledger	P
Notes, canceled	10
Note ledgers	P
Payroll register	7
Petty cash records	3
Plant ledger	P
Profit and loss statements	P
Property asset summary	10
Royalty ledger	P
Salesperson commission reports	3
Stock ledger	P
Tabulating cards and magnetic tape	1
Traveling auditor reports	15
Trial balance, accounts receivable	3
Trial balance sheets	P
Uncollectible accounts	7
Work papers, rough	2

ADMINISTRATIVE

Audit reports, internal	10
Audit reports, public and government	P
Audit work papers, internal	6
Classified documents; control, inventories, reports	5
Correspondence, accounting	5
Correspondence, advertising	3
Correspondence, credit and collection	7
Correspondence, engineering and technical	10
Correspondence, general	3
Correspondence, personal	6
Correspondence, sales and service	3
Correspondence, tax	20
Correspondence, traffic	6
Forms control	5
Inventory cards	3
Inventory, plant records	P
Organized charts	P
Requisitions	3
Research reports	20
System and procedure records	P
Telegram and cable copies	3
Telephone records	P

ADVERTISING

Activity reports, media schedules	5
Contracts	10
Contracts, advertising	7
Correspondence	5
Drawings and artwork	P
Estimates	2
House organs	P
Market data and surveys	5
Samples, displays, labels, etc.	P
Tear sheets	3

CORPORATE

Annual reports	P
Authority to issue securities	P
Authorization and appropriations for expenditures	3
Bonds, surety	10
Capital stock certificates	P
Capital stock ledger	P
Capital stock transfer records	P
Charters, constitution, bylaws, and amendments	P
Contracts, employee	P
Contracts, government	P
Contracts, labor union	P
Contract, vendor	10
Dividend checks	10
Easements	P
Election ballots	20
Election records, corporate	10
General cashbooks, treasurers', auditors'	25
Incorporation records and certificates	P
Licenses, federal, state, local	P
Permits to do business	P
Records of mergers, consolidations, acquisitions, dissolutions, and reorganizations	P

Reports to Securities and Exchange
Commission   P

Stock applications for issuance   P

Stock certificates, canceled   10

Stock, stock transfer and stockholders' records   P

Stockholder minute books,
resolutions   P

Stockholder proxies   10

Stockholder reports   P

Voter proxies   15

EXECUTIVE

Correspondence   2

Policy statements, directives   P

Projects, ideas, notes   P

Research reports   20

Speeches, publications   10

INSURANCE

Accident reports   11

Appraisals   P

Claims, automobile   10

Claims, group life and hospital   4

Claims, loss or damage in transit   7

Claims, plant   P

Claims, workers' compensation   10

Expired policy, accident   7

Expired policy, fidelity   7

Expired policy, fire   6

Expired policy, group   6

Expired policy, hospital   6

Expired policy, inspection
certificates   7

Expired policy, liability   7

Expired policy, life   7

Expired policy, marine   7

Expired policy, property   8

Expired policy, surety   10

Expired policy, workers'
compensation   10

LEGAL

Affidavits   10

Charters   P

Claims and litigation of torts and
breach of contract   P

Copyrights   P

Patents and related data   P

Trademarks   P

MANUFACTURING

Authorities for sale of scrap   3

Bills of material   5

Blueprints   30

Correspondence, engineering and
technical   10

Correspondence, production   2

Credit memoranda   5

Credit ratings and classifications   2

Drafting records   8

Drawings and tracings, original   P

Inspection records   5

Inventory records   16

Invoice copies   5

Invoices, received   7

Job records   10

Journals   10

Ledgers   P

Operating reports   10

Order register	6
Production reports	6
Quality control reports	5
Receipts, delivery	3
Reliability records	P
Specifications, customer	P
Store issue records	3
Time and motion studies	P
Tool control	5
Work orders	5

PERSONNEL

Accident reports, injury claims, settlements	11
Applications, changes, terminations	3
Attendance records	6
Clock records	4
Correspondence	6
Daily time reports	5
Disability and sick benefits records	8
Earnings records	P
Employee service records	P
Employee contracts	7
Fidelity bonds	3
File, individual employee, after separation	3
Garnishments	7
Health and Safety bulletins	4
Injury frequency charts	10
Insurance records: group, employee	6
Medical folders, employee	5
Paychecks	P
Payroll records, after termination	P
Pension plan	P
Pension plan, applications	P
Pension plan, claims	P

Pension plan, correspondence	P
Rating cards	5
Salary and rate changes	10
Salespeople auto records	2
Salespeople performance records	P
Salespeople expense accounts	4
Time cards	5
Time tickets	5
Time tickets, receipted	5
Training manuals	P
Union (collective bargaining) agreements after termination	6
Withholding exemption certificates after termination	8
Workers' compensation reports	10

PLANT AND PROPERTY

Appraisals	P
Damage reports	7
Deeds, titles	P
Depreciation schedules	3
Inventory records	6
Leases	6
Maintenance and repair, buildings	10
Maintenance and repair, machinery	5
Plans and specifications	P
Plant account cards, equipment records, historical folders	P
Purchase, lease records	1
Sales	7
Space allocation records	2
Taxes	P
Water rights	P

PURCHASING

Acknowledgments	3
Bids, awards	3
Contracts	5
Correspondence	5
Exception notices	6
Purchase orders	3
Purchase requisitions	1
Quotations	3
Receiving reports	6
Receiving slips	4
Vendors' contracts	P

SALES AND MARKETING

Claims (loss or damage)	5
Complaints	5
Contract progress reports	3
Contracts, customers	6
Contracts, representatives, agents, distributors, etc.	3
Correspondence	3
Discount rates	5
Guarantees, warranties	6
Invoices, copies	6
Invoices, received	7
Mailing and prospect lists	2
Market research studies and analysis	P
Market surveys	5
Orders acknowledgment	4
Orders filled	8
Price lists	P
Shipping notices and reports	4
Tax-exempt sales	5

TAXATION

Agent's reports	P
Annuity or deferred payment plan	P
Correspondence	20
Depreciation schedules	3
Dividend register	P
Employee withholding certificates (after termination)	8
Exemption status	P
Excise reports	5
Inventory reports	16
Real estate	15
Sales and use	P
Social Security	P
Tax bills and statements	P
Tax returns and working papers	P

TRAFFIC

Aircraft operating and maintenance	10
Bills of lading	3
Delivery of reports	3
Employee travel	1
Export declarations	4
Freight bills	5
Freight claims	5
Leases	6
Manifests	1
Receiving documents	5
Routing records	1
Shipping instructions	6
Shipping tickets	6
Title papers	P
Tonnage summaries	P
Tracer reports	P
Vehicle operation and maintenance	4

Appendix 4

SBIR OFFICES

The Office of Technology strengthens and expands the competitiveness of small high-technology research and development businesses in the federal marketplace. They coordinate the Small Business Innovative Research (SBIR) program and the Small Business Technology Transfer Research program (STTR) and also assist in achieving the commercialization of the results of both the federal research and development programs mandated by the Small Business Innovation Development Act of 1982 and the Small Business Research and Development Enhancement Act of 1992.

SBIR REPRESENTATIVES OF THE PARTICIPATING FEDERAL AGENCIES

U.S. DEPARTMENT OF AGRICULTURE

Charles Cleland, Ph.D., Director, SBIR Program
United States Department of Agriculture
Cooperative State Research, Education &
  Extension Service
Aerospace Bldg., 1400 Independence Avenue
  SW, Stop 2243—Room 328
Washington, DC 20250-2243
Phone: (202) 401-4002
Fax: (202) 401-6070
E-mail: CCleland@reeusda.gov

Ruth Lange, Assistant Program Director
U.S. Department of Agriculture
Cooperative State Research, Education &
  Extension Service

Aerospace Bldg., 1400 Independence Avenue
  SW, Stop 2243—Room 328
Washington, DC 20250-2243
Phone: (202) 401-1839
Fax: (202) 401-6070
E-mail: rlange@reeusda.gov

DEPARTMENT OF COMMERCE

Joseph Bishop, Ph.D., Program Manager
U.S. Department of Commerce
Office of Research and Technology
  Applications
1315 East-West Hwy., SSMC3, Room 11464
Silver Spring, MD 20910
Phone: (301) 713-3565

Fax: (301) 713-4100
E-mail: Joseph.Bishop@NOAA.GOV

T.J. Garcia, Director, Office of Small and Disadvantaged Business Utilization
U.S. Department of Commerce
14th and Constitution Avenue NW, HCHB, Room 6411
Washington, DC 20230
Phone: (202) 482-1472
Fax: (202) 482-0501
E-mail: Tjgarcia.doc.gov

Norman Taylor, Chief, SBIR Program Office
U.S. Department of Commerce
North Campus, 820 West Diamond Avenue, Building 820, Room 306
Gaithersburg, MD 20899-0001
Phone: (301) 975-4517
Fax: (301) 548-0624
E-mail: Norman.Taylor@NIST.GOV

Kelly Brickell, Assistant Program Manager, SBIR
SBIR Program Office, Department of Commerce
1315 East-West Hwy., Room 11464
Silver Spring, MD 20910
Phone: (301) 713-3565
Fax: (301) 713-4100
E-mail: Kelly.brickell@noaa.gov

DEPARTMENT OF DEFENSE

Jon Baron, DOD SBIR/STTR Program Manager
Office of Under Secretary of Defense, U.S. Department of Defense

1777 North Kent Street, Suite 9100
Arlington, VA 22209
Phone: (800) 382-4634
Fax: (703) 588-7561
E-mail: Baronj@acq.osd.mil

Ken Bannister, Ph.D., SBIR Program Manager
U.S. Army Research Office—Washington
Attn: AMXRO-W-SBIR
5001 Eisenhower Ave., Suite 8N31
Alexandria, VA 22333-0001
Phone: (703) 617-7425
Fax: (703) 617-8274
E-mail: aro-sbir@hqamc.army.mil

Kenneth L. Jones, Technology Integration Manager
U. S. Army
PO Box 12211
Research Triangle Park, NC 27709-2211
Phone: (919) 549-4200
Fax: (919) 549-4248
E-mail: Jones@aro-emh1.army.mil

Stephen J. Guilfoos, SBIR Program Manager
U.S. Air Force
1864 4th Street, Suite 1
Wright-Patterson AFB, OH 45433-7131
Phone: (937) 656-9021 or (800) 222-0336
Fax: (937) 255-2329
E-mail: Stephen.guilfoos@afrl.af.mil

Connie Jacobs, SBIR Program Manager
Defense Advanced Research Projects Agency
3701 North Fairfax Drive
Arlington, VA 22203-1714
Phone: (703) 526-4162

Fax: (703) 841-5158

E-mail: cjacobs@darpa.mil

Bill Burks, AM/SBIR

Defense Nuclear Agency

6801 Telegraph Road

Alexandria, VA 22310-3398

Phone: (703) 325-5021

Fax: (703) 325-2955

E-mail: Burks@HQ.DSWA.MIL

Thomas J. (Jeff) Bond III, BMDO SBIR
   Program Manager

Ballistic Missile Defense Organization

1725 Jefferson Davis Hwy., Suite 809

Arlington, VA 22202

Phone: (703) 604-3538

Fax: (703) 604-3956

E-mail: jeffbond@bmdo.osd.mil

Karen L. Pera, SADBU—SBIR Program
   Coordinator

U.S. Special Operations Command

7701 Tampa Point Blvd., SOAL-KS

MacDill AFB, FL 33621-5323

Phone: (813) 840-5514

Fax: (813) 840-5481

E-mail: Perak@socom.mil

Vincent Schaper, Navy SBIR Program Manager

Office of Naval Research

800 N. Quincy Street

BCT 1, Room 633

Arlington, VA 22217-5660

Phone: (703) 696-8528

Fax: (703) 696-4884

E-mail: Schapev@onr.navy.mil

John Williams, Deputy, Navy SBIR/STTR
   Program Manager

Office of Naval Research

800 N. Quincy Street

BCT #1, Room 633

Arlington, VA 22217

Phone: (703) 696-0342

Fax: (703) 696-4884

E-mail: Williajr@onr.navy.mil

Diane Baregas, Public Affairs Specialist

Office of Naval Research

800 N. Quincy Street, Room 915

Arlington, VA 22217

Phone: (703) 696-2868

E-mail: Banegs@onr.navy.mil

DEPARTMENT OF EDUCATION

Lee Eiden, SBIR Program Coordinator

U.S. Department of Education

555 New Jersey Avenue NW, Room 508 D

Washington, DC 20208

Phone: (202) 219-2004

Fax: (202) 219-1407

E-mail: Lee_Eiden@ed.gov

DEPARTMENT OF ENERGY

Robert E. Berger, Ph.D., SBIR/STTR Program
   Manager

U.S. Department of Energy, SC-32

19901 Germantown Road

Germantown, MD 20874-1290

Phone: (301) 903-3054

Fax: (301) 903-5488

E-mail: Robert.Berger@science.doe.gov

David E. Koegel, *Program Manager*
Office of Science, SC-32
19901 Germantown Road
Germantown, MD 20874
Phone: (301) 903-3159
Fax: (301) 903-6067
E-mail: David.Koegel@science.doe.gov

Julie Scott, *Support Specialist, SBIR/STTR*
Department of Energy, SC-32
19901 Germantown Road
Germantown, MD 20874-1290
Phone: (301) 903-0569
Fax: (301) 903-5488
E-mail: Julie.scott@science.doe.gov

Arlene M. De Blanc, J.D.
Department of Energy, SC-32
19901 Germantown Road
Germantown, MD 20874-1290
Phone: (301) 903-3199
Fax: (301) 903-5488
E-mail: arlene.deblanc@science.doe.gov

DEPARTMENT OF HEALTH AND HUMAN SERVICES

Verl Zanders, *SBIR Program Manager*
U.S. Department of Health and Human
  Services
200 Independence Avenue SW, HHH
  Building, Room 517D
Washington, DC 20201
Phone: (202) 690-7300
Fax: (202) 260-4872
E-mail: vzanders@os.dhhs.gov

Joanne Goodnight, *NIH SBIR/STTR Programs*
  Coordinator
National Institutes of Health
6701 Rockledge Drive
Rockledge Two, Room 6186, MSC 7910
Bethesda, MD 20892-7910
Phone: (301) 435-2688
Fax: (301) 480-0146
E-mail: Jg128w@nih.gov

DEPARTMENT OF TRANSPORTATION

Joseph D. Henebury, *SBIR Program Director*
  DTS-22
U.S. Department of Transportation
55 Broadway, Kendall Square
Cambridge, MA 02142-1093
Phone: (617) 494-2051 or (617) 494-2712
Fax: (617) 494-2497 or (617) 494-2370
E-mail: Henebury@volpe.dot.gov

ENVIRONMENTAL PROTECTION AGENCY

James Gallup, *SBIR Program Manager*
U.S. Environmental Protection Agency
401 M Street SW
Washington, DC 20460
Phone: ((202) 564-6823
Fax: (202) 564-2447
E-mail: Gallup.James@epamail.epa.gov

Marshall Dick
Office of Research and Development, EPA
401 M Street SW
Washington, DC 20460

Phone: (202) 564-6828
Fax: (202) 564-2447
E-mail: Dick.marshall@epamail.epa.gov

Michael Bender, Environmental Engineer/Project
Officer
EPA
401 M Street SW
Washington, DC 20460
Phone: (202) 564-6829
Fax: (202) 564-2446
E-mail: Bender.michael@epa.gov

NASA

Robert L. Norwood, Ph.D., Director,
Commercial Development
National Aeronautics and Space
Administration
300 E Street SW, Code XC
Washington, DC 20546-0001
Phone: (202) 358-2320
Fax: (202) 358-3878

Robert W. Nelson, Deputy Program Manager,
SBIR/STTR
NASA Program Management Office
Goddard Space Flight Center, Code 710
Greenbelt, MD 20771
Phone: (301) 286-0077
Fax: (301) 286-0321
E-mail: Robert.w.nelson@gsfc.nasa.gov

Paul Mexcur, Program Manager, SBIR/STTR
Technology Program Management Office,
Code 710.3

Goddard Space Flight Center
Greenbelt, MD 20771
Phone: (301) 286-8888
Fax: (301) 286-0321
E-mail: Paul.Mexcur@gsfc.nasa.gov

Carl Ray, Executive Director Commercial
Technology Program, SBIR/STTR
NASA
300 E Street SW, Code XC
Washington, DC 20546-0001
Phone: (202) 358-4652
Fax: (202) 358-3878
E-mail: CRAY@.HQ.NASA.GOV

Robert W. Nelson, Deputy Program Manager,
SBIR/STTR
Technology Program Management Office
Goddard Space Flight Center, Code 705
Greenbelt, MD 20771
Phone: (301) 286-0077
Fax: (301) 286-0321
E-mail: Robert.W.Nelson@gsfc.nasa.gov

Dr. James E. Kalshoven, Jr., SBIR Technical
Manager
Goddard Space Flight Center, Code 705,
Building 11
Greenbelt, MD 20771
Phone: (301) 286-8506
Fax: (301) 286-0321
E-mail: Kalshoven@gsfc.nasa.gov

NATIONAL SCIENCE FOUNDATION

U.S. National Science Foundation
4201 Wilson Blvd., Room 590
Arlington, VA 22230
Kesh S. Narayanan, Ph.D., Director Industrial
  Innovation Programs
Phone: (703) 306-1390
Fax: (703) 306-0337
E-mail: Knarayan@nsf.gov

Jean Bonney, SBIR Program Manager
Phone: (703) 306-1391 ext. 5250
Fax: (703) 306-0337
E-mail: jbonney@nsf.gov

Cynthia J. Ekstein, SBIR Program Manager
Phone: (703) 306-1390 ext. 5256
Fax: (703) 306-0298
E-mail: Cekstein@nsf.gov

Darryl Gorman, SBIR Program
  Coordinator/Manager
Phone: (703) 306-1390
Fax: (703) 306-0337
E-mail: dgorman@nsf.gov

Sara B. Nerlove, Ph.D., SBIR Program
  Manager
Phone: (703) 306-1395 ext. 5247
Fax: (703) 306-0337
E-mail: snerlove@nsf.gov

Bruce K. Hamilton, Ph.D., SBIR Biotechnology
  Program Manager
Phone: (703) 306-1391 ext. 5254
Fax: (703) 306-0337
E-mail: Bhamilton@nsf.gov

Deborah Crawford, SBIR Program Manager
Phone: (703) 306-1391
Fax: (703) 306-0337
E-mail: Dcrawford@nsf.gov

Ritchie Coryell, SBIR Program Director
Phone: (703) 306-1391
Fax: (703) 306-0337
E-mail: Rcoryell@nsf.gov

U.S. SMALL BUSINESS ADMINISTRATION

Office of Technology
409 3rd Street SW, Mail Code: 6470
Washington, DC 20416
Phone: (202) 205-6450
Fax: (202) 205-7754
Daniel O. Hill, Assistant Administrator
E-mail: Daniel.Hill@sba.gov

Arthur Collins, Deputy Assistant Administrator
E-mail: Arthur.Collins@sba.gov

Appendix 5

STATES WITH FRANCHISE AND/OR BUSINESS OPPORTUNITY LAWS

If you live in a state with franchise or business opportunity laws, take the time to contact the appropriate state office and ask whether the franchise or opportunity you are planning to purchase is registered in the state. The states with franchise opportunity laws are as follows:

CALIFORNIA (*filing required*)

Franchise Division
Department of Corporations
1115 11th Street
Sacramento, CA 95814
(916) 445-7205

HAWAII (*filing required*)

Franchise & Securities Division
State Department of Commerce
PO Box 40
Honolulu, HI 96813
(808) 586-2722

ILLINOIS (*filing required*)

Franchise Division
Office of Attorney General
500 South Second Street
Springfield, IL 62706
(217) 782-4465

INDIANA (*filing required*)

Franchise Division
Office of Secretary of State
One N. Capitol Street, Suite 560
Indianapolis, IN 46204
(317) 232-6576

MARYLAND (*filing required*)

Franchise Office
Division of Securities
200 St. Paul Place, 20th Fl.
Baltimore, MD 21202
(410) 576-6360

MICHIGAN (*only notice required*)

Antitrust and Franchise Unit
Office of Attorney General
670 Law Building
Lansing, MI 48913
(517) 373-7117

MINNESOTA (*filing required*)

Franchise Division
Department of Commerce
133 East Seventh Street
St. Paul, MN 55101
(651) 296-6328

NEW YORK (*filing required*)

Franchise & Securities Division
State Department of Law
120 Broadway, 23rd Fl.
New York, NY 10271
(212) 416-8211

NORTH DAKOTA (*filing required*)

Franchise Division
Office of Securities Commission
600 East Boulevard, 5th Fl.
Bismarck, ND 58505
(701) 328-2910

OREGON (*no filing required*)

Corporate Securities Section
Dept. of Insurance & Finance
Labor & Industries Building
Salem, OR 97310
(503) 378-4387

RHODE ISLAND (*filing required*)

Franchise Office
Division of Securities
233 Richmond Street, Suite 232
Providence, RI 02903
(401) 277-3048

SOUTH DAKOTA (*filing required*)

Franchise Office
Division of Securities
910 E. Sioux Avenue
Pierre, SD 57501
(605) 773-4013

VIRGINIA (*filing required*)

Franchise Office
State Corporation Commission
1300 E. Main Street
Richmond, VA 23219
(804) 371-9276

WASHINGTON (*filing required*)

Department of Financial Institutions
Securities Division
PO Box 9033

Olympia, WA 98507-9033

Phone: (360) 902-8760

Fax: (360) 586-5068

http://www.wa.gov/dfi/securities

WISCONSIN (*filing required*)

Wisconsin Securities Commission

Franchise Office

PO Box 1768

Madison, WI 53701

Phone: (608) 266-3364

http://www.wdfi.org

STATES WITH BUSINESS OPPORTUNITY LAWS

CALIFORNIA (*filing required*)

Attorney General's Office

Consumer Law Section

1515 "K" Street

Sacramento, CA 92101

(916) 445-9555

CONNECTICUT (*filing required*)

Department of Banking

Securities Division

44 Capitol Avenue

Hartford, CT 06106

(203) 566-4560 ext. 8322

FLORIDA (*filing required*)

Department of Agriculture & Consumer
  Services

Mayo Building, Room 110

Tallahassee, FL 32301

(904) 488-2221, (800) 342-2176 (in-state
  only)

GEORGIA (*no filing required*)

Office of Consumer Affairs

Martin Luther King Drive, No. 2

Plaza Level, East Tower

Atlanta, GA 30334

(404) 656-3790

ILLINOIS (*filing required*)

Illinois Securities Department

520 S. Second Street, Suite 200

Springfield, IL 62701

(217) 782-2256

INDIANA (*filing required*)

Attorney General's Office

Consumer Protection Division

219 State House

Indianapolis, IN 46204

(317) 232-6331

IOWA (*filing required*)

Securities Bureau
Lucas State Office Building, 2nd Fl.
Des Moines, IA 50319
(515) 281-4441

KENTUCKY (*filing required*)

Attorney General's Office
Consumer Protection Division
209 St. Clair
Frankfort, KY 40601
(502) 573-2200

LOUISIANA (*bond filing required*)

Office of the Attorney General
Consumer Protection Division
2610-A Woodale Blvd.
Baton Rouge, LA 70804
(504) 342-7900

MAINE (*filing required*)

Banking Bureau
Securities Division
State House, Station 121
Augusta, ME 04333
(207) 624-8551

MARYLAND (*filing required*)

Attorney General's Office
Securities Division
200 St. Paul Place, 20th Fl.
Baltimore, MD 21202
(301) 576-6360

MICHIGAN (*notice required*)

Department of the Attorney General
Consumer Protection Division
670 Law Building
Lansing, MI 48913
(517) 373-7117

MINNESOTA (*filing required*)

Department of Commerce
Registration Division
133 East 7th Street
St. Paul, MN 55101
(651) 296-6328

NEBRASKA (*filing required*)

Dept. of Banking & Finance
PO Box 95006
Lincoln, NE 68509
(402) 471-2171 or (402) 471-3445

NEW HAMPSHIRE (*filing required*)

Attorney General's Office
Consumer Protection Division
State House Annex
Concord, NH 03301
(603) 271-3641

NORTH CAROLINA (*filing required*)

Department of Justice
Consumer Protection Division
PO Box 629
Raleigh, NC 27602
(919) 733-3924

OHIO (*no filing required*)

Attorney General's Office
Consumer Fraud & Crime Section
30 East Broad Street, 25th Fl.
Columbus, OH 43266-0410
(614) 466-8831, (800) 282-0515 (in-state only)

OKLAHOMA (*filing required*)

Oklahoma Department of Securities
First National Center
120 N. Robinson, Suite 860
Oklahoma City, OK 73102
Phone: (405) 280-7700
Fax: (405) 280-7742
http://www.oklaosf.state.ok.us/~osc

SOUTH CAROLINA (*filing required*)

Secretary of State's Office
PO Box 11350
Columbia, SC 29211
(803) 734-2169

SOUTH DAKOTA (*filing required*)

Division of Securities
910 E. Sioux Avenue
Pierre, SD 57501
(605) 773-4013

TEXAS (*filing required*)

Secretary of State's Office
Statutory Documents Section
PO Box 13563
Austin, TX 78711
(512) 475-1769

UTAH (*filing required*)

Department of Commerce
Consumer Protection Division
160 East 300 South
Salt Lake City, UT 84111
(801) 530-6601

VIRGINIA (*no filing required*)

Consumer Affairs Office
101 North 8th Street
Richmond, VA 23219
(804) 786-0594, (800) 451-1525 (in-state
  only)

WASHINGTON (*filing required*)

Department of Financial Institutions
Securities Division
PO Box 9033
Olympia, WA 98507-9033
(206) 753-6928

Appendix 6

ASSOCIATIONS

There are thousands of associations and organizations that are of potential interest to businessowners. The list below is just a small sampling. You can locate many more industry associations from a searchable association directory available on the Business Know-How web site (http://www.businessknowhow.com). Local newspapers and local resources such as SCORE or a Small Business Development Center can help you locate associations in your area that might be beneficial to join.

411now.com Business Association
10400 Griffin Road, Suite 101
Cooper City, Fl 33328
Phone: (954) 252-9177
Fax: (954) 252-0279
http://www.411now.com

Advertising Mail Marketing Association
  (AMMA)
1901 N. Fort Myer Drive, Suite 401
Arlington, VA 22209-1609
Phone: (703) 524-0096

Fax: (703) 524-1871
http://www.amma.org

American Arbitration Association
140 West 51st Street
New York, NY 10020-1203
Phone: (800) 778-7879
http://www.adr.org

American Association of Franchisees & Dealers
PO Box 81887
San Diego, CA 92138-1887

Phone: (800) 733-9858
Fax: (619) 209-3777
http://www.aafd.org

American Association of Hispanic CPAs
    (AAHCPA)
100 N. Main Street, Suite 406
San Antonio, TX 78205
Phone: (203) 255-7003
Fax: (203) 259-2872
http://www.aahcpa.org/

American Association of Home Based
    Businesses
PO Box 10023
Rockville, MD 20849
Phone: (800) 447-9710
Fax: (301) 963-7042
http://www.aahbb.org

American Association of Legal Nurse
    Consultants (AALNC)
4700 W. Lake Ave.
Glenview, IL 60025
Phone: (847) 402-2562
Fax: (847) 375-6313
http://www.aalnc.org

American Association of Medical Assistants
20 N. Wacker Drive, #1575
Chicago, IL 60606
Phone: (312) 899-1500
http://www.aama-ntl.org/

American Association of Medical
    Transcriptionists
PO Box 576187

Modesto, CA 95357
Phone: (209) 551-0883
Fax: (209) 551-9317
http://www.aamt.org

American Bar Association
740 15th Street NW
Washington, DC 20005
Phone: (202) 662-1680
Fax: (202) 662-1683
http://www.abanet.org/dispute

American Boarding Kennels Association
4575 Galley Road, Suite 400A
Colorado Springs, CO 80915
Phone: (719) 591-1113
Fax: (719) 597-0006
http://www.abka.com

American Collectors Association
PO Box 39106
Minneapolis, MN 55439-0106
Phone: (612) 926-6547
Fax: (612) 926-1624
http://www.collector.com

American Consulting Engineers Council
1015 15th Street NW., #802
Washington, DC 20002
Phone: (202) 347-7474
Fax: (202) 898-0068
http://www.acec.org/

American Design Drafting Association
    (ADDA)
PO Box 11937

Columbia, SC 29211
Phone: (803) 771-0008
Fax: (803) 771-4272
http://www.adda.org

American Federation of Musicians
1501 Broadway, Suite 600
New York, NY 10036
Phone (212) 869-1330
http://www.afm.org

American Franchisee Association (AFA)
53 West Jackson Blvd., Suite 205
Chicago, IL 60603
Phone: (800) 334-4232
Fax: (312) 431-1132
http://www.franchisee.org/

American Home Business Association, Inc.
4505 South Wasatch Blvd., Suite 140
Salt Lake City, UT 84124
Phone: (800) 556-9150
http://www.homebusiness.com

American Institute of Certified Public
   Accountants
1211 Avenue of the Americas
New York, NY 10036
Phone: (212) 596-6200
Fax: (212) 596-6213
http://www.aicpa.org

American Institute of Graphic Arts
164 Fifth Avenue
New York, NY 10010
Phone: (212) 807-1990

Fax: (212) 807-1799
http://www.aiga.org

American Insurance Association
1130 Connecticut Avenue, NW, Suite 1000
Washington, DC 20036
Phone: (202) 828-7100
Fax: (202) 293-1219
http://www.aiadc.org/default.asp

American Intellectual Property Law
   Association
2001 Jefferson Davis Hwy., Suite 203
Arlington, VA 22202
Phone: (703) 415-0780
Fax: (703) 415-0786
http://www.aipla.org

American Management Association
1601 Broadway
New York, NY 10019-7420
Phone: (800) 262-9699
www.amanet.org

American Marketing Association
311 S. Wacker Drive, Suite 5800
Chicago, IL 60606
Phone: (800) AMA-1150
Fax: (312) 542-9001
http://www.ama.org

American Nursery & Landscape Association
1250 I Street NW, Suite 500
Washington, DC 20005-3922
Phone: (202) 789-2900
Fax: (202) 789-1893
http://www.anla.org

American Screenwriters Association
PO Box 12860
Cincinnati, OH 45212
Phone: (513) 731-9212
http://www.asascreenwriters.com

American Seminar Leaders Association
2405 E. Washington Blvd.
Pasadena, CA 91104
Phone: (800) 735-0511
Fax: (626) 798-0701
http://www.asla.com

American Society for Training and
  Development
1640 King Street, PO Box 1443
Alexandria, VA 22313
Phone: (800) 628-2783
Fax: (703) 683-1523
http://www.astd.org

American Society of Civil Engineers
345 East 47th Street
New York, NY 10017
Phone: (212) 705-7010
Fax: (212) 705-7712
http://www.asce.org

American Society of Composers, Authors
  and Publishers
One Lincoln Plaza
New York, NY 10023
Phone: (212) 321-6000
http://www.ascap.com/

American Society of Journalists and Authors
1501 Broadway, Suite 302
New York, NY
Phone: (212) 997-0947
Fax: (212) 758-7414
http://www.asja.org.

American Society of Landscape Architects
636 Eye Street, NW
Washington, DC 20001
Phone: (202) 898-2444
Fax: (202) 898-1185
http://www.asla.org

American Society of Mechanical Engineers
PO Box 2900, 22 Law Drive
Fairfield, NJ 07007-2900
Phone: (201) 882-1167
Fax: (201) 882-5155
http://www.asme.org

American Society of Travel Agents, Inc.
1101 King Street, Suite 200
Alexandria, VA 22314
Phone: (703) 739-8739
Fax: (703) 684-8319
http://www.astanet.com

American Stamp Dealers Association
3 School Street
Glen Cove, NY 11542-2548
Phone: (516) 759-7000
Fax: (516) 759-7014
http://www.asdaonline.com

Association of Bridal Consultants
200 Chestnutland Road
New Milford, CT 06776
Phone: (860) 355-0464
Fax: (860) 354-1404

Association of Computer Support Specialists
218 Huntington Road
Bridgeport, CT 06608
Phone: (203) 332-1524
Fax: (203) 333-6436
http://www.acss.org

Association of On-Line Professionals
6096 Franconia Road, Suite D
Alexandria, VA 22310
Phone: (703) 924-5800
Fax: (703) 924-5801
http://www.aop.org

Association of Stained Glass Lamp Artists
   (ASGLA)
5070 Cromwell Drive NW
Gig Harbor, WA 98335
http://www.asgla.com

Automotive Parts & Accessories Association
   (APAA)
4600 East-West Highway, Suite 300
Bethesda, MD 20814
Phone: (301) 654-6664
Fax: (301) 654-3299
http://www.apaa.org

Beauty and Barber Supply Institute
11811 N. Tatum Blvd., Suite 1085

Phoenix, AZ 85028
Phone: (602) 404-1800
Fax: (602) 404-8900
http://www.bbsi.org

Biotechnology Industry Organization (BIO)
1625 K Street NW, Suite 1100
Washington, DC 20006-1604
Phone: (202) 857-0244
Fax: (202) 857-0237
http://www.bio.org

Business Marketing Association
400 N. Michigan Avenue, 15th Fl.
Chicago, IL 60611
Phone: (800) 664-4262
Fax: (312) 409-4266
http://www.marketing.org

Canadian Authors Association
Box 419
Campbellford, Ontario K0L 1L0
Phone: (705) 653-0323
Fax: (705) 653-0593
http://www.CanAuthors.org

Chemical Specialties Manufacturers
   Association
1913 Eye Street NW
Washington, DC 20006
Phone: (202) 872-8110
http://prodapp1.eoweb.com/

Direct Marketing Association
1120 Avenue of the Americas
New York, NY 10036

Phone: (212) 768-7277
Fax: (212) 768-7277
http://www.the-dma.org

Direct Selling Association
1666 K Street NW, Suite 1010
Washington, DC 20006-2808
Phone: (202) 263-5760
Fax: (202) 463-4569
http://www.dsa.org

Editorial Freelancers Association
71 West 23rd Street, Suite 1910
New York, NY 10010
Phone: (212) 929-5400
Fax: (212) 929-5439
http://www.the-efa.org

Embroidery Trade Association
PO Box 612288
Dallas, TX 75261-2288
Phone: (800) 727-3014
Fax: (972) 906-6722
http://www.e-web.com

Equipment Leasing Association of America
4301 North Fairfax Drive, Suite 550
Arlington, VA 22203
Phone: (703) 527-8655
Fax: (703) 527-2649
http://www.elaonline.com

Foodservice Consultants Society
    International (FCSI)
304 West Liberty Street, Suite 201
Louisville, KY 40202

Phone: (502) 583-3783
Fax: (502) 589-3602
http://www2.fcsi.org/fcsi

FTD Association
33031 Schoolcraft Road
Livonia, MI 48150-1618
Phone: (888) 419-1515
Fax: (734) 466-8978
http://www.ftdassociation.org/ftda/home.nsf

Handweavers Guild of America (HGA)
Two Executive Concourse
3327 Duluth Hwy., Suite 201
Duluth, GA 30096-3301
Phone: (770) 495-7702
Fax: (770) 495-7703
http://www.weavespindye.org

Health Insurance Association of America
555 13th Street NW
Washington, DC 20004
Phone: (202) 824-1600
http://www.hiaa.org

Home Office Association of America
10 Gracie Station, PO Box 806
New York, NY 10028-0082
Phone: (800) 809-4622
Fax: (212) 535-7240
http://www.hoaa.com

Home Sewing Association
1350 Broadway, Suite 1601
New York, NY 10018
Phone: (212) 714-1633

Fax: (212) 714-1655
http://www.sewing.org

HTML Writers Guild
110 E. Wilshire Avenue, Suite G-12
Fullerton, CA 92832
Phone: (714) 526-4963
Fax: (714) 526-4972
http://www.hwg.org

Human Resource Planning Society
317 Madison Avenue, Suite 1509
New York, NY 10017
Phone: (212) 490-6387
Fax: (212) 682-6851
http://www.hrps.org/html/index.htm

IEEE Computer Society
1730 Massachusetts Avenue NW
Washington, DC 20036
Phone: (202) 371-0101
Fax: (202) 728-9614
http://www.computer.org

Incentive Travel and Meetings Association
PO Box 195
Twickenham, UK TW1 2PE
Phone: (44) 1-81-892-0256
Fax: (44) 1-81-891-3855
http://www.martex.co.uk/itma

Independent Computer Consultants
   Association
11131 South Towne Square, Suite F
St. Louis, MO 63123
Phone:(800) 774-4222

Fax: (314) 487-1345
http://www.icca.org

Independent Insurance Agents of America
   Incorporated
127 South Peyton Street
Alexandria, VA 22314
Phone: (800) 221-7917
Fax: (800) 221-7917
http://www.independentagent.com

Independent Medical Distributors
   Association
5800 Foxridge Drive, Suite 115
Mission, KS 66202-2333
Phone: (800) 398-5632
Fax: (913) 262-0174
http://www.imda.org

Independent Press Association
2390 Mission Street, Suite 201
San Francisco, CA 94110-1836
Phone: (415) 643-4401
Fax: (415) 643-4402
http://www.indypress.org

International Franchise Association
1350 New York Avenue NW, Suite 900
Washington, DC 20005-4709
Phone: (202) 628-8000
Fax:(202) 628-0812
http://www.franchise.org

International Virtual Assistants Association
   (IVAA)
8375 Leesburg Pike, PMB 433
Vienna, VA 22182

Phone: (703) 760-9543
Fax: (860) 974-1935
http://www.ivaa.org

International Webmasters Association
119 E. Union Street Suite E
Pasadena, CA 91103
Phone: (626) 449-3709
Fax: (626) 449-8308
http://www.iwanet.org

Knitting Guild of America (TKGA)
PO Box 1606
Knoxville, TN 37901-1606
Phone: (423) 524-2401
Fax: (423) 524-8677
http://www.tkga.com

Mothers' Home Business Network
PO Box 423
East Meadow, NY 11554
Phone: (516) 997-7394
Fax: (516) 997-0839
http://www.homeworkingmom.com

National Association for the Self-Employed
PO Box 612067
DFW Airport
Dallas, TX 75261-2067
Phone: (800) 232-6273
http://www.nase.org

National Association of Black
    Telecommunications Professionals, Inc.
1710 H Street NW, 10th Fl.
Washington, DC 20006-4601

Phone: (800) 946-6228
http://www.nabtp.org

National Association of Computer
    Consultant Businesses (NACCB)
1800 Diagonal Road, Suite 520
Alexandria, VA 22314
Phone: (703) 838-2050
Fax: (703) 838- 3610
http://www.naccb.org

National Association of Enrolled Agents
200 Orchard Ridge Drive, Suite 302
Gaithersburg, MD 20878
Phone: (301) 212-9608
Fax: (301) 212-9608
http://www.naea.org

National Association of Environmental
    Professionals
6524 Ramoth Drive
Jacksonville, FL 32226
Phone: (904) 251-9900
Fax: (904) 251-9901
http://www.enfo.com/naep

National Association of Executive Recruiters
    (NAER)
20 North Wacker Drive, Suite 550
Chicago, IL 60606
Phone: (312) 701-0744
Fax: (312) 630-9882
http://www.naer.org

National Association of Financial and Estate
    Planning
525 East 4500 South, # F-100

Salt Lake City, UT 84107
Phone: (801) 266-9900
Fax: (801) 266-1019
http://www.nafep.com

National Association of Fine Artists
PO Box 151311
Arlington, TX 76015-7311
Phone: (530) 470-0862
Fax: (530) 470-0256
http://www.artmarketing.com

National Association of Home Based
   Businesses
4205 Parnelle Road
Marietta, GA 30062
Phone: (800) 332-9252
Fax: (404) 971-6778
http://www.usahomebusiness.com

National Association of Home Inspectors
4248 Park Glen Road
Minneapolis, MN 55416
Phone: (800) 448-3942
Fax: (612) 928-4641
http://www.nahi.org

National Association of Independent Artists
   (NAIA)
PO Box 44008
Madison, WI 53744-4008
Phone: (847) 426-8532
http://naia-artists.org

National Association of Independent
   Publishers
PO Box 430

Highland City, FL 33846-0430
Phone: (813) 648-4420
Fax: (813) 648-4420
http://lcweb.loc.gov/loc/cfbook/coborg/nai.html

National Association of Independent Travel
   Agents
24 Eastern Road South Melbourne
Victoria, Australia 3205
Phone: (61) 3-9682-2388
Fax: (61) 3-9682-1979
http://www.rucc.net.au

National Association of Personal Financial
   Advisors
355 West Dundee Road, Suite 200
Buffalo Grove, IL 60089
Phone: (888) FEE-ONLY
http://www.napfa.org

National Association of Professional
   Employer Organizations
901 N. Pitt Street, Suite 150
Alexandria, VA 22314
Phone: (703) 936-0466
Fax: (703) 836-0976
http://www.napeo.org

National Association of Professional Pet
   Sitters
1030 15th Street NW, Suite 870
Washington, DC 20005
Phone: (202) 393-3317
Fax: (202) 393-0336
http://www.petsitters.org

National Association of Sales Professionals
8300 N. Hayden Road, Suite 207
Scottsdale, AZ 85258
Phone: (602) 951-4311
Fax: (602) 483-2860
http://www.nasp.com

National Association of Small Business
   Investment Companies
666 11th Street NW, Suite 750
Washington, DC 20001
Phone: (202) 628-5055
Fax: (202) 628-5080
http://www.nasbic.org

National Association of Tax Practitioners
720 Association Drive
Appleton, WI 54914-1483
Phone: (800) 558-3402
Fax: (920) 749-1062
http://www.natptax.com

National Association of Temporary and
   Staffing Services
119 S. Saint Asaph Street
Alexandria, VA 22314
Phone: (703) 549-6287
Fax: (703) 549-4808
http://www.natss.org

National Association of Webmasters
9580 Oak Avenue Parkway, Suite 7-177
Folsom, CA 95630
Phone: (916) 929-6557
Fax: (916) 987-3022
http://www.naw.org

National Association of Wholesalers
1725 K Street NW
Washington, DC 20006
Phone: (202) 872-0885
http://www.nawmeetings.org./am2000

National Association of Women Business
   Owners
1100 Wayne Avenue, Suite 830
Silver Spring, MD 20910
Phone: (301) 608-2590
Fax: (301) 608-2596
http://www.nawbo.org

National Association of Women in
   Construction
327 S. Adams Street
Fort Worth, TX 76104-1081
Phone: (871) 877-5551
Fax: (817) 877-0324
http://www.nawic.org

National Athletic Trainers' Association
2952 Stemmons Freeway
Dallas, TX 75247-6196
Phone: (214) 637-6282
Fax: (214) 637-2206
http://www.nata.org

National Bicycle Dealers Association
777 W. 19th Street, Suite O
Costa Mesa, CA 92627
Phone: (949) 722-6909
Fax: (949) 722-1747
http://www.nbda.com

National Business Incubation Association
20 East Circle Drive, Suite 190
Athens, OH 45701-3751
Phone: (740) 593-4331
Fax: (740) 593-1996
http://www.nbia.org

National Child Care Association
1016 Rosser Street
Conyers, GA 30012
Phone: (800) 543-7161
Fax: (770) 388-7772
http://www.nccanet.org

National Federation of Independent Business
53 Century Boulevard, Suite 300
Nashville, TN 37214
Phone: (615) 872-5300
http://www.nfibonline.com

National Federation of Paralegal Associations
PO Box 33108
Kansas City, MO 64114
Phone: (816) 941-4000
Fax: (816) 941-2725
http://www.paralegals.org

National Federation of the Blind
1800 Johnson Street
Baltimore, MD 21230
Phone: (410) 659-9314
http://www.nfb.org

National Funeral Directors Association
13625 Bishop's Drive
Brookfield, WI 53005

Phone: (800) 228-6332
http://www.nfda.org

National Magic Dealers Association
PO Box 7670
Auburn, CA 95604
Phone: (530) 823-7077
Fax: (530) 823-7078
http://www.magicdealers.com

National Mail Order Association, LLC
2807 Polk Street NE
Minneapolis, MN 55418-2954
Phone: (612) 788-1673
Fax: (612) 788-1147
http://www.nmoa.org

National Paralegal Association
PO Box 406
Solebury, PA 18963
Phone: (215) 297-8333
Fax: (215) 297-8358
http://www.nationalparalegal.org

National Pest Control Association
8100 Oak Street
Dunn Loring, VA 22027
Phone: (703) 573-8330
Fax: (703) 573-4116
http://www.pestworld.org

National Quilting Association (NQA)
PO Box 393
Ellicott City, MD 21041-0393
Phone: (410) 461-5733
Fax: (410) 461-3693
http://nqa.society.webjump.com

National Resume Writers Association
Fax: (512) 246-7433
http://www.nrwa.com

National Roofing Contractors Association
10255 W. Higgins Road, Suite 600
Rosemont, IL 60018-5607
Phone: (847) 299-9070
Fax: (847) 299-1183
http://nrca.net

National Small Business United
1156 15th Street NW, Suite 1100
Washington, DC 20005
Phone: (202) 293-8830
Fax: (202) 872-8543
http://www.nsbu.org

National Small Business Network
PO Box 223
Centereach, NY 11720
Phone: (631) 467-6826
http://www.businessknowhow.net

National Society of Professional Engineers
1420 King Street
Alexandria, VA 22314
Phone: (888) 285-6773
http://www.nspe.org

National Specialty Gift Association
PO Box 843
Norman, OK 73070
Phone: (405) 329-7847
http://www.giftprofessionals.com

National Venture Capital Association
1655 N. Fort Meyer Drive, Suite 850

Arlington, VA 22209
Phone: (703) 524-2549
Fax: (703) 524-3940
http://www.nvca.org

National Wood Carvers Association
PO Box 43218
Cincinnati, OH 45243
http://www.chipchats.org

Professional Association of Innkeepers
    International
PO Box 90710
Santa Barbara, CA 93190
Phone: (805) 569-1853
Fax: (805) 682-1016
http://www.paii.org

Professional Association of Resume Writers
3637 Fourth Street N., Suite 330
St. Petersburg, FL 33704
Phone: (800) 822-7279
Fax: (813) 894-1277
http://www.parw.com

Professional Photographers of America
229 Peachtree Street NE, #2200
Atlanta, GA 30303-2206
Phone: (404) 522-8600
Fax: (404) 614-6400
http://www.ppa-world.org

Public Relations Society of America
33 Irving Place
New York, NY 10003-2376
Phone: (212) 955-2230
http://www.prsa.org

Small Business Benefit Association
1112 East Range Road
Salt Lake City, UT 84117
Phone: (801) 446-1091
Fax: (801) 446-1092
http://www.sbba.com

Small Publishers Association of North
    America
PO Box 1306
Buena Vista, CO 81211
Phone: (719) 395-4790
Fax: (719) 395-8374
http://www.spannet.org

Society for Human Resources Management
1800 Duke Street
Alexandria, VA 22314
Phone: (703) 548-3440
Fax: (703) 535-6490
http://www.shrm.org

Software & Information Industry Association
1730 M Street NW, Suite 700
Washington, DC 20036-4510
Phone: (202) 452-1600
Fax: (202) 223-8756
http://www.siia.net

Software Support Professionals Association
11858 Bernardo Plaza Court, Suite 101C
San Diego, CA 92128
Phone: (619) 674-4864
Fax: (619) 674-1192
http://www.supportgate.com

Telecommunications Industry Association
1300 Pennsylvania Avenue, Suite 350
Washington, DC 20004
Phone: (202) 383-1480
Fax: (202) 383-1495
http://www.tiaonline.org

Travel Industry Association of America
1100 New York Avenue NW, Suite 450
Washington, DC 20005-3934
Phone: (202) 408-8422
Fax: (202) 408-1255
http://www.tia.org

United States Personal Chef Association
    (USPCA)
3615 Highway 528, Suite 107
Albuquerque, NM 87114-8919
Phone: (800) 995-2138
Fax: (505) 899-4097
http://www.uspca.com

United States Tour Operators Association
342 Madison Avenue, Suite 1522
New York, NY 10173
Phone: (212) 599-6599
Fax: (212) 599-6744
http://www.ustoa.com

Women in Packaging
4290 Bells Ferry Road, Suite 106-17
Kennesaw, GA 30144
Phone: (770) 924-3563
Fax: (770) 928-2338
http://www.womeninpackaging.org

Glossary

2/10 net 30   If this phrase or one like it appears on an invoice, it means that the purchaser of the goods may take a 2 percent discount if they pay the bill within 10 days. If they choose not to pay in 10 days, the full amount of the bill is due in 30 days.

Accounts payable   These are your bills—the money you owe suppliers and vendors.

Accounts receivable   Money (bills or account) that is owed to you for goods or services purchased by customers but not paid for at the time of sale.

Adjusted gross income (AGI)   On income taxes, your total income minus any adjustments to income. Taxable income is your adjusted gross income minus your deductions.

Agent (insurance)   An insurance agent is a salesperson who represents one or more insurance companies. An exclusive agent represents only one company; an independent agent is an independent contractor who is a sales representative for more than one insurance company. See also *broker*.

All-risk insurance policy   This term used to describe a type of insurance policy that protects you against all possible causes of loss except any specifically excluded and listed in the policy. Most companies now call these policies "special form" policies instead of "all-risk."

Amortization	A method of spreading out certain kinds of business costs over a period of years. Similar to depreciation, but usually the recovery period is longer.
AOD	Acknowledgment of delivery.
Arbitration	A way of resolving legal disputes without a formal trial. The disagreeing parties agree to have a third party or panel of experts hear both sides of the dispute and make an award or decision on how the dispute should be settled.
ASCII	American Standard Code for Information Interchange. This is a computer standard for creating text that can be read on any computer.
Asset	A business asset is something you buy or acquire or develop, has or is expected to have monetary value, and will use in your business for more than one year. Examples of assets are land, equipment, patents, buildings, and franchise rights.
Assumptions (financial—in business plan)	As used by financial types, assumptions are predictions about future circumstances and future business activities. If you are predicting what your sales will be next year, for instance, you have to make some predictions (informed guesses) about how many customers you will have and how many sales you will make to those customers.
Backup	A copy of computer data that can be stored independently from the hard disk or floppy disk which the data was originally stored. You need to back up your data so you can recreate the information if something happens to the data you originally created.
Balance sheet	A summary of your assets (what you own), your liabilities (what you owe), and what you are worth (the difference between the assets and liabilities).
Basis	The beginning figure for calculating depreciation, amortization, gain, loss, or depletion.
Baud	A term used to describe how fast modems and faxes transfer data.

Body copy
Body copy refers to the text of press releases, printed articles, or advertising.

Boilerplate
Standard information or forms, such as standardized contracts or personalized sales letters in which only a small amount of information (such as a name or address) changes from one document to another.

BOP
See *Businessowner's policy*.

Break-even analysis
An analysis of how many sales you have to make at a given price in order that your sales cover your expenses.

Broker (insurance)
An insurance broker is a marketing specialist who represents the buyer of insurance and selects proper coverage from among the offerings of many companies. See also *agent*.

Bulletin board system
An electronic communications center where messages can be posted for other people to read using their computers. Also called a message board.

Business interruption insurance
As the name implies, business interruption insurance offers insurance coverage against losses due to a temporary interruption of business due to fire or other insured risks. It covers lost net profits and continuing expenses such as rent.

Businessowner's policy
This is a special type of insurance policy for small businesses that combines many separate insurance coverages, such as fire, theft, and personal liability, into one policy. Often abbreviated BOP.

Card deck
Card deck advertisements are ads that are printed on index-sized cards and mailed to subscribers of certain magazines or people who are known to buy a certain type of product or service through the mail.

Cash flow
Literally, the flow of cash (money) through your business from outlays for supplies, products, raw materials, sales, and operating expenses to income from sales or other sources. A cash-flow analysis compares the income your daily operations generate to your expenses.

CEO

Chief executive officer. The chief executive officer of a company is usually the person who controls it.

CFO

Chief financial officer. This person is responsible for managing all the financial aspects of a company.

Chargeback

A chargeback is a credit card transaction that is literally "charged back," or billed to the business that made the original sale. Chargebacks occur when credit card holders dispute charges on their bill either because they never made the purchase or because they are dissatisfied with their purchase and the merchant refuses to correct the problem. The merchant is liable for chargebacks even if the merchandise was shipped.

Clip art

Artwork you license to use in your publications. You actually may cut or clip the art out of a book that is distributed to you, hence the name *clip art*. Clip art (artwork you have the right to reproduce) is available in various computer formats as well as high-quality printouts.

Close, closed, or closely held corporation

A private corporation as opposed to one that is publicly traded. Often its shareholders are close friends or family members. Special rules sometimes apply to closed corporations.

COBRA

See *Consolidated Omnibus Budget Reconciliation Act of 1985*.

Compliance audit

A compliance audit is an audit conducted under the Taxpayer Compliance Measurement Program (TCMP) to help the IRS determine who is most likely to cheat on which types of deductions. The audit looks in depth at all of your finances.

Confidentiality agreement

Also called a nondisclosure agreement. This is an agreement you may be asked to sign if you will have access to trade secrets of projects under development. It legally prevents you from disclosing trade secrets or other information to other parties.

Consideration (law)

Consideration is what you receive in return for doing something you don't have to do—usually money. If you agreed to write a technical manual for $5,000, the fee would be the consideration.

Consolidated Omnibus Budget Reconciliation Act of 1985	This law provides a way for people to continue health care coverage after they leave their jobs, divorce their spouse, or lose eligibility for health insurance through some other means. The law applies to companies with twenty or more employees.
Contingency fee	A fee that is paid when the outcome of something such as a lawsuit is successful.
Continuous form	Forms or computer paper that come in one continuous strip. It is usually perforated so it can be separated easily into page-sized sections. The edges on continuous forms have holes in them to allow them to be pulled through a printer by a mechanism that has sprocket or pins to grab and move the paper.
Copy	See *Body copy*.
Corporation	A separate entity chartered by the state to do business.
Covenant not to compete	Sometimes called a noncompete agreement. It is a contract employees or others sign stating they will not compete with the employer for a set period of time. There are a variety of state laws that govern such agreements, so if you plan to use one be sure to have an attorney look it over and make sure it is enforceable in your state.
Damages	Money awarded as the outcome of a lawsuit.
Data file	Any information or document you create with a computer program (letter, ad, drawing, etc.).
DBA	"Doing business as." A term used to designate the certificate one gets after registering a business name with appropriate local or state officials.
Debt financing	Debt financing simply means financing your business with loans. You borrow a specified amount and are expected to pay it back in a specified period of time at a specified interest rate.
Debt-to-worth ratio	Amount owed creditors divided by the value of the business.
Depreciate	A tax deduction that allows you to recover what you paid for property by deducting its cost over a period of years.

Download	To transfer information from a remote computer to your own and save it on disk.
Dunning letters	Letters demanding payment for bills.
Equity financing	Equity means ownership. Equity financing means trading ownership for money. How much ownership must be given up varies with the deal.
Estimated taxes	Estimated taxes are money you must pay in advance toward your expected year-end tax liability. You only have to pay estimated taxes if the income and Social Security tax (FICA) withheld from any wages you earn will not cover all the tax you will owe at the end of the year. Generally, if you expect to owe more than $500 in income and self-employment tax than you will contribute through salary withholdings, you will have to pay estimated taxes. The tax gets paid in four installments during the tax year.
Factor or factoring	Factoring is the sale of accounts receivable to a third party. It is a way of speeding up collection of receivables in which you sell your receivables (what's owed you) to a third party for a percentage of what the actual amount owed is worth. Once receivables are sold, the factor accepts all the risk for collection. Billing functions remain either with you or get transferred to the factor, depending on the individual arrangements.
FICA	The Federal Insurance Contributions Act, which made into law the withholding of Social Security contributions from employees' paychecks.
Financials	The financial projections and financial historical data used in a business plan.
Fiscal year	Any 12 consecutive months used for accounting for business activity. The fiscal year may or may not start and end at the same time as the calendar year.
Floor	In the preparation of income taxes, a floor is a base amount that expenses must exceed to be deductible. The floor is calculated as a percentage of adjusted gross income.

Floppy disk	Floppy disks store small amounts of computer data and are removable from the computer. Originally, floppy disks were thin and flexible, hence the name *floppy*.
Freeware	Software that is distributed for free use but for which the author retains the copyright.
Gross income	The total of all income with no expenses or deductions subtracted.
Guaranteed renewable	An insurance term meaning an insurance company cannot cancel or refuse to renew your policy as long as you continue to pay the premiums, and it continues to sell the kind of insurance you've purchased.
Hard disk	A hard disk is a type of mass storage device for computer data. It is used to store computer programs and data files.
Hardware	Pieces of a computer system you can actually touch, like the keyboard, printer processing unit, monitor (screen), hard drive, etc.
Health maintenance organization (HMO)	A managed health insurance plan where the insurer is also the health care provider. Usually HMOs cover only the fees of doctors or other providers who are part of the plan. If you go to a doctor or hospital outside the HMO, the insurance won't cover your costs.
HMO	See *Health maintenance organization*.
Income statement	Also called a profit and loss statement or operating statement. It summarizes the profitability of a business, showing what's left over (or lost) when you subtract cost of goods sold and operating expenses from the total sales.
Independent contractor	A self-employed individual who performs a specific job for a business either under a formal contract or by verbal agreement with the company. Generally, independent contractors offer their services to more than one business. In fact, people who work only for one company sometimes have trouble proving their independent contractor status to the IRS.

Inland marine insurance   A type of insurance that was originally designed to cover goods *after* they were taken off ships and were in transit inland. Now it is used to cover a wide range of perils including some for which nothing else is appropriate, such as electronic data processing equipment and media. Other things often covered by inland marine policies or floaters are goods in transit, jewelry, fine art, personal effects, as well as bridges, highways, and other things having to do with transportation or communications.

Internet   A global network of computers linked together for information exchange.

ISO   Independent Sales Organization. A distributor who buys products or services and resells them at a profit. ISOs operate in a variety of fields. Companies that offer merchant card processing services to vendors are one type of ISO.

Jaggies   Refers to the jagged edges that are produced when some computer printers print alphabetical characters or drawings with rounded edges.

Keogh plan   One type of tax-deferred retirement plan for the self-employed.

Letter of agreement   A letter of agreement sums up points you and another party agreed on. It can serve as a contract.

Liabilities   In accounting, all debts your business owes. This includes money you owe vendors (accounts payable), money you owe in income taxes, money you owe on long-term loans, etc.

Mediation   A way of attempting to settle disputes without a lawsuit. A third party (called a mediator) brings disagreeing parties together and encourages them to settle the dispute themselves.

Megabyte (MB)   A unit used to measure disk space and computer memory.

Merchant status   Authorization for a business to accept credit cards in payment for goods and services. A business with merchant status will have the charges processed through their "merchant account" with a bank or other credit card processor.

Message board	See *Bulletin board system*.
Modem	A device that converts computer data into a format that can be sent over telephone lines and converts incoming telephone signals into computer data on the receiving end.
Net income	Total income minus expenses; in other words, your profit.
NOL	Net operating loss (when sales minus expenses produces a loss).
Noncompete agreement	See *Covenant not to compete*.
Nonexclusive right(s)	A right to sell a product that may be granted to more than one person or organization at a time.
NSF	Nonsufficient funds (said of a checking account that doesn't have enough money in it to cover a check).
Online service	Any of a number of large, commercial computer services that offer information, news, searchable databases, discussion forums, and, in many cases, software you can download, store, and use on your own computer system. To access an online service you need a computer, a modem, a telephone line, and a subscription to the online service.
Overhead	Any expenses a business has that can't be directly tracked to a product or service. Examples of overhead costs are expenses you pay for heat, light, telephone, insurance, supplies, and indirect labor. Overhead costs should be allocated and included in the price of every product or service you sell.
Partnership	A legal form of business where two or more individuals share work and/or financial responsibility for running a business.
Phonorecords	A term the Copyright Office uses to denote musical records you play on a phonograph.
Port	A data passageway on a computer. In other words, a place to plug printers, scanners, and other devices into the computer system.

PPO	See *Preferred provider organization.*
Preferred provider organization (PPO)	A health care plan where you have the option of using any of the providers in a network of preferred doctors, laboratories, hospitals, and other providers or using doctors and other providers outside the system. Generally, there is a small copayment per visit ($2 to $10) for using the plan's providers; if you use providers outside the plan's network, you pay and send in the bills to the company to collect your share.
Prime contractor	The business that is responsible for successful completion of a government contract. Prime contractors usually subcontract (give work out to other companies) various parts of contracts.
Print spooler	Software that lets you print out work on a computer printer while you continue to work at the computer.
Pro forma	Projected or expected financial data.
Prorated	Proportioned or allocated. In figuring your taxes, you prorate an expense to the percent business usage of the item. For instance, if you bought a $2,400 computer for your home office and used it 60 percent of the time for business, the amount you could depreciate or expense would be 60 percent of $2,400, or $1,440.
Public domain	Works (artwork, writing, software, etc.) that do not have copyright protection.
RAM	Random access memory. The temporary memory a computer uses to process work. Every time you shut down the computer, and often when you change tasks, the contents of the RAM are lost.
S corporation	Formerly called subchapter S corporation. This is a special type of corporation that affects the way profits and losses are handled for taxation. Many small businesses are S corporations.
Sales projection	An estimate of the number and dollar amount of sales over a specific period of time and sometimes in a specific region.

Scanner

A computer device that converts images on paper into a format that a computer can read. Different scanners have different capabilities. Some can convert only pictures; others with the appropriate software can convert words into a format the computer can edit.

SCSI

Small computer system interface (pronounced "scuzzy"). A computer passageway (port) through which data can pass at very high speeds. A SCSI port is simply a place to attach a disk drive or some other device to a microcomputer.

Self-employment tax

Social Security tax and Medicaid tax individuals pay when they are self-employed.

SEP

See *Simplified employee plan*.

Shareware

Software that you can try before you buy. This can be downloaded from online services or local electronic bulletin boards or can be purchased in disks sold by mail order and sometimes on racks at novelty stores and bookstores. You can buy the disk for a few dollars, try the software, and, if you like it, buy it from the author of the program.

SIC

Standard industrial code. This is a code the U.S. government uses to classify businesses by industry.

Simplified Employee Plan (SEP)

A type of IRA retirement plan where the employer makes the contribution, not the employee.

Software

Programming (instructions) that tells the computer what to do with what you type at the keyboard.

SOHO

Small Office/Home Office.

Sole proprietorship

A business owned by only one person. The business may have employees, but the actual ownership is in one name.

Source code

Source code is a computer code that can be read like English.

Spool

See *Print spooler*.

Statute	A statute is a law created by a governing body.
Statutory damages	An amount of money specified by law. Often statutory damages are penalties; for instance, three times the amount set by a jury or three times the value of a property.
Telecommuter	An employee who works at home and uses a telephone and computer to communicate with the employer.
Telemarketing	Using a telephone to market or sell goods and services or to get appointments to meet with customers.
Trade secrets	Information such as customer lists or formulas that gives a business a competitive edge in the marketplace, provided the information is kept secret. Unauthorized use of your trade secrets can be against the law.
Turnkey business	A turnkey business is a business that is complete and ready to go. It is usually a business concept that comes with plans to follow, equipment, and perhaps some training videos or manuals. Like with a car, someone just has to get behind the figurative wheel of the business, turn on the key, and drive it.
Upload	To send information from your computer "up" to some other computer. In other words, to transfer information from your computer and store it on the remote computer system.
Useful life	The amount of time an asset is expected to last and be usable.
Weekly shopper	Weekly shoppers are publications that consist of almost all advertising and have little or no editorial content. They may be mailed or tossed on driveways or stoops and contain ads for plumbers, garage sales, hair salons, tire dealers, etc.
Widget	A term used by business writers to mean any type of gadget or product a business might sell.
Working capital	Your current assets minus your current liabilities.

Index

About the Author

JANET ATTARD is the owner of Attard Communications, Inc., in Long Island, New York, which provides writing, electronic information, and Web-development services to businesses and organizations. She also runs the Business Know-How Forum on America Online. A respected expert, she is often quoted in mainstream and computer publications.